PRESSING THE POLICE AND POLICING THE PRESS

PRESSING THE POLICE AND POLICING THE PRESS

THE HISTORY AND LAW OF THE U.S. PRESS-POLICE RELATIONSHIP

SCOTT MEMMEL

UNIVERSITY OF MISSOURI PRESS

COLUMBIA

Library of Congress Cataloging-in-Publication Data

Names: Memmel, Scott, 1992- author.
Title: Pressing the police and policing the press : the history and law of
   the U.S. press-police relationship / Scott Memmel.
Description: Columbia : University of Missouri Press, 2024. | Series:
   Journalism in perspective: continuities and disruptions | Includes
   bibliographical references and index.
Identifiers: LCCN 2023042341 (print) | LCCN 2023042342 (ebook) | ISBN
   9780826223067 (hardcover) | ISBN 9780826275011 (ebook)
Subjects: LCSH: Press law--United States--History. | Police and the
   press--United States--History. | Police-community relations--United
   States--History.
Classification: LCC KF2750 .M45 2024 (print) | LCC KF2750 (ebook) | DDC
   343.7309/98--dc23/eng/20231005
LC record available at https://lccn.loc.gov/2023042341
LC ebook record available at https://lccn.loc.gov/2023042342

Typeface: Minion Pro and Aktiv Grotesk

Journalism in Perspective: Continuities and Disruptions

Tim P. Vos and Yong Volz, Series Editors

Journalism is a central institution in the social, cultural, and political life of communities, nations, and the world. Citizens and leaders rely on the news, information, and analysis that journalists produce, curate, and distribute each day. Their work must be understood in the context of journalism's institutional features, including its roles, ethics, operations, and boundaries. These features are themselves the product of a history emerging through periods of stability and change. The volumes in this series span the history of journalism and advance thoughtful and theoretically driven arguments for how journalism can best negotiate the currents of change.

The volumes of this series are published through the generous support of the University of Missouri School of Journalism.

Dedicated to my family, friends, colleagues, mentors, and teachers, as well as those who inform us, protect us, and strive for a better world.

CONTENTS

PREFACE

THE STORY OF THE RELATIONSHIP between the press and police in the United States dates to the origins of the republic, with the modern conceptions of both institutions forming in the mid-nineteenth century, a time during which American society was upheaved by urbanization, industrialization, and foreign immigration. In the nearly two centuries that followed, the news media and law enforcement became fundamental institutions intended to serve the public in the United States and formed a close relationship with each other. Throughout each successive era, both the press and the police were affected by, and responded to, the same societal contexts, often in similar ways. In some cases, this allowed for greater cooperation, or at least a mostly peaceful coexistence, while at others it ignited heightened contentiousness or allowed for unique practices by both entities, raising especially problematic, though often hidden, effects.

In conducting the research for this project, I had expected to see significant differences in the U.S. press-police relationship between the eras that make up its centuries-long history. Instead, I found that at any given moment, the press-police relationship was, and still is, made up of interinstitutional cooperative coexistence, interinstitutional contentiousness, and unique practices bridging these categories of interactions. Within these categories lie primary interactions between the press and the police, including the press's coverage of police activities, the news media's efforts to hold law enforcement accountable, and the police's intentional or unintentional targeting of members of the press. Additional interactions also arise, including media ride-alongs in police vehicles and members of each institution posing as members of the other through various means and purposes.

Whatever one may make of the state of the press-police relationship, it now finds itself strained by significant pressure and scrutiny. Conflict between the press and police has only further increased between the two, with the press highly critical of law enforcement and journalists facing arrests, use of force, threats, and more by the police.

Despite the prominence and importance of the press-police relationship, as well as the very real problems both institutions currently face, its history and the legal landscape that have both shaped and been shaped by them remain largely unstudied. This book aims to remedy the situation by providing a comprehensive history of the press-police relationship, as well as by detailing the law surrounding and implicating the relationship. Each chapter focuses on the interactions between the press and police during a particular era and introduces important societal factors, as well as how the press and police evolved and responded, often in similar ways, to that societal context, with the goal of providing relevant details needed to understand the changing contexts in which the relationship functioned without bogging the reader down in overanalysis.

In telling the story of the press-police relationship and analyzing its legal landscape, I strive to ultimately convey practical, tangible recommendations to improve the relationship. Certainly, there are broader calls for reform of the press and police, especially following cases like the murder of George Floyd in 2020. Although this manuscript cannot adequately address all these calls and recommendations for change, it can, and does, offer recommendations targeting the press-police relationship that, when combined with broader reform efforts for each institution, allow both the news media and law enforcement to better serve all members of the public in the present and future.

ACKNOWLEDGMENTS

EVEN AS A CHILD I was fascinated by journalism. I would stand in front of the television pretending to be a weatherman or listen to the radio in my room to catch the latest sports news. From participating in the school news to competing in forensics and debate, I knew from a young age that journalism and mass communication would be a life-long passion of mine. My interest in the press has only further grown from working at WSUM 91.7 FM and for Magnum Media, as well as from earning my bachelor's degree from the University of Wisconsin School of Journalism and Mass Communication and my master's and doctoral degrees from the University of Minnesota Hubbard School of Journalism and Mass Communication. It was as a graduate student that I discovered there was scant research on the history and law of the press-police relationship in the United States despite the ongoing importance, influence, and relevance of both institutions. Although far from a form of policing, my work as a county park ranger has only further deepened my interest in law enforcement's connection to journalism. Finally, as a professor at the University of Minnesota and Marquette University, I have been fortunate to teach courses related to media history, law, ethics, and more, only further expanding my knowledge of, and passion for, these important topics, as well as for education and learning as a whole.

I have a great many "thank-yous" to give to all those who helped make this book, my goal for many years, possible. Thank you first and foremost to my parents, Rick and Cindy, and my brother, Eric. Thank you also to my maternal grandparents, Fred and Zelma (a.k.a. Grandpa and Grammy), and late paternal grandma, Anne (a.k.a. Florida Grandma), as well as the rest of my extended family. I am so fortunate to have had such a supporting and caring family throughout my life.

Thank you to my friends, classmates, and colleagues, from childhood, college, and graduate school through the present. I would not be where I am today without all of you. Thank you to my MA and PhD adviser, Professor Jane Kirtley, and dissertation committee members, Drs. Chris Terry, Sid Bedingfield, and Tom Wolfe. Your support and guidance on my dissertation, the basis of this book, were instrumental as I worked on the project, including in May 2020 when I could smell the smoke and hear the sirens just a few miles away from the protests surrounding the murder of George Floyd Jr. in Minneapolis by law enforcement. It is because of all the support and guidance that I received that I was fortunate to win the 2021 Association for Education in Journalism and Mass Communication (AEJMC) Nafziger-White-Salwen Dissertation Award and the 2020 University of Minnesota Hubbard School of Journalism and Mass Communication Ralph D. Casey Dissertation Research Award, honors tied to legendary journalism and mass communication scholars. Additionally, thank you to Journalism in Perspective series editors Tim Vos and Yong Volz, and everyone at the University of Missouri Press, especially editor in chief Andrew Davidson, for helping to bring this book to publication.

My thanks go out as well to all of the teachers, teaching assistants, professors, and staff members with whom I've worked and learned from throughout my years at Burleigh Elementary School, Pilgrim Park Middle School, Brookfield East High School, the University of Wisconsin, and the University of Minnesota. Education is one of the most important aspects of life, and I am truly fortunate to have had so many amazing people teach, support, and guide me.

Finally, thank you to members of the press and police across the nation whose daily work is essential to the well-being of our communities. The news media and law enforcement are fundamental institutions in U.S. society, affecting the American public as well as people around the world. Both institutions, individually and in concert, have positive goals, purposes, and functions and take actions in the name of serving the public. That said, both institutions currently face serious problems, the remedy of which, along with concrete actions, will require a deep reflection on their intertwined histories and the legal landscape generated by both. It is my hope that this book can play a small role in a process of positive change moving forward.

PRESSING THE POLICE AND POLICING THE PRESS

Understanding the U.S. Press-Police Relationship

ON SEPTEMBER 3, 1833, THE *New York Sun* reported the story of a man named John Evans, who caught the attention of the press and law enforcement alike for throwing stones at the home of a woman, Eliza Vincent, who had "refused him admittance."[1] The *Sun*, which reported the story under the heading "Police Office," quoted a watchman, an early form of law enforcement officer, who said he had "advised [the] prisoner to desist." When Evans called him "a rascal," the watchman responded by saying that if he did not "clear out," he would "get a devil of a flogging." The watchman then arrested Evans and "walked him up to the watch-house."

At first glance, this appears to be a routine crime story written by a journalist and distributed to a public fascinated by criminals and wrongdoing, a tradition dating back to the first American newspapers. However, the story was part of a series of firsts, including the first of nine crime stories that appeared in what was the first issue of the *New York Sun*. This newspaper, established by Benjamin Day, a former printer's apprentice in Massachusetts who moved to New York City and opened his own printing business in 1831, is heralded by media historians as the first successful newspaper constituting the "penny press"—what would become a new wave of newspapers featuring coverage of crime and sensational stories that sold for only one penny, rather than the five or six cents traditional papers of the day fetched, and often regarded as the beginning of the modern conception of "news."[2] Therefore, the story about Evans throwing rocks at Vincent's house marks the first modern reported crime story and the beginning of "police news," as this same period also saw the formation of modern police departments.

Reporting on crime and police matters represents just one facet of the complicated but important relationship between the press and police in the United States, which dates to the American colonies. Today, "the press" and "news media" both refer collectively to professional reporters, anchorpersons, photographers, and others employed by local, regional, or national print, radio, television, or internet-based news organizations. "Police" and "law enforcement" comprise federal agencies, namely, the Federal Bureau of Investigation (FBI), statewide authorities such as state and highway patrols and capitol police, and, at local levels, municipal, county, tribal, and regional police and sheriff departments, as well as transit authority, school district, housing authority, airport, harbor, university, and hospital police.

It is important to note that the press-police relationship goes well beyond press coverage of crime and police proceedings. There are also countless instances of the press investigating and even "exposing" law enforcement agencies, officials, and officers in order to try to hold them accountable for their actions. For example, on July 22, 2018, nearly 185 years after the *Sun* published the first modern crime story, the *Minneapolis Star Tribune* published the first part of a special report, "Denied Justice: Minnesota's Failed Rape Investigations," in which the news outlet reported that "sexual assault cases in the Twin Cities and across Minnesota [were] being investigated [by the police] poorly or not at all, leaving many women feeling betrayed by a system they once trusted."[3] The *Star Tribune*'s report ultimately led to greater scrutiny of the police across Minnesota and calls for reform of their practices.[4]

It does, however, work the other way as well. Members of the press often find themselves the target of the police, both intentionally and unintentionally, which often leads to contentiousness and divisiveness— sometimes even physical altercation. Such contentiousness was perhaps most visible recently during the demonstrations following the death of George Floyd—a forty-six-year-old Black man—while in the custody of Minneapolis Police Department (MPD) officers on May 25, 2020. As racial justice protests spread across the United States in the coming days, weeks, and months, in some cases journalists reporting on what was taking place were met with arrests by law enforcement, as well as threats of and the actual use of force, including tear gas and other chemical agents, rubber bullets, flashbangs, riot batons, and being tackled to the ground. During racial justice protests between May 2020 and January 2021 in at least seventy-nine cities, there were 170 attacks of journalists by police and at least 115 arrests, among multiple cases of searches and seizures, damage to equipment, and surveillance.[5]

Finally, in some instances, the respective goals of the press and the police, as well as their purposes, functions, and actions, overlap in problematic ways. For example, in April 1992, the U.S. Marshals Service and Montgomery County (Maryland) Police Department, while executing three arrest warrants, entered the home of Charles Wilson, whose son, Dominic, had violated his probation on three felony charges.[6] The elder Wilson, wearing only a pair of briefs, ran into the living room to investigate, yelling at the police. The officers, mistaking Charles for his son, wrestled him to the floor as his wife, Geraldine, entered the room wearing a nightgown. During the confusion, a *Washington Post* reporter and a photographer took several photos and observed what took place. As it turned out, the two staff members of the *Post* had been participating in a "media ride-along" as part of their coverage of "Operation Gunsmoke," an initiative to arrest dangerous criminals. The Marshals Service had recently adopted a policy allowing journalists to ride along with police officers to observe and record operational missions. When the Wilsons later challenged the media presence during their encounter with the police under the Fourth Amendment, the Supreme Court held in *Wilson v. Layne* (1999) that the presence of the reporter and photographer violated the Wilsons' Fourth Amendment protection against unlawful search and seizure. This case demonstrates one of the unique practices that goes beyond cooperation and divisiveness between the press and police, raising especially problematic, though often hidden, negative effects.[7]

Taken together, these examples speak to the complexity of the press-police relationship in the United States, namely, the different ways the press and police interact without incident while responding to the societal context around them. Yet they also point to interinstitutional tensions and the types of interactions that spark them, in many ways the same types of division balanced with partnerships inherent throughout the long history of the relationship. Importantly, the often overlapping purposes and functions of the press and the police see them come into contact and interact with one another in many different settings, including public events, crime scenes, emergency scenes, news and press conferences, and other locations of breaking or ongoing news stories.

Ultimately, one might divide the functions and actions of the press and the police into two broad categories, which manifest as four types of interinstitutional interactions. The first category, "Cooperative Coexistence,"[8] comprises interactions during which the press and police find themselves at the same place at the same time, but manage to go about their respective activities without interfering with one another. In some such instances, the two institutions may even end up successfully working together, or at least toward the same goal, such as solving a complicated case or finding a missing person, while still maintaining independence as separate entities. Moreover, the press and police may sometimes act in ways to help the other to do its job properly, such as when the news media chooses to hold back on the reporting of certain details of a criminal investigation, in case doing so might tip off a suspect. In much the same way, police officials and officers can agree to act as sources, helping journalists gather and report news. In these types of instances, the press-police relationship has been described over time as a "symbiotic" one, an "[u]nholy [a]lliance," a "working relationship," and exhibiting "[h]ints of a [p]artnership," "trust," goals that "coincide," or a "complex loop of interdependence."[9]

At times, however, cooperation can border on problematic, especially if such actions undermine what might best serve the interests of the public that both institutions are charged with serving. For example, in some cases, the press may praise law enforcement or provide overly positive coverage of their activities while ignoring, whether purposefully or not, the interests of some members of a community. As discussed further in the pages that follow, there are also practices that appear cooperative but raise negative consequences that include potentially straining the press-police relationship. One can trace cases in which cooperation has gone "too far" throughout the history of the press-police relationship and are separate from forms of cooperation in which the press and police do not undermine their respective roles in serving the public.

Cooperative coexistence manifests in the first type of interaction: press coverage of police. This refers to the press covering crime and police activities, personnel, or other matters at a crime scene, emergency, or other location in a way that simply details what took place. Importantly, such coverage does not include criticism or otherwise critical reporting or an investigation of law enforcement. Such reporting is also not intended to place significant pressure on police, but simply to inform the public of recent happenings. Part of press coverage of police is the news-gathering activities of journalists—including interviewing law enforcement sources, attending press conferences, and other practices—while the police are performing their activities. The result is that the press and police are in this vein working together or, at the very least, coexisting at the same locations without targeting or interfering with one another.

The second category of interactions, "Contentiousness," includes those interactions during which the press-police relationship is strained or that occur during a situation that ends up putting the two institutions at odds, with one of them acting counter to the other's wishes, impeding its responsibilities, or both. For example, whereas the press may aim to obtain information to inform the public, law enforcement may avoid sharing that same bit of information to preserve an investigation or protect their own reputation. In other instances, one institution may target the other, intentionally or not. Previous literature has referred to the press-police relationship, when contentious, as "not always so symbiotic," "controversial," "asymmetrical," "adversarial," "always [having] tension," "conflicted," "strained," and "hostile," being prone to "get[ing] in one another's way," or "not always work[ing] cooperatively."[10] Some authors have provided potential reasons for such divisiveness, including, at times, conflicting purposes and functions, or negative perceptions of one another, often based on past events.[11]

Contentiousness typically manifests in two types of interactions between the press and police. The first, "press accountability of the police," refers to instances wherein journalists directly investigate and critically report on the police or when they investigate crimes and societal events in a way that puts a bad light or added pressure on law enforcement in a pointed effort to hold police accountable for their actions and procedures. This differs from basic press coverage of police in that the press seeks not only to inform the public but also to hold police accountable in some way. For example, in covering a crime, the press might take the next step of critically reporting on the police's response to and handling of a matter. The press can also hold police accountable by reporting on the misconduct and wrongdoing of police officials and officers, such as often happens in coverage of police-involved shootings. Naturally, the result in these cases is increased divisiveness, perhaps even conflict.

The second type of interaction falling under contentiousness, and third overall, arises when police target, intentionally or not, journalists and news organizations through arrests; threats of arrests, violence, or both; use of force, including with tear gas and other chemical agents, rubber bullets, riot batons, flashbangs, and tackling journalists to the ground; searches and seizures of journalists themselves or their homes, offices, sources, information, materials, newsrooms, electronic devices, and digital communications and accounts; enforcing subpoenas and related court orders; and surveillance, including mass surveillance, wiretapping, and bulk data collection, as well as secretive searches, seizures, and subpoenas. These actions, regardless of whether they lead to a journalist being convicted of a crime, mark clear intrusions into press independence, also generally leading to greater contentiousness.

Finally, there are also unique practices largely absent from previous literature that bridge cooperative coexistence and contentiousness, comprising the fourth type of interactions between the news media and law enforcement. "Impersonation" refers to the press or police representing, in some fashion, as the other to accomplish certain goals. In such cases, members of the press or police go beyond acting *like* the other and instead act *as if* they are part of the other institution to further their respective purposes. A media ride-along refers to the practice of journalists or other members of the media accompanying police officials or officers in their police vehicles. Both practices are similar, unique parts of the press-police relationship that have long histories dating back to the nineteenth century.

In the present, police impersonation of the press, press impersonation of police, and media ride-alongs each raise significant negative effects that one can trace throughout the entire history of each practice. In the case of press impersonation of police, despite the relative secrecy of the practice, the negative effects almost immediately gave rise to criticism and efforts to limit it, though the practice continued into the twenty-first century. Conversely, with police impersonation of the press, it took longer for criticism to arise, though it did increase by the twentieth century as word got out about the federal government's large-scale use of the practice, though still not going far enough to eliminate it at the federal, state, and local levels. Media ride-alongs, meanwhile, raise significant negative effects that date back to the 1880s, but generally saw little criticism until recently in the twenty-first century, with such criticism of the practice still being inadequate to address the problems arising from it. It is necessary to note that the effects of each of these practices may not have violated norms and values in different eras, one reason it took some time for widespread criticism to arise. Throughout the respective histories of the practices, the potential benefits of impersonation and media ride-alongs also often overshadowed potential problems and issues, leading some to perhaps not recognize or even ignore the negative effects, explaining why criticism still remains uncommon or inadequate to address the problems arising from the practice. And in the case of impersonation, the often secretive nature of the practice meant that any negative effects it engendered were likely hidden from public view.

But ultimately, it is important to tell the story of police impersonation of the press, press impersonation of police, and media ride-alongs given their importance to fully understanding the press-police relationship. Although other interactions and practices between the press and police fall under the same type of interaction as impersonation and media ride-alongs, the latter in particular represent important cases bridging co-operative coexistence and contentiousness. They are practices in which cooperation, willing or not, becomes problematic to the point where the practice itself and the negative effects that arise risk straining the press-police relationship, leading to even greater division and conflict. The practices also undermine the respective purposes and functions of the press and police, as well as their independence, in addition to other negative effects ranging from physical danger to the undermining of public trust. The result of these negative effects implicates not only the press, police, and the relationship between the two, but also the public unless necessary and adequate action is taken.

Seemingly, the press and police have a lot in common, including the mission of both to serve the American public, often leading to cooperative coexistence. But some of their respective purposes and functions intrinsically lead to contentiousness, especially when one purposely targets the other. And in between cooperative coexistence and contentiousness lie actions that undermine their responsibilities and create negative effects, including straining the press-police relationship. Significantly, one can discern these two categories and four types of interactions throughout the history of the press-police relationship despite changes to the practices of each institution over time. In some eras, cooperative coexistence seemed to pervade, while in others the pendulum tended to swing further on the side of contentiousness. Impersonation and media ride-alongs add a further layer of complexity. The result is that one can divide the press-police relationship into key eras reflective of how the relationship worked and evolved across different historical moments. But even during those times when one category or type of interaction pervaded, the others still occurred, providing consistent trends and characteristics across the more than two-century story of the U.S. press-police relationship.

At the foundation of that relationship is the story of how the two separate entities underwent changes across different eras in response to the societal context—including political, economic, social, cultural, and technological changes, as well as factors related to race, class, and gender—to eventually become the independent institutions as we conceive of them today. In particular, as social institutions, both the press and the police sought to carve out their role and authority in the United States, including by figuring out their internally shared values, assumptions, and practices that are the basis for their authority. Put differently, the press and police, like "all professions," sought to "engage in boundary maintenance"[12] and define their institutional identity over time, including through "boundaries between journalists and nonjournalists."[13] At times, such efforts helped hone the borders and independence of the institutions. But both the press and the police also have and continue to face identity crises, such as when policing struggles to embrace recommended reforms or the rights of underrepresented communities or when the press tries to make room for nonmainstream news organizations or tame the digital frontier.

This book therefore seeks to detail how the press and police responded, often in similar ways, to significant societal changes across several historical eras, including following the modern origins of both in the mid-nineteenth century, eventually becoming independent institutions in the twentieth century, and continuing to evolve, in many ways together, through the present. This book then analyzes how the changes undergone by the press and police over two centuries shaped their current purposes and functions.

Significantly, this coforming of institutional identities has important implications on not only the press and police as separate entities but also their relationship with each other, sometimes leading to greater cooperation, or at least coexistence, while at other times leading to division and opposition. This, then, serves as the key focus of the book, namely, how the changes the press and the police underwent throughout different historical eras affected their relationship with each other, using case studies to illuminate these interactions and show how they ebbed and flowed, but remained largely consistent over time. These case studies include recent occurrences and apply social responsibility theory (SRT),[14] the press's "collaborative role,"[15] First Amendment theory, and other theoretical and empirical literature to help detail the press's and police's interactions in the present in an attempt to explain why they are a mixture of cooperative coexistence at one moment and contentiousness the next. Doing so also reveals the effects and consequences of the press's and police's interactions on each other, their relationship, and the public.

It is important that we study the history of the press-police relationship and that of the law pertaining to it, and study it *now*. First, both institutions are fundamental players in American society that wield significant influence. The press is charged with serving as "society's primary information system," while the police are to serve as society's "primary system for legitimizing values and enforcing norms" and ensure public safety.[16] The press-police relationship therefore has and will continue to implicate all of us as members of the public, raising important questions, issues, and insights related to race, class, and gender. Additionally, the actions of both institutions touch on constitutional rights, among them the First Amendment protections of free speech and freedom of the press, Third Amendment protection from quartering soldiers, and Fourth Amendment protection from illegal searches and seizures. The influence of the press-police relationship on these rights demonstrates the significant ways both institutions affect the public.

Second, both institutions currently face significant political, economic, social, and technological tension, pressure, and scrutiny. For their part, the U.S. news media face antipress rhetoric and actions by politicians, economic pressures ranging from decreased resources to layoffs to the shutting down of local newspapers, accusations of bias and fake news, growing distrust by the public, and technological changes that influence where Americans get their news. Similarly, law enforcement faces a sharply decreased level of trust by the public, especially the Black community. Officer-involved shootings of unarmed suspects and other forms of police misconduct have led to increased scrutiny of law enforcement and urgent, widespread calls for significant reform and change.

In addition to such concerns, a heightened level of contentiousness has arisen between the two institutions, especially since the murder of George Floyd, to the point of a significant reckoning seemingly on the horizon for both institutions. Certainly, the murder of Floyd and subsequent events can mark a moment of departure for a new period of redefining the press-police relationship. But at the same time, it also

marks the continuation of conflict and dysfunction between the two institutions dating back throughout the press-police relationship, including during the tumultuous 1960s. Unfortunately, this continued discord
between the press and police only further limits the two, meaning both
cannot, and presently do not, serve and benefit the public as best they
might. The press and police not only augmented self-introspection but
also increasingly looked at their relationship, marking a key moment in
its history and raising questions about whether meaningful change will,
or even can, arise.

Finally, although past research has focused on other aspects of the
press-police relationship,[17] its history and law remain understudied.[18]
No single volume tackles the history and law of the relationship, necessitating this book, which aims to provide the most comprehensive history
and legal analysis of the press-police relationship to date. This book
takes lessons from this history and law and also holds out tangible ways,
despite the questions and concerns named earlier, in which to improve
the press-police relationship as each institution continues to reflect on
the events surrounding the murder of George Floyd.

Chapter 1 begins the story of the press-police relationship in the
United States by going back thousands of years to the ancient antecedents of journalism and policing before turning to how both arose in
Great Britain's North American mainland colonies. The first American
newspapers, combined with forms of law enforcement like sheriffs and
constables, as well as day and night watches, marked the beginning of
interactions between the press and police in what would become the
United States, namely, cooperative coexistence through press coverage
of police and contentiousness arising from press accountability of police
and law enforcement targeting the press.

These same interactions continued into the nineteenth century with
the rise of the modern press and modern police in the United States. Like
the press and police both tracing their roots to colonial America, it is no
coincidence that their modern origins both arose around the same time
in the 1830s–'50s as urbanization, immigration, and industrialization
created a perfect storm for journalism and policing to evolve as rising
crime, economic disparities, and other societal factors created new opportunities for newspaper reporting by the penny press and necessitated
changes to law enforcement leading to new urban police departments.
As the nineteenth century continued, it is also no surprise that the press

and police evolved and developed together, often in similar ways, such as newspaper reporters and police officers both being assigned to specific locations or responsibilities, known as "beats," as well as the use of badges by both the press and the police. Significantly, newspapers and law enforcement through the mid-nineteenth century were not without their problems, including both having and creating significant issues and division with marginalized communities. Amid these trends and others, which would continue for years to come, the colonial era through the rise of the modern press and police set the foundation for the press-police relationship in the United States, marked by cooperative coexistence and contentiousness from the very beginning.

The political, economic, and social upheaval stemming from the Civil War and its aftermath had, like in other eras, significant implications for the press, police, and their relationship, again, not surprisingly, often in similar ways. Chapter 2 illustrates first how each navigated the Civil War and then how, following the conflict, both entities expanded with new forms of journalism and the continued spread of modern police departments. Significantly, the second half of the nineteenth century saw the rise of unique practices by the press and police that added a new, complicated layer to the press-police relationship. With the invention of horse-drawn patrol wagons designated for law enforcement use came reporters riding with the police, marking the advent of the media ride-along, a practice still used more than 150 years later. Early instances of members of the press and police impersonating each other for their own specific purposes also arose, also setting the foundation for a practice still raising important implications to this day. But even amid such significant change, trends dating to the American colonies, namely, cooperative coexistence and contentiousness, also continued, as well as problems related to greed, politics, race, class, and gender, increasing calls for change that grew louder and louder as the twentieth century approached.

An era of reform emerged across American society in the first decades of the twentieth century with the rise of the Progressive movement. Chapter 3 details how the press and police were not immune to change, each undertaking their own forms of professionalization and reform, though with mixed results and often still failing to adequately serve marginalized communities. Both the press and the police also underwent institutionalization, meaning efforts toward defining their boundaries and becoming independent institutions. Combined with dealing with World War I, new and renewed types of aggressive critical reporting by the press, and new strategies, like public relations, by law enforcement, the result was an era of greater separation and division, though cooperative coexistence, impersonation, and media ride-alongs each remained key parts of the story of the press-police relationship.

Then came a significant change: the rise of greater partnerships between the press and police in the 1920s–'50s, marking an era of symbiosis and trust otherwise unseen in the history of the U.S. press-police relationship. Chapter 4 tells the story of how amid the "Roaring Twenties," Prohibition, the Great Depression, World War II, and other major societal developments, the press and police once more underwent changes with notable connections that collectively allowed for a greater level of trust between the two. It was an era where a game of dominoes in the police department's press room was not out of the question or reporters "borrowing" a police vehicle with little punishment was within the bounds of what could be expected. Cooperative coexistence was therefore quite common during the time period, including as crime and policing became common subjects in film, radio, and television news and entertainment in the first half of the twentieth century, contributing to the positive relationship between the press and police. However, this did not mean that contentiousness simply went away. Far from it. By the end of this era, cracks were beginning to show, foreshadowing a major shift on the horizon.

That dramatic swing came in the 1960s–'70s, the basis of chapter 5. The era of heightened partnerships and trust devolved into an era of division, conflict, and distrust between the press and police during a tumultuous time across the United States, in which members of the public increasingly distrusted the government amid the Vietnam War, civil rights movement, Watergate, and other major developments. Both the press and the police also struggled, as in the past, to fully and properly serve marginalized communities, with law enforcement in particular undergoing a "crisis," in which television coverage revealed police brutality and other problematic actions against Black individuals and civil rights movement protesters. Contentiousness therefore defined this era, as the news media and law enforcement more often targeted each other, the press through critical, adversarial, and investigative reporting and the police through arrests, use of force, searches and seizures, subpoenas, and surveillance directed at the press. Impersonation and media ride-alongs only further problematized the relationship, over-shadowing cooperative coexistence.

Chapter 6 brings the story of the press-police relationship to the present, focusing on four decades in which the news media and law enforcement returned to a more balanced combination of partnerships and division amid a new era of political, economic, social, and technological changes and influences. Although this era is hundreds of years removed from the rise of the press-police relationship in the colonial era and the creation of the modern forms of each entity in the mid-nineteenth century, it nevertheless marks the continuation of the trends dating back to those eras, namely, cooperative coexistence and contentiousness. Not surprisingly, other trends and practices, including impersonation and media ride-alongs, as well as problems tied to political influences, fluctuating resources, and division with marginalized communities, also continued. Chapter 6 aims to uncover why this is the case, namely, why members of the press and police can get along or even cooperate at one moment, but then be embroiled in conflict the next. The chapter discusses the current purposes and functions of the press and police, as well as the current state of, and reasons for, the interactions between the institutions and the effects they raise.

Chapter 7, as part of this long history of the press-police relationship, briefly details elements of the evolution of the law surrounding it. Doing so clarifies—for members of the news media, law enforcement, and public—the legal considerations of the different ways in which the press and the police interact and further reveals why the press-police relationship continues as a cooperative coexistence in some cases, while in others as a contentious one, with impersonation and media ride-alongs adding another layer of complexity. It also reveals important ways in which the law affects not only the press and the police but also their relationship and the public.

Finally, the conclusion focuses on how the history and law of the press-police relationship informs the future of both institutions, namely, how it might be improved moving forward amid other reform efforts individually targeting the press and police. This chapter argues that cooperative coexistence is the ideal, as it best allows the press and the police to function and accomplish their purposes. However, the chapter also acknowledges that contentiousness is a natural part of the relationship, though action needs to be taken by both institutions to minimize division to the greatest extent possible. Additionally, the conclusion argues that significant action needs to be taken to address the negative effects arising from impersonation and media ride-alongs in particular. Although there have been instances, and even eras, of heightened tension and conflict between the press and police, there have also been a great many times marked by a spirit of cooperation and coexistence, even in periods of heightened contentiousness. This suggests that change is possible and that the press-police relationship might indeed improve, curtailing negative effects and ensuring that both institutions are better able to serve and benefit the public moving forward.

Rise of the Modern Press and Police, 1630s–1850s

THE ORIGINS OF JOURNALISM AND policing, and the relationship between them, date back tens of thousands of years.[1] Oral cultures arising as early as 150,000 BCE saw the beginning of "news," meaning the conveyance of information about happenings in a community, spread through word of mouth. Such information included topics such as local misbehavior by certain individuals, marking an antecedent to crime news. Written cultures developed in ~3,000 BCE, in some cases covering official corruption, a precursor to the press holding government accountable. Printed news arose first in sixteenth-century imperial China and Korea, with the first instances of printed news and sensationalism on crime arriving in Europe in the 1570s. Meanwhile, policing first arose in ancient Babylon, where individuals with military backgrounds were generally tasked with enforcing what were among the earliest legal codes.[2] Ancient China, Egypt, Rome, and Greece each had forms of policing, with other civilizations and countries developing forms of law enforcement in ensuing centuries. This, of course, includes the United States, beginning with the country's origins as a colony of Great Britain, and continuing with the rise of the modern press and police in the first half of the nineteenth century, setting the foundation for a centuries-long history of the U.S. press-police relationship.

Colonial Newspapers and the Partisan Press

One can trace the press-police relationship in the United States back to before the founding of the republic to the formation of Great Britain's North American mainland colonies, in which colonists scrambled to set up forms of communication, as well as methods of maintaining law and order. Journalism began with the establishment of printing presses in the New World, including first in Cambridge, Massachusetts, in 1638.[3] From the 1630s through about 1762, much of the materials circulating in the colonies were European books, diaries, letters, religious texts, and newspapers. The first materials published by American presses were government decrees, legal documents, opinion or political pamphlets, almanacs, educational materials, and religious writings. Among other content, these publications contained reports of current events, which included coverage of wrongdoings and the resultant punishments, such as public hangings.

In 1690, Benjamin Harris, an English bookseller and writer regarded as the first journalist in the American colonies, published the first newspaper in America, titled *Publick Occurrences*. In order to constitute a "newspaper," a publication must be published regularly or frequently, carry news and information about a variety of events or topics, display content using a "consistent and recognizable" format or title, and be disseminated to a wide readership.[4] Harris wrote in the one and only issue of *Publick Occurrences* before it was shut down by British colonial authorities that its purpose was to regularly cover "such considerable things as have arrived upon our notice."[5]

From the creation of the *Boston News-Letter* in 1704 through the following decades, several additional newspapers arose in New England. They mainly focused on European affairs and verbatim European political stories, as well as commercial and trading information. However, they also included some coverage of crime and local happenings, catering to colonists who, thanks to evolving education systems, had an increasingly higher literacy rate and a growing desire for local news. Newspapers also appeared in the southern colonies, though somewhat later than in the North due to the establishment of more farming units than populous towns.

As the Revolutionary War approached and enveloped the colonies, newspapers and pamphlets shifted their focus to debates related to independence from England, among other issues of the day.[6] Following the war, newspapers aligned themselves with one of the two newly emerged political parties, the Federalists and Anti-Federalists. Known as the "partisan press," or "party press," printers took sides on issues in public discourse, often becoming "outrageously partisan" to vilify the opposing side.[7] Newspapers also provided a forum for the first debates over the meaning of free speech and a free press, eventually leading to the drafting of the First Amendment. This period therefore saw the continued growth of criticizing public officials in print, as well as increased coverage of major political issues. Further changes included increased coverage of domestic news, as opposed to events in England and the European continent, the introduction of daily newspapers, and the creation of editors and correspondents generally assigned to cover doings in the U.S. capital city. In 1792, Congress passed the Postal Act, which not only formally established the U.S. Postal Service as a publicly owned entity but also helped expand the dissemination of newspapers through direct federal subsidies.[8] The partisan press perhaps reached its zenith in the early nineteenth century, a period called the era of "black journalism" or the "Dark Ages of Partisan Journalism."[9]

Meanwhile, the press continued to grow outside New England. In the South, several weekly papers were established following the Revolutionary War.[10] However, the number of newspapers still lagged New England, including because the population in the South was more spread out, newspapers only reached plantation owners and educated individuals, and there was less infrastructure, such as roads, to support the regular delivery or sale of papers. As the United States expanded westward, so too did the "Frontier Press." Although disorganized, the Frontier Press was characterized by small newspapers in settlements and towns, often relying on the Pony Express and still developing U.S. Postal Service for information and circulation.[11]

Colonial Law Enforcement

The antecedents of policing in the United States were also found in the respective American colonies, which had several different types of law enforcement.[12] One relied on informal methods such as members of the local church or family members handling disputes and instances of bad behavior. In many cases, individuals took law enforcement into their own hands or formed vigilante committees or "brotherly watches." Colonial law enforcement also came to include sheriffs—county officials appointed by the colonial governor for the purposes of criminal law enforcement, who were also often responsible for collecting taxes, conducting elections, maintaining bridges and roads, and other duties. Constables, who were sometimes elected while at other times appointed, generally had similar tasks to sheriffs, namely, being tasked with enforcing the law and maintaining order in a city or town, though also focusing on health and sanitation, among other civic tasks. Collectively, sheriffs and constables were meant to keep the peace in their communities, including dealing with unwanted or excessive drinking, gambling, and prostitution. However, both were often ineffective. They were rarely trained, and in requiring sheriffs and constables to also handle administrative matters, such as holding elections or collecting taxes, officials placed less emphasis on crime prevention, with little incentive to deal with crime. Adding to these problems was political corruption, with officials favoring their families and friends, resulting in officers taking bribes, fixing juries, or assaulting citizens without any cause.

Perhaps the aspects of colonial law enforcement closest to modern conceptions of policing were day and night watches, which date back to the first night watch established in Boston in 1634.[13] Under the watch system, men patrolled the community on the lookout for fires, suspicious individuals, or riots. Details of the watch system varied by locality, though they were generally authorized by a city or town government and service was voluntary, with watchmen being overseen by constables. However, some localities tried compulsory service, including as a form of punishment. Some localities, including Boston and New York, paid watchmen a fee, though most officers did not receive a salary but instead were paid by private citizens from their town. Ultimately, any adult male could enlist or be enlisted, regardless of qualifications. Watchmen, like sheriffs and constables, were also subject to political interference, were poorly paid, and garnered little respect from the local community. The result was that watchmen were often unprepared and ineffective, being found more often in bars, brothels, or asleep than patrolling the streets. And when they encountered situations too much to handle, the military or state militia was called in, as well as the U.S. Marshals beginning in 1779.

Rise of the Modern Press and Police

In the 1830s, major cities saw significant political, economic, social, and technological changes amid a dramatic increase in urbanization and immigration. New York City, for example, saw its population jump from fewer than 100,000 in 1810 to more than 200,000 two decades later, with city and town populations across the United States nearly doubling in the 1840s.[14] In the first decades of the nineteenth century, the number of immigrants from around the world entering the United States was only about 5,000 per year.[15] By the 1830s, that number had increased to 600,000, predominantly made up of people from Germany, Ireland, and Scandinavia. By the 1840s, 1.7 million immigrants were entering the

United States each year, with the total reaching more than 2.6 million by 1860. The great influx of new residents resulted not only in the rapid growth of many U.S. cities but also in the formation of ethnic enclaves within them. The result was larger, increasingly literate low-income communities, but also greater diversity and economic inequality.[16] Growing with the rise in immigration, industrialization in the United States also upheaved and reordered U.S. society, sparking new innovations, but also new tensions, violence, and conflict both regionally and between rural and urban America.

The result, therefore, of these larger societal trends and upheavals was greater crime, for which there were several reasons, especially in urban centers. First, the mid-nineteenth century saw conflict between different racial and religious groups, including white violence targeting the Black community. In particular, major cities, though especially New York City, "were the main points of racial conflicts" and "furnished the means for constant misunderstanding among religious and racial groups that eventuated in mob force."[17] Such conflict, including by gangs formed by Irish settlers and later others in New York City, arose as an "outgrowth of intense hatred and prejudice that were based on ignorance and fear." Second, increased crime arose amid "unbalanced sexual proportions . . . in the larger industrial centers of the East," leading "to an increase in sexual crimes."[18] Third, the second quarter of the nineteenth century saw significant income gaps and inequality, especially within major cities, provoking greed, tension, and division. Furthermore, the rise of the banking system in major cities led to new forms of crime, including "embezzlement," and "the transportation of large sums of money from place to place helped increase highway robbery." Finally, political corruption in major cities certainly led to increased graft and wrongdoing by politicians and those they encouraged to do so, whether in relation to gambling, prostitution, and more. All of these factors, combined with the lack of a strong law enforcement presence, lack of punishment for offenses, and lack of sanitation and good living conditions during this time period, including and especially by the 1850s in New York City, led to increased conflict and wrongdoing, prompting greater calls for something to be done.[19]

It was against this backdrop that the press and the police came to take their modern forms. As mentioned, in 1833, Benjamin Day established the *New York Sun*, heralded as the first successful penny-press newspaper, or "penny paper."[20] It was not long, however, before Day had several competitors, including James Gordon Bennett's *New York Herald* and Horace Greeley's *New-York Tribune*. In time, penny papers became known as the "popular press," as they appealed to and were affordable for all members of the public, including laborers and those from low-income communities. The penny press and technological innovations of the day, including the steam press, also led to the rise of daily issues and the commercialization of the newspapers, with newsboys (and some newsgirls) selling the "daily" on the city streets. Additionally, penny papers came to rely on broad circulation and advertising revenue to turn a profit, rather than the subscriptions or political subsidies of the past. Partisanship did not, however, completely exit the picture during this time, and by the 1850s, even the original penny papers had clear political alliances.

Other modern journalistic practices arose during this time, including attribution of sources and follow-up stories, even though penny papers still evinced a good amount of sensationalism and self-promotion.[21] The era of the penny press also saw the advent of the telegraph, invented by Samuel Morse in 1844, as well as the subsequent rise of the Associated Press, formed by representatives of five New York papers in 1846 to function as a formal news "wire-service,"[22] so called because of their connection to the telegraph. AP correspondents spread throughout the nation to gather news to dispatch via telegraph lines, greatly broadening the acquisition and dissemination of news across the United States.

At around the same time that the early press was transforming into its modern version, in London in 1829, Sir Robert Peel founded the first modern police force, known as the Metropolitan Police Department.[23] Peel's force had three primary characteristics, namely, a mission of crime prevention; a military ethos, including the use of military ranks and titles; and the use of uniforms, patrols, and designated assignments of territories to patrol, known as beats. Despite concerns that a police force resembling a standing army was antithetical to American values, several U.S. cities adopted Peel's "modern"[24] style of policing, including Boston, which created the "Day Police" in 1838, the precursor to the Boston Police Department, formally founded in 1854. Other cities followed suit, including New York City in 1845, Cincinnati in 1852, Philadelphia in 1854, and Chicago and Milwaukee in 1855.

Interestingly, growing U.S. cities adopted such police measures for many of the same reasons that influenced the creation of the penny press, including the aforementioned rise in urbanization, immigration, and industrialization that, beginning as early as the 1830s, fueled both ethnic diversity and growing economic disparities.[25] The resultant rise in crime prompted local government to seek new means of crime prevention, including those devised by Peel. Economic interests also played a role in the adoption of modern police departments, including in Boston, where businesses that previously hired individuals to protect their property and commercial goods came to expect such service from the city police.[26] In this way, Boston merchants realized a way to save money, by transferring the costs of such protection from their books to the city's. Early police forces were therefore formed to protect the property interests of wealthy white Americans, largely emphasizing social control and a stable workforce, rather than to prevent or adequately address crime in the interests of all citizens.

And just as many of the factors had prompted both the press and the police to begin a significant transformation during roughly the same time, so too did both institutions embrace the same types of changes. For example, some of the characteristics U.S. police departments adopted from Peel's model would later be adopted by the press as well. For example, members of both the press and the police were assigned to specific locations, responsibilities, or both,[27] so it is not a coincidence that both institutions, starting with law enforcement, would come to use the same word to describe these assignments: *beats*. Peel assigned officers to specific geographic areas, in which the respective "bobbies" were responsible for trying to prevent and address incidents of crime. For the press, the similar idea of establishing beats is generally credited to editor Charles E. Chapin, who at the end of the nineteenth century drew a checkerboard pattern on a map of New York City and assigned reporters to expressly cover events within their assigned beats. There was, however, precedent for this idea, as the first reporters employed by the penny press were sent to report on happenings in specific locations of New York City as part of their daily tasks.

The use of badges by both the press and the police followed a similar story line.[28] Part of the uniform advocated for and implemented by Peel was a numbered badge for each officer, another policy adopted by newly established police departments in the United States. In fact, in New York City and other jurisdictions, officers' badges were made from copper, garnering them the nickname "cops." Press badges, too, can be traced back to at least the second half of the nineteenth century, with some of the earliest ones being used by the newsboys selling papers on the street. A major impetus for their use was lobbyists in Washington, D.C., posing as journalists to gain access to politicians. The D.C. press corps summarily established rules about who could access Capitol press galleries and telegraph facilities, with White House reporters following by the twentieth century and convening the White House Correspondents' Association in 1914. Although this meant greater access for some journalists, it meant exclusion for others, particularly people of color.

Although the police departments of U.S. cities largely adopted the policies and practices outlined by Peel, two key differences distinguished U.S. police from their London counterparts. First, officers in the United States were given "unchecked discretionary power," therefore providing them more autonomy than those in England, which meant less direct oversight of their activities by already unqualified or outnumbered commanding officers, who could cover only so much ground in monitoring and communicating with their subordinates.[29] One result of wielding more discretionary power was that one might find U.S. police officers in bars, gambling dens, and brothels rather than patrolling the streets or preventing crime, much like colonial law enforcement officials and officers.

Second, U.S. police were influenced by powerful local governments and politicians operating under the "boss system," such as Tammany Hall in New York City.[30] Under this arrangement, politicians hired new police officers based on political connections rather than their qualifications. Indeed, jobs as police officers were considered a major reward under the so-called spoils system that politicians could dispense. In return, police officers largely put the carrying of the wishes of politicians, such as beating or arresting political opponents, ahead of their duty to serve and protect the public. Politicians also offered kickbacks and payoffs to police officers for turning a blind eye, namely, not shutting down or interfering with illegal drinking, gambling, and prostitution, as well as not "targeting" or looking into the affairs of their benefactor's political allies. The lack of accountability of individual officers was therefore also tied to bossism and the relatively few commanding officers on a typical force often being backed politically. Departments were therefore staffed by unqualified officials and officers who despite having significant discretionary power had motivations for political gain, rather than serving the public and preventing crime. In this way, the police's principal charge to maintain social order was subverted into a political game, with officers frequently committing criminal activity—including instances of police brutality—rather than preventing it. In the end, early modern police forces were rife with corruption, ineffectiveness, and violence despite the hope of quelling growing crime in expanding cities.

Connection to Underrepresented and Marginalized Individuals and Communities

Significantly, the colonial press, partisan press, and penny press, as well as colonial law enforcement and modern police departments, all raised significant problems and concerns in relation to marginalized individuals and groups. Both the colonial press and the partisan press came to be run almost exclusively by white men and cater to the wealthy—also mostly white and male, something entrenched by the late eighteenth and early nineteenth centuries—and offered few, if any, opportunities for women and people of color, following broader trends in U.S. society.[31] This resulted in problematic coverage of people of color, including describing Native Americans and enslaved persons in ways that focused, frequently unfairly, on violence and crime. The post office also played a role in perpetuating the white racial narrative in that it did not deliver antislavery publications in the South and as early as 1803 hired only white persons to deliver mail.

As the modern press was developing in the mid-nineteenth-century United States, the problematic coverage of marginalized people and communities, combined with an overall lack of reporting on topics and issues most important to these groups and people, helped prompt the creation and growth of several alternative newspapers and presses, often those providing dissenting voices in American society.[32] Although the penny papers advocated more for the average reader than had papers in the past, the former still included racist views and featured inconsistent coverage of people of color and lower-income communities. For example, newspaper articles often depicted violence as the fault of Black men. Furthermore, telegraph and AP dispatches frequently contained unfavorable coverage of Black and low-income communities, especially as related to involvement in crime and riots. Such coverage helped "sow racial hatred . . . and spearheaded bloody mob attacks against non-white communities and their abolitionist supporters."[33]

In 1827, a group of free Black men in New York City founded *Freedom's Journal*, the first Black-owned newspaper in the United States.[34] It generally focused on abolishing slavery and challenging racial bigotry in American society, including that seen in coverage by white newspaper editors at the time, before ceasing publication in 1829. The 1840s saw a more outspoken generation of Black editors and publishers, including Frederick Douglass, arise in the North, all of whom made passionate calls for emancipation and a new national framework of Black freedom advocates. The *Liberator*, published by William Lloyd Garrison from 1831 to 1865, marked the nation's first integrated paper. The growth of the Black press included the years following the Civil War with the rise of several new Black newspapers,[35] including the *People's Advocate* founded in Virginia in 1876 by businessman and politician Traverse B. Pinn Sr., who served as its first publisher and business manager, and lawyer, historian, and civil rights activist John Cromwell, who served as its first editor.

The Black press also expanded west, with the region's oldest Black newspaper being the *California Eagle*, founded in Los Angeles in 1879 as the *California Owl* by John James Neimore, who created the newspaper as a teenager after moving from Texas to California. The newspaper aimed to provide Black settlers with important information in their transition to the West, including posting job and housing information. Charlotta A. Bass assumed control of the newspaper following Neimore's death in 1912, becoming what many scholars believe to be the first Black woman to own and operate a newspaper in the United States. Bass previously worked selling subscriptions to the *Providence Watchman*, a Rhode Island Black newspaper, before moving to California in 1910 and taking a job at the *Owl*, which she renamed the *California Eagle*. Under her control, the newspaper focused more on campaigning against discrimination and segregation. In ensuing decades, the Black press built on this foundation, providing a voice for the Black community through the present.

One year after the creation of *Freedom's Journal*, the General Council of the Cherokee Nation worked with the Reverend Samuel Worcester of the American Board of Commissioners for Foreign Missions and missionary to the Cherokee Nation to build a printing office for a new newspaper, the *Cherokee Phoenix*, which is regarded as the first Native American newspaper.[36] Elias Boudinot, a writer who grew up in Cherokee Territory and was raised by parents of mixed Cherokee and European ancestry, along with other leaders of the Cherokee Tribe, helped raise money to found the paper. Boudinot edited the first edition, printed in both Cherokee and English. The *Cherokee Phoenix*, and other Native newspapers launched by the 1850s, provided a contrasting view to coverage of Native Americans in the commercial press, which reinforced negative stereotypes when bothering to cover political, economic, and social issues important to Native Americans at all.

The rise of the alternative press in the United States in the 1820s–'50s also included Spanish-, German-, French-, and Chinese-language papers.[37] By the start of the Civil War, immigrants and people of color published more than one hundred newspapers in the United States, challenging narratives based in white bias.[38] By the twentieth century, ethnic communities published thousands of volumes of newspapers.[39]

This era also saw the rise of the labor press, including the *Mechanics Free Press* and the *Working Man's Advocate*, each of which criticized the treatment and exploitation of workers by big business.[40] By the 1830s, there were approximately fifty labor weeklies, and that number increased as the decade advanced with each new wave of urbanization and industrialization. By the end of the nineteenth century and well into the twentieth, the number of working-class and labor advocacy newspapers grew exponentially, with 1880–1940 seeing "thousands of labor and radical publications circulated, constituting a golden age for working-class newspapers."[41]

The first "women's magazine" in the United States was the *Lady's Magazine and Repository of Entertaining Knowledge*, founded in 1792 in Philadelphia by a "Society of Literary Characters."[42] Although it lasted for less than a year, the *Lady's Magazine* and later women's magazines that followed in the 1820s–'30s, such as *Godey's Lady's Book*, founded in 1830 by former newspaper editor Louis A. Godey, included stories and features related to household management and child care, but also addressed issues such as child labor and women's legal rights. During the 1820s–'50s, known as the "period of expansion" for magazines in America, which included those produced for and by women, there was greater emphasis on marketing to women readers. There were also technological advancements, increased literacy, and an emphasis on original contributions, each of which contributed to more women entering the printing industry in the second half of the nineteenth century. Although women rarely held positions as reporters at mainstream newspapers in the nineteenth century, there were some notable exceptions, including Margaret Fuller, an advocate for women's rights who became the first woman reporter for Greeley's *New-York Tribune* in 1844. Significantly,

editors of Black press newspapers and Native American magazines
devoted space for original works by women. Douglass, an outspoken
supporter of women's rights, "backed up his rhetoric by providing space
in his newspapers for several black women writers."[43] Among them was
Mary Ann Shadd Cary, who in her writings advocated for the Black
community and challenged corruption, in addition to supporting the
women's suffrage movement and improving education, among other political and social topics. Shadd Cary later became the first Black
woman publisher of a newspaper in North America after launching the
Provincial Freeman in Windsor, Ontario, in March 1853.

The colonial era and early nineteenth century also marked the beginning of the long history of conflict and division between the police and
marginalized communities, especially the Black community. During the
era, police corruption, ineffectiveness, and brutality were common.[44]
People of color, including enslaved persons, were often the target of violence by early forms of policing, with the first deaths of Black men in
America at the hands of law enforcement dating back to 1619, when the
first slaver full of kidnapped Africans landed at Point Comfort in the
Virginia Colony.[45]

One of the earliest forms of policing in the United States, slave patrols
became a main system of law enforcement in the South, beginning with
South Carolina in 1704. These forces searched roads, inns, and other
locations for Black individuals who did not have a pass allowing them
to be away from the plantation after curfew. If they found an individual without proper documentation, or who was acting suspiciously, the
patrols took them into custody and held them for appearances before
magistrates or freeholders. Slave patrols also went a step further and
"provide[d] a form of organized terror to deter slave revolts," as well as
punished slaves, outside the law, for breaking plantation rules.[46] These
forces remained active in the South until the Civil War, marking an antecedent to statewide police forces that developed in the early twentieth
century.[47] In addition to a partial resemblance to the modernizing police
developing at the time in New England, including staffs of uniformed
municipal employees, slave patrols also helped lead to the development
of modern police departments in the South, such as New Orleans's new
force in 1840.[48]

Slave patrols ultimately demonstrated significant division between
law enforcement and marginalized communities, as the very purpose
of such patrols was the prevention of crime and insurrection by slaves

against the white community in the antebellum South.[49] Law enforcement also continued protecting the interests of wealthier individuals and groups. From the very beginning, then, starting with slave patrols and continuing through the formation of modern police departments, law enforcement in the South was a primary means of maintaining the political and social status quo, which included white supremacy. Because modernizing police departments in the North also served largely to protect foremost the economic interests of the wealthy, control over underprivileged individuals, laborers, and anyone else who challenged societal norms has been an integral feature of the history of U.S. law enforcement, a significant problem pervading policing for years to come and to this day.

Amid the disorganized beginnings of the press and the police, as well as a growing partisanship, entrenched racism, and other changes in the young republic, came some of the interactions that would come to define the press-police relationship for more than two centuries. Such interactions would continue and evolve with the changes brought about by major societal shifts and the resulting rise of the modern press and police.

Cooperative Coexistence from the First American Newspaper to the Modern Press and Police

The origins of cooperative coexistence between the press and the police in the United States, namely, press coverage of crime and law enforcement—the first type of interaction between the two institutions—dates back to the first American newspaper, *Publick Occurrences*, with the sole issue including an account of a kidnapping of two children by Native Americans, as well as two fires, one of which destroyed a printing press. As newspapers expanded across New England, so too did reporting on crime and law enforcement. In 1704, the *Boston News-Letter* published the first "extra" in America, detailing the exploits and ultimate hanging of "Quelch the pirate."[50] In 1703, Massachusetts governor Joseph Dudley sent the *Charles*, a ship under the command of Captain Daniel Plowman, to attack French and Spanish vessels near Newfoundland and Arcadia. Before the ship could leave Massachusetts, Plowman fell ill and was locked in his quarters by the rebelling crew, which included John Quelch, the man chosen to be the new captain of the *Charles*. Between August 1703 and February 1704, Quelch and the crew went on a "piracy spree against Portuguese ships in the Caribbean and off the coast of South America . . . stealing a wide variety of goods and valuables and committing a number of other crimes including murder."[51] After a trial, six men, including Quelch, were ultimately hanged in Boston. Although law enforcement did not play a direct role in the crimes committed by Quelch and the crew, the *Boston News-Letter*'s reporting demonstrates how colonial papers covered crime and wrongdoing, which would, in other cases, implicate law enforcement.[52]

Such newspapers included the *American Weekly Mercury*, which was founded by Andrew Bradford in Boston in 1719 and dedicated more space for local news, including crimes like murder, stealing, and smuggling. In 1801, Fisher Ames, a noted writer, teacher, and attorney elected to the first United States Congress, published a piece in the *New-England Palladium*, a newspaper based in Boston, addressing U.S. printers, in which he asserted that "there seems to be a rivalship among printers, who shall have the most wonders, and the strangest and most wonderful crimes."[53] Although he wrote that such coverage "raise[s] curiosity, and we desire nothing so much, as the particulars of terrible tragedies," Ames actually implored printers "to banish as many murders, and horrid accidents, and monstrous births and prodigies from their gazettes," contending that they "make each particular hair stiffen and stand upright in the reader's head," as well as raise "terrour," "horror," and "disgust." But despite concerns raised by Ames and others, newspapers continued to cover "reports of 'shocking accidents,' 'horrid murders,' suicides, and other crimes."[54]

With the rise of the penny press, press coverage of police took center stage. Perhaps the most significant change brought about by the penny press was the beginning of the modern concept of "news," particularly through the increased publishing of stories about crime and coverage of police doings.[55] Although the penny press did not invent reporting on crime, it did focus on such news more regularly than ever before. For the first time in the United States, the press printed reports from law enforcement, the courts, the streets, and private homes, "pioneer[ing] the coverage of the criminal, especially in reporting police news."[56] This came amid a societal context that provided a "perfect storm," so to speak, for the coverage of crime and policing. Urbanization and immigration meant a growing, diverse body of readers never far from the call of a newsboy or newsgirl. Industrialization made innovations like the steam press possible, allowing for daily issues of penny papers. And growing crime meant no shortage of stories to track down and cover. The result was these papers appealing daily to a growing public, like today, captivated by crime and police news, leading to ever-increasing circulation numbers for penny papers. It is perhaps not a coincidence that Edgar Allan Poe's "The Murders in the Rue Morgue," published in *Graham's Magazine* in 1841 and regarded as the first modern detective story, arose during the same era. Three decades later, it was Sherlock Holmes, the most famous fictional detective ever, when told that he was "a walking calendar of crime" and that he "might start a paper along those lines. Call it the 'Police News of the Past,'" who recognized the appeal of news on crime and policing, remarking, "Very interesting reading it might be made, too."[57]

The penny papers covered crime and police through the first paid American reporters, who, along with some editors, independently sought and gathered news, including at crime scenes, police courts, and police departments. For example, George Wisner, who was hired by Day at the *New York Sun* as the first full-time police reporter, would often go early in the morning to police stations and police courts to obtain the latest news, before publishing it the same day. During this era and in ensuing decades, it was therefore common to find reporters in police departments and regularly interacting with officials and officers. Editors also went to greater lengths to get news, including the use of speedboats, messenger pigeons, the Pony Express, and, eventually, the telegraph. In some cases, reporters even arrested criminals, such as in 1838 when "a well dressed white scoundrel . . . was brought to the police office . . . by two respectable newspaper reporters, who arrested him."[58]

Perhaps the most famous crime coverage during the penny-press era arose on April 10, 1836.[59] At three in the morning, the body of twenty-three-year-old prostitute Helen Jewett was found in her bed in a luxury brothel. Jewett had been struck three times in the head before her bed was set on fire, charring a large portion of her body. The *New York Herald* provided the most complete coverage of the murder and ensuing trial. James Gordon Bennett, who was known to go to crime scenes to conduct his own investigations, provided significant detail of the crime scene. He also conducted several interviews with people connected with the case. Bennett, and soon other editors and reporters, wrote that nineteen-year-old clerk Richard P. Robinson, a frequent visitor of Jewett, was accused and charged with the crime. On the morning of April 10, police entered Robinson's home and took him to the crime scene, a common practice at the time. During the investigation and trial, newspapers played up sexual and gruesome details and even falsified evidence. They also editorialized, with each paper providing a different opinion, implicit or explicit, about whether he was guilty. Ultimately, a jury acquitted Robinson, but not before Bennett had already concluded he was the target of a conspiracy involving the police and was innocent of the crime. The reporting by Bennett and others proved significant, as it set the stage for continued coverage of crime, sex, and scandals by the penny press and future eras of journalism.

As the penny press was expanding in New England, newspapers in the South and West also covered crime and policing. For example, early newspapers in Houston, including the *Telegraph and Texas Register*, covered the mounting violence plaguing the city in the late 1830s and 1840s.[60] Assaults were a common occurrence on the streets, often emanating from the young city's many brothels and saloons, prompting increased attention by both the government and the press. Like the penny papers in the North, their counterparts in the South and West often portrayed Black individuals in inaccurate or unfair ways, demonstrating the link between crime coverage and racial injustice that would continue in ensuing eras.

Contentiousness Also Defines Early Press-Police Relationship, Modern Press and Police

Early American newspapers went beyond simply reporting on crime and law enforcement by criticizing and otherwise holding accountable to varying degrees the different forms of government and law enforcement in the colonies, the second type of interaction found throughout the history of the press-police relationship.[61] In pointing out the deficiencies of law enforcement, newspapers contributed to the growing calls for changes and reforms by the 1830s. For example, in 1757 the *New York City Gazette* referred to the Citizen's Watch, the form of law enforcement in the city at the time, as a "parcel of idle, drinking, vigilant Snorers, who never quell'd any nocturnal Tumult in their Lives."[62] In addition to calling attention to the ineffectiveness of the watch system, the *Gazette* contended that its members "would, perhaps, be as ready to join in a Burglary as any Thief in Christendom." Criticism of law enforcement continued through the turn of the nineteenth century, such as in 1812 when the *New York Evening Post* targeted "the abominable practices of the marshals, constables, low attornies [*sic*]."[63] The *Post* called the officials and officers "the worst blood-suckers that prey upon the vitals of a great part of the community."

Amid the growing conflict between printers and the authorities, early examples arose of law enforcement targeting members of the press, the third type of interaction between the press and police. Arrests of members of the press in the United States can be traced back to the arrests of printers in the colonial era.[64] Under the 1798 Alien and Sedition Acts, law enforcement arrested a total of twenty-five individuals, including several printers and others tied to newspapers. But perhaps the most notable arrest and prosecution of a printer came in 1735 when John Peter Zenger, a German immigrant in New York City and printer of the *New York Weekly Journal*, was arrested for seditious libel after his newspaper criticized a local government official.[65] The case arose after the *Journal*, an early partisan press newspaper, accused royal governor William S. Cosby of rigging elections, among other claims. Zenger, as the publisher of the *Journal*, did not write the remarks but determined to keep the authors of the articles in question anonymous, leading him to be arrested and jailed for seditious libel. During Zenger's trial, his lawyer, Andrew Hamilton, convinced the jury to find his client not guilty, arguing that New York's seditious libel law was unjust and against the values of freedom, including being able to criticize the government. Hamilton also argued that the claims about the officials were true, making truth as a viable defense in libel actions.

The press and law enforcement targeting each other expanded with the rise of the modern press and police. Police corruption, ineffectiveness, and violence created opportunities for editors and reporters to investigate, criticize, and otherwise hold accountable law enforcement. Although the general view of the free press during this time did not emphasize the ideal of the press holding the powerful accountable, at least not to the extent it does in the twentieth and twenty-first centuries, government and law enforcement remained targets of press scrutiny. The penny press began a trend in which "modern police forces have been the target of media scrutiny since police first established ranks in urban centers."[66]

Newspapers targeted several issues arising from law enforcement, including "absolute police despotism"[67] and ineffectiveness.[68] The press also targeted corruption in law enforcement, with the *National Police Gazette* being among the publications to do so.[69] Founded in 1845 by attorney Enoch E. Camp and George Wilkes, a clerk in Camp's law office and a journalist who previously started a four-page paper, the *Subterranean*, in 1844, the *Police Gazette* had the express purpose of focusing on crime and law enforcement. In its early years, the publication "was very much an organ of artisan and working-class culture, upholding the virtues of natural rights, republicanism and the public good, condemning not only those who committed crimes against individuals and their property, but also corrupt public officials."[70] Thus, the *Police Gazette* would, at times, target police with criticism and otherwise critical coverage. For example, in 1847, the *Gazette* reported that some on-duty New York City police officers were hard to locate, suggesting they were not adequately performing their jobs. To top it off, some of these officers received more in rewards than the rest of the nearly one thousand men in the department, demonstrating the problematic nature of policing at the time.

By the time of the Civil War, the *Police Gazette*—first under the control of former New York City chief of police George Matsell from 1866 to 1877 and then Belfast immigrant and journalist Richard Kyle Fox from 1877 to 1922—shifted to a more tabloid-style publication, falling in the same category as the growing number of newspapers reporting on sensationalized crime and focusing on lurid murders and western outlaws. Combined with helping pioneer sports coverage and celebrity gossip columns, the *Police Gazette* also marked an antecedent to modern tabloid and sensational outlets, though with its central focus always on crime and police.

The penny press held law enforcement accountable to the public in several ways, contributing to changes and reforms in law enforcement. Perhaps most significantly, the increased "publicized crimes of the day [by penny papers], coupled with extreme collective violence, indicated to citizens that cities needed to be secured, and public officials moved to secure them by implementing urban police systems,"[71] namely, the modern police departments first found in New York City and Boston. Furthermore, in conducting their own investigations and "crusades," penny papers in several cases actually solved crimes before the police.[72] In doing so, the penny press's "pyrotechnic entry" only further increased "the normal pressure on the police to solve gruesome murders [and other crimes]," as "prying, fact-hungry reporters . . . asked questions that penetrated more deeply" and "peer[ed] over the shoulders of police as they attempted to solve crimes."[73] Penny-press editors and reporters digging deeper into crimes than previous newspapers therefore also "increased pressure on police officials to commission crime-solving specialists— detectives"—as part of modern police departments, including the first such unit in Boston in 1846.[74] Finally, even in cities with already established police departments, the penny press helped prompt changes and reforms, namely, through criticism of police.[75] For example, the *New York Herald* "fought for the adoption of uniforms by the city police," a policy that when ultimately adopted "added much to the respect for law and order in New York."[76]

In addition to the press holding law enforcement accountable, the early years of the modern press-police relationship were made more contentious by instances of police targeting editors and reporters. Arrests of journalists continued during this time, often while or for doing their jobs. For example, in 1842, Rev. Charles Torrey—an abolitionist and freelance reporter for several northern newspapers in 1841 and 1842—attended a slaveholders' convention in Annapolis, Maryland, where he sought to report on the organized efforts to defend slavery.[77] Torrey was, however, arrested after refusing to leave during a closed session of the meeting even though he "was engaged in a lawful exercise of his profession as a reporter."[78] Torrey spent six days in jail, an experience that only strengthened his resolve to confront slavery directly in slaveholding states. And in Torrey's case, the prosecution went a step further in that the court examined notes he had taken, including of private conversations with slaves.

In ensuing years, police continued to arrest editors and reporters for allegedly "excit[ing] to riot and treason"[79] and libel.[80] Police also targeted members of the press for actions that fell outside their typical work habits, including when law enforcement thought they had gone too far to get a story. Between 1855 and 1860 alone, police arrested editors and reporters for perjury, robbing a post office, disorderly conduct, and being "dangerous characters," among other charges.[81] Regardless of whether members of the press were arrested for conduct related to journalistic functions, the result was the same: increased contentiousness.

The level of contentiousness in the press-police relationship was also ratcheted up by instances of editors and reporters facing threats and violence from not only public officials, rival journalists, and members of the public but also police officers.[82] For example, in 1850, James Corbitt, a member of the night watch, reportedly assaulted *Nashville Reporter* editor Thomas Buckley.[83] The attack came in Buckley's office, where he was "severely beaten." No further details were provided, but the episode nevertheless demonstrated the risk of violence that editors and reporters faced during this time period.

Members of the press also faced searches and seizures by police, often in relation to arrests. In several cases, police conducted searches of newsrooms,[84] at times even going a step further and searching journalists' offices or private homes. For example, in 1857, *Chicago Democrat* editor James O. Brayman was arrested for "robbing the post office drawer of McNally & Co., of valuable letters,"[85] this after two Chicago police officers watched Brayman take letters out of the McNally & Co. box in addition to the *Democrat's* drawer. The officers searched Brayman, finding the letters as well as a key to McNally & Co.'s drawer in his pocket. Shortly thereafter, Brayman's "house and his room at the *Democrat* office were searched by officers, but none of the missing letters were found" there. In recounting these events, the *Chicago Daily Tribune* proclaimed, "The above statements [were] as detailed to us by the officers, there being no legal investigation of the affair. They may or may not be true," suggesting that the newspaper, and by extension the public, was skeptical of the police account, something that would become more deeply ingrained in the second half of the twentieth century and up to the present. This case also demonstrated part of a trend through the present of law enforcement's willingness to search a member of the press, as well as their newsroom and home.

Law enforcement also played a role in the long history of government efforts, including subpoenas, to compel journalists to divulge their sources and certain acquired information. Perhaps the first case of a reporter being jailed for contempt came in 1812 when Nathaniel Rounsavell, an editor of the *Alexandria (VA) Herald,* refused to identify member(s) of the House of Representatives with whom he spoke for an article.[86] He was remanded to custody of the House sergeant at arms until a representative identified himself as Rounsavell's source.

Another noteworthy case arose on March 26, 1848, when the U.S. Senate arrested and imprisoned a journalist.[87] Earlier that month, the *New York Herald* published details of a secret treaty between the United States and Mexico amid ongoing disputes between the two nations over the former Republic of Texas, which the United States had annexed in 1845 but to which Mexico still held claim. Despite significant questioning by senators, correspondent John Nugent repeatedly refused to identify his sources. Nugent was released only when the Senate publicly cited "the face-saving grounds of protecting his health," even though he "spent his captivity in comfort, receiving a doubled salary while issuing his regular columns" and enjoying meals at the sergeant at arms's home.[88]

Although law enforcement was not directly tied to this arrest, it would be in future cases of subpoenas filed against journalists, pitting the press against the police and raising contentiousness in their relationship.

The rise of the modern press and police in the United States did not happen by accident. The penny press and urban police departments came amid a perfect storm of urbanization, immigration, and industrialization. Each was a reaction to the context around them, with the result that both entities evolved from their colonial roots with the expanding United States. And in doing so, they implicated their relationship in crucially important ways. But significantly, practices first seen in the colonial era, falling under cooperative coexistence and contentiousness, continued in largely similar ways even with the rise of the modern forms of both entities. What to make of this? This consistency across eras ultimately demonstrates how the colonial era and first half of the nineteenth century provides a foundation for a relationship that would continue to evolve for another 150-plus years. As the United States hurtled toward the Civil War, as well as a new wave of urbanization, immigration, and industrialization in the second half of the nineteenth century, the story of the press-police relationship would continue, along with it the trends of cooperative coexistence and contentiousness, but also introducing changes and new practices that would usher in a new dimension to their relationship.

CHAPTER 2

New Opportunities, New Problems, 1860s–1890s

IN AN ERA MARKED BY division, conflict, corruption, violence, and greed, what would societal upheaval mean for the newly established modern press and police? And, in turn, what would that mean for their relationship? The second half of the nineteenth century began with the United States having just expanded its territory by roughly a half-million square miles in the aftermath of the Mexican-American War, this as Americans stood on the cusp of the Civil War, which would cause political, economic, and social upheavals affecting all aspects of American society, including the press and police. The postwar eras of Reconstruction, the Gilded Age, and Jim Crow saw Americans embroiled in ongoing social problems and questions related to race relations and other cultural issues that the war had failed to settle. In the final decades of the nineteenth century, American society in general and the press and police in particular were met with new problems and responsibilities, this amid growing governmental oversight and, at times, intervention. The result was the expansion of both institutions—including new forms of journalism building on historical antecedents and further adoption of modern police forces—amid other similarities in how each responded to the societal context as calls for change and reform grew louder by the turn of the century. Nevertheless, trends dating to the American colonies, namely, cooperative coexistence and contentiousness, would continue, though with new unique practices adding a new layer to the press-police relationship.

Press and Police during the Civil War Era

During the Civil War, the press scrambled to provide coverage of the immense conflict. Although the Mexican-American War had featured some of the first instances of war correspondents, this type of journalist became more common during the Civil War, providing eyewitness accounts of battles by using telegraph lines, bringing in stories on horseback, and traveling, or "embedding," with soldiers in the field, including in combat, for a time.[1]

Although some level of partisanship endured during the penny-press era, the renewal of a very heated partisan press in the second half of the nineteenth century occurred in two phases.[2] Prior to and during the Civil War, debates around slavery, suffrage, and other fervent issues of the day brought renewed political influence and editorializing. Following the Civil War, partisanship remained, especially surrounding the "spoils system" of federal, state, and city government and contentious issues such as the impeachment of Andrew Johnson and the extralegal segregationist laws passed in southern states during the rise of Jim Crow.

Heightened partisanship also led to efforts by the government in both the North and the South to influence the press, namely, through imposing censorship.[3] Union censorship evolved in three stages. The first stage, 1861–62, saw uncertainty as the government searched for a workable solution, as well as voluntary self-censorship by the press. The second stage, 1862–64, was marked by government clarification of censorship regulations, though it remained a subjective decision about what to restrict. During this time, all telegraph lines were placed under government supervision, and correspondents, who generally needed to be accredited or recognized, agreed to submit copy to a provost marshal for approval. The third stage, 1864–65, saw correspondents increasingly cooperate with the federal government, though problems arose when military commanders placed pressure on publishers deemed to be traitors. Meanwhile, in the South, Confederate officials destroyed or censored several newspapers. At a minimum, the Confederacy closely oversaw the southern press, limiting the scope of its coverage.

The Civil War also occurred in the partisan and political era of policing, leading to new and renewed problems for law enforcement as well as a growing proclivity for government to try to exert political influence, and even control, of police forces, North and South. In the North, the war halted the progress of law enforcement, as the conflict tasked police officers with addressing war-related matters, including the apprehension, arrest, and detainment of deserters and bounty jumpers; the guarding of military shipments; and temporarily helping to care for wounded soldiers.[4] Police officers also dealt with protests and riots sparked by disagreement over conscription and emancipation, as well as a rise in gambling and prostitution. In trying to coordinate their actions, the police increasingly used the telegraph to communicate, although the system remained under the control of the federal government.

Additionally, the task of providing security for and protecting President Abraham Lincoln fell to local law enforcement when the president came to their respective city. In 1865, the Secret Service was founded as a small policing unit under the Treasury Department, though it was not until after the assassinations of Presidents Lincoln (1865), James A. Garfield (1881), and William McKinley (1901) that the Secret Service shifted to also providing occasional guards for the president, even though there were no funds for the agency to do so.[5] In 1903, the assignment of the guards to protect the president became permanent, though only five agents were assigned to the detail until 1914, when the number began gradually to increase.

In the South, police, like the press, found themselves under Confederate control, which manifested in law enforcement charged with suppressing disloyalty to the Confederacy.[6] The result was the targeting of dissenting voices, including those in the press; renewed tension between Black and white individuals; and increased violence between those believing in the legitimacy of slavery and those who considered it both unsustainable and immoral. Police in certain towns and cities were also tasked with military or paramilitary duties whenever invasion seemed imminent, though at other moments police yielded to soldiers in the patrol of cities. Significantly, the Civil War also led to the questioning of the legitimacy and efficiency of slave patrols, a catalyst for more southern cities to adopt modern police departments like those in the North after war's end.

During the second half of the nineteenth century, however, the problem facing police in the North and South was that departments, officials, and officers "did not have either the doctrine [or] the materials to deal with disorder in any way other than violence."[7] Compounding the problem was that police forces saw a decrease in personnel as many police officers volunteered or were required to serve as soldiers. The combined result during the Civil War era not only produced greater inefficiency and ineffectiveness, but also increased police brutality against the public, as well as increased violence waged against the police.

Societal Changes in the 1870s–1890s Implicate Press and Police

In the decades following the Civil War and up to the turn of the twentieth century, the United States experienced new waves of urbanization, industrialization, and immigration.[8] The result was new forms of journalism and the continued adoption of modern police departments in cities and towns throughout the United States in an attempt to squelch growing crime rates arising from similar factors leading to increased crime in the first half of the century, including economic inequalities as well as a white nativist fear of foreign immigrants, marginalized individuals, and unskilled workers. Between 1870 and 1920, approximately twenty-four million people immigrated to the United States.[9] Over this same span, approximately eleven million people moved from rural areas to major U.S. cities. In 1880 to 1900 alone, major U.S. cities grew by approximately fifteen million people, owing in large part to rising immigration.

And it was in the 1870s–'90s that the United States also saw the rise of three new forms of journalism: "yellow journalism," "serious journalism," and "advocacy journalism." The phrase *yellow journalism* was coined by a cartoon strip by Richard F. Outcault, whose main character, the "Yellow Kid," lived in New York's slums. A battle over control of the cartoon between the owners of New York City's two leading newspapers, Joseph Pulitzer of the *New York World* and William Randolph Hearst of the *New York Journal*, ensued after Hearst persuaded Outcault to leave the *World* for the *Journal*. The new style of newspaper publishing and reporting pioneered by Hearst and Pulitzer, including the layout of the papers and the types of stories they featured, became known as yellow journalism.[10] This style of journalism included sensationalism, exaggeration, lurid details, and shameless self-advertising. Michael Schudson, a journalism professor at the Columbia Journalism School and adjunct professor in the Department of Sociology, has called this style of journalism the "Ideal of the Story," or "action journalism," the goal of which was to spread newspapers to as many readers as possible by focusing on entertainment, shock, and emotionality, as well as offering each issue at a much lower price.[11] The result was the development of mass circulation, as the work of yellow journalists appealed to and reached a far wider audience, including the residents of underrepresented ethnic and lower-income communities to whom the traditional papers had not cared about reaching. The newspapers of the yellow press were also among the first to include photographic images, one of several technological advances in the industry alongside the increased use of telephones by reporters, who now could easily and quickly communicate with newspaper offices to deliver leads on breaking stories.[12]

A very different form of journalism of the day was evinced by the *New York Times*, which was founded in 1851 as a penny paper titled the *New-York Daily Times* by Henry J. Raymond, a journalist and associate editor at several newspapers, including Horace Greeley's *New-York Tribune*. His cofounder was George Jones, who also worked at the *Tribune*, among other newspapers, but was working as a banker in 1851 before establishing the *New-York Daily Times*. The *New York Times* from its inception took a more serious, fact-based approach to reporting.[13] Raymond founded the paper to provide news from around the world with morality and without personal or party bias. In 1860, the *Times* emphasized that its "proper business is to publish facts."[14] However, the *Times* faced bankruptcy until Adolph S. Ochs, the son of German immigrants whose successful career as a newspaper publisher began when he worked as an office boy for the *Knoxville Chronicle*, took over the *Times* near the turn of the century, aiming to provide a trustworthy, dignified, and nonpartisan paper. Under Ochs, the *Times* gained great notoriety during World War I for repeatedly obtaining government documents, a practice it started in the 1890s. Schudson called the Times' style of journalism the "Ideal of Information" because it underscored the press informing the public through verifiable facts and details.[15] Significantly, in doing so, serious journalism also served as an agent of the public by uncovering and singling out abuses across society, including by "critically examin[ing] local governments" and municipal corruption by emphasizing impartiality and facts and by using more and creative sources.[16]

The third form of journalism to emerge in the last decades of the nineteenth century was advocacy journalism, which although not an entirely new form, became increasingly prominent and aggressive in the second half of the century and carried on the muckraking tradition throughout the Progressive Era of the early twentieth century.[17] Advocacy journalism took pride in targeting wrongdoing and corruption in the United States, attempting to alter the composition of public institutions in the spirit of reform of the day. Notable reporters who engaged in this style of reporting included female reporters such as Nellie Bly, who in one instance posed as a patient of an "insane asylum" at Blackwell's Island to expose the routine maltreatment of the residents at the hands of the staff of the facility. Following three of her friends—business owners

Calvin McDowell, Thomas Moss, and Henry Stewart—being lynched in Memphis in 1892, Ida B. Wells, a journalist, author, activist, and co-founder of the National Association for the Advancement of Colored People (NAACP), continuously reported on the lynching of Black men, this during the reign of the Jim Crow South, a time when white journalists paid little attention to these heinous crimes.

In some cases, more mainstream newspapers carried the work of advocacy journalists. For example, Bly, in an industry dominated by white men with few women reporters, began writing for the leading newspaper in Pittsburgh at the time, the *Pittsburgh Dispatch*, in 1885 and later worked for the *New York World*, which published her exposé on Blackwell's Island. Bly not only reported on abuses and wrongdoing, prompting reform, but also broke barriers by writing about significant political and social issues, again in an era where women had few positions in the press and, when they did, were often forced to cover topics related to fashion, housework, and other topics and traits ascribed to women at the time.

Advocacy journalism also found its way into alternative presses, including the Black press and immigrant and labor presses, each of which continued to grow from their roots in the first half of the century. A new alternative press during the second half of the century was the suffrage press, with the *Revolution* marking the first major newspaper.[18] Influential suffragists Susan B. Anthony and Elizabeth Cady Stanton established the newspaper in 1868 and were among its editors until February 1872, when it was absorbed by the *New York Christian Enquirer*. The *Woman's Journal*, founded in 1870 in Boston by abolitionist and suffragist Lucy Stone and her husband, reformer Henry Browne Blackwell, became the *Revolution*'s direct competitor in 1870, serving as an official publication of the American Woman Suffrage Association.

Much like the press, law enforcement continued to expand amid urbanization, immigration, and industrialization in the second half of the nineteenth century. By the 1890s, most large U.S. cities had their own police forces, with smaller towns and localities beginning to follow suit. As modern police forces spread throughout the South and West, they showed significant similarity to their New England counterparts, including the adoption of elements of the English tradition of policing.[19] In the years following the Civil War, Chicago, Detroit, San Francisco, and several other big cities followed the example set in New England, resulting in a remarkable degree of similarity in police departments across the United States, especially in terms of preventive policing, unified administration, officer uniforms, and around-the-clock patrols.

Along with similarities in structure and policy, across the growing United States new police departments came to face similar hurdles, including bossism and keen partisanship under which the early police departments in New York City, Boston, and other major cities found themselves operating.[20] The result, once again, was corruption in law enforcement, especially in New York City under the ongoing influence of William Magear "Boss" Tweed's Tammany Hall. Inefficiency and ineffectiveness in police forces also continued apace, as police officials and higher-ranking officers continued to struggle, as their counterparts in the first half of the century had, to supervise patrolmen after they left the station to work their beats.

At the same time, the United States saw an increase in crime and violence, this in a growing nativist-charged fear among established white Americans of the "dangerous classes" in society, by which they meant immigrants, residents of ethnic enclaves, Black and Hispanic communities, and the unskilled workers who worked in the burgeoning factories, many of whom were recent immigrants from Europe.[21] Conflict also arose from the stark and increasing inequalities in economic opportunities associated with the age of industrialization.[22] From 1880 to 1900, approximately thirty-five thousand workers died annually in work-related accidents, with hundreds of thousands more injured on the job—especially in textile mills and on the assembly lines—during these decades. Poor pay and lack of workplace safety saw the rise of labor unions, whose members staged a series of walkouts and strikes, protests that often led to confrontations and even violence between disgruntled workers and management's hired security forces and police.

One of the most sensational of these violent clashes occurred in Chicago in 1886, an incident that became known as the Haymarket Affair.[23] On May 1, news outlets reported that 80,000 workers peacefully marched up Michigan Avenue as part of a series of nationwide demonstrations and strikes in support of an eight-hour workday. On May 3, however, the protest turned violent, as Chicago police attacked and killed several picketers at the McCormick Reaper Plant. In response to the attacks by the police, the protesters held a meeting in Haymarket Square, in the Near West Side of the city, on the evening of May 4. By the end of the meeting, fewer than 200 people remained gathered, but they were approached by 176 rifle-toting policemen with orders to disperse the crowd. Amid the ensuing chaos, an unidentified individual threw "the first dynamite bomb ever used in peacetime history of the United States," causing police to shoot indiscriminately.[24] In the end, 7 policemen lay dead, in one case directly accountable to the detonation of the bomb, as did 4 workers, with approximately 70 others injured.

In the days that followed, governments across the United States and even the world pointed to the events that transpired in Haymarket Square to take measures, even radical ones, to suppress labor movements, including those by unions. Ultimately, urbanization, industrialization, and immigration fueled already significant political, ethnic, and class tensions, leaving police to address rising crime despite finding themselves working in departments that in some cases were corrupt, ineffective, and abusive to the very public they were charged to serve and protect. And what's more, they did so among a complicated news media environment in which some radical editors criticized antilabor actions, including by police, while other editors who dominated the mainstream press demonized the labor movement, including the work of those radical editors. The result was that the affair marked a complicated tangle of contention and cooperation within and between institutions.

Amid this backdrop, police in the different regions of the United States both raised and faced unique concerns. In the South, policing was inextricably tied to race given the historic role of slavery and white supremacy in southern society and the rise of extralegal "Jim Crow" laws in the wake of Reconstruction, legislation, and Black codes that persisted well into the twentieth century.[25] Chicago was considered a "western" city throughout much of the nineteenth century, and in its early history it did indeed face many of the issues of a frontier town, including widespread violence and struggles over morality, including who would determine certain behaviors as immoral and who would enforce such judgments.[26]

The same sorts of phenomena played out throughout different territories and towns stretching west from Chicago all the way to California over the course of the nineteenth and twentieth centuries, including in San Francisco and the nearby placer mines during the Gold Rush of 1849. Nascent law enforcement in the West included little organized policing, as many parts of the vast region started to boom before the establishment there of formal government. This wide-open atmosphere led to vigilantism at the hands of frontier settlers, as well as the formation of private detective and security agencies, including those of the infamous Pinkerton Agency, whose hired guns at times acted outside the law in the protection of railroads and other privately held business-es. The second stage of policing in the West, after the creation of local law enforcement agencies, drew on the long-standing systems of justice of the region's Hispanic and Native American cultures, as well as some of the characteristics of American colonial systems of law enforcement. While an area remained a territory, before its annexation by the United States as part of a state, law enforcement therein was overseen by the U.S. Marshals Service. Small towns sometimes appointed a local police-man, though these figures generally did not have the legal authority to deal with criminals. Once a territory became part of a state, local law enforcement typically was composed of sheriffs who primarily collect-ed taxes, maintained order on the streets of town, ran local jails, and executed other administrative duties, as opposed to apprehending and arresting bandits and other outlaws. The third stage saw the founding of formal police departments in established cities with standardized gov-ernment, including in San Francisco in 1856 and Dallas in 1881. As in New England, the modernized big-city police departments were often corrupt, ineffective, and violent, including against Native Americans and Latina/os. Together, these problems prompted calls for reform in the ensuing decades of the Progressive Era, which ushered in the fourth stage of police development in the West.

The evolution of policing in Washington, D.C., was in some ways unique, as the "problems faced in the policing of any large city were compounded by the peculiarities of policing the nation's capital."[27] In particular, the D.C. police were closely tied to the federal government, especially in times of war when the force more closely resembled a lo-cal militia or the U.S. military. However, the D.C. police department still evinced some of the ills of its big-city counterparts, including cor-ruption and ineffectiveness. The Metropolitan Police Department of the District of Columbia (MPDC) was founded in 1861 as the prima-ry law enforcement agency for Washington, D.C., this after President Lincoln, amid increasing violence in the capital city, sent an emissary to New York to learn about its new-styled criminal justice system. The U.S. Capitol Police, a federal law enforcement agency separate from the MPDC, was established by Congress in 1828, though its origins date back to 1800, when a single watchman, John Golding, was hired to pro-tect the Capitol Building. Several additional law enforcement agencies later followed, including the District of Columbia Protective Services

Division and Metro Transit Police, as well as the U.S. Park Police, Mint
Police, and others.

The Press's and Police's Division with Marginalized Communities

The politically charged and divided nature of U.S. society in the years
surrounding the Civil War, combined with a new wave of immigrants
and other societal factors in the years leading to the turn of the century, had an additional effect on both the press and the police, namely,
poor or strained relations with people of color. In the press in particular and society in general, European immigrants to the United States
over time managed to shed their stigmatization as suspected criminals
or anarchists as they acculturated. However, when the press bothered
to cover issues facing Black communities in the first place, Black persons, including the great many newly freed persons in the aftermath of
the Civil War, could not and remained the targets of problematic press
coverage.[28] During Reconstruction, newspapers, especially those in the
South, frequently stereotyped Black politicians and voters. They also
covered crimes in ways that portrayed Black individuals as violent, in-
ferior, and a threat to the white race, the narrative fitting neatly into the
larger and centuries-old trope that Black men posed a continual threat
to white women. Coverage of the lynching of Black men, in the South
as well as in the North, and even by newspapers that condemned the
practice, including the *New York Times*, provided "minute and gory details of the atrocities," and sometimes tried to rationalize the extralegal,
overtly racist vigilante violence. In the South, several newspapers either
did not condemn the practice of lynching or encouraged its further use.
In ensuing decades, and even well into the Progressive Era, racial issues
like segregation were largely ignored by newspapers, even if individual
reporters like Wells provided crucially important coverage of both race-
and gender-related issues of the day.

A key moment in the historic distrust between the police and the Black
community in the United States came in 1865 with the ratification of the
Thirteenth Amendment, which reads, "Neither slavery nor involuntary
servitude, except as a punishment for crime whereof the party shall have
been duly convicted, shall exist within the United States, or any place
subject to their jurisdiction." Although the amendment formally ended
slavery, it did not provide the Black community protection from the
re-creation of systems of exploitation and brutality that developed in
the so-called reconstructed former states of the Confederacy in the final

decades of the nineteenth century as southern whites desperately tried to maintain a white supremacist society.

One such system was "peonage," in which "an employer compels a worker to pay off a debt with work."[29] There were different means and methods by which Black men, and in the case of sharecropping whole Black families, were swept into this never-ending cycle of indebtedness and labor, including prisoners, many of whom had been arrested and convicted by racist law enforcement, whose labor was leased out to commercial businesses, being paid little to nothing even as the prison profited.[30] Local police were the primary enforcers of the new systems, which spanned from the 1870s to World War I, arresting Black men for minor crimes such as "loitering" or purely fabricated charges and forcing them to pay off high fines and court fees through forced labor, the equivalency in some ways to enslavement. Black codes, which date back to at least 1865–66, were another means of restricting African Americans' freedom and forcing them to work for no or minimal wages. Law enforcement played a major role in enforcing, for example, vagrancy laws, arresting Black individuals unable to prove that they were employed.

Following the Reconstruction era in the late nineteenth century was the extralegal legislation and judicial system known collectively, and colloquially, as "Jim Crow," under which the South underwent "regimes . . . predicated upon white fears of black crime," or at least the "myth" of Black crime.[31] Significantly, law enforcement functioned as a central part of this extralegal system of segregation and disenfranchisement that reinforced white supremacy by reducing the Black community's political, economic, and social power. Additionally, the 1870s–'90s saw police use physical force to control or suppress peaceful demonstrations or other forms of political events by political dissidents, women, and communities of color, a practice that would continue well into the twentieth century.

Further contributing to growing division between the police and the Black community was lynching, with the incidences of the vile practice actually increasing after Reconstruction.[32] In 1892, the number of lynchings of Black men peaked at 156, with the frequency not declining significantly until the 1930s, despite repeated calls for the end of the practice by Black newspaper editors, reporters, and others. Although some local police officers tried to stop lynching and other forms of mob violence, many others made no effort to stop it or, worse, actively engaged in the brutality. In many cities, especially in the South, violence against Black individuals was "almost totally unchecked by police," with police instead participating in the violence through actions like clubbing individuals with nightsticks or blackjacks.[33]

Concerns related to race, combined with other problems arising for the press and police, led to a final similarity at the beginning of the new century. Both the sensationalism from yellow journalism and the continued police corruption, ineffectiveness, and violence across the United States prompted increased calls for change and reform, setting the stage for the Progressive Era. In the meantime, cooperative coexistence and contentiousness between the press and police continued, though perhaps most significantly the societal context, as well as technological advancements, such as the creation of police vehicles, also gave rise to new practices between the press and police that would have important implications for years to come.

Cooperative Coexistence Continues in the
Second Half of the Nineteenth Century

Despite the societal turmoil in the years surrounding the Civil War, newspapers still sought and published crime and policing stories, continuing the tradition of printers, editors, and reporters before them, including sensational reporting on murders and police responses to draft riots in major cities.[34] But starting in the 1870s–'90s, newspapers began to focus more heavily on human-interest stories, like the penny press, though in their continued coverage of crime and police activities, all three new forms of journalism proceeded in different ways.[35] For its part, serious journalism tended to eschew sensationalism in its thorough coverage of crime. The *New York Times*, for one, took a "scientific approach to crime, showing a genuine concern for causes and punishment."[36]

Yellow journalism was in part typified by a significant increase in crime coverage, including countless examples of reporting on murders, fights, shootings, thefts and burglaries, scandals, and more—often in a sensational manner.[37] As discussed later, yellow journalists went so far as to take on the role of detectives. Although this led in some cases to cooperation between the press and police, it also placed significant pressure on law enforcement, including drawing attention to the mistakes and shortcomings of individual officials and officers. Advocacy journalism likewise touched on law enforcement as part of its reform-minded reporting.

Changes to Press and Police Do Not Slow Contentiousness

Contentiousness remained a part of the press-police relationship in the second half of the nineteenth century, with the press continuing to hold law enforcement accountable before, during, and after the Civil War, including with newspapers criticizing the ineffectiveness of police and detectives.[38] For example, in 1858 the *New York Times* expressed concern over the possibility that "every Policeman is to be an absolute monarch . . . with complete power of life and death over all within his range, and armed with revolvers to execute his decrees on the instant."[39]

Following the example of penny-press editors and reporters, their counterparts in serious journalism, advocacy journalism, and yellow journalism put more time and effort into investigating crimes, which in effect also led to greater accountability of law enforcement. In terms of serious journalism, the *New York Times* became a "local crusader," exposing facts and calling for the "righting of wrongs."[40] In the early 1870s, the *Times* gained prominence by exposing the Tweed Ring in New York City, demonstrating the paper's ability to create change not only in government but also in the city's police force.[41] William Magear "Boss" Tweed was the political boss of his "Tammany Hall" political machine, his control over his many cronies giving him a large measure of control over New York politics and the Democratic Party. Even though his machine was well oiled by thievery, fraud, and graft, he effectively controlled public works contracts, patronage jobs, and numerous other projects and responsibilities around New York City. Except for Thomas Nast's critical political cartoons in *Harper's Weekly*, few contemporary journalists dared speak out against Tweed, at least until 1870 when George Jones, who had recently become publisher of the *Times* after the death of its founder and Jones's partner, Henry J. Raymond, determined that the *Times* would take up the mantle and expose Tweed and his associates. After Jones's epiphany, editorial writer Louis Jennings along with reporter John Foord began to write pieces and stories investigating and analyzing the doings of the Tweed Ring's financial empire, in so doing revealing corruption and therefore forcing police to act. After the exposé, in the November 1871 election, all the Tammany Hall candidates were defeated except Tweed, who retained his seat in the state senate. He was, however, later indicted on multiple counts, leading to his arrest in December 1871 and trial in 1873. Found guilty, he was sentenced to twelve years in prison, though he served only one year before being rearrested in connection to a civil suit. Tweed would later die in his prison cell at the age of fifty-five.

The *Times*, among other newspapers, also increasingly reported on police brutality beginning in the 1860s.[42] Although there were instances of the press defending the use of police brutality, including against certain strikers, protesters, and rioters, reporters often condemned such actions. For example, on June 28, 1881, the *New-York Tribune* reported that "Policeman Montgomery Ditmars of the Nineteenth Precinct, arrested no less than seven persons" in a single day.[43] Among those targeted by Ditmars were John McDonald and his wife, Anna. The couple was sitting outside their home when Ditmars ordered them to go inside. The McDonalds contended that they had been caring for a sick child and were sitting outside simply to get some fresh air. Ditmars countered, however, that they were drinking beer outside on a Sunday, pointing to a tin pail on the stoop. When John McDonald told the officer to "mind his own business" and refused to go inside, Ditmars "gave McDonald a terrible beating" with his club. Both McDonalds were arrested for disorderly conduct and taken to the police station, and John's head was "covered in cuts and bruises and dripping with blood." The McDonalds both spent the night in jail cells. The following day, Ditmars appeared before Justice Benjamin Wandell at the Yorkville Police Court, who listened to the stories of some of the individuals arrested by Ditmars. Upon hearing the McDonalds' story, Wandell "became very indignant and lectured Ditmars severely on his brutal conduct." The *New York Times* also covered the beating of McDonald and called it a "pompous show of authority."[44] Such reporting provided a "crude form of citizen oversight," as reporters "used their access to New York Police Department headquarters, station houses, and courts to churn out numerous accounts of official violence [and] . . . the rough-and-tumble world of nineteenth-century policing."[45]

Advocacy journalism also targeted abuses implicating law enforcement. For example, in reporting on lynching, Wells helped demonstrate the complicit nature of police in allowing, or even participating in, these heinous crimes, especially in the South.[46] She wrote in 1893, "Masks have long since been thrown aside and the lynchings of the present day take place in broad daylight. The sheriffs, police, and state officials stand by and see the work done well," often with "not a hand . . . lifted" to stop the violent crimes by police officers and sheriffs.[47] She later called for federal policies to protect Black people from lynching, contending that even in the limited cases where white people were arrested and charged for the crime at the local level, they could easily be acquitted by a jury consisting of their peers.

Nellie Bly, in a February 24, 1889, article titled "Nellie Bly a Prisoner," detailed how she had herself arrested by police in order to gain entrance to the station house.[48] She did so to investigate "how women—particularly innocent women—who fall into the hands of the police are treated by them, and, second, what necessity, if any, there is for providing station-houses with matrons." Bly devised a plan in which a woman, another newspaper reporter, would accuse her of stealing money, leading to her arrest. The plan worked, as detectives ultimately took Bly and the fake accuser to the Thirtieth Street station house where a detective named "Hayes" heard the accuser's story and instructed a woman working as a "lodger" to search Bly, who was also ordered to undress in a separate room. Bly reported that she believed a male officer peered through a "crevice" in the door or wall, leading her to later contend that "a regular woman-searcher should be employed in station-houses" and that "male officers should be given no opportunity of squinting through a peep-hole at women who are being searched," among other conclusions. Upon being found with several bills on her person, Bly was taken to a small cell in a building adjacent to the station house, which Bly described in detail along with her experiences as a prisoner, concluding that "innocent women who fall into the hands of the police are not necessarily badly treated," though some reform may be needed.

Yellow journalists similarly conducted investigations and "crusades" against local abuses and wrongdoing, including by local government and police, often in sensational ways.[49] In some instances, the press's reporting on police even helped lead to changes in law enforcement. One example arose in 1882 when the *New York Sun* linked the Washington, D.C., detective bureau with "the uninterrupted success" of gambling operations.[50] The D.C. commissioners later launched their own investigation and suspended two detectives, who were later acquitted. Nonetheless, in making their case, the D.C. commissioners also requested that Congress abolish the D.C. detective force, which it did in 1883.

Significantly, Pulitzer and Hearst also went a step further and "undertook active detective work in locating criminals" and solving crimes, therefore placing greater pressure on the police, who often proved less effective in doing so.[51] Hearst in particular sought to create "New Journalism," largely predicated on "excel[ling] in running down criminals."[52] In some cases, editors or reporters would even arrest criminals themselves, or at least attempt to do so.[53]

Additional examples of newspapers undertaking such detective work abound,[54] though one example that perhaps best illustrates how Hearst and Pulitzer not only covered crime and conducted investigations but also acted as detectives was the "Guldensuppe mystery."[55] On June 26, 1897, a group of kids found a headless torso in New York's East River. The next day, another bundle of body parts washed up along the Harlem River, prompting sensational stories and investigations by Pulitzer's *New York World* and Hearst's *New York Journal*, which vowed to stop at nothing to solve the mystery. Hearst immediately hired divers to find the missing head. He also formed a "Murder Squad" of reporters "who were ready to resort to flashing badges and pistols to make citizen's arrests."[56] Pulitzer was not to be outdone, with the *World* "st[ealing] evidence from the Guldensuppe murder scene by shaving off a piece of a floorboard, testing it, and proclaiming BLOOD IN THE HOUSE OF MYSTERY." Pulitzer offered $500 to any reader who could solve the case, prompting Hearst to offer $1,000. Both newspapers were also accused of manufacturing a fake head, both denying they falsified evidence. The head was never found.

A key moment came when reporters for both papers identified the pattern on a piece of oilcloth in which a part of the body of the murdered man had been wrapped. Hearst assigned thirty reporters to find the purchaser of the cloth. In no time, they found the merchant who sold the fabric, who tied its purchase to Augusta Nack, the wife of William Guldensuppe, the murdered man. The fabric discovery, as well as the investigation by police at the crime scene at a house rented by Nack, led to her arrest and that of her lover, Martin Thorn, who had earlier been discovered together by Guldensuppe. Nack, who pinned the crime on Thorn, was later convicted and spent ten years in Auburn Prison in New York. Thorn was executed by electric chair in the Sing Sing prison, also in New York.

On the one hand, journalists' taking on the role of detective appears like cooperative coexistence in that they had significant access to crime scenes and evidence. Additionally, the press sometimes assisted police in tracking a criminal or helping in their capture, also suggesting cooperative coexistence. However, on the other hand, detective work by yellow journalists often went beyond reporting on policing. Through such reporting, the press provided "a check on the more exuberant of the force, who fear more to see their misdeeds spread forth by [the reporter's] trenchant pen, than to receive a stern admonition of their superiors," echoing the press's watchdog role. In fact, the press's success led "every police commissioner in New York [City to] frankly [admit] the great assistance of the press" and instilling in police officers "fear [of] exposure of their incompetence by the daily press."[57]

In adopting detective duties, yellow journalists also succeeded where the police could not by delving "deeper even than the detectives . . . into the hidden workings of crime," the result of which often placed further pressure on law enforcement.[58] An example of yellow journalists succeeding in breaking a case before the police is that of the "*Argus*, of Albany, New York, [solving the case] after the police . . . were completely baffled in an attempt to locate a kidnapper." The *Argus* reporters "not only found the child, but also captured the criminal."[59] In another example, the *New York Journal*, after having solved a challenging murder case, argued in an editorial that it succeeded where the police had not, writing that it was the "duty of a newspaper to do anything whatever that will promote the public interests."[60] The editorial concluded that the *Journal* therefore had effectively become "a detective force at least as efficient as that maintained at public expense by this or any other city," with a network of millions of readers to help in their efforts, an "instrument of detection of incomparable power." In another editorial, the *Journal* went so far as to say that it worked faster than professional detectives and "investigated along its own lines, examining every [clue], tracing every rumor and unravelling every theory."[61] The result was that New York City and Newark, New Jersey, detectives were often "compelled to accept its views of the subject.'" Ultimately, journalists who undertook detective duties "fancied themselves super-sleuths. Time and again [they] proved themselves better detectives than the professional policemen," contributing to pushes for reforms and changes to law enforcement.[62]

As in previous eras, in the late nineteenth century law enforcement at times targeted members of the press, adding to contentiousness in their relationship. Sometimes police officers arrested journalists for doing their jobs, including in instances wherein reporters were critical of police. On August 28, 1873, the *Evening Star* in Washington, D.C., received a telegram from Philadelphia explaining that a reporter for the *Age* in Philadelphia was arrested and incarcerated three days earlier due to "his revelations concerning [the detectives'] wrongdoing." The telegram noted that Philadelphia's "detective department . . . ha[s] become so thoroughly incensed at the repeated expositions of their nefarious schemes that they now waylay and arrest reporters whose duty it is to travel the streets at a late hour, and prefer charges against them of a trifling character, that they may be subjected to the ignominy of prison confinement."[63]

In several cases, reporters were arrested when they went too far in seeking to get a story, including in 1887 when reporter S. G. Hopkins, assisted by reporter Arthur B. Sperry, "worked up [a] sensational story" in which they sent a "little paper box" to Chief Justice Morrison Waite of the Supreme Court.[64] The box contained what first appeared to be an "infernal machine," meaning one meant to explode like a bomb, in the mail. It turned out to be a "hoax, gotten up by a sensational newspaper man" to get a dramatic story, matching the style of reporting by yellow journalists during this era. Hopkins and Sperry were both arrested, and Hopkins later confessed to the scheme, hoping to escape prosecution, claiming that they put in only enough ink and powder "to burst the phial and alarm the person who might open the package." Sperry had called Chief Justice Waite at his home to inquire whether he had received a suspicious box, which he showed to a policeman who happened to be nearby. Chief Justice Waite said he opened the box and found nothing dangerous, calling it "a perfect sham" and saying he involved the police only because an officer inquired about the package.

In addition to this sensational case, police also arrested members of the press in some cases for actions outside their roles as editors or reporters, including for counterfeiting, fighting each other, public drunkenness, and a false accusation of murder.[65] Such arrests, although less problematic in that they did not target reporters for news gathering, still led to greater contentiousness.

Adding to the conflict and divisiveness between the press and police were cases of law enforcement threatening to, and actually using, force against journalists, including when the latter were in the act of trying to gather news.[66] In 1875, firefighters responded to reports of a fire in the cellar of a men's clothing store in Pittsburgh.[67] Although the fire was quickly extinguished, the cause of the flame could not be determined. A *Pittsburgh Commercial* reporter endeavored to cover the fire by "obtain[ing] a station upon the sidewalk in front of the burning building for the purpose of securing the required information." At the time, the Pittsburgh Fire Commission rules permitted members of the press "to pass within the lines if any be drawn" blocking access to members of the public. As the reporter "pushed forward through the crowd to a position as near the scene of the fire as possible," he "was resisted by the police," prompting him to argue that he had "the privileges of getting as near as he could to the burning building." However, as the reporter pleaded his case, "an officer, Lieutenant Tyre, sprang forward, threw him upon the sidewalk, and, had it not been for the interference of citizens, would no doubt have inflicted bodily harm." Following the incident, the "bullying policeman" made a claim that would be made by police officers for many years to come and into the twentieth and twenty-first centuries: he had not known the man he tackled was a reporter. He reportedly "put in a plea in self-defense, to this effect, 'You didn't say you were a reporter.'" The "riled" reporter claimed that Tyre "had committed an assault and battery upon him, and expressed his intention of prosecuting him for that offense." However, Officer Joseph McCoy had taken the arm of the reporter, stating, "I want you to come with me." Rather than Tyre, it was the reporter who was ultimately taken to the police station, where he was ordered to pay ten dollars or be charged for disorderly conduct. The *Pittsburgh Commercial* ultimately determined that the episode "was certainly regarded by spectators as an outrage of the first magnitude."

During this time, police also searched reporters, often in connection to arrests.[68] In 1896, two *Daily Picayune* reporters rode their bicycles on the pavement around Lee Circle in New Orleans.[69] The previous week, the city council had passed an ordinance allowing bicycles in the circle. However, the reporters were "held up" by a police officer, referred to as "No. 2," and "were about to be sent to jail" when one of them "remembered that he had a copy of the law in his pocket." Upon showing it to the police officer, the latter was "loathe to believe . . . that such was the law," but ultimately let the reporters go. Later in the day, another *Daily Picayune* reporter was stopped while cycling in the circle by No. 2, who arrested and detained him. When another officer arrived, he told No. 2, "You ought not to have done dat; dat man's a reporter, and dem fellers always knows de law. Youse too quick and tomorrow de chief and de jedge [*sic*] will ask you what youse trying ter git through you." No. 2 countered that "bicyclers were nuisances, and . . . had no right on the Lee Circle pavement" and argued that he wanted "to make a test case." The officers debated whether to search the reporter at the scene, but ultimately decided to do so at the police station, taking the reporter there in the patrol wagon. The *Daily Picayune* noted that "reporters have written

many times about how it feels for other people to be carried to jail in a
patrol wagon, but they have seldom themselves been obliged to take the
same free ride."

Upon arriving at the police station, "the search [of the reporter] was
ordered and the policeman placed his hands in the prisoner's pockets,
and otherwise examined him to be sure there were no howitzers or dynamite cartridges about him." The reporter was later released, though
the episode led his fellow journalists to contend that the arrest was due
to the reporter having criticized the officer earlier that afternoon. The
Daily Picayune contended that No. 2 made the arrest "not because he
had not found it to be a fact that such an ordinance had been passed
and promulgated in the official city newspaper, but because, as he said,
the reporter in the afternoon had been a little flip and had the audacity
to say to him (the policeman) that he was ten years behind the time,
and would hear of the law probably next June, or after he had annoyed
innumerable wheelmen."

Finally, law enforcement also continued to play a role in the subpoenaing of journalists for refusing to disclose certain of their sources, including those in law enforcement.[70] In 1886, *Baltimore Sun* reporter John T.
Morris uncovered information suggesting that some Baltimore officials
and police officers, including Sheriff Henry G. Fledderman, were connected to illegal gambling operations and bribery. The *Sun* published
an article containing the information, which was read by members of a
Baltimore grand jury investigating the alliance between illegal gambling
and law enforcement. The grand jury, suspecting a leak, subpoenaed
Morris and demanded he disclose his source's identity. Morris refused
and ultimately spent five days in the city jail. Following the events, which
prompted calls for change by press advocates, in 1896 Maryland became
the first state to pass a shield law providing protections for journalists
against compelling disclosure of their confidential sources and information, one facet of the complicated legal landscape surrounding the
press-police relationship, to be discussed in later chapters.

Impersonation and Media Ride-Alongs Arise

As varying degrees of cooperative coexistence and contentiousness
continued to define the press-police relationship, a new development
forever changed the interactions between the two institutions. The
1870s–'90s saw the rise of several documented examples of police impersonation of the press and vice versa, as well as media "ride-alongs"

with police. These practices, particularly impersonation of one another to serve their immediate purposes, may have occurred earlier in the nineteenth century, as there are reports of members of the press and police going undercover, posing as other members of society on the job.[71] The 1870s–'90s, however witnessed recorded instances of these practices, providing a starting point for their respective histories, that have remained part of the fabric of the press-police relationship ever since.

In each era, newspaper accounts have documented these interactions, providing a source to discover more about impersonation and media ride-alongs, including the purposes of the practices, how and why they took place, reactions to them, and the effects of their use.[72] The result is that the accounts are generally from the perspective of the journalists covering the instance(s) of impersonation and media ride-alongs, requiring that we be cautious about the conclusions we draw due to bias in favor of the press. However, these accounts still provide meaningful details about these key practices and their implications, helping us study a crucially important part of the press-police relationship that would otherwise be largely invisible, forgotten, or ignored without the journalists' work across different eras.

Police Impersonation of the Press
In the 1970s, it was revealed that Central Intelligence Agency agents had been impersonating American journalists and news organizations since the early 1950s.[73] Although the CIA is not strictly a law enforcement agency, the revelations marked a significant moment in that from that point forward, greater attention was given to the practice of police impersonation of the press. However, the practice dates back at least a century earlier to the 1880s, when it became an established, if often secretive, practice. Although one can find examples of private detectives impersonating journalists as early as 1880,[74] a report by *Cedar Rapids (IA) Gazette* on November 13, 1889, constitutes what may be the first clear instance of police impersonating the press.[75] The newspaper reported that "twenty-five policemen" had attended an "anarchist meeting . . . disguised as reporters" and "took notes" on one of the "incendiary" speeches. In this case, the police officers conducted the impersonation by disguising themselves as journalists, mimicking the actions of a reporter taking notes, what would become an ongoing tactic. The purpose of this behavior was to investigate individuals or groups without alerting them to their presence as law enforcement officers. In this case, the

investigation apparently went a step further, with the article claiming the individual who gave the speech would "be called to account for it," suggesting the officers potentially intended to arrest him. One year later, the *Buffalo (NY) Express* included a two-sentence snippet explaining that police had "act[ed] as reporters at Irish Nationalist meetings."[76]

Another investigation conducted through police impersonation of the press occurred in 1895, when Denver police chief Hamilton Armstrong and two members of his detective force posed as art critics and "occupied a box at the Broadway Theater" to "pass judgment on the 'living pictures' to which the Police Board and ladies of the W.C.T.U. [Women's Christian Temperance Union] ha[d] objected." After the exhibition, Armstrong informed management that portions of the films would have to be modified.[77]

One year later, impersonation of a reporter came amid the Republican primaries, a political contest described by the *Brooklyn Daily Eagle* as "the hottest ever held in this city."[78] Amid the tumultuous results of the election, which saw several incumbents defeated, were claims that jobs and other lucrative positions had been held out to ballot goers in exchange for their votes. Sheriff Buttling reportedly called the tax office and "impersonat[ed] a reporter of a New York paper" in order to determine the winner of one of the primaries. This example is therefore significant in that on the call, Buttling specifically identified himself as a reporter, demonstrating another way in which police were able to impersonate the press: by identifying themselves as and verbally telling others that they are members of a real or fake news organization.

Thus, the final decades of the nineteenth century not only provide the foundation of the story of police impersonation of the press, but also display key aspects of the practice, including how and why police used it. In ensuing years, the ways in which the police carried out their impersonation of the press (including the use of fake credentials, acting like reporters, and actually identifying themselves as journalists) and the purposes behind the practice (investigation and surveillance, the ending of standoffs and hostage situations, and trying to find out what the press already knew about a case) remained largely the same. However, the significant effects of the practice—including the undermining of the press's credibility, source relationships, news-gathering functions, independence, and physical safety, as well as straining of the press-police relationship—despite largely existing beginning in the nineteenth century, would not garner significant criticism until much later. Like with media ride-alongs, this is perhaps because aspects of the practice did not violate norms and values in different eras. Alternatively, it is likely that the purported benefits of the practice overshadowed the problems that could arise. And given the largely secretive nature of the practice by law enforcement, the practice as a whole likely was not at the center of public attention, meaning the negative effects could remain hidden. But by the twentieth century, as word got out about the federal government's large-scale use of the practice, criticism would increase, though the practice would continue into the twenty-first century, warranting further examination and action.

Press Impersonation of Police

On March 30, 1877, under the headline "Brevities," the *Pittsburgh Post-Gazette* published a single sentence stating that a "City Hall clerk and a reporter impersonated police officers, Wednesday evening."[79] Although no further details were given, this incident provides a starting point for the centuries-long history of press impersonation of police.

Two years later, a *San Francisco Chronicle* reporter "rushed in the direction" of a "pistol shot . . . on a deserted commercial street."[80] Upon arriving, the reporter found a man "shaking all over and [holding] a still smoking revolver in his hand." The reporter "arrest[ed] him at once in the interest of sensational journalism, and on the way to the [police] station got from the quaking man, who never doubted that he was an officer, the name of the person he had fired at." After a "real policeman" took control of the suspect, the reporter continued to investigate the story, including surreptitiously entering the home of the shooting victim. Thus, in this case, a reporter seeking a sensational story deceived, or at least misled, a shooting suspect into thinking he was a police officer, thereby leading him to identify the target.

In 1896, the sensational murder trial of Alonzo Walling, accused of assisting in the murder of Pearl Bryan, a twenty-two-year-old pregnant woman, drew national attention.[81] Following reporter Edward Anthony's testimony, an attorney for Walling accused the journalist of having prior to Walling's arrest "impersonated a police officer, and exercised the same influence over Walling as an actual officer, Walling being ignorant of the impersonation." A judge summarily threw out Anthony's testimony, "taking away the most damaging evidence against Walling that [had] yet been produced." This constitutes an early instance of legal action stemming from the practice, one of the negative effects of press impersonation of police. Although there is no indication that Anthony was charged or arrested for his impersonation, the accusation alone led to the throwing out of his testimony, demonstrating that the practice, even in the nineteenth century, was not taken lightly. This further suggests that the press's use of the practice could, and would, strain the press-police relationship as well, a negative effect arising for years to come.

If the practice of press impersonation of police saw its foundation with that single line in the *Pittsburgh Post-Gazette* in 1877, the many variations of how the practice occurred would by the twentieth century come to include the use of fake police badges, reporters acting like and identifying themselves as police officers or officials, and, in some rare cases, police actually aiding the press in using impersonation of law enforcement. The purposes behind the practice would also remain largely the same after the turn of the century, with the primary one remaining news gathering. In some cases, however, the press impersonated law enforcement to try to aid the police, bringing their independence into question and whether they were adequately accomplishing their own purposes in doing so. Significantly, press impersonation of police would also give rise to additional adverse effects, including journalists becoming the targets of police investigations, arrests, and legal action, sometimes leading to jail time or fines (or both), the straining of the press-police relationship, threats to physical safety, and, again, an undermining of public trust in both institutions. In general, it did not take long for the press, police, public, and others to recognize the potential problems arising from the practice, with criticism being found throughout its history, especially amid legal proceedings.

Media Ride-Alongs

In 1881, the first police vehicle—meaning a mode of transportation specifically intended and in some cases designed and manufactured for use by police—in U.S. history was introduced in Chicago.[82] The new horse-drawn patrol wagon followed the example of wagons used by city fire departments, but its use by police meant that for the first time, police officials and officers might ride to a crime or emergency scene in a vehicle designated for the exclusive use of law enforcement.[83] For the next 140-plus years, as police vehicles evolved, members of the press, and the media more generally, would, on occasion, come to accompany police in their patrol wagons, automobiles, and cars. In time, the practice was seen in popular culture and even debated by the Supreme Court. Over the history of media ride-alongs—a term not formally introduced until 1964 but used throughout this book to refer to a member of the press riding with law enforcement officials or officers in or on a police vehicle—aspects of the practice remained largely consistent, despite changes to police vehicles and other developments.

The story of media ride-alongs begins on October 26, 1881, when several Chicago officials, including the chief of the Chicago Police Department (CPD), "witnessed an exhibition of a new fire and police patrol wagon," which had been built in Cincinnati, Ohio, the previous year.[84] Although Chicago already had fire patrol wagons, and there were some wagons sometimes used by police,[85] the *Chicago Tribune* proclaimed that "this is the first wagon built" expressly for the police, "a model in its way."[86] The wagon, which went into service sometime between November 1880 and July 1881, was drawn by two horses and contained a box for passengers. Two lanterns were affixed to the front of the wagon, which could be taken off and used as handheld lights by police officers on foot. Several additional patrol wagons went into service soon thereafter.

Two months earlier, on August 23, 1881, St. Louis chief of police Ferdinand B. Kennett traveled to Chicago to look at the "recently inaugurated" patrol wagon, "the best thing in the way of police innovation" that he saw during his trip.[87] He further explained how the wagon worked, including that the horses were "kept in stalls as fire-engine horses and [were] hitched up at the signal, much of the time-saving apparatus employed at the engine-houses being in use for the police patrol." Kennett added that three officers would accompany the wagon, which would "astonish you to see," and that there was "hardly any limit to [its] benefits."

One year later, a reporter for the *Chicago Tribune* was with a police wagon when it "turned into Archer avenue with . . . a crowd of over 1,000 . . . following it, and one drunken harridan [who] was throwing mud and filth with both hands."[88] The woman "succeeded in covering several police officers and the *Tribune* reporter with mud." It is not clear whether the reporter was with the officers in the patrol wagon or was on foot covering the attendant crowd. At the very least, the case suggests that reporters were covering events very near the patrol wagon, even if they were not riding in it. The same year, reporter Mike Wasserman rode in one of the CPD's new patrol wagons during a parade honoring the police and politicians.[89]

Less than two years after the introduction of the patrol wagon came what might be the first detailed report on a media ride-along in U.S. history. On June 20, 1883, a *Chicago Times* reporter recounted his night spent on "The Red Wagon."[90] In it, he relayed that he had "stationed himself in the patrol barn . . . waiting for something to turn up." Shortly thereafter, the ride-along began: "The wait was not a long one, for in a few moments a reverie was interrupted by the 'b-r-r-r-r-r-r-r-r,' of the electric annunciator. . . . By an ingenious electric appliance, when the alarm-bell was rung, the doors of the horses' stalls were thrown open, and the intelligent animals were in a second at their places by the harness. . . . All of this was done in about two seconds. . . . Down Harrison street goes the big wagon." The police proceeded to pick up an "old, drunk woman," who had been involved in a fight. Before the reporter's ride was over, the police also stopped the wagon to pick up injured persons and transport them to safety. The reporter called his time riding the wagon "a strange experience," suggesting the novelty of the practice for reporters, but he also praised the opportunity to see up close the "Laddies and Their Work."

One aspect of media ride-alongs that has remained consistent over time is that members of the press who ride with police do so at their invitation or with their permission to do so. And this was indeed the case with the *Chicago Times* reporter on that late-spring evening in 1883, whose article indicated no resistance whatsoever by officials or officers. In fact, the article ended with a description of the reporter watching the sunrise with the officers, to which one responded, "Yes, it's a daisy."

Law enforcement's willingness to allow journalists to ride along with them became increasingly common as the use of patrol wagons spread across the country. On May 4, 1889, several Lincoln, Nebraska, officials, including "Mayor Graham . . . [and] Chief [of Police] Newbury," along with a reporter, "chartered the [police department's] patrol wagon, and . . . proceed[ed] on a tour of investigation" related to a report from several eyewitnesses that a church, which was being relocated by the use of cedar blocks, had "begun to break the concrete over the gas and sewer trenches [of the city streets]."[91] One year later, San Francisco chief of police Patrick Crowley asked a *Chronicle* reporter, "Would you like to try a trip [on the patrol wagon]?"[92] The reporter "almost before the words had left the chief's lips . . . found himself deposited in the [patrol] wagon, the horses were whipped up and in a jiffy the team was rattling down Kearny street toward the Folsom-street station." In this case, there was an explicit invitation by an official for a reporter to join him on a patrol wagon, suggesting that in some cases the police not only allowed reporters to ride with them but encouraged it.

By the turn of the twentieth century, ride-alongs by journalists became an accepted practice. This was evidenced in Detroit, where it was common "when an alarm of fire or disaster sounded in the press room" for "journalists to rush downstairs to the paddy-wagon station and grab . . . seats . . . with the cops" in the "Black Maria," the Detroit Police Department's early patrol wagon.[93] In these instances as well, media ride-alongs with police took place precisely because law enforcement had granted them access to do so, which suggests that the police, too, expected to get something out of the practice, including improved community relations. It is possible, of course, that the police may even have acted differently when journalists were riding along, this to ensure the journalists did not see "bad things" happen, so that the resulting coverage might show the police in a good light. At the same time, members of the press would have wanted to retain this type of access to law enforcement. Therefore, reporters were careful to avoid doing something that might lead to the revoking of their ride-along privileges. Taken together, one might infer that from the start of the practice, media ride-alongs constituted a give-and-take, mutually beneficial arrangement. On the one hand, this would allow both entities to accomplish purposes and functions they may not have been able to otherwise. However, on the other, as this and future eras would come to demonstrate, negative effects lurked below the surface of this type of arrangement.

As part of the symbiotic nature of ride-alongs, the press participated with several purposes in mind, the most common of which was to cover the police, meaning when law enforcement itself was the main focus of the story. Journalists often recounted their experiences on a ride-along, otherwise reported on individual police officials and officers, or detailed police functions, strategies, actions, and new technologies, including the vehicles themselves. An example of the latter was demonstrated in the story on the *Chicago Times* reporter's experience on Chicago's new patrol wagon in 1883, in which he was "detailed to write up the patrol-wagon system" and "very faithfully accomplished his assignment."[94]

Additionally, the reporter covered the actions by the police on the patrol wagon over the course of the night, such as when dealing with "drunk and disorderlies" and responding to a fire.

The *Chicago Times* reporter's experience was not an isolated incident.[95] Within three years of Chief Kennett marveling at Chicago's patrol wagon, St. Louis had purchased its own.[96] On July 26, 1884, the *St. Louis Post-Dispatch* detailed a reporter's "night spent with the patrol wagon." The night began slowly, as "a sleepy stillness reigned throughout the [Central District Station]." Officer Billy Sims told a *Post-Dispatch* reporter waiting at the station house that he would be better suited to "go out with the patrol boys to-night." Moments later, a "gong" rang, and the officers scrambled to prepare the wagon. The reporter provided his account of the preparations of the wagon and his ride with the officers to the scene of the disturbance. In this account, too, the journalist therefore provided readers with an intimate glimpse into city police.

Significantly, the *Post-Dispatch* reporter included an early instance of a journalist including praise and positive coverage of police or their vehicle following a ride-along, writing that "a midnight gallop with the . . . police . . . is absolutely exhilarating."[97] Similarly, in his July 26, 1884, description of his ride-along with Chief Crowley, a reporter for the *San Francisco Chronicle* wrote extensively on the "complete" success of the new alarm system targeting "the city's toughs, sneak thieves, burglars, and intellectual criminals," even though it had only been tested.[98]

Another, if somewhat less common, purpose motivating journalists to go on ride-alongs with the police was, and continues to be, using the practice as a method of covering a news story. In these instances, the press focused on what was happening at crime scenes, in emergency areas, and on the roads rather than on the police per se. Naturally, though, even in such cases, the police were part of the story and were often depicted in a positive, or at least neutral, light. Once such instance occurred in 1885 when police received a call that a man had committed suicide in Minneapolis.[99] The "patrol wagon, with Officer Fitzgibbon and a Tribune reporter, was sent to the place designated, where the self-murderer was found." In this case, the reporter had been stationed at the police department in the hope of using a ride in the patrol wagon to obtain information for a story to include in the next edition of the paper. Because of the resurgence of sensational crime news during the time, it is not surprising that reporters sought to use ride-alongs to get their next sensational story.

It was not long, however, before the two most common reasons for journalists participating in ride-alongs—covering the police and obtaining news stories—began to illuminate a negative effect of media ride-alongs, one that would continue in ensuing decades: the practice proved to be an ineffective means to provide complete, unbiased coverage of law enforcement and hold police accountable for their actions. More specifically, when it came to ride-alongs, the resulting stories were far more likely to include praise and positive coverage of the police, or at the worst neutral treatment, than critical reporting of police. This is largely due to the press not wanting to lose access to law enforcement vehicles and sources. In addition, coverage stemming from ride-alongs generally provided the point of view of police officials or officers, who may, as mentioned, have been acting in certain ways, including the avoidance of negative actions, in order to influence the coverage.

The give-and-take arrangement of media ride-alongs also provides a clear demonstration of the second overarching negative effect of the practice: whenever the members of either institution were engaged in helping the other accomplish its own purposes or functions, they necessarily were not fully focused on their own important role in society. This was further evidenced in a third purpose of media ride-alongs arising in the 1880s–'90s: the press directly and specifically aiding police with the functions of law enforcement.

For example, in 1895 a large mob in St. Paul, Minnesota, gathered around the patrol wagon as it was dropping off prisoners at the police station.[100] The mob reportedly "gave a yell and made for the [policemen]." The police captain recounted the events, explaining that a reporter "helped us (the police) Although the reporter tried to push his way into the patrol wagon but failed to get in it due to his being "a little fellow," he subsequently "jumped to the steps of the station house and into it and pulled the call for help, and stationed himself outside the door . . . picking out a man now and then with his gun as cool as you please," it being not uncommon for journalists to carry guns during this time period. The reporter, who had been riding with police prior to the forming of the mob, failed to get back into the vehicle, but still shot at the violent protesters seeking to attack a group of officers, "help[ing the police] out in a tight place." Although a sensational case by contemporary standards, as well as appearing to be a helpful decision and series of actions by the reporter on the surface level, and perhaps was in the moment, whenever the press is directly helping police accomplish its purposes, and vice versa, neither institution is focused on its own goals and functions.

The ineffectiveness of media ride-alongs for the press and police to fully and adequately accomplish their purposes and functions is compounded by additional negative effects of the practice, including the physical danger posed to members of both institutions and the undermining of public trust and confidence in both. Media ride-alongs increase the chances of physical harm to both the journalists and the police officers involved, especially if officers become the target of violence or otherwise come to be part of a confrontation. Certainly, reporters and police officers may be the target of violence outside media ride-alongs; however, the risk is generally higher for reporters during the practice. The risk may also be higher for the police, as the presence of the press can increase the unpredictability of those with whom officers interact, as well as police needing to worry about the safety of the journalists joining them.

Such dangers can be traced back to at least 1895. During a trolley railroad strike in Brooklyn, several reporters went to the scene to cover "the perils to which new motormen, conductors, the police, and the militia were subjected."[101] Reporters, who at times rode to and from the strike in police wagons in order to gain access to the sites, explained that they faced "risks . . . in gathering the news" and ensuring that the "reading public was kept fully informed." Certainly, news gathering during this time was already "a particularly hazardous business." However, what made it even more dangerous for reporters in this instance was being so close to the crowd's other potential target of violence: the police. This was also the case in those volatile situations in which a mob gathered around the police and patrol wagon, such as when it was dropping off prisoners at the police station.[102] Significantly, there were no special precautions taken to protect members of the press who accompanied police on patrol wagons. As the New York Times noted on March 17, 1895, a "newspaper reporter learns, after a few days of such adventure, how to prepare for them, and how best to avoid dangerous consequences."[103]

Media ride-alongs can also lead to decreased public trust and confidence in both the press and the police. This is evident whenever members of the public questioned why journalists were in a police vehicle, wondering whether they had been arrested or were working with law enforcement. For example, when Chief Crowley invited a San Francisco Chronicle reporter to join him on one of the new patrol wagons, the reporter noted that he "caught audible speculations from the pedestrians . . . as to the exact nature of the crime he . . . had committed to earn a seat in the patrol wagon in such distinguished but suggestive companionship."[104] One member of the public said, "Poor fellow, he's going up for seven years sure." Although it is not clear whether the sight of the reporter in the patrol wagon decreased his credibility, it is possible that some members of the public would be less willing to trust a ride-along reporter and their coverage.

In fact, less than a year later, a similar set of circumstances prompted the *San Francisco Examiner* to raise concerns about a journalist's credibility. On March 15, 1891, the paper noted that one of its reporters had spent twenty-four hours with a patrol wagon, during which "people glanced at the wagon and pitied the reporter as they drove by, and his friends pretended not to notice him."[105] The article contended that although "popular pity was on his side," so too was "popular contempt," because it was considered "bad" for a reporter "to be seen in a patrol wagon."

The final decades of the nineteenth century saw the beginning of media ride-alongs in the United States as the first police vehicles came into service. Media ride-alongs have remained part of the fabric of the press-police relationship ever since. Significantly, as with impersonation, the negative effects arising from media ride-alongs, combined with how and why it was conducted, would remain consistent for years to come and demonstrate the problematic nature of the practice and how it can undermine the ability of both the press and the police to benefit and serve the public. However, criticism of media ride-alongs remained almost entirely missing until the twenty-first century and remains inadequate, necessitating this work. Certainly, what we view as problematic today may not have violated norms and values at the time. Alternatively, as in the present, the purported benefits of the practice overshadowed the problems and issues that could, and would, arise. In any event, the negative effects arising from media ride-alongs in the present can be traced back more than a century, yet the practice, which remains largely missing from existing literature, continues, necessitating action.

The second half of the nineteenth century marked the expansion and evolution of the relationship between the modern press and police in the United States. Amid major societal events like the Civil War and renewed urbanization, the press and police, and their relationship, underwent changes ranging from new forms of journalism and expanding urban police forces to, perhaps most notably, the rise of impersonation and media ride-alongs. Nevertheless, despite the tumultuousness of the era, the trends associated with cooperative coexistence and contentiousness first seen in the American colonies continued. But so too did the problems with the evolving press and police, resulting in renewed calls for change and reform as the United States entered the twentieth century.

CHAPTER 3

Reform and Separation, 1900s–1910s

THE FIRST DECADES OF THE twentieth century were a time of great change in the United States as the Progressive Era saw political, economic, and social reforms throughout American society. How would this movement shape the press and police, along with their relationship? The press and police were not immune to these changes, undergoing reforms and changes largely in response to problems arising in the second half of the nineteenth century, including yellow journalism and police corruption, ineffectiveness, and violence. Ultimately, new and renewed types of reporting, new strategies by law enforcement, and efforts toward greater independence and institutionalization by both the press and the police resulted in an era with augmented separation and contentiousness that often overshadowed, but did not eliminate, cooperative coexistence, impersonation, and media ride-alongs.

Press and Police Undergo Changes amid Progressive Era Reforms
Fitting into, and contributing to, this context of reform and change was a new style of journalism known as muckraking.[1] President Theodore Roosevelt coined the term in a 1906 speech criticizing journalists whom he thought to be too fixated on problems and issues in society. He drew on a character from *The Pilgrim's Progress* written by English writer John Bunyan in 1678, namely, "the Man with the Muck-rake . . . who could look no way but downward with the muck-rake in his hands; who was offered a celestial crown for his muck-rake, but who would neither look up nor regard the crown he was offered, but continued to rake to himself the filth of the floor." The muckrakers, like the advocacy journalists and others before them, were reform minded, exposing

corruption and mistreatment of immigrants, residents, and workers in growing U.S. cities, prison inmates, and others. Muckraking magazines included most notably *McClure's*, which was published by S. S. McClure, an Irish American immigrant who grew up in poverty in Indiana before later founding the first U.S. newspaper syndicate, McClure Syndicate, in 1884.

Meanwhile, one of the most significant effects of yellow journalism was the criticism it received from many in the newspaper industry, including Pulitzer. The result was a push toward objectivity in the first decades of the twentieth century, marking a turn toward increased focus on facts and impartiality, therefore moving away from the practices of yellow journalism, though those would remain in "jazz journalism" during the 1920s and tabloid publications through the present. Journalists increasingly saw themselves as mediators between government officials and the public, ensuring Americans were not manipulated, and continuing the crusade of the muckrakers to expose political and social problems, though perhaps to a lesser extent.

There was also a greater push for the independence of the press, namely, through institutionalization.[2] During this period, the press gained an independent role in democratic society, becoming its own institution, like the sciences, independent from outside influences. The press also shifted toward professionalization, resulting in better education and training of reporters, including at newly formed schools of journalism.[3] Professionalization also emphasized ethics and trustworthiness, as well as creating professional organizations, academic publications, and changes to newsroom structure, including hiring more women and providing more autonomy for reporters. The ultimate goal was to "[uplift] the practice of journalism" as researchers, journalists, and the public recognized the power of news.[4]

The Progressive Era marked the beginning of the reform era of policing as changes across society came to law enforcement.[5] The key figure who brought reform to policing was August Vollmer, the chief of police in Berkeley, California. Vollmer introduced professionalization of law enforcement, which included several key characteristics. First, it aimed to decrease the influence of government and politics on policing, instead requiring officials and officers to follow the rule of law and to protect individual rights. Second, Vollmer advocated for the creation of a central bureaucratic command structure for each department, including the election of qualified officials who ensured accountability of all members of police departments. Third, Vollmer called for the continued use of military ethos, including parades, drills, titles, and uniforms. Fourth, professionalization called for the training of intelligent and healthy officers, who were significantly more qualified than their predecessors. Universities began researching criminal justice as a formal area of study to help provide such training. Fifth, key figures in the professionalization movement drafted codes of ethics for departments to follow and helped create police commissions in some jurisdictions. Sixth, Vollmer advocated for departments to create special units, often replacing ineffective detective units and improving social service functions. For example, a special unit was created to address juvenile problems, leading to perhaps the first examples of women being hired on police forces.

Seventh, public relations efforts by law enforcement began developing in the first decades of the twentieth century, marking a clear response to the investigations by the press.[6] Early public relations campaigns aimed not only to provide a good public image of police but also to begin adapting to working with the press, such as providing access to police files in exchange for more favorable coverage. Public relations was ultimately a key element of Vollmer's philosophy, with a reemphasis on social service functions as a means of connecting with a local community, marking an antecedent to community-centered policing that would arise by the 1970s. Public relations efforts during the Progressive Era also marked an antecedent to public information officers, which arose in the 1960s–'70s.

Finally, professionalization brought significant change to the technology of policing, including placing greater emphasis on science being used in policing, such as for fingerprinting and other forensic practices.[7] Police communication technology can be traced back to the eighteenth and nineteenth centuries with night watches using "rattles" as an alarm to alert citizens. Perhaps the first major innovation, however, was the police's use of the telegraph to share information on fugitives and other issues with neighboring law enforcement authorities in the 1850s. However, the use of the telegraph was largely inefficient, including because all communications had to go through the chief's office. The 1880s–'90s saw greater implementation of "call boxes" or "signal boxes," which were placed in several locations around the city, allowing citizens close to the boxes to call if they encountered or witnessed problems, while also deterring criminals. Communication technology further improved through increasing police use of telephones by the first half of the twentieth century, resulting in members of the public calling police departments directly from their homes and other locations to report emergencies, crimes, and other problems. Reporters similarly began using telephones to communicate with their newsrooms while gathering news. In the 1920s, departments also instituted the use of the two-way radio, which allowed departments to contact officers to respond to the scenes. In addition to allowing officials to better oversee officers on their beats, a major departure from policing in the previous century, law enforcement radio communications allowed reporters seeking their next story to listen in, a practice that continues in the present with the use of police scanners.

Because the public could now call the police from wider geographic areas, and criminals were gaining access to faster forms of transportation, officers had to be able to respond more quickly, leading to the adoption of police vehicles.[8] As discussed in the previous chapter, police used patrol wagons and, eventually, cars and other vehicles to get to crime scenes as fast as possible. In fact, the New York Police Department (NYPD) created an aviation unit in 1929, which would include four planes by March 1930 and its first helicopter in 1947.

Another significant technological development during the Progressive Era was the formalized use of firearms by police.[9] Previously, in the 1850s through about the 1880s, officers carried revolvers, though often without the authority to do so. Although it was more common for officers to carry clubs, increasing violence against the police slowly led city governments to approve the use of handguns, such as in the 1890s in New York City. However, it was not until the first decades of the twentieth century that police more consistently, and legally, used firearms, including both revolvers and machine guns.

In addition to professionalization, the first decade of the twentieth century saw three additional significant developments. First, the founding of the federal Bureau of Investigation followed several antecedents, including postal inspectors, the Secret Service, and the U.S. Marshals. The Bureau of Investigation, as it was referred to until 1934, was founded in 1908 by President Roosevelt through an executive order after Congress initially feared that the law enforcement body would become "a political spy force" targeting political enemies over actual criminals.[10] The new agency, which allowed the federal government to "enter the police picture," was assigned its first main responsibilities with the passage of the Mann Act, which made it a federal crime to transport an individual over state lines for immoral purposes.[11] However, it was not until the 1920s–'40s that the bureau would gain increased authority, as well as a greater presence in American society and life, discussed more in the next chapter.

Second, formal state police forces, beginning with Pennsylvania's establishment of the "Black Hussars" in 1905, replaced sheriffs and constables who still had jurisdiction over large areas outside major cities.[12] These forces, which initially closely resembled the military, followed several antecedents, including slave patrols in the colonial South, the Texas Rangers, and Massachusetts's experimental state police force, the Massachusetts District Police. Formal state forces were created due to urbanization and industrialization connecting interdependent communities. Statewide law enforcement was also needed to reach a wider area due to the development of railroads, improving roads, and automobiles as a large number of criminals traveled across the country, including to more rural and remote areas. The rise of automobiles also meant that these new state forces, along with their local counterparts, increasingly handled growing traffic regulations and busier roads. Despite conflicts with local police, often over jurisdictional issues, this arm of law enforcement would continue to develop in ensuing decades, with Wisconsin being the last state to adopt such a force in 1939.

Finally, the first decades of the twentieth century saw increased calls for police unions amid low pay and poor working conditions, especially prior to professionalization efforts. Police unionization had antecedents dating back to the late nineteenth century, but came to a head with the Boston Police Strike of 1919.[13] Police commissioner Edwin Upton Curtis forbade the Boston police force from applying for a charter with the American Federation of Labor, which was chartering police departments across the United States. When Curtis suspended several union leaders after the force disobeyed his order, more than three-quarters of Boston police officers refused to work. The result was four days and nights of rampant crime across the city, leaving nine people dead and eventually leading Massachusetts governor and future vice president and president Calvin Coolidge to call in the Massachusetts State Guard. Coolidge famously said, "There is no right to strike against the public safety by anybody, anywhere, anytime." The fallout of the strike led to the firing of more than a thousand police officers and a chilling effect on further unionization efforts until the second half of the twentieth century.

Progressive Era Reforms Extend to Underrepresented
Communities with Mixed Results

Amid the press and police undergoing significant reforms in the early twentieth century, some changes and improvements arose in relation to underrepresented communities, including by the press. Journalists and writers like Ida B. Wells continued to target abuses in society, including the epidemic of lynching and hatred directed at Black individuals through aggressive advocacy journalism dating back to the late nineteenth century. Advocacy journalism of the nonwhite press and muckraking journalism developed in a "parallel, though segregated tracks." The development of both traditions was parallel in that they each targeted abuses in society. However, the paths diverged in that muckrakers' publishers largely ignored the works by the Black press and failed to cover racial segregation, among other critical topics and issues. Ultimately, Progressive Era reformers and the muckrakers accomplished a great deal but "fell short in two key areas: they failed to build public support for closing the growing divide between workers and capitalists in America, and they did almost nothing to confront the spread of racial segregation."[14]

Advocacy journalists, including Wells and José Martí, a correspondent for several newspapers in Latin America and occasional contributor to the *New York Sun*, also helped create social justice journalism, a new form of reporting arising during the Progressive Era. Journalists in this new tradition paved the way for similar reporting during the civil rights movement, covering issues such as white men going unpunished for sexual assaults of Black girls and women, while Black men were lynched for mere allegations of assaulting a white woman. Black newspapers in particular criticized the federal government for inaction related to violence against Black people and other marginalized groups. Social justice journalism by the nonwhite press was therefore "a separate but vibrant wing of the country's muckraking press," but, like advocacy journalism to a large extent, it "remained largely invisible to white society," allowing for the further "consolidation of the white racial narrative."[15]

Despite the reforms and changes to policing during the first decades of the twentieth century, division between law enforcement and marginalized communities also continued.[16] In the 1910s–'20s, a spike in race riots marked a key moment in the history of Black resistance to the police. In the first decades of the twentieth century, racial oppression, white supremacist terrorism, and segregation were commonplace across

U.S. cities and towns.[17] During World War I, Black people, including those moving to cities as part of a larger trend of urbanization, were met with violence by white individuals amid greater competition for the job and housing markets. Such violence included the bombing of twenty-four homes owned by Black families in South Chicago in 1917. In St. Louis, white workers killed 39 Black people and injured hundreds more, driving another 5,000 people out of the city. Two years later, the summer of 1919, referred to as the "Red Summer," saw violent uprisings by white people, including the growing Ku Klux Klan (KKK), against Black communities in at least twenty-six cities across the United States, though especially in the South. For example, in Elaine, Arkansas, white landowners, in what became known as the "Elaine Massacre," attacked hundreds of Black sharecroppers who tried to join a union, resulting in the deaths of at least 100 Black people and as many as 240.

A U.S. House of Representatives Special Committee in 1918 found that police were often complicit in the riots, concluding that "instead of being guardians of the peace they became a part of the mob by countenancing the assaulting and shooting down of defenseless negroes and adding to the terrifying scenes of rapine and slaughter."[18] The committee cited several examples, condemning the police's actions as well as their ineffectiveness in addressing the turmoil. Additionally, the Chicago Commission on Race Relations found that during riots in the summer of 1919, police had been ineffective at preventing the violence against Black people and instead more readily arrested and used force against Black individuals. Other officers left the scene without addressing the violence and often without any explicit reason for doing so.[19] As discussed more later in the chapter, the press extensively covered the violence, though often in problematic ways, such as implying that socialists were behind the violence or that Black communities were entirely to blame. For example, even the *New York Times* reported in 1919 that "bloodshed on a scale amounting to local insurrection" was evidence of "a new negro problem."[20] In other reporting, the *Times* suggested that socialists were trying to push Black communities to respond with violence, rather than the peaceful demonstrations that were largely planned by the NAACP and others.[21]

By the 1910s–'20s, police had also implemented "third-degree" violent interrogation tactics to elicit confessions. In particular, law enforcement used physical and psychological violence to elicit confessions from suspects, often leading to false confessions. Especially in the South, police

most frequently used such tactics against Black people, with white people largely being reluctant to put police on trial.[22] Even when white police officers were prosecuted, the result was largely the same: acquittals
by white juries. Although the tactics were not without criticism dating
back to the first decades of the twentieth century,[23] it was not until the
1930s that federal and state appellate courts, including the U.S. Supreme
Court in 1936, reversed convictions stemming from "confessions shown
to have been extorted by officers of the State by brutality and violence,"
finding that they violated the Due Process Clause of the Fourteenth
Amendment.[24] It was not until at least the 1940s–'50s that the FBI began
investigating the practice as political pressure to do so grew.

Press and Police Feel the Influence of World War I
World War I was a significant moment for the United States and the
world, implicating a wide range of institutions, to which the press and
police were no exceptions. In terms of the press, despite the push for
objectivity arising in the first decades of the twentieth century, the years
around World War I also marked greater interpretation and political
commentary amid government efforts to censor and otherwise target
journalists.[25] During the war, Congress passed the Espionage Act, the
Trading with the Enemy Act, and the Sedition Act, through which they
targeted publishers and dissenting voices, often with arrests or jail time.
The Committee on Public Information aimed to mobilize press and
public cooperation by controlling wartime information, imposing censorship, and spreading propaganda.

Falling during the police reform era, World War I also had several
effects on law enforcement, including much like the Civil War, leading
police officers in several cities to act like soldiers, while other officers
actually served as soldiers, reducing departments' personnel. This came
as the war brought increased visitors and criminals to cities, especially
those serving as a site of military training, leading to violence, straining law enforcement even further, and resulting in multiple cases of
police brutality. Police violence was also seen in increasing confrontations with marginalized groups and dissenting voices during speeches,
protests, riots, and more.[26] Law enforcement also wiretapped several
hundred suspected criminals' and marginalized individuals' phones,
leading state legislatures to conduct reviews of departments' wiretapping policies.

Cooperative Coexistence Holds On amid Reform and Change

Press coverage of police continued across the United States in the first decades of the twentieth century, including notable examples like the reporting on the 1910 *Los Angeles Times* bombing. As the building went up in flames in the middle of the night following the explosion of sixteen sticks of dynamite planted below the building, several inside died jumping out of windows to escape the flames, while others could not escape the inferno. The fire, which engulfed the building due to the blast hitting a natural gas line, was tied to the "Dynamite Conspiracy," a nationwide campaign to dynamite more than one hundred antiunion buildings and establishments, including the *Times* under Harrison Gray Otis and his son-in-law and right-hand man, Harry Chandler, both known to be aggressively opposed to organized labor. Ultimately, the blast killed twenty-one newspaper employees and injured one hundred more, leading to the federal indictment of fifty-four union men and prompting the *Los Angeles Times* to call it the "crime of the century."[27] Between 1900 and 1920, journalists also covered train robberies, gang activity, disappearances, and more as police aimed to accomplish their purposes and functions.

**Progressive Era Changes Prompt Greater
Division between Press and Police**

However, given the institutionalization by both the press and the police, among other factors and changes, contentiousness also arose during this time period, at times overshadowing cases of cooperation and coexistence. In particular, the press doubled down in holding police accountable amid the rise of public relations efforts by the police. Most notably, one of the targets of the muckrakers was law enforcement and police corruption.[28] In January 1903, muckraker Lincoln Steffens, who became managing editor of *McClure's* in 1901 after nearly a decade working as a journalist in New York City, wrote the magazine's cover story, "The Shame of Minneapolis."[29] Steffens analyzed police graft in the city, namely, the paying off of police officials to allow illegal operations of gambling rooms, brothels, and opium dens. Steffens wrote that corruption even included a "police baseball team, for whose games tickets were sold to people who had to buy them." He questioned at the end of the article, "Can a city be governed without any alliance with crime? It is an open question," noting that the new mayor at the time, David P. Jones, had reorganized the police force and emphasized that there be "no gambling, with police connivance, in the city of Minneapolis," though he had served for only four months and "certainly would reconsider this [position]" given a longer term in office.

Newspapers also continued reporting on police brutality, including of Black individuals in several large cities.[30] In many cases, the press condemned the actions of officers, placing most of the blame on high-level police officials, including in the NYPD. Steffens wrote in his 1931 autobiography that he and other reporters were increasingly "appalled at how baton-wielding police brutalized suspects while their supervisors sought to conceal the injured victims from public view."[31]

Additionally, the press reported on killings involving police officers. In 1912, the *New York World* and other newspapers covered the arrest and trial of NYPD lieutenant Charles Becker and others for the murder of gambling bookmaker Herman Rosenthal.[32] The case arose after Rosenthal complained to the *World* that Becker and his associates had raided his operation too many times and were negatively affecting his business. After being subsequently interrogated and ordered to appear before a grand jury by Manhattan district attorney Charles Seymour Whitman, who later became governor of New York, Rosenthal went to the Hotel Metropole at Broadway and Forty-Third Street for a drink early in the morning on July 16, 1912. But on his way, Rosenthal was gunned down by a group of men in a vehicle that quickly sped away, marking one of the first instances of a "hit squad" making a getaway by automobile.[33] Jack Rose, a gambler connected to Becker, turned himself in in an attempt to get leniency and revealed the names of the four shooters, each of whom were paid $1,000 by Becker to silence Rosenthal. On July 29, Becker was arrested at his desk in the Bathgate Avenue station house in the Bronx. Although some stories of the ensuing trial were sensational, Becker's "entire nineteen-year police career was put under a microscope by the press," which obtained bank statements and other incriminating materials. As the investigations into payoffs by police in connection to gambling operations played out, eighteen officers were indicted and four inspectors went to prison. Becker and the four gunmen were found guilty of first-degree murder and sentenced to death. Although Frank Cirofici, one of the convicted shooters, issued a statement clearing Becker of any responsibility in the shooting, Judge Samuel Seabury, the presiding judge in the case, refused to admit the statement in a second trial of Becker, who was once again found guilty and sentenced to death.

In 1915, Becker was put to death by the electric chair, the first police officer in the United States to receive the death penalty.

Contentiousness also arose as law enforcement continued arresting journalists, often in the course of journalistic functions.[34] Most notably, the passage of the Espionage Act in 1917—which was drafted to prohibit the obtaining, recording, or copying of information that could cause harm to national defense or foreign relations—and subsequent arrests and prosecutions of several printers and dissenting voices tested the bounds of First Amendment protections, including in Supreme Court cases *Schenck v. United States* (1919), *Debs v. United States* (1919), and *Abrams v. United States* (1919).[35] In fact, in *Frohwerk v. United States* (1919), the Court upheld the conviction of Jacob Frohwerk, the editor of the Missouri German-language newspaper *Staats Zeitung*, under the Espionage Act for writing articles published in the newspaper denouncing and opposing U.S. involvement in World War I. Frohwerk was convicted of eleven counts of attempting "to cause disloyalty, mutiny, and refusal of duty" in the military. As discussed in the next chapter, these cases were generally losses for the press and dissenting voices, though they still marked a turning point, as things would begin to change as the 1920s saw a turn toward pro–First Amendment sentiments.

As in past eras, some arrests were for actions outside journalistic purposes and functions;[36] however, the greatest contentiousness arose when arrests came during journalists' news-gathering efforts. In 1900, a reporter was arrested for allegedly bribing a police officer in an effort to obtain "confidential information in the possession of the Police Department for the purpose of . . . scoop[ing] its contemporaries with exclusive police reports."[37] An official furnished the reporter with false information, which the newspaper published. Although the *Buffalo (NY) Evening News* published an editorial criticizing the reporter for making other newspapers look bad and failing to uphold ethical values, which started to take hold during this era, it also condemned law enforcement's actions, contending that they made the arrest only to cover "their own incompetency."

Further adding to contentiousness were cases of police use of force and threats of violence against reporters in the course of news gathering, such as in 1910 when Topeka, Kansas, chief of police R. W. Eaton "in a sudden fit of passion at the police station . . . resorted to the methods employed by primeval men and present day inhabitants of the 'underworld'" and punched reporter C. A. Sloan.[38] The assault came after Sloan went to the police station to pose questions for his next story about a recent unidentified "incident." The reporter claimed that he had been at the police station "every day and several times a day" and had learned nothing of the incident, to which Eaton countered that he and his force "have other things to do than run to the papers with our troubles." Sloan added, "I simply want the news and all the news, and I mean to get it" before Eaton "made some angry exclamation not understood by the reporter and added, 'Take that, you . . . fool,' and struck a blow in the reporter's face with his clenched fist." Eaton then said, "You'll get what's coming to you all right if you hang around here" before "add[ing] a vicious kick and order[ing] the reporter out of the station."

Three years later, the *Marshalltown (IA) Times-Republican* carried a story from Davenport asserting that "in a desperate and futile effort to suppress the news and to prevent the publication of the numerous crimes that from day to day are a matter of record in Davenport, the latest tactics of Davenport police officials are to assault newspaper men."[39] In one particular instance, a Davenport police officer, Sergeant Walker, "forgot himself and made an uncalled for attack upon a reporter, violently ejecting him from [the police station]." The officer then shouted, "Ve don't vant dot stuff published, do you heerd dat," to which the unnamed reporter responded, "It matters not to us what your desires are. . . . We print the news regardless of your threats." The reporter had been seeking information in connection with a shooting the night before in which several individuals narrowly escaped the gunfire, though adding another in a line of shootings and violence in the neighborhood." The *Times-Republican*'s article covering the confrontation went so far as to contend that the assault was "not new to the local officers as it seems to have been a customary thing when a [suspect] is brought to the station," suggesting police violence against not only the press but also members of the public.

Police also subjected reporters to searches and seizures, including in 1911 when Vic Mauberret, the boss of the Fourth Ward in New Orleans, became "enraged by the presence of two Times-Democrat reporters" near the Second Precinct police station as they sought "to see what the effect [of their presence] would be," meaning how the politicians would respond to their reporting on a local election that was taking place.[40] Mauberret, convinced that the reporters were spying on him, "made an assault upon one of the reporters," breaking his glasses, and ordered a police officer to search the other reporter for a gun. Although the reporter emphasized that he did not have a gun, the officer searched him, finding that he was, in fact, unarmed. Mauberret then accused the reporter he attacked of being a "dangerous and suspicious character" before driving off in a vehicle with Captain William J. Hardee, who claimed to have not seen the assault and declined to arrest Mauberret for the attack at the request of the reporter.

Law enforcement also continued to play a role in subpoenas issued against journalists compelling their testimony in court.[41] Most notably, in 1911, police were directly tied to a subpoena when *Augusta (GA) Herald* reporter T. J. Hamilton refused to disclose to a police review board the name of an officer who had allegedly leaked information about a recent murder in the city.[42] A state court ruled in favor of Hamilton after he appealed the decision to hold him in contempt, finding that the police review board could punish an individual for not appearing, but not for refusing to testify. However, the Georgia Supreme Court reversed the ruling, finding in favor of the police review board. Hamilton was ultimately fined fifty dollars and served five days in jail.

A key development in the first decades of the twentieth century, particularly during World War I, was the federal government's "monitoring" of journalists.[43] The U.S. Department of Justice (DOJ), U.S. Post Office, and other agencies kept allegedly suspicious journalists and members of the Black press under surveillance. In particular, the government and law enforcement, including the Bureau of Investigation, actively monitored newspaper content and press telegrams during World War I, looking for and investigating dissenting voices that could sway public opinion or otherwise negatively affect loyalty to the United States and the war effort.

New Era of Impersonation and Media Ride-Alongs Continues Trends from Nineteenth Century, Raises New Considerations

Amid an era of significant reform, the press and police continued practices falling outside the interactions found more squarely under ongoing cooperative coexistence and contentiousness. And despite the profound changes occurring during this period, many of the trends arising from impersonation and media ride-alongs in the nineteenth century continued as well. Significantly, in the case of police impersonation of the press and media ride-alongs in particular, the effects of the practices, although problematic by our current standards, were either not in violation of the norms at the time or, alternatively, hidden in ways that meant members of the press, police, and public may not have seen or discussed them. It is also possible that the negative effects of the practice were not recognized or were ignored given the perceived benefits of impersonation and media ride-alongs. In any event, however, the continuation of trends first seen in the nineteenth century would help further set the foundation for future eras where such problems and issues would more clearly violate norms and values, often in ways hidden below the surface, though in some cases generating greater attention and criticism, especially closer to the twenty-first century.

Police Impersonation of the Press

In October 1910, a standoff occurred in Winter, Wisconsin, when a man named John Dietz refused to surrender to police and exit his home.[44] Although a St. Paul, Minnesota, man was permitted to go to Dietz's home to try to talk him into surrendering, the news media and others were not permitted near the house. Detective William Baxter who "had been masquerading as a reporter for a Chicago newspaper . . . presented his plea for passage through the cordon but was bluntly turned down by the sheriff." Nevertheless, Baxter "attempted to run the blockade." Although it is unclear whether Baxter was a private detective or a member of a police department, his actions suggested a new purpose for impersonating the press: ending a standoff or hostage situation, which would become increasingly common later in the century.

Additional cases of impersonation continued trends beginning in the previous era, showing the wide range of ways in which the police, by posing as journalists, conducted investigations into public and private figures, often leading to consequences for the individuals being investigated.[45] In 1912, police used impersonation to detain an individual and bring him before a government proceeding. The underlying legal case was against Jim Larkin and former assemblyman Benjamin Gitlow, who were both out on bail after being indicted for criminal anarchy due to their participation in alleged communist activities.[46] During the subsequent trial, Larkin reportedly "told of his recent 'honor' of being arrested in his home by a detective, 'a being of a low mental type,' who, he asserted, was masquerading as a newspaperman in order to reach him" and bring him before a legislative hearing. The case ultimately proved significant in that it led to a U.S. Supreme Court ruling in 1925 that the Fourteenth Amendment extended First Amendment rights and protections to the states.[47]

A final example of law enforcement using impersonation of a journalist for investigative purposes occurred in 1918 when a "government sleuth" sought information about a man who recently deserted from the military.[48] The detective reportedly located the home of the deserter's sister where he said to her, "I just wanted to get something about him for a newspaper sketch—I'm a reporter, you know." The sleuth alleged that "in the half hour's talk I had with her I learned everything I needed to know, and she was not conscious of having given anything away." Thus, the detective purposely misled an interviewee into giving him information by misrepresenting himself as a reporter.

Press Impersonation of Police

In 1901, litigation once again brought press impersonation of police to the forefront. During the trial of several "charity swindlers," a defense attorney accused a newspaper reporter of having "impersonated a detective officer."[49] However, it turned out that a police official had "asked the reporter to pose as an officer and search the room of [one of the defendants] for evidence," to which the reporter refused. Although the accusation ended up being untrue, it demonstrated that press impersonation of police was frowned upon during this period, like in the 1880s–'90s, potentially straining the press-police relationship. Significantly, this example also suggests the possibility that a journalist impersonated a police officer in order to aid law enforcement in some way, meaning the reporter may not have been fully accomplishing their own purposes and functions. Whether the police are willing or unwilling participants, the use of the impersonation by the press in this case undermines the independence of both institutions and complicates the nature of their relationship, including their ability to accomplish their own important purposes and functions.

The 1911 trial of Rev. Clarency V. T. Richardson for murder provided the backdrop for another accusation of press impersonation of police.[50] In this case, Chief Inspector John Dugau "declared that when his inspectors went to the pastor's rooms, they found everything in a state of chaos, the result of a general ransacking which occurred prior to the police visit." Although it was "not known who was responsible for this," newspaper reports indicated that a "reporter impersonated an officer and gained entrance to the apartment." As with earlier examples, the article represented an accusation, in this case against an unknown reporter, who likely entered the home for news-gathering purposes. This case therefore suggests the second, and most common, purpose behind press impersonation of police: reporting and news gathering, including acquiring information for a story, gaining access to a location, or interviewing a source.

Finally, in 1916, two reporters' actions once again demonstrated how press impersonation of police can lead to negative effects on journalists and the press-police relationship. In this case, two unnamed reporters allegedly used Tulsa, Oklahoma, police chief Ed L. Lucas's phone and his name to call the editor of a weekly magazine in the community.[51] The reporters told the editor to "come at once to the chief's office." Upon hearing that the reporters used his name and phone, likely as part of a rivalry with the other publication, Lucas expressed the need "to conduct a serious investigation into the matter," calling it a "serious offense." In doing so, Lucas demonstrated once more that at least some police officials and others did not condone the practice, meaning that it could strain the press-police relationship when used by members of the press. Furthermore, this example also demonstrated that press impersonation of police could result in legal action against reporters, a negative effect first seen a decade earlier and that, like other consequences, would continue for years to come.

Media Ride-Alongs

In 1899, officials in Akron, Ohio, introduced what many scholars now refer to as the first police car in existence. By January 1900, the new automobile, "the first horseless patrol wagon ever made" and "first automobile to be put to use as a police patrol wagon," was in operation.[52] For the first time, a police wagon was "propelled by electricity," with a top speed of twenty miles per hour. The *Akron Beacon Journal* reported that at least three officials rode in the automobile accompanied by "a few others," likely including a reporter given the historic nature of its introduction.[53]

Within ten years, several cities had adopted motorized patrol vehicles, including police "automobiles" or "cars," which ran on gasoline as opposed to electricity and steam.[54] An early instance of a reporter riding in a police automobile in the United States came on April 26, 1907, when the new patrol wagon in Indianapolis "was taken out for its initial trial spin" despite poor weather and "slippery" streets.[55] Chief

Robert Metzger invited five newspaper reporters to join him, with the *Indianapolis News* later calling it "a great ride up to a certain point" when the wagon struggled to reach the top of a hill, though it eventually did so after some quick repairs. The wagon broke down again before ultimately returning to the city.

Amid the rise of horseless patrol wagons and motorized police vehicles, the 1900s–1910s saw the continuation of several trends seen in the previous era. First, police officers and officials, like Metzger, continued to invite or grant permission to reporters to join them on ride-alongs. Second, journalists rode with police to cover law enforcement and news stories, often resulting in coverage praising police or portraying them in a positive light. In 1917, *Des Moines Evening Tribune* reporter W. D. Harrison recounted his experiences "in a police automobile equipped to run down traffic law violators."[56] In his story, Harrison described the vehicle and his experiences, which provided "enough thrills . . . to last through the season." Harrison also contended that despite their public perception, "a traffic man is not necessarily a bully; he may be a gentleman," explaining that Detective Hollibaugh did not get into a single "row" during the ride-along. Based on a single shift, Harrison praised the officer he rode with, as well as law enforcement more broadly.

Third, journalists also participated in ride-alongs in order to cover a news story, such as on May 2, 1905, when a *Charlotte (NC) Observer* reporter "saw the police wagon starting out with three coppers, the driver, and little Peter Black. The little boy was perched on the driver's seat."[57] The reporter believed it to be "such an important occasion," namely, a case of child abuse or domestic violence, that he "ran and swung up behind" the wagon in order to quickly go to the scene and report on what was taking place with the young boy. The "Black Maria" ultimately stopped at a water tower, with the reporter jumping off "to get the first glimpse," though the police could not find the suspect for whom they were searching.

Fourth, there were some limited examples of critical coverage of law enforcement resulting from media ride-alongs, though they remained far less common than positive coverage of police.[58] For example, the *San Francisco Chronicle* reported in 1901 that "a Chinese keeper of a lottery den . . . [claimed] that he had bribed Captain George Wittman of the San Francisco Police." Upon hearing the allegation, Wittman, "in tragic tones, declared that he would go get his trusty sledge, break in the door of the place and bring forth the concealed Pagan 'on his own responsibility.'"[59] Several reporters summarily "scrambled into a patrol wagon with Wittman and his sledge." However, when Wittman arrived at the scene and broke down the door, "the place was empty." The *San Francisco Chronicle* called the events a "futile raid" and a "fiasco," providing at least some accountability of the official.[60] Five years later, Wittman was fired from the San Francisco Police amid allegations that the police had not adequately addressed gambling in Chinatown, among other claims.

Fifth, in some instances, reporters aided police on a ride-along. In one case, a reporter "assisted [a] wounded young man while the [police] wagon was stalled with two [tire] punctures."[61] Here, the reporter may not have solely intended to help the police while riding on the patrol wagon; however, that quickly became his purpose as the officers focused on other tasks. Although it may not have been the case here, if journalists are too busy helping the police with their activities, they cannot fully accomplish their own responsibilities.

Finally, the 1900s–1910s saw threats to the physical safety of journalists. This was perhaps best apparent in examples of reporters being caught in the crossfire between police and criminals in a shoot-out. For example, in 1913, a reporter joined several police officials and officers as they responded to a robbery at a local store.[62] As the group approached the scene, "two men—lookouts stationed at the corner—opened fire. Policeman Anderson, who sat on the front seat, was first to return shots. Captain Mayo and Policeman Watson . . . also opened up." The reporter was carrying a revolver, but it failed to fire, leaving "the only logical thing he could be expected to do under the circumstances[:] climbing over the back of the [automobile]."

Connected to physical danger was a lack of precautions taken to protect members of the news media, including in January 1909 when a reporter for the *Washington (D.C.) Evening Star* spent a night on the patrol wagon.[63] Having asked for permission to ride on the wagon, the reporter was told by the driver, "'I have no objection to your going. . . . But I can't guarantee you safety any more than I can an interesting time.'"

In 1917, the dangers of riding along with police played out when F. A. Scott and Horace Karr, reporters for the Times-Mirror Company and the Herald Publishing Company, respectively, "accompanied [E. P. Bradley, then the police chauffeur] in the police car to the home of Mrs. Francis Harrison, who was slain."[64] But on the way, John T. Jordan, a mail carrier, "was struck and injured by the police car," leading to a

$25,000 lawsuit against Bradley, as well as Scott, Karr, and the companies for which they worked. Judge Charles Wellborn ruled in favor of Jordan, finding that a "police or fireman chauffeur has no more right to exceed the speed laws than a private driver." Scott and Karr were later "exonerated." Nevertheless, the episode demonstrated not only the dangers of police vehicles but also the threat of legal action that can arise from a media ride-along, a new negative effect arising from the practice that would continue for years to come.

For the press and police, there was no escaping the vast and significant changes sweeping across the United States during the Progressive Era, especially following an era of yellow journalism and continued police wrongdoing. Each entity underwent its own separate, though in many ways similar, reforms, including professionalization, which saw the establishment of distinct, separate borders as the press and police became independent institutions. The resulting effect on their relationship was one of separation. Institutionalization, muckraking and advocacy journalism, new public relations efforts, and other developments led to greater division and tension between the press and police, including as impersonation and media ride-alongs continued. However, cooperative coexistence was far from gone. Instead, an era of partnerships was approaching in which cooperative coexistence would become the predominant category of interactions between the press and police in ensuing decades as their relationship would continue to evolve amid a new series of societal changes and upheavals.

CHAPTER 4

Greater Partnerships, 1920s–1950s

AS THE UNITED STATES ENTERED the "Roaring Twenties," it saw a period of prosperity in the years following World War I, bringing a variety of changes to American life, ranging from Prohibition to the rise of pro–First Amendment feelings and court rulings. However, in 1929, the Great Depression devastated the United States and the world, bringing human suffering, significant economic losses, and other profound changes. World War II and the beginning of the Cold War marked two additional major worldwide events, once again sending ripple effects across different aspects of American life. As with past major societal events, the press and police were not immune to significant changes, each undergoing respective transformations, again often in similar ways, implicating their relationship. Most notably, by the 1940s–'50s, an era of greater cooperative coexistence reached its zenith as greater partnerships and trust between the two institutions reached a level not yet seen, or seen since, in the United States. However, it did not take long for cracks to begin to show as contentiousness remained a key aspect of the relationship, ushering in a new era altogether in the 1960s–'70s.

Major Societal Events Promote Greater Partnerships between Press and Government

The 1920s marked a "liberal turn," falling between the Progressive Era and the 1930s New Deal, setting the stage for greater partnerships and trust between the press and government, including law enforcement.[1] In an era in which conservative politics and forces generally controlled federal politics, a separate trend of liberal ideas, including favoring civil liberties, urban culture, and more, created a "cultural conflict." Falling under this context, society increasingly favored pro–First Amendment considerations. Beginning in 1919, federal courts, as well as Congress to a lesser degree, "began to develop a more protective legal framework for free speech." The push for civil liberties and liberal ideas broadly, and First Amendment rights more specifically, carried on the tradition of the free-speech movement during the Progressive Era, in which groups like the Industrial Workers of the World, a workers union, carried out dozens of free-speech demonstrations across the United States. The Free Speech League was a defender of Free Expression in the first decades of the twentieth century, prior to the development of the American Civil Liberties Union (ACLU) in 1920, the same year that the Democratic Party platform emphasized the need for freedom of speech and the press.

In 1989, Norman L. Rosenberg, then a professor of history at Macalester College in St. Paul, Minnesota, drew on previous scholarship and wrote that First Amendment law was "reconstructed, if not invented, between 1919 and 1927."[2] He pointed to two opinions in particular: Justice Oliver Wendell Holmes Jr.'s dissent in *Abrams v. United States* (1919) and Justice Louis D. Brandeis's concurring opinion in *Whitney v. United States* (1927). *Abrams* arose when Jacob Abrams and four fellow Russian immigrants distributed two leaflets in New York City criticizing the United States' involvement in the Russian Revolution in 1917 that overthrew the imperial government and put the Bolshevik political party in power. The U.S. Supreme Court ultimately upheld the immigrants' twenty-year prison sentence under the Espionage Act, applying the clear-and-present-danger test articulated by Justice Holmes in *Schenck v. United States* (1919), meaning that speech would raise "substantive evils that Congress has a right to prevent. It is a question of proximity and degree." However, in a dissenting opinion in *Abrams*, Justice Holmes advocated for a more libertarian version of the test, finding that the immigrants' actions presented no immediate or real danger to the war effort or national security. Justice Holmes also articulated the marketplace of ideas theory, writing that "the ultimate good desired is better reached by free trade in ideas—that the best test of truth is the power of the thought to get itself accepted in the competition of the market, and that truth is the only ground upon which [people's] wishes safely can be carried out. That at any rate is the theory of our Constitution." The theory, still cited by First Amendment scholars more than one hundred years later, posits that ideas and arguments should be allowed to compete in a free market, where, hopefully, truth and "good" speech prevail. Put differently, the marketplace of ideas calls for free speech with limited, if any, government intrusion, allowing for the free flow of ideas and information.

Whitney centered around Charlotte Anita Whitney, a young woman from Oakland, California, who was a member of the local branch of the Socialist Party. In 1919, she attended the party's national convention in Chicago, where she was part of a group that split from the Socialist Party and established the Communist Labor Party of America. Whitney was arrested and convicted under the California Criminal Syndicalism Act of 1919 for her role in helping establish and participating in the CLP, which advocated for violent revolution. The U.S. Supreme Court ultimately upheld the conviction, finding that the California statute did not violate the First and Fourteenth Amendments. However, Justice Brandeis wrote a concurring opinion cited by many scholars as among the greatest defenses of free speech in the history of the United States. He wrote, in part, "Those who won our independence believed . . . that freedom to think as you will and to speak as you think are means indispensable to the discovery and spread of political truth; that, without free speech and assembly, discussion would be futile; that, with them, discussion affords ordinarily adequate protection against the dissemination of noxious doctrine. . . . Recognizing the occasional tyrannies of governing majorities, they amended the Constitution so that free speech and assembly should be guaranteed." Justice Brandeis's opinion, like Justice Holmes's dissent in *Abrams*, would be cited by the Supreme Court, lower courts, scholars, and others for years to come, paving the way for stronger protections for freedom of speech and the press as the twentieth century continued.

The press covered a variety of societal events and changes arising during the Roaring Twenties, perhaps most notably Prohibition following the passage of the Eighteenth Amendment and the National Prohibition Act of 1919, known as the Volstead Act. The press covered a variety of angles related to the nationwide ban on the production, transportation, and sale of alcohol, including covering local businesses' stances, as well as how the government and law enforcement responded to its effects, necessitating at least some cooperation.

The following decade was characterized by the United States entering and responding to the Great Depression, affecting the press, like all American institutions, in several different ways.[3] Amid the economic disaster, newspapers were generally able to maintain circulations but saw significant decreases in advertising. Newspapers also dealt with increased competition from the growing radio industry, discussed further later in the chapter. Nevertheless, the press covered the poor economic conditions and government responses, complicated stories of which the public had a deep interest. Such reporting required government sources and information, which were complemented by President Franklin Delano Roosevelt's semiregular press conferences beginning in 1933. Although some reporting still included interpretation and criticism, the 1930s continued the trend toward greater partnerships between the press and government.

The 1940s were marked by World War II, which became known as the "First Broadcast War."[4] This was exemplified by the famous radio broadcasts, including by CBS journalist, war correspondent, and broadcast pioneer Edward R. Murrow from the rooftops of London, as well as a team of war correspondents spread across Europe, Asia, and North Africa who came to be known as the "Murrow Boys." Additionally, war correspondents moved toward more aggressive reporting, stemming from coverage of major events like the landing on the beaches of Normandy. But at the same time, FDR's administration sought to influence and limit the press through the Office of Censorship, the central gatekeeper of war news in the United States, and the Office of War Information, which produced and distributed war news and propaganda. After the United States entered the war, the federal government imposed a formal system of censorship, review of journalists' materials, and monitoring and tracking journalists as it had during World War I.

The rise of greater cooperation between the press and government broadly can be traced to 1913 when President Woodrow Wilson establishing semiweekly press conferences open to all correspondents and reporters.[5] President Warren G. Harding, who owned a newspaper in Ohio and was known to talk freely to journalists, revived the practice in 1921. The liberal turn, as well as reporting on Prohibition and the Great Depression, further moved the press and government toward greater trust and partnerships. However, the greatest cooperation was seen during World War II and the beginning of the Cold War when the press and government had an "uneasy alliance," even amid censorship and surveillance.[6]

There were several reasons that likely contributed to the "broad immunity granted to FDR and [the government] in general."[7] First, in terms of World War II, reporters and correspondents did not want to risk the lives of American soldiers or the success of the war effort. They were, therefore, largely willing to self-censor or submit their reports to prior review. Even during the early years of the Cold War, the press did not want to undermine the government's efforts. Additionally, the news media "helped to create and sustain the Cold War consensus" in the early years of the conflict, making members of the press "associates, not adversaries."[8] Second, reporters wanted to maintain access to government sources, information, and press conferences. Although found in earlier decades, the first half of the twentieth century in particular saw journalists forgo a political voice to maintain access to the inner workings of government. Finally, objectivity helped foster greater cooperation between the press and government. Journalists focused less on scandals and also refrained from elaborating on or challenging statements by government officials, which was largely seen as biasing the news. The result was protecting the status quo.

However, even in the 1940s, some editors still expressed frustration about censorship and the banning of information about diplomatic negotiations, enemy propaganda, and more.[9] The 1950s in particular saw the beginning of gradual distrust between the press and government, including because growing public relations efforts by the federal, state, and local governments meant reporters increasingly dealt with intermediaries, namely, public relations experts, which would more formally arise with public information officers in the 1960s–'70s. The result was growing resentment by the press toward the government, though the 1950s still marked numerous instances of the press working directly with government sources.

A "low point of press-government relations in the 1950s" came with President Harry Truman's 1951 executive order creating a classification system of government information.[10] The system, which expanded the amount of information deemed secret, confidential, or classified, was adopted in similar ways at the federal, state, and local levels. This led several reporters and editors to push against the withholding of information in peacetime, calling it unnecessary, against the values of a free press, and a means of allowing greater scandals and wrongdoing in government. Litigation increased as news organizations sought to open records and meetings, which often prompted government agencies and officials to refuse to disclose information.

This context led many journalists, scholars, and others to begin questioning the goal of objectivity in the 1950s, especially in light of the tumultuous nature of society and politics during the Cold War.[11] This era therefore marked an increase in interpretation in journalism, which, although not new, allowed greater latitude for reporters to provide critical reporting, commentary, and opinions about the government, which it was increasingly growing to distrust. Nevertheless, the "fissure" between the press and government that developed in the 1950s "was evident, but not great."[12] It was in the 1960s–'70s that "this breach would . . . reach great proportions."

Prohibition, the Great Depression, and World War II Challenge Law Enforcement

Prohibition, the Great Depression, and World War II all proved to be seminal moments in the history of U.S. law enforcement. Although objections to alcohol, and responses by police, can be traced to at least the 1830s, the passage of the Eighteenth Amendment and Volstead Act meant control of Prohibition fell to local law enforcement and the politicians who controlled the police.[13] Law enforcement was therefore tasked with enforcing prohibitions on speakeasies and bootlegging, as well as the rise of organized crime and gangs. However, enforcing Prohibition was difficult, especially because officers, who lacked training and adequate pay, were under the control of politicians associated with gangsters. The result was new challenges in addressing crime, though also frequent citizen complaints of police harassment and brutality.

The Great Depression saw the continued growth of professional and organized crime, necessitating police action of which there was "very little organization" in turn.[14] Police violence also continued, especially targeting those most affected by economic hardships, namely, marginalized individuals, unemployed workers, and dissenting voices. Although economic problems led to limited technological advancements, departments instituted other reforms, including becoming more centralized. There was also an increased number of qualified police recruits as they could not find jobs elsewhere due to the economic downturn.

World War II also affected law enforcement in several ways. As in World War I, police often acted as an internal defense in anticipation of a possible Axis attack, adding to the responsibilities of officers.[15] Other officials and officers served in the war, straining departments as they sought to address increased political and social protests. Also like World War I, law enforcement became increasingly involved in the surveillance, monitoring, and suppression of dissenting voices at protests and other events and locations.

Types of Media, Federal Law Enforcement Further Expand
Amid the significant societal events falling in the first half of the twentieth century, the press saw the rise of three new media for news and entertainment. Film, radio, and television each had earlier developments but in the 1920s–'50s changed how the media created and distributed news and entertainment. Following several decades of technological advances, the modern film industry began in the 1890s as films began to reach large numbers of people, though they were initially silent, shorter than a minute, and shown in storefronts, libraries, and recital halls.[16] By the 1920s–'30s, motion pictures were a full industry, moving to cinemas and now containing sound, though production slowed during the Great Depression. Newspapers increasingly covered movie stars and films, expanding their entertainment sections. Additionally, film was used for propaganda during World War I.

Developed around the turn of the twentieth century, radio brought both entertainment and news into listeners' living rooms.[17] The public listened to entertainment shows, as well as serious reporting of World War II by the likes of Murrow. Presidents Coolidge and Roosevelt used radio to address the nation, such as Coolidge's public addresses to Congress and FDR's "Fireside Chats"—a series of evening radio addresses in which the president directly addressed the nation in a more conversational, informal way as Americans listened from home on a variety of topics ranging from the Great Depression to Pearl Harbor and World War II. These developments led radio to be the first national medium, changing the U.S. media system from being solely "news*papers*" to "the news *media*."[18] However, the rise of radio also led to government regulation, justified on the basis that there were a limited number of electromagnetic frequencies available to broadcasters, known as spectrum scarcity. As a result, Congress passed legislation like the Radio Act of 1927, which established the Federal Radio Commission, later becoming the Federal Communications Commission (FCC) with the passage of the Communications Act of 1934.

Delayed by World War II, development and sales of televisions boomed in the 1950s to the early 1970s, known as the "golden age of television."[19] Like radio, television brought a rise in entertainment and news, ranging from *I Love Lucy* to Murrow's marveling that CBS could simultaneously show live images of the Brooklyn Bridge and the Golden Gate Bridge. Also like radio, television brought government regulation, including limitations on what could be shown on broadcast stations. Government also used, or appeared on, television, including the September 26, 1960, presidential debate between Democratic nominee John F. Kennedy and Republican nominee Richard Nixon, the first such debate on television. Scholars have contended that people who listened to the debate on radio generally thought Nixon had won, or the debate was at least a draw. However, those who watched the debate on television concluded that Kennedy was the decisive victor, citing that he looked healthier given his wide smile and tan, whereas Nixon came across as more pale, tired, and aggressive. In the 1960s–'70s, television would gain a more prominent role in news, politics, and entertainment, a trend continuing into the twenty-first century.

Meanwhile, in the 1920s–'40s, federal law enforcement came into its own. In 1924, J. Edgar Hoover, who was born and raised in Washington, D.C., and was hired in 1917 as a file reviewer by the Justice Department immediately after completing his law degree at George Washington University, was appointed head of the Bureau of Investigation, which became the Federal Bureau of Investigation in 1934.[20] Previously, from 1919 to 1921, Hoover served as the head of the Bureau of Investigation's new General Intelligence Division, which was referred to as the "Radical Division" due to its monitoring, investigating, and targeting those considered "radical" and "dangerous" by the federal government. Such individuals included alleged socialists and communists during the first "Red Scare"—a movement driven by Americans' fears that the Bolshevik Revolution in Russia, a coup d'état leading to the adoption of a socialist government under Vladimir Lenin—would spread to the United States.

Among Hoover's early tasks was the introduction of public relations efforts, such as portraying an FBI agent to be educated, highly trained, and a "champion of law and order."[21] Hoover also developed close relationships with numerous opinion leaders in government, law enforcement, the press, and other institutions, allowing for two-way communication.[22] In return for defending the FBI, or looking the other way, when the agency was challenged, those courted by the bureau would be given greater access to FBI information and materials, among other potential benefits. In 1930, Hoover gained control of the Uniform Crime Reports System and the federal fingerprint system. Two years later, the bureau opened its scientific crime lab, allowing for the examination of hair samples, blood specimens, firearms, and other evidence. The following decade included additional efforts by Hoover to gain power for the FBI as it acquired jurisdiction over several other crimes, ranging from kidnapping to drug use.

However, the FBI was also involved in several problematic actions, including, in the 1930s, practicing political spying, such as conducting illegal wiretapping, break-ins, burglaries, and forging documents. The FBI also frequently exaggerated accomplishments and glorifying crime in popular media, as well as focusing on and augmenting public hysteria around the second "Red Scare" during the Cold War, a movement led by Senator Joseph R. McCarthy, the junior senator from Wisconsin, who in February 1950 claimed to have a list of 205 card-carrying Communists employed in the U.S. Department of State. McCarthy subsequently held hearings on supposed communist subversion in America.

At the same time, the FBI gave little attention to organized crime, even as local police failed to address, or were complicit in, mob violence, until at least the late 1950s. Even by the 1960s and 1970s, investigations into organized crime and efforts to take down those involved in the Mafia were disorganized and largely ineffective, at least until the FBI began prosecuting mob leaders under the Racketeer Influenced and Corrupt Organizations Act in the 1980s. But despite the problems arising from and created by the FBI, it was not until the press increasingly investigated the bureau during the 1960s–'70s that its operations and authority began to change moving forward.

Amid the press's and police's responses to Prohibition, the Great Depression, World War II, and the beginning of the Cold War, as well as new forms of media and an increasingly powerful federal law enforcement agency, the news media and government broadly saw greater cooperation and trust. This would come to include the press-police relationship, which saw greater partnerships in the 1940s–'50s in particular,[23] though contentiousness, as well as impersonation and media ride-alongs, certainly did not go away.

Cooperative Coexistence Comes Roaring Back, Overshadows Contentiousness

The 1920s–'50s saw the continuation of a trend dating back to the nineteenth century in which it was common for members of the press to have significant access to police departments, often having their own dedicated space.[24] For example, in 1944, the *Houston Post* explained that it was common for police officers to visit the "press room" where "off-duty reporters could be talked into a game of dominoes."[25] The practice of reporters spending "their days in the station house" created an environment where journalists "admire[d] policemen, and the police . . . usually reciprocated this feeling."[26] Connected to access to police departments and other locations was the press having a "perpetual pragmatic concern over access."[27] The press therefore aimed to maintain the cooperation of police officials and officers as sources, sometimes self-censoring stories that portrayed law enforcement in a negative way, much like the press did with the federal government.[28] Furthermore, reporters and police officers often came from similar backgrounds, allowing both institutions to socialize and maintain the status quo.

As reporters looked to maintain access to police sources and locations, they still remained vigilant for a story, especially about crime and policing.[29] For example, during Prohibition and the Great Depression, the news media reported on speakeasies and homemade "hooch," as well as organized crime and gangster killings, lynchings, robberies, and more. As in the nineteenth century, reporters were even known to arrest criminals in some cases.[30] In the years around World War II, the press continued to cover crime and policing, including reporting on murders, robberies, arson, the attempted assassination of President Harry Truman in 1950, a shooting at the U.S. Capitol in 1954, and the 1958 bombing of the Hebrew Benevolent Congregation Temple in Atlanta, among numerous other examples from around the country.

Perhaps the most notable crime coverage in the first half of the twentieth century arose on the night of March 1, 1932.[31] At approximately ten o'clock at night, Charles Lindbergh, a world-famous American aviator best known for making the first nonstop flight from New York City to Paris in 1927, and his wife, Anne, discovered that their twenty-month-old son, Charles Augustus Lindbergh Jr., was missing from his nursery. A search of the premises by law enforcement soon followed in which a ransom note demanding $50,000 was found on the nursery windowsill. Reporters and photographers immediately flocked to the Lindbergh estate, while "sightseers trampled the area, possibly destroying clues and evidence."[32] In fact, a group of photographers went so far as to "[install] a portable darkroom in an ambulance, [pose] as medics, and dr[i]ve onto the grounds." In ensuing weeks, the New Jersey State Police, assisted by the FBI, conducted the investigation into the missing child, drawing further press coverage and sensationalism, billing it the "Crime of the Century."

John F. Condon, a retired schoolteacher and well-known individual in New York City, became the intermediary between the kidnapper and Lindbergh, including through newspaper ads. On April 2, Condon delivered $50,000 to a man identified as "John." The ransom included gold certificates, of which the serial numbers were recorded by police. However, on May 12, the body of Lindbergh Jr. was accidentally discovered fewer than five miles from the Lindbergh home in a state of advanced decomposition. The medical examiner ultimately determined that the baby died from a skull fracture likely occurring soon after he was kidnapped. The investigation into the kidnapping and murder persisted for another two years, continuing to draw press attention. Then, in 1934, police arrested and charged Bruno Richard Hauptmann, a German-born carpenter, after he used a $20 gold certificate that was part of the ransom money. When he was arrested, Hauptmann had another bill in his wallet and an additional $14,000 of the ransom money stored in his garage, among other evidence.

At least two hundred journalists from numerous news organizations representing newspapers, radio, and newsreels flocked to a small county courthouse in Flemington, New Jersey, where the "Trial of the Century" began in January 1935, only a few miles from the Lindberghs' home. The AP installed four teletype machines used to transmit trial transcripts to newspapers in New York, Philadelphia, and other major cities. More than one hundred Western Union telegraph wires were hung in the courthouse attic. While awaiting the jury's verdict, some reporters "smuggled portable radio transmitters into the courtroom to instantly 'flash' the verdict using a predetermined code."[33] Meanwhile, a crowd of ten thousand people had gathered outside the courthouse awaiting the verdict, yelling and screaming when the guilty verdict was read, with the jury recommending the death penalty, by a press messenger boy. Hauptmann's conviction was eventually upheld by New Jersey appeals courts, and on April 3, 1936, he was executed in the electric chair after turning down an offer from a Hearst newspaper for a confession.

Ultimately, the coverage of the "Crime of the Century" and "Trial of the Century" proved significant in that it was "the first time we see the three pillars of the modern media—print journalism, radio, and newsreels, which later become television and digital media—all coming together," namely, to cover a significant, breaking news story.[34] It was not all good news for the press, however, as following the trial, many federal and state courts across the United States banned press access to trials, contending that it could undermine a defendant's Sixth Amendment rights to a fair trial, especially in a high-profile case with significant media attention. To this day, free-press versus fair-trial rights remains a contentious debate and a complicated legal landscape, though many federal and state courts have allowed press access once more, especially in criminal cases where the First Amendment generally protects courtroom access.[35] The kidnapping also proved significant for law enforcement in that the FBI demonstrated to the press and public its ability to handle forensic evidence, at least better than the New Jersey State Police, which "so badly bungled evidence and handled the case with extraordinary incompetence."[36]

Sometimes, reporters went to great lengths to cover crime and police. This was perhaps best evidenced in a case involving two reporters who spent "a long evening at police headquarters" and "played a hunch which got them a whale of a story and also landed them in the pokey for a few hours."[37] The story went that one night, a desk sergeant received a call from a woman, whom he assumed to be intoxicated and told her to "go to bed and sleep it off." However, the reporters "smelled a story" and "decided to quietly check the call." However, neither had a means of transportation to get to the woman, so they "did the only thing good reporters on the way to get a story could do. There was a shiny Model T marked 'Police Department' parked at the curb, so they climbed in and drove off." Upon reaching the home of the woman, they found that her husband had been murdered, providing them "a terrific exclusive." But it came at great risk not only because they ended up in jail for "stealing" the police vehicle, but also because they had caused an "uproar" in the police department by making the police "look silly," risking future access and source relationships that defined the first half of the twentieth century.

Crime and policing were also common subjects in both news and entertainment in film, radio, and television in the first half of the twentieth century, contributing to the positive relationship between the press and police. An antecedent to depictions of police in film, radio, and television was the dime novel, which was popular among youths and workers.[38] These inexpensive books, which became the first profitable form of U.S. mass literature, "reflected and helped shape society," such as through depictions of crime and law enforcement.

Early films, which were generally meant for those who could not afford to attend traditional theater performances, often depicted "topics
represent[ing] slices of daily life," including related to crime and police.[39] For example, *The Great Train Robbery* (1903) is regarded as one
of the first crime dramas. It centers, with exaggeration and split-second
timing, on a gang of outlaws breaking into a train station and then holding up and robbing passengers on a steam locomotive in the American
West. The four bandits are then pursued by a sheriff's posse, ending
with one of the gunmen escaping and shooting toward the camera, as
if to shoot at members of the film's audience. In the first decades of the
twentieth century, some films went beyond entertainment and showed
newsworthy events, such as President William McKinley's inauguration
in 1897. Newsreels, ten-minute productions that showed news events
before films in theaters, combined actual news images with staged reen-
actments and human-interest material, including crime.

As the film industry came into its own in the 1920s–'30s, some films
depicted interactions between the press and police. For example, *The
Front Page* (1931) included both comedic and dramatic depictions of
the press-police relationship.[40] A humorous scene was when Officer
Woodenshoes came to the press room in the Criminal Court Building
with a story he thought the press "might be interested in." However, the
reporters, who were depicted playing poker, ignored the officer, instead
sending him to get hamburgers. A more serious interaction occurred
when reporters heard gunfire as Earl Williams, who was accused of killing a police officer, escaped from prison, prompting them to rush to the
scene by hopping onto police cars.

News and entertainment about crime and police soon became part
of radio programming beginning as early as the 1920s.[41] For example,
radio executives created the format of having thirty- to sixty-second
"news spots" presenting different categories of news, including related
to crime. Radio also contributed to coverage of breaking news stories.
In fact, the CBS network affiliate in New York was the first to cover the
1932 Lindbergh kidnapping, representing an instance of radio's coverage beating newspapers to the first information on stories.

In terms of entertainment, radio dramas of the 1930s–'40s included programming centered on crime fighting and detectives, including
shows like *Dragnet* and *Gang Busters*.[42] Significantly, radio allowed
listeners to create mental images that could not be shown in film at
the time, foreshadowing the violent, graphic images later found on

television. However, radio programs were not without their problems, including stereotyping Black individuals and lacking context related to Jim Crow, discrimination, and more. Additionally, although early amateur radio in the first decades of the twentieth century saw more diverse involvement than is generally acknowledged, women and people of color were almost entirely shut out of radio ownership following the Radio Act of 1927, as their presence on the air was also significantly reduced.

Although crime news and entertainment were never a dominant part of radio programming, they still played an important role in paving the way for such content on television. Beginning in the 1950s, television crime shows "became a staple of prime time television entertainment."[43] Local crime news would take longer to develop, but by the late 1970s, it had become common on local broadcast channels, and soon on cable television.

Entertainment depictions of law enforcement, as well as increased news coverage of crime and policing on radio and television, carried several significant effects. On the one hand, the police and the media industry saw greater collaborations, echoing the larger trend of this period. But with such collaboration come problems and issues. Beginning in the 1920s, law enforcement agencies "worked closely with media producers in order to rehabilitate their image."[44] A major reason for this was Hollywood needed the cooperation of law enforcement, particularly the Los Angeles Police Department, to preserve its stars' reputations, even after they were alleged to have committed crimes. The result was that the media across the United States increasingly focused on the "heroic" cop, such as with *Dragnet* in 1951, in which the LAPD reviewed every script and could have any portion they disliked removed. There were, and continue to be, significant downsides to depictions of police solely in overly positive, heroic ways, including that these entertainment depictions provided a one-sided view of law enforcement, which still exhibited corruption, ineffectiveness, and brutality.[45] At best, the public received conflicting views of police in that there were some instances of critical coverage of law enforcement by the press, as discussed more later. However, negative reporting, which would become more common in ensuing decades, was often overshadowed by positive coverage given the greater partnerships between the press and police during this period. And in depicting police as always doing the right thing, the press and media largely ignored the voices of those targeted or otherwise affected by law enforcement, namely, marginalized individuals and communities. Instead, these communities were depicted in stereotypical, inaccurate, or otherwise problematic ways.

Contentiousness between Press and Police Foreshadows Ensuing Era
Greater partnerships did not mean contentiousness between the press and police completely went away. During the 1920s–'50s, journalists continued investigating law enforcement, sometimes helping prompt changes and reforms. For example, in September 1921, the *New York World* ran a series of articles providing extensive coverage of the Ku Klux Klan in Brooklyn.[46] The first article, published on September 6, 1921, and titled "Ku Klux Klan Wars on Catholics, Jews; Reap Rich Returns," began detailing the inner workings of the group, as well as its recent increase of more than five hundred thousand members. Multiple newspapers around the country picked up the coverage, including the *St. Louis Post-Dispatch, Boston Globe, Milwaukee Journal,* and *Minneapolis Journal.* Among other effects, the reporting prompted law enforcement action to remove the KKK's "foothold" in New York City, as well as investigations into police officials' and officers' involvement in the group.

The press also helped prompt change through its coverage of ongoing cases of police brutality.[47] For example, in the early 1950s, civil rights activists were "frustrated and perplexed" by the indifference of federal authorities regarding allegations of police brutality against Black individuals.[48] In 1953, the *New York Sun* and *World-Telegram* uncovered that the DOJ deferred investigations into civil rights complaints filed against the NYPD and allowed the department to do its own investigations. Although the U.S. House of Representatives Judiciary Subcommittee's final report concluded that the secret agreement was simply an administrative misunderstanding, largely dismissing the civil rights violations, the NYPD still instituted some reforms. They included the appointment of its first Black deputy commissioner, George Redding, and greater training for police officers. The events, and New York newspapers' reporting, also led to the creation of a Civilian Complaint Review Board, which required deeper investigations of police misconduct, penalties for undermining investigations, and legal representation for both police officers and complainants.

The 1950s also marked early instances of television helping expose corruption and lead to reforms, including related to the police.[49] For example, from 1950 to 1951, the U.S. Senate Crime Committee, known as the Kefauver Committee, conducted a nationwide investigation into organized crime and police corruption, focusing on cities such as Kansas City and Chicago. Public interest in the proceedings reached its peak when the March 1951 hearings were televised across the country, amplifying the reach and attention given to the committee's proceedings and findings of rampant illegal gambling, elected officials profiting from criminal activities, and criminal syndicates currying favor with local law enforcement through bribes.

Also leading to greater divisiveness were renewed instances of law enforcement arresting members of the press. In 1927, police arrested Jay Near, the editor of the *Minneapolis Saturday Press*, under the 1925 Minnesota public nuisance law after he published a series of articles criticizing Minneapolis officials, including asserting that "a Jewish gangster was in control of gambling, bootlegging, and racketeering in Minneapolis, and that law enforcing officers and agencies were not energetically performing their duties."[50] Floyd B. Olson, the Hennepin County attorney and future governor of Minnesota, was one of the targeted officials. He sought to enjoin publication of the *Saturday Press* permanently as "malicious, scandalous and defamatory." The case ultimately reached the U.S. Supreme Court, which held that the press's "constitutional right" to publish protected it from government imposition of prior restraints and censorship, except in limited circumstances, a significant victory for press freedom. Chief Justice Charles Hughes cited the "need [for] a vigilant and courageous press," concluding that "interference with the . . . freedom of publication" would mean "the constitutional protection [of freedom of the press] would be reduced to a mere form of words."

On March 28, 1952, city detectives in Birmingham arrested Earl Chapman, a twenty-seven-year-old Black reporter from Greenville, Alabama, under the state's vagrancy laws, which remained in place from the Jim Crow era.[51] Chapman had been covering the impeachment proceedings against Birmingham police commissioner Eugene Connor for *Freedom*, a monthly publication founded the previous year by Paul Robeson, a political activist, bass-baritone concert artist, and professional football player. According to the AP, the vagrancy charges stemmed from allegations that he did "not have a reputable means of support." Police also alleged that Chapman possessed "left-wing newspapers, magazines, and books." On March 31, Chapman was released after prosecutors dropped the charges against him.

Additional reasons for arrests, some related to journalistic functions and others not, ranged from attempting to take photographs of mine picketers to testing the effectiveness of U.S. Customs security.[52] One significant development was arrests of journalists for allegedly interfering in police activities, in some cases wrongfully, a trend that continues through the present.[53] For example, in 1931, policeman H. E. Yannell arrested *Los Angeles Examiner* reporter Otis Wiles "in an effort to suppress details of the Hollywood 'candy shop murder.'"[54] On September 25, Wilma McFarland, the twenty-two-year-old sales girl at a candy store in Hollywood, was killed by an unknown assailant. Her body was found in a small washroom in the shop by the manager, R. H. Austin, with a bullet wound in her head along with a towel twisted around her neck. Wiles was arrested and charged for allegedly "blocking the sidewalk and resisting an officer" when seeking to gather details into the murder, but refused to leave the scene. Wiles was held in jail for two and a half hours before being released. The charge against Wiles was dismissed on October 3. Six days later, Wiles filed a $25,000 lawsuit against Yannell, claiming the officer "arrested him without reason while the reporter was endeavoring to ascertain facts in [the] Hollywood slaying."[55] The lawsuit further alleged that Wiles was falsely imprisoned after being placed in a police car and compelled to go to the police station.

As in past eras, members of the press also faced violence and threats from law enforcement, often amid news gathering and sometimes when reporters attempted to cover civil unrest and other noteworthy events, setting the stage for the turbulent 1960s–'70s.[56] For example, in 1928, reporters in Memphis sought to take pictures and report on Black individuals voting in a local primary election.[57] However, the *Commercial Appeal* and *Evening Appeal* reporters "were assaulted by police, bootleggers and ex-convicts," as well as the attorney general of the county. Police also searched the reporters and seized their cameras, destroying the film, as well as the reporters' notes and papers. Additionally, officers called a different reporter "vile names, threatened to beat him up if he got out of his car, ordered him away from the polling place, and threatened to kill him if he returned."

Searches and seizures remained another way in which law enforcement, including the FBI, targeted members of the press.[58] In 1959, FBI agents from the Washington, D.C., field office "entered the Washington hotel room of a[n unnamed *New York Post*] reporter to search his belongs for clues to his news sources and for evidence of impropriety in his personal life."[59] The agents were instructed to search for information about FBI officials and employees with whom the reporter may have been talking, as well as for "signs that he might have had a female in the room or was drinking heavily." On top of the search, the agents conducted "full-time" surveillance of the reporter "all over the city." The search and surveillance, both of which were ordered by J. Edgar Hoover "because of his concern over an investigation of the bureau then being conducted by *The New York Post*," failed to uncover any wrongdoing or information about his sources. Nevertheless, the search and surveillance marked one of many "surreptitious entries" carried out by FBI agents in the years following World War II."

Reporters also continued to face subpoenas for their confidential sources and information.[60] *Garland v. Torre* (1958) arose after *New York Herald Tribune* columnist Marie Torre refused to name a CBS executive whose statements about actress Judy Garland, according to her $1,393,333 lawsuit against CBS, "were false, defamatory, and highly damaging to [her] professional reputation."[61] In a January 10, 1957, article titled "Judy Tosses a Monkey Wrench," Torre cited several statements by an unnamed CBS "network executive" about the plaintiff, including that she thought herself to be "terribly fat." In November 1957, U.S. District Court judge Sylvester J. Ryan of the Southern District of California found Torre "in criminal contempt of court" and sentenced her to ten days in prison.[62] On appeal, the U.S. Court of Appeals for the Second Circuit upheld the ruling. When the Supreme Court ultimately refused to grant Torre's appeal, she served her ten-day prison sentence in 1959. Nevertheless, the case marked perhaps the first instance of a journalist citing the First Amendment as a defense against a challenge to disclose a confidential source, known as the "reporter's privilege," discussed more in chapter 7.

World War II marked the continuation of government surveillance of journalists and members of the public, just like during World War I.[63] In particular, the Office of Censorship, created following the December 1941 attack on Pearl Harbor to censor and protect sensitive war information, monitored mail, radio, and other communications entering and leaving the country for anything that could threaten the war effort or was against the values of patriotism (or both). In 1942, the Office of Censorship issued the "Code of Wartime Practices for the American Press," which detailed for newspapers, newsreels, and radio broadcasts what information needed prior authorization by the federal government to be published or broadcast. Such efforts of surveilling and restricting the press, which included at least some limited participation by law enforcement, contributed to the increased divisiveness between the press and government in the 1950s. Thus, even in an era of cooperative coexistence, cases still existed of significant conflict between the press and police, setting the stage for the following decades.

Impersonation and Media Ride-Alongs Follow Past Trends While Evolving in an Era of Cooperation

In the 1920s–'50s, it is perhaps unsurprising that impersonation and media ride-alongs continued amid greater partnerships and trust. In the case of ride-alongs and some cases of impersonation, it was willing cooperation as the press and police carried out such practices for their purported benefits. In other cases, especially impersonation, the practices were used in secret without the other entity knowing. However, despite the potential benefits of the practices, problems arising from the practice also continued as in past eras, though not always in ways that were visible to the public or generated a significant amount of criticism. Such concerns would still take longer to develop, though all three practices saw at least some level of pushback during this period as the effects arising from the practices more directly violated the norms and values of the time, especially as the adversarial 1960s–'70s approached.

Police Impersonation of the Press

In many ways, the 1920s–'50s saw the continuation of trends in police impersonation of the press dating back to the nineteenth century, including the purposes of using the practice and how it was conducted. This was evident in 1958 when the United Press International (UPI) published a story titled "Gun-Toting Grandma Outfoxed as Police Pose as Reporters."[64] Despite the levity of the headline, the coverage focused on a tense standoff between Lomie Puckett and sheriff's deputies after she refused to leave her home, which was set to be demolished for a Golden State Freeway extension. To end the standoff, Sergeants Carl Slem and Robert Chapman acted like journalists by "walk[ing] into the [home] casually, along with 30 other reporters and cameramen, posing as newsmen." By posing as reporters and surrounding themselves with real journalists, the officers were able to escort Puckett, the widow of a policeman, from her house.

Police also used impersonation of the press to investigate and surveil political officials, protesters, and underrepresented individuals and groups, just as law enforcement had in the nineteenth century. For example, in 1933, a group of state troopers, "disguised as newspapermen, attended [a] conference" hosted by Pennsylvania governor Gifford Pinchot in which they surveilled "a delegation of the recent invading jobless marchers."[65] To do so, they sought to disguise themselves as protesters, in this case "'arm[ing]' [themselves] with copy paper and pencils." However, whereas the "bona fide newspapermen jotted down important details . . . the troopers were taking mental notes," exposing the ploy.

However, the 1920s–'50s also marked an era of change related to police impersonation of the press. One such change was the role of Prohibition.[66] In 1928, Detective William F. Burke "declared himself to be a correspondent of a New York newspaper" in order to "trap" two men "whom he arrested and charged with transportation and possession of liquor."[67] Burke reportedly "telephoned Mrs. Saunders [at whose home the two men were arrested] saying he was a newspaper man." He also "called the number [of the two suspects] and announced himself as 'Mr. Moore,' of a New York newspaper."

Significantly, Burke's actions also provided an important development in that the press advocates raised concerns with the practice of the police posing as journalists. Upon hearing about the impersonation, the National Press Club board of governors lodged a formal "protest against . . . members of the police vice squad in posing as newspaper men [to] Maj Edwin B. Hesse, chief of police." Paul Wooten, the chairman of the board of governors, called it an "outrage that members of the police department should act in a manner such as Burke is said to have done" and requested a "complete explanation of the incident." In doing so, Wooten demonstrated that impersonation had strained the relationship between the two institutions.

Similarly, in 1930, "considerable resentment was caused in newspaper quarters" when the press learned that NYPD commissioner Grover Whalen had "disguised a number of his detectives as reporters, even equipping them with special press badges" in order to quell a demonstration of more than seventy-five thousand socialist protesters in Union Square.[68] The police ultimately succeeded in dispersing the demonstration through tear gas and use of force, though leaving several police officers and protesters injured. Once again, the case raised concern among journalists, suggesting that it could, and did, strain the press-police relationship. This example was also significant in that the detectives wore fake press credentials, marking another way police impersonated the press in this era and the future.

Behind a veil of secrecy, the 1940s–'50s marked the beginning of CIA impersonation of the press,[69] marking the most extensive use of the practice by government and law enforcement in U.S. history and eventually prompting greater scrutiny and criticism.[70] In 1948, Frank Wisner, who had served during World War II as the head of operations in southeastern Europe for the Office of Strategic Services, the predecessor to the CIA, was brought into the federal government to plan "black operations" against communist influence. He called his operation the "mighty Wurlitzer," because it incorporated, and exploited, charitable organizations, labor unions, book publishers, and the press. In the 1950s, the CIA adopted several of Wisner's policies, including using and partnering with several media organizations, such as the *New York Times* and CBS. Allen Dulles, who became the director of the CIA in 1953, aimed to establish a "recruiting-and-cover capability" within several journalistic institutions. By the 1970s, the CIA worked with more than eight hundred print, radio, and television organizations and individuals.

There were numerous "uses" of journalists by the CIA, including "to help recruit and handle foreigners as agents, to acquire and evaluate information, and to plant false information with officials of foreign governments."[71] But perhaps most significantly, reporters and news organizations also provided cover for CIA agents to pose as journalists. Multiple news organizations provided jobs and press credentials to CIA operatives abroad, allowing agents to impersonate members of the press. This impersonation of journalists in the CIA likely began around 1953 when Dulles stipulated that one purpose of using the press was for impersonation because "CIA operatives abroad would be accorded a degree of access and freedom of movement unobtainable under almost any other type of cover." The CIA even ran a formal training program in the 1950s to teach its agents to be journalists, including how "to make noises like reporters." Media organizations continued to provide "cover" for agents who impersonated journalists throughout the 1950s to the 1970s, resulting in "the traditional line separating the American press corps and government [being] often indistinguishable."[72] Because the practice would not be revealed until the 1970s, this era therefore marked the calm before the storm, as ensuing decades would see not only the revelations of the CIA's practices, but also an increase in reported instances of police impersonation of the press, prompting renewed and new concerns.

Press Impersonation of Police

The 1920s–'50s marked a complicated era for press impersonation of police in that it led to contentiousness between the two institutions in some moments and improved relations at others. In 1922, Los Angeles County district attorney Thomas Lee Woolwine characterized William Randolph Hearst's reporters as "presumptuous, dangerous and dastardly" after he accused two *New York American* reporters of going to the home of Henry Peavey, a Black man accused of killing motion picture director William Dean Taylor, for whom he worked as a servant.[73] The reporters allegedly "represent[ed] themselves to be officers from New York" and "took [Peavey] away in an automobile and attempted to bully and terrorize him." They also "held him prisoner for nearly twelve hours in the office of [the *Los Angeles Examiner*]." Peavey testified during the trial that he told the men, "I am not doing any talking to newspaper reporters," to which one of them replied, "Newspaper reporters? We are not newspaper reporters, we are officers from New York, and we have authority to come down here and get you and have you go over your statements."

Although a sensational example by contemporary standards, this instance provides important insight into press impersonation of police, namely, one way it was accomplished—journalists identifying themselves verbally as officers—and the main reason for doing so was to gather news, in this case a confession by Peavey. The sensational means of doing so were not uncommon, as some reporters were "known to have desk drawers full of fake official forms, such as subpoenas and warrants, as well as fake badges, including of detectives, police, sheriffs, and federal agents." Such tactics fell as part of "muscle" journalism, as named by reporter Frank Carson, the city editor at the *Chicago Herald & Examiner*, meaning reporters and editors did whatever it took—including kidnapping, wiretapping, burglary, bribery, and more—to get a story.[74] In fact, by the 1920s, Frank Carson, one of Hearst's editors, had "gained so much renown in solving crimes that he was called in to help the police on many occasions" and would be "granted privileges [by lawmen] denied [to] others because [the police] knew that all he wanted was the story and that he was generous in giving the glory to the police."[75]

Two reports by the *New York Times* in 1928 detailed among the most important moments in the history of press impersonation by police.[76] The *Times* reported that *New York Daily News* reporter Robert Barber "was arrested . . . for impersonating a police officer." Barber allegedly "posed as a member of the New York City Homicide Squad" during an investigation into the murder of state trooper Carl Wilder and used the information in a subsequent news story. Barber was summarily charged with violating Section 931 of the Penal Code, leading to a fifty-dollar fine and a suspended sentence. Six days later, the *Times* reported that "Justice of the Peace Elijah Pringle . . . fined [Barber] and then suspended sentence on [the] charge of impersonating an officer." Thus, Barber, like other reporters before him, was attempting to get information for a news story. However, in this case, the police went beyond investigating a reporter, instead also arresting and charging him for the impersonation, of which he was found guilty. This demonstrates not only the perceived severity of the crime but also the significant consequences faced by a reporter, including in New York where the practice was illegal under state law.

But adding to the complicated nature of this case was that the police had, allegedly, incorrectly concluded that Barber posed as an officer. *Daily News* night city editor Frank Dolan told the *Times* that "Barber was the victim of a misunderstanding," contending that "Barber had . . . presented himself to the troopers . . . and had been mistaken by them for a detective who was expected from the Homicide Squad." According to Dolan, Barber at no point "attempt[ed] to impersonate an officer." Whether this was true or not, it suggests that members of the press may not intend to impersonate a police officer but can still be perceived to have done so by law enforcement, nevertheless straining their relationship. In future years, another concern raising uncertainty would be members of the public being unable to differentiate a journalist from a law enforcement agent due to the possibility of impersonation.

In the years following World War II, it was "not uncommon for reporters to impersonate police officers . . . in the quest for a good story."[77] Significantly, amid increased partnerships between the press and police, there is evidence that the practice was more accepted than in the 1928 example. In 2002, *Chicago Tribune* correspondent Ellen Warren covered the tearing down of the original police headquarters in Chicago.[78] At one point, Warren discussed how reporters, during an era of a "chummy relations[hip]" between the press and police, "didn't just ride shotgun with police" but also wore "stars and interrogated prisoners" as if they were police officers. Besides connecting press impersonation of police with media ride-alongs, Warren asserted that the police allowed, or even encouraged, impersonation as reporters handled crime prevention and other law enforcement activities rather than, or in addition to, their own.

Media Ride-Alongs

By the 1930s, police cars were commonplace across the United States, particularly Ford's Model 18 introduced in 1932.[79] In the 1950s, several car manufacturers, including Ford, Chevrolet, and Dodge, began offering custom-built police cars, which included flashing lights and improved radios, to police departments. In doing so, they set the stage for innovations in police vehicles, including sedans, SUVs, and special weapons and tactics (SWAT) automobiles, as well as to the equipment within them, which have continued to evolve ever since. Amid this evolution, the trends found in the first decades of media ride-alongs continued, including the negative effects.

As in past eras, journalists generally gained access to ride-alongs through invitations or permission by police, therefore limiting how or what the press could cover. For example, in 1938, the police officer "whose job it was to roll out the 'Maria'" asked a group of reporters, "Want to go along?"[80] The reporters did not hesitate and "hop[ped] in the back" as "nothing could have stopped [them]." Permission to ride with police also came in other ways. A unique case arose on December 31, 1925, and January 1, 1926, when a reporter for the *Kenosha (WI) Evening News* "experienced being a member of the Kenosha police department."[81] In fact, the reporter was "sworn in as a member of the force" and drove the police vehicle.[82]

Conversely, some police officials, in rare instances, did not give permission to reporters, such as in 1938 when "Patrolman Roy M. Keller, substitute patrol wagon driver, . . . admitted he . . . took a civilian [and] a newspaper reporter, along on the patrol wagon in violation of department orders."[83] Following the ride-along, the Harrisburg City Council investigated why the wagon took a man to jail instead of the hospital, leading to his death. The council primarily targeted Keller, suggesting how actions tied to ride-alongs can result in potential legal repercussions or, at the very least, internal discipline within a department. Although the reporter was not investigated in this case, future examples of media ride-alongs would demonstrate that legal actions could also target members of the press.

In the 1920s–'50s, journalists continued covering police through media ride-alongs, often resulting in positive coverage. An example occurred when the *Kenosha (WI) Evening News* reporter rode "with the patrol wagon on its calls."[84] In addition to covering what took place, the reporter told the newspaper staff that "he enjoyed his night's work immensely" and "that there is only one thing better than being a news reporter, and that is being a police officer." Given an overall lack of critical coverage of law enforcement stemming from media ride-alongs, these examples fit into the larger historical trend of media ride-alongs being an ineffective means of fully informing the public about police activity, as well as being able to hold law enforcement accountable through the practice. This is only further apparent in one reporter's comment that "sooner or later a . . . police reporter succumbs to the favorite sport ascribed to police reporters by the movies. He goes for a Saturday night ride with the detectives on the homicide squad."[85]

During this era, the press also continued using ride-alongs to cover newsworthy events. In 1928, Walter Claffey, the night captain at the Indianapolis police headquarters, "received word . . . that a band of bandits had been holding up motorists [and] . . . were heading toward Indianapolis."[86] Newspaper reporters, "seated in the auxiliary seats of the police car," went to the scene to interview motorists and investigate what had taken place. At least one arrest was made in the case, which raised concerns of suspected gang activity in the area.

There were also limited instances of reporters aiding police on a ride-along. In 1938, Keller, the member of the police force in Harrisburg, Pennsylvania, who allowed a reporter to join him on the patrol wagon despite its being against department policy, said that one reason he did so was to "[take] 'him along to help; we were short-handed.'"[87] As in past eras, this demonstrates how one institution does, or participates in, the work of the other, potentially neglecting their own. Whether this violated the norms of the time given the congenial relations between the press and police, it still set the stage for the continued use of media ride-alongs in ways that would not fully benefit the public.

Finally, the 1920s–'50s saw instances of journalists facing danger while participating in a ride-along, including in 1921 and 1928 when reporters were involved in serious police vehicle accidents.[88] But perhaps the most extraordinary scene unfolded in 1928 when a reporter joined police on a call of "bandits . . . holding up motorists" near Anderson, Indiana.[89] Upon arriving at the scene, one bandit "swung about in the driver's seat [of the car the police had forcefully pulled over] and opened fire, the bullets from a heavy caliber revolver passing between the heads of newspaper reporters seated in the auxiliary seats of the police car." The reporters were caught in the middle of a "thrilling revolver and machine gun fight [between a gang and] police emergency squad," leading to the death of at least one bandit and testing the nerves of everyone at the scene.

In the 1920s–'50s, the right ingredients came together for the peak of cooperative coexistence between the press and police not seen prior to this era or in any that followed. Greater partnerships and trust between the government amid major global events and conflicts bled into the press-police relationship, which had its own reasons for being increasingly amicable. However, contentiousness, as well as impersonation and media ride-alongs, did not simply go away. Instead, significant and dramatic change was coming not just for the press and police but also for people and institutions across the United States. The general trend of positive relations between the news media and law enforcement slowly began to change in the 1950s, paving the way for greater contentiousness during the tumultuous 1960s–'70s. It would mark the peak of divisiveness and conflict in much the same way the 1920s–'50s marked the zenith of partnerships and trust that could never fully be rebuilt.

CHAPTER 5

Adversarial Relationship, 1960s–1970s

IN A TUMULTUOUS TIME IN the United States, the press-police relationship would change in ways that still reverberate to this day. The 1960s–'70s saw the press-police relationship undergo a significant and, in many ways, violent change as an era of partnerships gave way to the complete opposite: an era of conflict, tension, and divisiveness matching the character of the United States as a whole. During this period, the American public increasingly distrusted government and turned to the press to find information about the Vietnam War, the civil rights movement, Watergate, and other major developments. In turn, the new media became increasingly adversarial, which translated to investigative journalism and subsequent greater divisiveness with government. At the same time, law enforcement faced a crisis as division with marginalized people, especially the Black community, reached a crescendo, with police violence on display for millions of Americans as they watched television in their homes. Certainly, positive change would arise from the era amid racial justice protests and calls for equality, but reforms could not, and would not, be a panacea.

The division between the press and government broadly included adversarial relations with law enforcement, with several factors, including the events surrounding the assassination of President John F. Kennedy in 1963, playing a role in unraveling the broad trend of partnerships seen in previous decades. Ultimately, as the press increasingly targeted the police, and vice versa, contentiousness defined the era, with impersonation and media ride-alongs only further problematizing the relationship as cooperative coexistence decreased significantly in prominence, raising questions about how the relationship would move forward.

118   Chapter 5

Rise of the Adversarial Press and Conflict with Government

The divisiveness that began to show between the press and government in the 1950s reached its peak in the 1960s–'70s amid tumultuousness and upheaval across society.[1] These decades were marked by an adversarial press that carried an "antiestablishment ethos," denying government a level of trust that it had in the past and leading to greater critical coverage.[2] The result was two submerged traditions in journalism gaining renewed support. First, the "literary tradition" of journalism, in which reporters told compelling human-interest stories to the public, led to the development of "new journalism." This new emphasis on literary journalism included feature-length and long-form stories containing action, dialogue, emotionality, subjectivity, and detailed descriptions.

Second, the advocacy and muckraking traditions gained renewed support in the 1960s–'70s with the rise of investigative reporting, which also went a step further and included questioning power relations and structures.[3] Becoming more predominant in the 1960s, the press increasingly criticized the federal government as administrations placed greater controls on information and sources. President Kennedy's claims and efforts to have a more open government, including through live televised press conferences and government officials as sources, halted with the Bay of Pigs invasion in 1961, in which the CIA, first authorized by President Dwight D. Eisenhower and then by President Kennedy, attempted to oust Cuban leader Fidel Castro through equipping and training a guerrilla army composed of Cuban exiles, who invaded the Bay of Pigs—an isolated spot on the southern shore of Cuba—but ultimately surrendered as coral reefs sank some of their ships, a radio broadcast on the beach detailed all of their movements, and Castro's troops pinned them to the beach. Throughout the planning and execution of the plan, the federal government sought to conceal and control information, and often lied about the operation.

Tight controls of information only increased with the 1962 Cuban missile crisis, a thirteen-day standoff between the United States and the Soviet Union that brought the world to the brink of nuclear war after the latter secretly installed missiles in Cuba to potentially attack U.S. cities. The crisis ultimately ended in an agreement by Soviet premier Nikita Khrushchev to cease further development and withdraw the missiles in return for Kennedy agreeing to withdraw missiles from Turkey and never invade Cuba.

In ensuing years, the press's relationship with authority was only further complicated by President Lyndon B. Johnson's struggles with dealing with the news media and President Nixon's antipress rhetoric and actions, discussed further later in the chapter. Each of these administrations also augmented public relations efforts, cutting officials off from the press.

Investigative journalism came into its own with the work of *Washington Post* reporters Bob Woodward and Carl Bernstein during the Watergate scandal. Woodward and Bernstein revealed information about the 1972 break-in to the Watergate Hotel headquarters of the Democratic National Committee, as well as details provided by "Deep Throat" and other sources. The revelations about lies by President Richard Nixon eventually led to charges of obstruction of justice and his resignation.

Investigative journalism also focused on the civil rights movement, as detailed later, and the Vietnam War, including the *New York Times'* and the *Washington Post's* publishing of portions of the Pentagon Papers, which, following a favorable First Amendment ruling by the Supreme Court, helped expose lies and other embarrassing information about the federal government and the war effort. The Pentagon Papers were a U.S. Department of Defense study detailing the history of U.S. activities in Vietnam and containing embarrassing information for the federal government.[4] The documents were at the center of *New York Times v. United States* (1971), in which the Supreme Court was tasked with determining whether the *New York Times* and the *Washington Post* could publish the DOD study, which was leaked by military analyst Daniel Ellsberg to these newspapers and others.[5] The Court, in what has become known as the *Pentagon Papers* case, ruled that the Nixon administration had not overcome the "heavy presumption" under the First Amendment against prior restraints, meaning efforts by the government to prohibit publication of certain information or materials. In his concurring opinion, Justice Hugo Black explained that the "power to censor the press was abolished so that the press would remain forever free to censure the government."

The result of the rise in investigative reporting was a sharp division between the press and government, including a "break between government sources and the news media."[6] Journalists increasingly saw themselves as adversaries of political power and "champions of truth and openness, checking the tendency of the powerful to conceal and dissemble."[7] As discussed later, this division would extend to the press-police relationship.

But despite the great antiestablishment stance of the press, the 1960s–'70s included only mixed results in the relationship between the news media and marginalized communities. On the one hand, television coverage revealed police brutality and other problematic actions against Black individuals and civil rights movement protesters. Additionally, the civil rights movement, feminist movement, and other cultural changes helped prompt several press reforms, including the hiring of Black and female reporters, as well as increases in minority ownership of media companies, though people of color and women remain underrepresented.[8] The era also led the press to have greater awareness of how to cover racial and social issues in ensuing decades, a sign of at least some progress.

But on the other hand, press coverage of race, gender, and socioeconomic status, despite this heightened awareness and new hiring practices, continued to have significant problems, stemming from the 1940s–'50s when the press provided more coverage of racial violence, though often in inaccurate or misleading ways.[9] During World War II and the beginning of the Cold War, the mainstream press largely ignored the growing issues and protests against segregation, including by the Black press, which was once again leading the coverage of important issues at the time, but was also the subject of surveillance and censorship by the federal government. During much of the 1950s and even during the height of the civil rights movement, many members of the mainstream press also failed to cover growing protests against racial segregation, despite evidence of police misconduct and brutality raised by the NAACP, ACLU, and others. Instead, the press increasingly focused on what was perceived to be an "epidemic of street crimes" and "hysteria of Japanese Americans and internment."[10]

By the 1960s–'70s, the mainstream press "wrestled with race and gender on two fronts: first, the question of employment opportunities and discrimination in the newsroom, and second, whether and how to change news coverage."[11] New employment opportunities for women and people of color marked a step in the right direction, though they still remained underrepresented in the mainstream press. This lack of diversity in news organizations proved significant given biased news coverage against people of color in particular. One such instance occurred when Mississippi governor Ross Barnett blocked James Meredith from registering as a student at the University of Mississippi, despite a legal order by Justice Black, the White House, and federal marshals. Violence erupted within an hour of Meredith arriving on campus, with a mob composed of students and militant segregationists attacking federal agents with bricks, Molotov cocktails, and guns. Much of the press coverage of the event, rather than focusing on the reasons for desegregation, focused on arguments against Meredith registering. Coverage was also generally biased against Meredith and the Black community, falling as part of a trend of "how often the white press portrayed the victims of [white mob violence and massacres against nonwhite communities] as the instigators or perpetrators of violence."[12] As discussed later, racial bias also became increasingly common on local television news and entertainment, only further undermining press coverage of the Black community and other marginalized individuals and communities.

Police Undergo a Significant "Crisis"

As the civil rights movement, political assassination, counterculture, and public disorder heightened division, conflict, and momentous change in the United States, law enforcement underwent a "crisis" in the late 1960s through about 1975.[13] During this period, there was little improvement by the police across the United States in addressing crime and civil unrest. Especially pronounced, however, were worsening race relations, particularly in the South where local police used violence and intimidation against Black men and women. Across the country, relations between law enforcement and marginalized people, especially the Black community, became more divisive due to new strategies such as more aggressive patrol tactics and warrantless searches, practices most prevalent in Black neighborhoods. Law enforcement also increasingly targeted protesters with violence, including to suppress demonstrations by people of color, a trend dating back to previous eras.

In 1968, the National Advisory Commission on Civil Disorders, established by President Johnson and led by Illinois governor Otto Kerner Jr., investigated urban violence and race riots in the United States.[14] After a seven-month investigation, the "Kerner Commission" released a report stating that the top problem facing U.S. society was police brutality and the separating of "white" and "black" cultures. The commission also found that rioting was the worst in cities where the police were perceived to have strong leadership but lacked control over use of force, problematizing professionalization. Significantly, the commission also found that the press had not adequately covered problems of race in the United States and that it had "too long basked in a white world looking out of it, if at all, with white men's eyes and white perspective." It therefore made a series of recommendations for the press as well, including increased coverage of the Black community and hiring more people of color.

There were several additional federal actions directed at law enforcement, including the President's Commission on Law Enforcement and Administration of Justice, which sponsored research on the criminal justice system.[15] The National Commission on the Causes and Prevention of Violence was founded to investigate violence in the United States following the assassinations of Rev. Martin Luther King Jr. and Senator Robert F. Kennedy. Last, the federal government provided funding to local departments and to universities to teach criminal justice through the Law Enforcement Assistance Administration.

Because of the problems associated with the police "crisis," some reform efforts beyond those by the federal government began in the 1960s–'70s, including the hiring of people of color by police departments.[16] The era also saw the creation of citizen review boards, new control over police discretion, and increased research tied to criminal justice. In general, there was also a heightened public consciousness of the link between race, crime, poverty, and policing. Additionally, the era saw the gradual rise of police unionization, following antecedents in the late nineteenth and early twentieth centuries. Actions like the federal legalization of collective bargaining, amid the backdrop of rising violent crime, prompted the creation and increased political power of police unions, including in New York City in 1964. Police unions, although beneficial for improving conditions for law enforcement officials and officers, also immediately opposed accountability of police, making meaningful reform and change, including in relation to marginalized communities, more challenging during this era through the twenty-first century, as discussed further in the next chapter.

Another element associated with police efforts to improve community relations beginning in the 1960s, though never a panacea, was the expansion of public relations efforts with antecedents dating back to the beginning of the century. Perhaps the most significant development in the 1960s–'70s was the creation, within police departments, of public information officers, individuals responsible for communication with the press, public, and other law enforcement agencies. One of the recommendations in the Kerner Report was that the press "improve co-ordination with police in reporting riot news through advance planning, and cooperate with the police in the designation of public information officers, establishment of information centers, and development of mu-tually acceptable guidelines for riot reporting and the conduct of media personnel." Police departments across the country therefore launched dedicated "press offices or public information units . . . to help police deal more effectively with the media and to appear more open with the pub-lic in communicating information."[17] For example, the Louisville Police Department appointed its first public information officer in November 1971.[18] In 1979, the Commission on Accreditation for Law Enforcement Agencies was formed to establish guidelines and standards for public in-formation, including how to involve and interact with the news media. The commission's 1999 standards read, "To convey information, agen-cies often rely on the news media. The information should be conveyed accurately. . . . In large jurisdictions where media contacts are frequent and often of a sensitive nature, a full-time public information officer may be needed to coordinate activities; where the community served is small and media contacts infrequent, the assignment of the function to an individual as a part-time responsibility may suffice."[19]

Cooperative Coexistence Holds On

Against this backdrop of cultural upheaval and changes surrounding the press and police, contentiousness became the dominant category of interactions between the two institutions, though cooperative coexis-tence remained. Importantly, the press still needed to cover the news of the day, including on crime and policing, as law enforcement sought to complete their own functions and actions. The 1963 assassination of President Kennedy marked perhaps the most notable example, signaling a key moment in the rise of broadcast news professionals and also rais-ing important implications for the press-police relationship. The news media, including print publications, radio, and television, also covered a variety of crimes ranging from murders and kidnappings to robberies across the United States.

The 1970s saw the rise of local television crime news, which, along with television entertainment programming, would hit its stride in the 1980s–'90s.[20] In particular, the "eyewitness news" format emphasized journalists reporting from the scene of events, leading to a greater em-phasis on crime coverage. Local television news in particular, though other forms of media as well, followed the historical antecedents of finding, and in some cases exploiting, the most gruesome and outrageous crimes and tragedies to draw in a larger audience, exemplified by the phrase "If it bleeds, it leads." Several television shows, including *Columbo* and *Hawaii Five-O*, and numerous films, such as *Dirty Harry* and *Serpico*, also focused on or included elements of crime and policing.

However, the 1960s–'70s marked the beginning of a trend in which television news and entertainment raised significant concerns about the positive depictions of police versus the problematic representation of marginalized individuals and communities. Television news in the 1960s–'70s either failed to cover the Black community or treated it in insulting or derogatory ways, prompting challenges to some television stations' licenses.[21] Such coverage disproportionately focused on the Black community despite a decline in violent crime by Black individuals beginning in the early 1970s. Crime films and television programs similarly depicted Black people as generally violent, while television crime dramas, such as *F.B.I.*, continued to depict police in heroic ways, ignoring the real-world problems of policing during this period.[22] These concerns would become especially pronounced in ensuing decades as television news and entertainment became even more popular, as discussed further in the following chapter.

Contentiousness Defines a Tumultuous Era

However, the 1960s–'70s were defined by a sharp decrease in partnerships and trust between the press and police for several reasons.[23] First, the significant increase in investigative reporting included targeting law enforcement, placing an emphasis on press accountability of police. In doing so, the press provided the public with more information about police departments, officials, and officers, some of which challenged law enforcement and resulted in changes and reforms.[24] The rise of investigative reporting also meant that police increasingly feared that media reports would negatively affect their investigations or reputations, resulting in a decline in the media's access to police activities, information, and officials and officers themselves.

For example, the *New York Times* developed a more adversarial relationship with police in New York City in the late 1960s.[25] Previously, the *Times* had "a tacit understanding with the police force: the paper got special treatment and news tips, and the police got sympathetic coverage." More specifically, the police provided the *Times* with stories before other newspapers and "looked the other way" when *New York Times* delivery trucks blocked traffic, for example. In return, reporters did favors for officials and officers in hopes of later receiving a scoop. However, in 1968, the *New York Times* no longer ignored the corruption in the NYPD. Reporter David Burnham revealed that police officers frequently slept on the job, rather than patrol their beats, during overnight shifts. Although the *Times* lost the friendly treatment by the NYPD, its reporting prompted several officials to resign, as well as a commission to be appointed.

Similarly, after the *New York Times* published a series of reports in the late 1960s exposing widespread police corruption in the NYPD gambling and narcotics units, New York City mayor John V. Lindsay established in April 1970 a special investigating commission led by U.S. District Court for the Southern District of New York judge Whitman Knapp.[26] Following a two-and-a-half-year investigation, the Knapp Commission in 1972 made several findings, including detailing significant corruption, a cover-up by Mayor John Lindsay, police brutality, and the "Blue Code of Silence" prohibiting officers from disclosing wrongdoing. The commission's findings ultimately led to the resignation of police officials and officers, as well as policy changes by the NYPD and other departments.

Press accountability of police was also evident in investigations of the FBI, namely, its virtually unchecked power.[27] For example, the *New York Times* and the *Washington Post* exposed Director Hoover's official and confidential files containing sensitive information about political leaders that he could use to guarantee his position as director. Referred to as the "secret files," they were compiled over Hoover's forty-eight-year tenure as head of the FBI and stored in his office. Unlike with other files maintained by the FBI, Hoover never discussed his official and confidential files publicly and referred to them as "confidential," denoting further secrecy. Significantly, Hoover likely used the files against politicians and others for the purposes of blackmail, namely, uncovering compromising information and leveraging it to influence actions by legislators and other influential people inside and outside politics. Hoover even had compromising information against presidents, in one case in March 1962 informing President Kennedy that through wiretapping, the FBI had uncovered an affair with Judith Campbell Exner, a divorcée who was twenty-six years old when her two-plus-year relationship with Kennedy began. Although no officials ever claimed to have been blackmailed by

Hoover, it is unlikely anyone would have done so given the compromising information held against them.

By the late 1960s, Hoover and the FBI conducted "violent surveillance" of civil rights leaders and organizations, among other violations of their rights.[28] A covert 1967 surveillance operation targeted civil rights groups and Black leaders, including the Black Panther Party, NAACP, Martin Luther King Jr., Malcolm X, and many others. An FBI memo stated that the main objective was to "expose, disrupt, misdirect, discredit, or otherwise neutralize" the fight for Black rights. Actions ranged from spreading rumors of violence to maintaining detailed files of Black figures and organizations. The FBI surveillance, which also included wiretapping and the use of undercover informants, fell under a larger program targeting alleged communists across the country, providing a means of monitoring and undermining racial protests.

Second, the events surrounding the assassination of President Kennedy marked a key reason for the decreased partnerships between the press and police.[29] Prior to the assassination, the Dallas Police Department, among other departments across the country, was quite open with the press and often allowed reporters to enter the department with few limitations. Reporters were even able to walk up to President Kennedy's body at Parkland Hospital. Additionally, fewer public relations experts or spokespeople meant police officials and officers remained journalists' primary sources.

However, this openness and trust changed after newspapers in Dallas and across the nation printed information about Lee Harvey Oswald after he was charged with assassinating President Kennedy. Law enforcement criticized such coverage and argued that the press had contributed to Jack Ruby shooting Oswald and that, even if Oswald had lived, he would not have received a fair trial. The "perp walk," in which police escorted Oswald in front of numerous reporters and television cameras, further led police to criticize the press and, as a result, change their practices, such as eliminating the custom. Another change was the implementation of police-press and bar-press guidelines around the country, which aimed to establish how and what journalists could report regarding police investigations and defendants' Sixth Amendment rights. But most significantly, journalists began to lose access to the police not only in Dallas but across the United States. Police and government officials increasingly kept the news media at a greater distance and focused more closely on what information was made public.

Third, television coverage augmented contentiousness of the press-police relationship. In particular, televised images of police brutality against civil rights marchers increased public distrust and anger toward the government and policing. In May 1963, civil rights protesters gathered in Birmingham, Alabama, attempting to march into the downtown area.[30] On May 2 and May 3 alone, hundreds of protesters were arrested, prompting Commissioner Eugene "Bull" Connor to direct local law enforcement and fire departments to use force to halt further demonstrations. Police summarily used high-pressure fire hoses, clubs, police dogs, and more to disperse civil rights protesters. Television cameras were present to record the events, broadcasting them to millions of shocked and outraged Americans. Newspapers also covered the violence, reaching a national and international audience.

Another notable case arose on "Bloody Sunday" on March 7, 1965, when twenty-five-year-old activist and future congressman John Lewis led more than six hundred civil rights marchers in Selma to fight for equal voting rights. However, Alabama governor George Wallace ordered state troopers "to use whatever measures are necessary to prevent a march." As the protesters sought to cross the Edmund Pettus Bridge, named for a Confederate general and grand dragon of the Alabama KKK, they were met by a wall of state troopers, who advanced toward the marchers and struck them with clubs. The troopers also fired tear gas and used horses to trample those trying to cross the bridge. Once more, television cameras captured the violence. That night, ABC newscaster Frank Reynolds interrupted the airing of the television premier of *Judgment at Nuremberg*, a 1961 film focused on the military tribunal in Nuremberg, Germany, in which four German judges and prosecutors stood before a three-judge panel accused of crimes against humanity as part of the Nazi regime. In a matter of moments, nearly fifty million viewers went from watching the atrocities and violence of Nazi Germany to the events of "Bloody Sunday," with "the juxtaposition str[iking] like psychological lightning in American homes."[31]

Distrust of government and law enforcement only grew with news outlets' broadcast of stark and violent images of the Vietnam War, known as the first "television war" and "living-room war," reaching millions of Americans as they watched in their homes.[32] Until 1968, the television networks generally did not criticize military operations and edited out bloody, violent scenes. However, in January 1968, North Vietnamese troops and the Vietcong broke a cease-fire by launching surprise attacks on multiple cities in South Vietnam, known as the Tet Offensive. Television coverage, perhaps for the first sustained period of the war, depicted the violent confrontations, leading Americans to question whether the United States was actually winning the war.

When news of the conflict arrived at CBS headquarters, *The CBS Evening News* anchor Walter Cronkite, who had generally supported the war behind the cameras, exclaimed, "What the hell is going on? I thought we were winning the war!" The following month, Cronkite, known as the "most trusted man in America" and proponent of objectivity, went to Vietnam to uncover the impact of the Tet Offensive, finding that what he saw on the ground contrasted with official accounts. At the end of an hourlong primetime broadcast titled *Report from Vietnam: Who, What, When, Where, Why?* on February 27, 1968, Cronkite, after acknowledging what he was about to say was "subjective," declared, "It seems now more certain than ever that the bloody experience of Vietnam is to end in a stalemate. ... [I]t is increasingly clear to this reporter that the only rational way out then will be to negotiate, not as victors, but as an honorable people who lived up to their pledge to defend democracy, and did the best they could." President Johnson reportedly responded to the report, "If I've lost Cronkite, I've lost Middle America." Although Gallup polls suggest that public support for the war remained largely static until the end of 1968 despite Cronkite's broadcast, it marked a significant shift in that Cronkite "mainstreamed antiwar sentiment."[33] It also prompted the press, including investigative journalists, alternative newspapers, and radio stations, to increasingly contradict government statements and views of the Vietnam War, influencing the public and eventually helping lead to the end of American involvement.

In addition to covering the war itself, television coverage also focused on police violence against Vietnam War protesters, including the "Dow Riots" at the University of Wisconsin.[34] On October 18, 1967, student leaders organized an antiwar protest after learning that Dow Chemical, a company that manufactured napalm and Agent Orange during the Vietnam War, was sending recruiters to campus. Hundreds of students conducted a sit-in at the Commerce Building (now Ingraham Hall) where Dow planned to hold interviews, leading most to be canceled. However, when students refused to leave the building, Chancellor William Sewell called the Madison Police Department despite being against the war himself. Violence erupted after police fired tear gas outside the building and struck several students in the head, stomach, and legs, leading to at least seventy people, including nineteen police officers, being hospitalized. In addition to leading students previously indifferent to or in favor of the Vietnam War to change their position, the riots, marking perhaps the first time an antiwar demonstration on a major U.S. campus turned violent, also attracted national attention through extensive television and newspaper coverage.

Police corruption was another target of television news, including in 1961 with the airing of the CBS documentary *Biography of a Bookie Joint*, narrated by Cronkite.[35] The program depicted several Boston Police Department officers and one detective "entering and leaving with great frequency a South Boston Horse Parlor," implicating the officers in illegal bookmaking and gambling. Following the documentary, Police Commissioner Leo J. Sullivan eventually resigned in 1962 during public hearings focused on his removal from office. There were also a number of changes to the Boston Police Department, including shifting the power to appoint the police commissioner from the Massachusetts governor to the mayor of Boston. A survey of the department was also completed, determining additional reforms to be made in later years. Politicians and others praised the changes, including Dwight S. Strong, the executive secretary of the New England Citizens Crime Commission and who played a role in the CBS documentary and told the *Boston Globe*, "The wrath of an aroused public to the continued revelation of wrongdoing and conflict of interest is growing and can do more to bring about changes than any other single factor."

Finally, contentiousness between the press and police was once again raised by instances of law enforcement targeting members of the news media, continuing practices that can be traced back more than a century earlier. Perhaps to a greater degree than in the past, journalists faced arrests, use of force, and threats by law enforcement, including for disturbing a lawful meeting, trespassing, and other reasons related or unrelated to news gathering.[36] One significant development was arrests of journalists attempting to cover protests.[37] In such cases, journalists were often met with use of force, such as being tackled to the ground, hit with a police baton, or targeted with a chemical agent or rubber bullet, with police often contending that journalists interfered in their activities.[38] Amid arrests and use of force, police also continued to threaten reporters with violence.[39]

It was against this backdrop that the press-police relationship reached a boiling point, namely, at the 1968 Democratic National

Convention (DNC) in Chicago.[40] As the convention played out inside the International Amphitheatre, large protests erupted nearby, leading to 125 arrests, significant damage, and hundreds of injuries, most of which were at the hands of police. Among those injured were members of the press, resulting in twenty-two media representatives filing brutality charges against law enforcement. Although the press covered police violence against antiwar and civil rights protesters during this period, the events at the 1968 DNC hit especially close to home because the violence targeted reporters and white people. And like with the antiwar and civil rights protests, it was aired on network television news, with the police response being to defend the officers' actions while blaming reporters for being attacked, exaggerating what had taken place, and generally "gang[ing] up" on police officers at the convention.[41]

Significantly, journalists and news organizations began questioning whether they could trust the police.[42] In fact, just one year later, two *Chicago Sun-Times* reporters were arrested for "resisting, opposing and interfering with a deputy U.S. marshal in the performance of his duties" during the trial of seven individuals charged with conspiracy to incite riots during the 1968 DNC.[43] But at the same time, the events and ensuing coverage also marked an early, if not founding, moment of criticism toward the "liberal media," with letters to CBS and NBC overwhelmingly condemning their coverage of the convention and surrounding events as politically biased.[44] Thus, as journalists increasingly questioned whether they could trust law enforcement, many Americans, perhaps even members of law enforcement, raised similar concerns as to whether they could trust the credibility of the press.

Journalists also continued to face searches and seizures,[45] with the most notable example arising after a violent protest at Stanford University in 1971.[46] Several demonstrators had seized Stanford University Hospital's administrative offices, occupying them for several hours. As officers from the Palo Alto Police Department and the Santa Clara County Sheriff's Department attempted to force their way into the offices, a group of demonstrators emerged from a separate set of doors and attacked the nine officers with sticks and clubs. Two days later, on April 11, 1971, a special edition of the *Stanford Daily*, the university's student newspaper, carried articles and photographs regarding the protest and violent confrontation between the protesters and the police. On April 12, four officers, citing public safety and an active investigation into the confrontation, executed a search warrant on the *Daily*'s newsroom, searching the newspaper's laboratories, filing cabinets, desks, and wastepaper baskets, finding notes and correspondence. In response to the newspaper's lawsuit challenging the search, the U.S. Supreme Court held in 1978 that the First Amendment does not grant special protection from newsroom searches, as discussed more later. *Zurcher v. Stanford Daily* (1978) provides another good illustration of how searches and seizures can target not only journalists themselves but also their newsrooms and materials, practices dating back to at least the nineteenth century.

During President Nixon's administration in particular, there was a significant increase in subpoenas seeking to compel journalists to reveal confidential sources as part of investigations into journalists, editors, and others.[47] For example, in 1971, *Baltimore Evening Sun* reporter David Lightman went undercover to investigate reports that teenagers were openly buying drugs. Lightman reported that a shop clerk offered him marijuana while a police officer did not take any action. Lightman was sentenced to thirty days in jail for refusing to disclose the name of the clerk, though he later revealed the name of the shop in a compromise with local authorities. The result of multiple instances of such subpoenas targeting journalists was a "press uproar," further demonstrating the strained relationship between the press and government, including police.[48]

Law enforcement also targeted the press with surveillance. For example, in 1971, the FBI surreptitiously investigated Neil Sheehan of the *New York Times* and Ben H. Bagdikian of the *Washington Post* regarding their publishing of excerpts of the Pentagon Papers. The FBI not only "examin[ed] the activities" of both reporters, but also "used intrusive techniques to gather information about the actions of Bagdikian" in particular. The FBI secretly reviewed Bagdikian's phone, hotel, airline records, employment data, immigration file, and more.

Press-Police Relationship Further Complicated by Impersonation and Media Ride-Alongs

In the 1960s–'70s, the increased adversarial relations between the press and police had implications for impersonation and media ride-alongs. In particular, decreased partnerships between the two institutions, combined with the revelations of the CIA's impersonation of journalists and news organizations, led the news media to increasingly raise and report on negative effects of police impersonation of the press. Although the negative effects raised by the press and public can be traced back to the nineteenth century, it was not until this era that more widespread recognition of how these effects violated norms and expectations garnered increased attention. Meanwhile, press impersonation of police became less common during the 1960s–'70s as the divisive relationship between both institutions made the practice increasingly risky for reporters as it was less accepted by police. Finally, this era marked an important period for media ride-alongs with the creation of the first formal ride-along program in which members of the press and public could ride with officers in their squad cars. Once more, negative effects would arise, though again generally not garnering attention and criticism given the perceived benefits of the practice. Ultimately, despite these key changes in impersonation and media ride-alongs, each practice still saw the continuation of trends from previous eras, including the ways each was accomplished, the purposes for doing so, and multiple effects on both institutions, their relationship, and the public.

Police Impersonation of the Press

By the early 1970s, the CIA's impersonation and use of journalists and news organizations began to decrease as the CIA increasingly came under scrutiny by investigative journalists for other practices and issues.[49] In 1973, then-CIA director William Colby, who had been "disturbed" by the extensive impersonation and use of journalists in the 1950s–'60s, made several public disclosures about the practices, though he downplayed the extent of their use.[50] He also called for the "operational use of fulltime correspondents and other employees of major U.S. news magazines, newspapers, wire services, or television networks . . . to be avoided."

In 1976, the Senate Select Committee on Intelligence under Chairman Frank Church outlined how the CIA and FBI regularly used and impersonated journalists, among other abuses by the agencies.[51] Although the Church Committee's final report was circumscribed under CIA pressure and did not disclose several "important discoveries," the portion discussing CIA use of journalists further brought to public attention the practices by the agency.[52] The final report concluded that "United States publications provide[d] cover for CIA agents overseas," with at least a few news organizations being "unaware that they provided this cover."[53]

Two months before the Church Committee published its report, on February 11, the CIA announced new guidelines governing its relationship with U.S. media organizations.[54] Then-director George H. W. Bush stated that the CIA would no longer "enter into any paid or contractual relationship with any full-time or part-time news correspondent accredited by any U.S. news [organization]."[55]

Nevertheless, federal, state, and local law enforcement continued to employ impersonation of the press, leading to increased concerns from journalists, scholars, and advocacy organizations, as well as tangible negative effects.[56] The first effect was the undermining of the credibility of members of the press, meaning the reduction of the public's trust and confidence in journalists, news organizations, and the press as a whole. This effect was discussed in 1970 by *Washington Post* columnist William Raspberry, who reported that at an antiwar demonstration near the U.S. Capitol, "two men, both in casual dress . . . were filming the proceedings with a video tape unit."[57] Although both men "wore red stenciled badges reading 'Press,'" a "small identification sticker on the side of their camera read 'U.S. Capitol Police,'" exposing the ruse. Raspberry wrote that this "far-from-isolated incident . . . threatens the credibility of the press," as it made the news media the "unwilling agent of the police." Significantly, the undermining of the press's credibility affects not only the press but also the public. In order for the press to inform the public and hold government accountable, it requires the trust of those reading, listening to, or watching their coverage. If the public loses even some of its trust and confidence in the press due to police impersonation of the press, the news media's purposes and functions become more difficult, if not impossible.

Another effect implicating both the press and the public is the undermining of reporters' source relationships. In 1970, the *Grand Rapids Press* filed a formal protest with the Detroit Police Department for allowing an officer to pose as a newspaper photographer during a General Motors Corporation stockholder meeting.[58] *Grand Rapids Press* editor Werner Veit argued that "any news source, no matter how proper and innocent, would be reluctant to speak out freely to a news photographer—or reporter—who could be suspected of" working with the government, including "gathering information solely for the purpose of compiling a police department dossier." Later in the decade, the *Fort Lauderdale News* explained that impersonation could raise doubt for sources as to whether they "are speaking to an objective reporter or a government agent whose goal is prosecution," resulting in sources "refus[ing] to talk with newsmen."[59]

A third and related effect of police impersonation of the press is the undermining of journalists' and news organizations' ability to gather news. When the two law enforcement officers posed as journalists at an antiwar demonstration near the U.S. Capitol in 1970, Raspberry argued that such actions "[threaten] [the press's] freedom to function."[60] The *Fort Lauderdale News* added in 1979, "Any time an investigator for a government or even a police agency masquerades as a reporter, the ability of all journalists to gather news is eroded," thereby failing to fully inform and serve the public.[61]

Police impersonation of the press also creates the threat of physical danger for reporters, a fourth negative effect of the practice. Amid significant commentary about this concern in the 1960s–'70s,[62] there were multiple cases of physical violence aimed at reporters stemming from impersonation by police. In 1972, *Christian Science Monitor* editor Erwin D. Canham, in reporting on a recently revealed case of impersonation of the press by the Army Security Agency at the 1968 DNC, noted that some political extremists had, across the United States, "sometimes attack[ed] news people physically because they [were] believed to be [members of law enforcement]."[63] Although journalism can often be a dangerous profession, impersonation is especially problematic because reporters do not get to decide whether to place themselves in the dangerous situation; the decision is made for them by police using impersonation.

A fifth negative effect of police impersonation of the press is the straining of the press-police relationship, an effect evidenced in that members of the press and media advocacy groups criticized and called for explanations or changes following the use of the practice. For example, the instance of impersonation in Detroit in 1970 prompted Veit to call for assurances that the police would not use the practice any further.[64] Law enforcement departments and agencies took different approaches to handling press complaints about the use of impersonation. On the one hand, Tampa police chief J. G. Littleton attempted to order the press to "not expose his officers to demonstrators" after a group of officers posed as reporters at an antiwar protest.[65] On the other hand, some departments and agencies changed their policies to purportedly prohibit impersonation following complaints by the news media and press advocates.[66] For example, in 1968, Attorney General Ramsey Clark issued an order "instructing FBI agents not to impersonate reporters during investigations" after CBS news bureau chief in Washington, D.C., Bill

Small "complained on behalf of the three major networks."[67] However, instances of the FBI impersonating reporters would continue in ensuing decades, discussed more in the next chapter. In other cases, the police issued an apology for impersonating the press, suggesting a recognition of the potential harm it caused to the relationship.[68] Although purported policy changes and apologies may have been superficial and did not lead to the elimination of the practice, they still suggest that the press-police relationship was strained to the point that some sort of action or apology was needed.

A final overarching effect of police impersonation of the press is the undermining of both institutions' independence.[69] In 1972, the *Louisville Courier-Journal* reported that at an antiwar rally outside a new federal building, Louisville Police Department detectives Marty Green and Bobby Branham "identified themselves as representatives of newspapers."[70] Green told Jon Petrovich, a local reporter for WHAS-TV, that he worked for "The Shelbyville (Ky.) Express," but no such paper existed. Branham said she worked for the *Jefferson Reporter*, though the news editor denied anyone from the paper was covering the rally. In a letter to Louisville police chief Edgar Paul, WHAS executive vice president Ed Shadburne contended that "the practice of police identifying themselves as representatives of the news media confuses the public and constitutes a threat to the credibility and independence of the press," calling the actions "reprehensible and intolerable."

Press Impersonation of Police

The 1960s–'70s saw fewer documented examples of press impersonation of police than in previous eras. However, there are some clues as to why the practice became less common or journalists did not write about it to the extent they had in the past, reflecting the changing nature of the press-police relationship.

First, press impersonation of police was likely less common or less reported because it was illegal across the United States by this time. In 1975, writer David Ellis noted that "a reporter cannot impersonate a police officer in order to gain a story," even though "there is no law against a police officer impersonating a reporter to gain an arrest."[71] The fact alone that it was illegal to impersonate the police may have been enough to deter most reporters from the practice, or at least lead them to be more secretive about it, especially given the adversarial press-police relationship at the time.

Second, *Chicago Tribune* correspondent Ellen Warren's 2002 article about the tearing down of the original police headquarters in Chicago provided evidence as to why press impersonation of police may have been less common in the 1960s–'70s.[72] She wrote that, at least in Chicago, the "chummy relationship between police and press . . . was [frayed] after police bashed reporters' heads during the [DNC] . . . in 1968." One result was that it became less common for reporters to work with the police, a decrease in cooperation that would have likely meant the return of law enforcement investigating or condemning instances of press impersonation of police, necessitating that reporters either end or hide the practice.

Finally, in 1979, *Los Angeles Times* reporter David Shaw suggested another negative effect of press impersonation of police in the 1960s–'70s that would limit its use: the undermining of the press's and police's credibility.[73] According to Shaw, "In previous generations . . . [m]any reporters routinely posed as police . . . to get a story." However, several editors in the second half of the twentieth century "were bothered" by ethical and practical concerns with the practice, including "deception, misrepresentation, falsification and possible invasion of privacy." Each risked undermining the public's confidence in not only the press but also law enforcement. As with police impersonation of the press, the public questioning whether they are talking to the press or police is a significant concern arising from the two institutions undermining their purposes and functions. Thus, in addition to the legal risks around the practice, as well as angering law enforcement, the press itself moved away from the practice, given the implications of undermining credibility and trust.

Despite the reasons making press impersonation of police an especially risky and problematic tactic during this period, its use still continued, through often surreptitious means and without coverage. For example, in a 1979 interview with Shaw, *Philadelphia Inquirer* executive editor Gene Roberts recalled "using a variety of misleading tactics when he covered civil rights in the South for *The New York Times* in the late 1950s and 1960s." Such tactics included "deliberately stuff[ing] a thick notebook in the inside breast pocket of his jacket, knowing that the resultant bulge clearly resembled those made by the shoulder holsters worn by FBI agents." The result, according to Roberts, was that "people thought I was an FBI agent, too, and I was able to move around some pretty hostile crowds more easily than I could have as a reporter."

Similarly, former CBS anchor Bob Schieffer recounted that in the years around the assassination of President Kennedy, he "always wore a snap-brim hat in those days because I wanted to look like the police; if people assumed we were detectives, we'd let them."[74] In one instance, Schieffer drove Lee Harvey Oswald's mother to the Dallas police station, where he allowed the police to think he was an officer until Captain Will Fritz questioned who he was "with" and ultimately uncovered he was a newspaper reporter. Fritz immediately ordered Schieffer to leave, demonstrating that the practice was frowned upon, though also suggesting that it was likely still used by reporters often in unreported or secretive ways. Although they represent the experiences of only two journalists, Roberts's and Schieffer's discussions suggest that reporters may have still used impersonation of police, but in more surreptitious ways, likely given the possible consequences they would face if law enforcement found out. For that same reason, other reporters may have avoided writing about the practice or steered clear of it altogether.

It is therefore not surprising that the practice would likely be limited to only the most aggressive reporters. In 1956, sportswriter Dan Cook, along with Texas boxing promoter Jimmy Parks, posed as police officers when they went to the homes of two individuals suspected of stealing $300,000.[75] Cook said he and Parks "roughed up the pair in order to find out where [they] had hidden the money." Officers later raided the homes and recovered $95,000 tied to the robbery, acknowledging the efforts of Cook, who was initially charged with robbery until the police believed his story. Because Cook allegedly went to great lengths to pull off the practice, and did so in order to "get his 'big story,'" it suggests that it was not a common practice and was something to be done by a particularly enterprising reporter under special circumstances and at the risk of legal consequences, straining relations with the police and undermining credibility.

Media Ride-Alongs

A foundational moment in the history of media ride-alongs came in 1964 with the first formal ride-along program in the United States, also marking the first official use of the terminology *ride-along*.[76] On December 10, 1964, Chicago police superintendent O. W. Wilson announced the creation of the program.[77] The *Chicago Tribune* reported the following day that "prominent and influential citizens [were] invited to ride in squad cars and view the day-to-day tasks of the beat patrolman." Wilson was quoted as saying, "It is hoped that public officials, lawyers, and businessmen may gain new insight into the problems of policing our city and develop a better understanding of what constitutes probable cause for arrest and search."

As similar programs spread around the country in ensuing years, largely for public- and community-relations purposes, they moved from targeting prominent citizens and city leaders to adults more generally, as well as youth, especially from marginalized communities.[78] In some ways, the introduction of formal ride-along programs offset some of the contentiousness during this era between the press and police as reporters also took part in the programs. In fact, about a month after Chicago's program was created, in January 1965, *Chicago Tribune* reporter Ronald Koziol "spent a working day . . . with . . . homicide detective [John Loftus] to learn something of the experiences of these men."[79] As the new programs spread, so too did trends dating back to the nineteenth century, with the purported benefits of the practice outweighing the negative effects that remained almost entirely unaddressed.

During this era, reporters continued receiving invitations or permission to ride with police, often in relation to the formal ride-along programs. For example, in 1967, *Chicago Tribune* reporter Ann Plunkett had "an opportunity to watch [the police] in action" through the city's "unique program called 'Ride Along.'"[80] Plunkett rode with police through the Eighteenth District with Officers Patrick Kelly and Gregory Demas in the morning and Sergeant James White in the afternoon. Plunkett detailed several traffic stops, as well as quoting the three officers who each detailed their views on the "most dangerous situations police face daily," including traffic stops and domestic violence calls. On the one hand, it is perhaps surprising that the police granted such access to journalists amid the rocky relationship during this period. But on the other hand, it is not unusual given that, as in past eras, police expected to get something out of media ride-alongs, namely, improved community relations. The police may have acted differently knowing the press was present to ensure positive coverage. Plunkett not only provided a forum for the police officers to discuss the dangers of their job, but also quoted White, who asserted that the ride-along program "would encourage respect for and cooperation with the police."[81]

Members of the press, in turn, often provided positive or neutral coverage of police following a ride-along, as they had in previous eras, in order to retain future access. Some reports, purposefully or not, read more like press releases than news coverage of policing in a community, even amid public criticism and concerns.[82] For example, in 1972, *New York Amsterdam News* reporter Lee Cook detailed his "night in a patrol car," in which he joined the integrated team of Willie Williams and Roy Peron.[83] Cook wrote that he was "struck by Williams' adept handling of the youth: it is an act which seems alien in the prevailing community atmosphere of hostility and suspicion toward police." Cook also went a step further and included commentary by several police officers that the "problems of the police image in the community [were] distorted" and that the inner city was "frightening" on a Saturday night.

Reporters also continued using media ride-alongs to cover newsworthy events, just as they had for nearly a century. In 1968, reporter Tom Tiede reported on the aftermath of the conflict and violence between law enforcement and the press and public during the DNC in Chicago.[84] Tiede noted a heavily damaged police vehicle from the protests as he rode along with police, among other observations. On the one hand, Tiede's reporting—namely, highlighting how "two dozen newsmen were reportedly manhandled by Chicago cops and officially 22 media representatives filed brutality charges"—fell under a trend of the press seeking to hold law enforcement accountable during this era. On the other hand, though, the reporting still favored the police to at least some degree in that Tiede included several quotes from police officers either downplaying the violence against the press or questioning the "debatable" charges filed against law enforcement officers.

Some additional examples of critical reporting through a media ride-along occurred during this period, likely fueled by the tension between the press and police across the country, though these cases remained overshadowed by praise and positive or neutral coverage.[85] This was the case in 1969 when the *Chicago Tribune* reported on the rise of new "aggressive patrols" used in the "Crime War" in Chicago.[86] Reporter Casey Banas focused on the Chicago Police Department's emphasis on "'aggressive preventive patrol' . . . to deter crime on the streets," meaning that "policemen stop citizens on the street for questioning and even searching if their behavior supposedly is suspicious. Policemen justify these stops on grounds they are looking for weapons and narcotics." Banas briefly noted that these actions sometimes "br[ought] charges by [Black men and women] that their civil rights [were] violated" and also concluded that "left in doubt was whether the task force methods did any good or [had instead] violated citizens' rights." He also cited one officer who "suggested that 'some people have to suffer' in the fight against crime." However, even within this critical coverage, Banas included some praise of police officers, calling them "aggressive, but tactful." He also did not delve deeper into the targeting of Black men and women beyond the short acknowledgment toward the beginning of the article.

Additional negative effects first seen in previous eras also continued, though generally without criticism as they were overshadowed by the purported benefits of the practice. First, journalists continued to face dangers outside their normal duties when riding with police. On the one hand, the creation of formal ride-along programs led to greater safety precautions.[87] But despite such efforts, the dangers to those riding along were still present, as police could, and would, encounter situations that seemed benign on the surface, but became volatile without any warning. This was apparent in 1969 when *Chicago Tribune* reporter Joseph Boyce rode along with police to investigate gang violence in Chicago.[88] Boyce recounted his experiences, including that at one point, two suspected gang members "walked over to the squad car." Joyce explained that "one was angry" and called him an "Uncle Tom," accusing him "of a 'double cross' by not printing facts." The angry individual also turned to one of the officers and reportedly said, "Why should I talk to you. You're . . . my worst enemy." Although the men walked away, their actions nevertheless demonstrated how potential danger can arise at any moment and a reporter can become a target. And in covering the dangers faced by police, reporters not only risked getting caught in the middle, but also often provided a pro–law enforcement view of officers as heroes and risking their lives for the public.[89] There is truth to this, but it does not tell the full story, especially amid significant division between police and marginalized communities in the 1960s–'70s.[90]

If the 1920s–'50s marked the zenith of cooperative coexistence between the press and police, the 1960s–'70s marked the pinnacle of contentiousness. Beginning in the 1950s, and especially in the 1960s–'70s, the press-police relationship changed dramatically as both institutions followed and adapted to larger societal changes stemming from major conflicts, economic fluctuations, and fights for racial justice. Partnerships gave way to increasingly adversarial and divisive relations, with each institution increasingly targeting the other. Nevertheless, cooperative coexistence remained part of the press-police relationship as journalists continued to report on crime and police activities, including as local television news began to rise in prominence. The result was that the remaining partnerships and trust, although overshadowed by contentiousness, provided enough of a foundation for improved relations in the coming decades, though divisiveness and conflict, as well as impersonation and media ride-alongs, also endured and continued to affect the press police relationship through the present.

CHAPTER 6

Rebuilding a Complicated Relationship, 1980s–2020s

FOLLOWING THE TUMULTUOUS 1960S–'70S, A variety of events, trends, and transformations brought significant changes across the United States. As in past eras, the press and police were not immune to these societal shifts, responding to political, economic, social, and technological influences often in similar ways with new tactics, improved technology, and efforts at reform. However, both institutions also faced problems tied to political influences, fluctuating resources, and division with the public, especially marginalized communities, as evidenced by major events like the May 2020 murder of George Floyd in Minneapolis.

The press-police relationship, in responding to a sixty-year period marked initially by increased partnerships and then by increased divisiveness, returned to a more balanced combination of cooperative coexistence and contentiousness, demonstrating how two categories of interactions that defined the early press-police relationship still exist today. But the existence of both categories also raises the question once again: What accounts for members of the press and police getting along or even cooperating at one moment, then embroiled in conflict the next? We have all watched the evening news and seen journalists reporting from a crime scene, sometimes interviewing police officers or attending a press conference. But then at other moments, perhaps even just a short time later, we see journalists face arrests, use of force, and more at the hands of the police. Why is this the case? And equally significant, what effects do these practices continue to raise in the present? And what happens when impersonation and media ride-alongs continue to occur? The answers to these questions are not easy ones, but our present moment provides critical details and information—including the press's and police's current purposes and functions, their interactions with each other in the present, the reasons for such practices, and the effects of such interactions—that help us make sense of where the press-police relationship stands today, learning from the past and informing the future.

Political and Social Factors Prompt Problems
and Changes for Press and Police

Politically, the 1980s–2020s saw carryover from President Nixon's antipress rhetoric and actions.[1] For example, President Donald Trump frequently referred to journalists and news outlets as the "fake news media" and "enemies of the people." His administration also took several antipress actions, including attempting to suspend *Playboy* magazine senior White House reporter Brian Karem's press credential, revoke CNN reporter Jim Acosta's White House press pass, and ban CNN reporter Kaitlan Collins from a press availability with the president.

President Trump was not alone, as other politicians and influential individuals throughout the past forty years have criticized the press for alleged bias and unfair reporting, among other claims, sometimes legitimate, but often unwarranted or for political gain. Some have even gone so far as to physically threaten or attack members of the press, such as on May 24, 2017, when *Guardian* political reporter Ben Jacobs asked Representative Greg Gianforte (R-MT), then congressman-elect, about the Republican health-care plan at a campaign event.[2] Several reporters described how Gianforte then "slam[med Jacobs] to the ground while shouting 'Get the hell out of here.'" After tackling Jacobs, Gianforte reportedly punched him as well, breaking Jacobs's glasses. Jacobs, who showed no physical aggression toward Gianforte and was taken to the hospital for X-rays, filed a police report, resulting in a misdemeanor assault charge.

But despite the assault and charge, on May 26, Gianforte won the special election for Montana's open U.S. House of Representatives seat. On June 12, Gianforte pleaded guilty and was sentenced to a 180-day deferred sentence, forty hours of community service, twenty hours of anger management, and a $300 fine along with a $85 court fee. As part of a deal with Jacobs to avoid a civil lawsuit, Gianforte agreed to donate $50,000 to the Committee to Protect Journalists. Jacobs responded in a statement that he hoped the sentencing would help demonstrate the important role of the press. "While I have no doubt that actions like these were an aberration for Congressman-elect Gianforte personally,

I worry that, in the context of our political debate, they have become increasingly common. . . . This needs to stop," he wrote.

Another important factor is political polarization. Although far from a new development, evidence suggests it is perhaps getting worse in the twenty-first century compared to the final decades of the twentieth century and other eras in U.S. history, building on growing divides seen in the 1960s–'70s.[3] In 2014, the Pew Research Center found that "Republicans and Democrats are more divided along ideological lines—and partisan antipathy is deeper and more extensive—than at any point in the last two decades," adding that "these trends manifest themselves in myriad ways, both in politics and in everyday life."[4] A 2020 study by Brown University found that "Americans' feelings toward members of the other political party have worsened over time faster than those of residents of European and other prominent democracies." Political polarization is also seen in Congress. Pew reported that, in 2022, "on average, Democrats and Republicans are farther apart ideologically today than at any time in the past 50 years." The analysis further found that "both parties have moved further away from the ideological center since the early 1970s. Democrats on average have become somewhat more liberal, while Republicans on average have become much more conservative."[5]

The rise of political polarization in recent years can be attributed to several reasons,[6] including the especially contentious elections in 2000 and 2016, political rhetoric by both parties, and differences between each, including race, religion, and more. Political systems, such as the makeup of the U.S. Senate in which Wyoming and California have the same number of senators, also contribute to polarization, as do technological changes, such as social media echo chambers and filter bubbles, and the increasingly rapid spread of misinformation online. Certainly, there are other explanations as well, and there is ongoing research about the extent to which each of these reasons accounts for polarization and how to combat it. But there are certainly tangible effects, including in public trust in both the press and the police, as well as the relationship between them and their attitudes toward each other.

Meanwhile, the news media has and continues to face decreasing trust and confidence from the general public amid the context of "fake news" allegations and the increase in misinformation and disinformation online. In the 1970s, the press was viewed as one of the most respected institutions, with public trust ranging from 68 percent to 72 percent in Gallup surveys.[7] However, this number declined in the 1990s, though it remained more than 50 percent until 2004, when it dipped to 44 percent. After hitting 50 percent in 2005, it has not risen above 47 percent. Then in 2016, Gallup reported a 32 percent record low amid the divisive presidential election campaign between Hillary Clinton and Donald Trump. Only 32 percent of respondents reported a "great deal" or "fair amount" of trust in the news media's ability to report the news fully, accurately, and fairly.[8] An October 2021 Gallup Poll found that only 7 percent of U.S. adults say they have "a great deal" of trust in the news media, while 29 percent reported "a fair amount" of trust and confidence in newspapers, radio, and television reporting.[9] A Pew Research Poll in August 2021 found a "widening of the partisan gap in trust of the media," noting that "in just five years, the percentage of Republicans with at least some trust in national news organizations has been cut in half—dropping from 70% in 2016 to 35% this year."[10] Conversely, 78 percent of respondents identifying as Democrats and Democratic-leaning independents said they had "a lot" or "some" trust in the information that comes from national news outlets, 43 percent higher than Republicans and Republican-leaning independents.

Antipress sentiment, rhetoric, and actions have significant effects, including undermining the press's ability to serve the public.[11] Put simply, if Americans do not trust the news media or do not consume fair, accurate news, they lose important sources of information and means of holding the powerful accountable. The result is a less informed, increasingly polarized electorate, implicating not only democracy as a whole but also all Americans' daily lives.

Amid decreasing public support, there were changes and reforms in the 1980s–2020s aimed at the press's coverage of and working with race in particular. Newsrooms, to varying degrees, set goals to place greater emphasis on community voices, decrease reliance on official sources and accounts, hire greater diversity in newsrooms and leadership positions, and rethink certain ethical norms and practices. However, many questions related to race, class, and gender still remain unresolved.[12] This includes problematic depictions of people of color in news and entertainment, discussed more later. Insufficient diversity in newsrooms and media ownership also continues and, in some ways, has even gotten worse.[13] Furthermore, the twenty-first century risks seeing "the nation's persistent class and racial inequalities [be] replicated in cyberspace," such as by expanding the "digital divide," thereby denying access to news, as well as jobs and opportunities in journalism for marginalized and lower-income individuals and communities.[14]

Police also faced political and social challenges, including related to decreased public trust, over the past four decades. The tumultuous 1960s to early 1970s for law enforcement gave way to the "conservative era" from 1975 through the present, which included a significant shift to an "anticrime mood."[15] Supreme Court rulings demonstrated this shift to greater police power in that the Warren Court (1953–69) generally recognized equal protection and greater due-process rights,[16] while the Burger (1969–86) and Rehnquist Courts (1986–2005) generally favored crime-control measures.[17]

But perhaps most notably, the new push for "law and order" and being "tough on crime" was exemplified by the escalating "War on Drugs."[18] In June 1971, President Nixon declared drug abuse to be "public enemy number one" and therefore increased the size and resources for drug enforcement agencies, including the U.S. Drug Enforcement Administration, established in 1973. President Ronald Reagan further augmented efforts targeting drug use, including by signing several pieces of legislation like the Anti-Drug Abuse Act of 1986, which allocated $1.7 billion to drug enforcement and further established a system of mandatory minimum prison sentences for a wide range of drug offenses. Significantly, while possession of five grams of crack cocaine led to an automatic five-year sentence, it took five hundred grams of powder cocaine to receive the same sentence. Because the Black community accounted for 80 percent of crack-cocaine users, the result was unequal incarceration of Black and white people. The result was the rise of mass incarceration, particularly of Black people, discussed more later.

Driving the expansion on the War on Drugs was increased public concern about drug use. In 1985, polls showed that only 2–6 percent of Americans viewed drug abuse as the top problem facing the country. However, by 1989, that number reached 64 percent. Increased media coverage of drug use almost certainly contributed to public concern, especially through television coverage that sensationalized drug use, exaggerated the "epidemic" nature of such use, and overrepresented criminalized Black men. Other media coverage intentionally or unintentionally glamorized drug use, such as in May 1977 when *Newsweek* ran a story stating that "a little cocaine, like Dom Perignon and Beluga caviar, is now de rigueur at dinners. Some partygivers pass it around

along with the canapes on silver trays. . . . [T]he user experiences a feeling of potency, of confidence, of energy."[19] The piece was later criticized
for romanticizing drug use and failing to fully discuss its dangers. Press
coverage and the moral panic around drug use ultimately contributed to
efforts like First Lady Nancy Reagan establishing her "Just Say No" campaign seeking to educate schoolchildren on the dangers of drug use. Los
Angeles police chief Daryl Gates, who would spend forty-three years in
the LAPD, including fourteen as chief, founded the DARE drug education program in 1983, which similarly sought to prevent drug abuse by
educating elementary school students.

Further driving the greater emphasis on law and order was the
September 11, 2001, terrorist attacks.[20] Amid the chaos of the attacks,
NYPD police officers were depicted as heroes in their efforts to save
as many people as possible. However, in the wake of the attacks, augmented fear and public safety concerns across the United States led to
several changes in law enforcement. The federal government, among
numerous other actions domestically and abroad, placed greater emphasis on, and committed greater resources to, federal, state, and local
law enforcement to focus on counterterrorism and national security.
Such tactics included, and still include, increased surveillance through
license plate readers and mobile X-ray vans, as well as greater emphasis
on detaining and arresting Americans, often from marginalized communities. Studies demonstrate that Islamophobia by law enforcement
increased significantly in the post–September 11 world, fueled by stereotyping and negative portrayals of in the mainstream press and entertainment programs. Arab, Middle Eastern, Muslim, and South Asian
communities were illegally arrested, beaten, and killed in the days and
weeks following September 11. The NYPD also sent undercover officers to predominantly Muslim neighborhoods and used informants to
monitor community and religious events. As discussed later, September
11 also contributed to greater police militarization, adding weaponry,
vehicles, and technology that resemble that of a military force rather
than domestic policing. Ultimately, law enforcement moved away from
community policing following September 11. The tactics and technology stemming from the augmented law enforcement efforts following the
terrorist attacks are still used in the present, disproportionately affecting
marginalized communities, and often for reasons completely unrelated
to counterterrorism.

Connected to the War on Drugs, September 11, and other political and social changes were the continued division and violence between police and marginalized communities despite some reform efforts in response to the 1960s–'70s.[21] The conservative era saw the rise of "community-oriented" or "problem-oriented" policing, with the goal being law enforcement working closely with community residents, instead of being an inward-looking bureaucracy. Officials and scholars reasoned that the development of police vehicles meant a decrease in foot patrols through which officers could better interact with members of the community, among other justifications.

Although the 1980s–2020s saw greater protections, legal and otherwise, for women and people of color, there were also new reasons for division, especially with the Black community.[22] One such moment arose after Rodney King, a twenty-five-year-old Black California resident, led police on a high-speed chase.[23] Bystander video footage, shown nationwide by CNN, captured "at least a dozen officers surrounding the man after he left his car, kicking him and inflicting more than 40 blows with nightsticks as he lay on the pavement." On March 15, 1991, four officers, including Sergeant Stacey Koon and Officers Laurence Michael Powell, Timothy Wind, and Theodore Briseno, were indicted by a grand jury in Los Angeles for assault with a deadly weapon and use of excessive force. But despite the video evidence, on April 29, 1992, the officers were acquitted. Seventeen other police officers, who were present at the beating, but were not shown participating in the video footage, were not indicted.

Riots broke out throughout Los Angeles, lasting for five days and leaving nearly sixty people dead and more than two thousand injured. Nearly twelve thousand people were arrested, and estimated damage in the Los Angeles area exceeded $1 billion. Unrest spread across the nation, during which Rodney King made a television appearance and called for peace in Los Angeles, famously asking, "Can we all get along?"[24]

The division between police and the Black community was also apparent in the rise of mass incarceration of Black Americans in the second half of the twentieth century.[25] The War on Drugs led to a dramatic increase in incarcerations for nonviolent drug offenses, from fifty thousand in 1980 to four hundred thousand in 1997. Recent statistics indicate that Black men and women constitute only about 13 percent of the nation's population, yet they account for about 45 percent of those incarcerated. As a result, civil rights activists argue that felony convictions have "replaced the explicit use of race as the mechanism to deny black Americans their rights as citizens."[26] And given the role of law enforcement, these actions further contribute to distrust of police by the Black community.

Division between the police and Black community was further augmented by killings of several unarmed Black men and women by law enforcement. On August 9, 2014, Michael Brown, an eighteen-year-old amateur rap musician, was walking down the middle of Canfield Drive in Ferguson, Missouri—a city with a predominantly Black population though an almost entirely white police department—with his twenty-two-year-old friend Dorian Johnson.[27] The pair was approached by police officer Darren Wilson, who told the young Black men to use the sidewalk. Wilson and Brown then exchanged words, with some witnesses and Wilson claiming that Brown reached into the police car and punched the officer, fighting for his gun. Johnson and other witnesses countered that Brown was never inside the vehicle and that the officer had grabbed Brown around the neck from inside the vehicle. Wilson fired two shots, one of which grazed Brown's right thumb and another lodged into the driver's side door. Brown and Johnson then fled the scene. Wilson and some witnesses claimed that after a short pursuit, Brown charged at the officer, leading him to open fire. Johnson and other witnesses, meanwhile, contended that Brown had stopped and had his hands raised after Wilson shot at his back. Johnson alleged that Wilson then shot Brown several times until he fell to the ground. Two autopsies later reconfirmed that Brown was shot six times in total, including once in the hand at close range and the fatal shot on the top of his head from at least thirty-five feet away.

On November 24, a grand jury decided not to indict Wilson, prompting protests outside the Ferguson Police Department that grew increasingly intense throughout the night. Demonstrators threw objects at police officers in riot gear, who in turn fired tear gas and smoke to disperse people. Several buildings and at least one automobile were set on fire around the city. Demonstrations continued for several weeks, frequently resulting in confrontations between police and protesters, as well as journalists.

Another notable case arose on May 25, 2020, when George Floyd was restrained and killed while in Minneapolis Police Department custody.[28]

Bystander video showed Floyd lying on his stomach with Officer Derek Chauvin pressing his knee on the back of Floyd's neck for nearly nine minutes, causing Floyd to fall silent and unresponsive. Chauvin was charged with, and found guilty of, second-degree murder, third-degree murder, and second-degree manslaughter and sentenced to 22.5 years in prison. In July 2022, Chauvin was sentenced in the federal case against him to 252 months in prison on two civil rights charges after previously pleading guilty. Officers J. Alexander Kueng, Thomas Lane, and Tou Thao, the other three officers at the scene, faced charges of aiding and abetting. In a federal case, Thao was sentenced to 42 months in prison and Kueng 36 months for depriving Floyd of his constitutional rights. At the time of publication, the state trial of the officers remained ongoing. Floyd's death prompted widespread protests, with the epicenter being Minneapolis as demonstrations eventually spread across the United States to at least sixty-four cities and twenty-four states, with more protests continuing into 2021, among other cases of police killing unarmed Black individuals.

Economic Changes Place Pressure on News Media and Law Enforcement

Economic trends and changes in the 1980s–2020s contributed to significant changes in how the press gathered and reported news, as well as how law enforcement utilized generally increased resources and funding. The rise of "big media" began in the 1980s as news organizations reached larger audiences, but also consolidated, "went public," or both.[29] Following a broader trend across Wall Street of a "frenzy of mergers and acquisitions . . . media consolidation began in earnest in 1985, placing more and more journalism properties inside giant companies that sometimes had little interest in news." For example, that year, Capital Cities Communication bought ABC for $3.5 billion, and General Electric bought RCA and its NBC division for $6.3 billion. Such moves continued in the 1990s, with the 1995 purchase of CBS, the latest move for the historic network, by Westinghouse for $5.4 billion and the 1996 purchase of Cap Cities/ABC by Disney Corporation for approximately $19 billion. In the early 2000s, consolidation further expanded as "even the giants wanted to get bigger." Chains like Gannett, Knight-Ridder, and McClatchy bought previously independent newspapers. Clear Channel bought thousands of radio stations. The result was and remains a significant decrease in the number of individual owners of media outlets, therefore decreasing diversity and points of view in exchange for large, publicly traded companies generally owned and controlled by wealthy white men.[30]

The rise of big media had, and still has, a variety of effects on journalism, including blurring the lines between the editorial side of a news organization, namely, the behind-the-scenes work and decision-making related to news gathering and reporting, and the business interests of the company or individual that owns the news organization.[31] Sometimes, ownership by wealthy conglomerates and individuals led to significant resources supporting important reporting. However, in other cases, the result could be a conflict of interest or unwanted business pressure on the editorial side. What happens if a reporter uncovers damning information about their bosses or the company that employs them? What about if the conglomerate pushes a news organization to cover a story a certain way? In any event, the independence of journalists as a professional ideal was undermined. In fact, even the appearance of a conflict of interest and lost independence could be enough to damage the credibility of a journalist or news organization, making news gathering and source relationships even more challenging. And even if the news side of a conglomerate enjoys First Amendment protections, other parts of that corporation may be subject to regulation, such as by the Federal Communications Commission.

A significant problem tied to the rise of big media is the parallel decline of newspapers, especially at the local level, as they faced decreased resources, newsroom closures, and layoffs. The statistics bear this out: More than 2,500 newspapers across the United States, representing a quarter of all newspapers nationwide, have closed since 2005.[32] From the start of the COVID-19 pandemic through the summer of 2022 alone, more than 360 newspapers closed. From 2008 to 2020, newsroom employment dropped by more than 26 percent, from 114,000 employees to fewer than 85,000.[33]

There are several reasons for the decline in newspapers, including that they generally had high fixed costs, meaning that each day, in order to produce and distribute a newspaper, came with high costs.[34] At the same time, publishers also had additional expenses arising from mergers and acquisitions, including paying the interest on the debt arising from being part of a chain or conglomerate. Combined with paying pensions, costs associated with launching and maintaining news websites, operation of a manufacturing plant for the production of the newspaper, and more, newspaper publishers had and have to make difficult financial decisions. Adding to problems was a steady decrease in advertising revenue, subscriptions, and circulation, especially as young people stopped reading newspapers and instead headed to television or, eventually, online where they could more easily find the information they wanted over a newspaper with set boundaries and categories of news. Although some newspapers, including giants like the *New York Times*, owned by the Sulzberger family through the New York Times Company, and the *Washington Post*, purchased in August 2013 by Amazon founder Jeff Bezos, and regional papers like the *Minneapolis Star Tribune*, have figured out how to survive and thrive in the current media market, significant concerns remain for the future of newspapers and the important journalism they do.

Since 2004, the number of journalists employed by newspapers was cut in half. There are several negative effects stemming from the loss of local news, namely, the creation of "news deserts."[35] Half of the 3,143 counties in the United States have only one newspaper, usually attempting to cover several communities at once with limited resources. Approximately 200 counties have no newspaper at all. The result is the loss of access to reliable and timely local news, calendars of local events, advertising, community forums, and much more, often for the most vulnerable and already underrepresented communities.

Much like the press, police across the country faced significant economic influences and changes over the past four decades. Across this period, federal, state, and local police forces generally received increased funding and resources due to the emphasis on combating crime. In 1960, state and local governments spent approximately $2 billion on police.[36] During that time, there were about 1,887 crimes per 100,000 Americans. By the 1980s, state and local governments spent $14.6 billion on law enforcement as crime rates increased to 5,950 crimes per 100,000 Americans. Although crime rates fell to around 4,000 crimes per 100,000 Americans over the next two decades, funding spiked to more than $67 billion. By 2018, crime rates had fallen to 2,580 crimes per 100,000 people, but spending reached $137 billion, not adjusted for inflation.

Meanwhile, federal funding of law enforcement also dramatically increased. In 1968, President Johnson signed the Omnibus Crime Control and Safe Streets Act of 1968, which earmarked $400 million for law enforcement purposes.[37] Four years later, President Nixon announced that his administration, in the three years since he became president, had provided more than $1.5 billion in funding for state and local law enforcement grants. Between 1982 and 2015, federal spending increased by 354 percent, faster than state and local spending combined.[38] In 2015, federal spending accounted for about 20 percent of law enforcement funding, while local governments paid just under 70 percent and state governments 11 percent. Federal funding largely comes from two sources, the Community Oriented Policing Services program—established as part of the Violent Crime Control and Law Enforcement Act, often referred to as the 1994 Crime Bill, signed by President Bill Clinton—and the Byrne Justice Assistance Grants, known as Byrne JAG, established as a part of the Anti-Drug Abuse Act of 1988, signed by President Reagan. Combined, the two grants from the DOJ accounted for more than $700 million of funding for law enforcement as of 2020.

Following the murder of Floyd and other high-profile cases of white police officers killing unarmed Black men and women, debates raged across the United States about whether and how to reform policing moving forward, including calls to "defund" federal, state, and local law enforcement. The movement advocated for reduction in government spending in policing, not necessarily the complete elimination of law enforcement. It also called for shifting responsibilities, such as responding to people experiencing mental health crises, away from departments to education, social services, health care, and other community groups and resources. Conversely, other Americans pushed for increased funding of law enforcement, citing violent crimes in major U.S. cities. The debate around funding, and police reform more broadly, remains heated across the United States, continuing trends dating back centuries.

Technological Changes Bring Both Opportunities and Challenges

A particularly significant technological change influencing how the press covered newsworthy events and conducted investigative reporting was the beginning of cable news in 1980 with the creation of CNN. In addition to being the beginning of news found on cable television, CNN and other cable news channels that followed, including both MSNBC and Fox News in 1996, introduced the twenty-four-hour news cycle soon adopted by regional and local news outlets.[39] News no longer came only from fixed parts of the day, but instead focused on newsworthy events as they happened through live coverage and breaking news. This was perhaps best exemplified by the nationwide and worldwide coverage of the trial of O. J. Simpson, an actor and former professional football player, for the murder of his ex-wife, Nicole Brown Simpson, and her friend Ronald Goldman.[40] The case arose on the night of June 12, 1994, when Brown Simpson and Goldman were stabbed to death outside her Los Angeles condominium. Soon after, police investigating the murders named Simpson the prime suspect. But rather than surrender to police, on June 17, Simpson hid in the back of a white Ford Bronco, a sport-utility vehicle, driven by his friend A. C. Cowlings, leading to a notorious "slow-speed" chase ending at Simpson's home in Brentwood, California, where he was arrested. The chase was televised nationally with an estimated 95 million viewers watching the events unfold live as they were recorded by helicopter cameras.

The trial began on January 24, 1995, with Judge Lance Ito of the Los Angeles County Superior Court serving as the presiding judge. Lasting eight months, the trial garnered worldwide media coverage, including from the courtroom where Court TV broadcast every moment of the proceedings, including the pivotal moment in which Simpson tried on the bloody leather glove found at his home, with the defense team arguing that it could not have been his because it appeared too small for him. CNN dedicated a significant amount of coverage to the trial, as did other national, regional, and local broadcast and print outlets. But the cable networks also went a step further and broadcast substantial commentary and editorializing about what took place. Across the United States, Americans watching the nearly endless coverage came to different conclusions about Simpson's guilt or innocence, which largely fell along racial lines. Whereas Black Americans generally believed Simpson to be innocent, white Americans believed him to be guilty. Ultimately, on October 3, 1995, Simpson was found not guilty by the jury. It is believed that more than 150 million viewers, accounting for 57 percent of the country, tuned into the live broadcast of the verdict.

The media coverage of the chase, arrest, and trial of Simpson has several noteworthy effects, including further ushering in, and making a permanent fixture, the twenty-four-hour news cycle, live reporting, cable news commentary, reality television shows, and more. Press coverage also likely contributed to shifts in public opinion during and following the trial, including the racial tension and nationwide debates arising from whether people believed Simpson was innocent or guilty.

The media coverage also provided platforms for many key players in the trial who would go on to seek and achieve further stardom.

Another effect was the clear illustration of the blurring of news and entertainment, especially related to crime, arising beginning in the 1980s.[41] During this era, news was more accessible, emotional, and entertaining. The combination of these factors was evident in the coverage of Simpson's trial, where the emphasis was often placed less on the newsworthiness of what was taking place, but instead on the entertainment value and enthralling Americans more than their soap operas or sporting events to gain as large an audience as possible. What some called a "media circus" around the trial therefore led to greater scrutiny of the press and, much like following the Lindbergh trial, many experts and others calling for changes in how the media was allowed to cover trials and whether cameras should be allowed in courtrooms.

Then came the internet and digital media, marking the digital revolution. Digital media—including cell phones, laptops, desktop computers, tablets, and other forms of media connecting to the internet and using electronic devices for distribution—increasingly implicated journalism in numerous, wide-ranging ways, especially as more and more Americans gained reliable access to computers and the internet in the late 1990s and into the twenty-first century.[42] Innovation in press activities included increased multimedia journalism, requiring journalists to become proficient in print, audio, video, and online reporting all at once. Journalists were also increasingly expected to have a presence on social media and comments sections on online news articles, allowing for greater connections with the public. Digital media also gave journalists access to more tools for news gathering and publishing. The easy portability of laptops and smartphones allows for easy access to the internet, the storage of files, and easier communication with newsrooms, as well as containing cameras, editing software, and much more.

In some cases, the internet therefore provided opportunities for journalists, including new sources of revenue. However, as discussed earlier, in other cases, the internet meant newspaper audiences could go elsewhere for information, forcing newspapers to adapt and move online, some being more successful than others. Complicating matters was a more fragmented audience less willing to pay for information as more and more was made available for free online, meaning traditional forms of subscriptions and paywalls may not suffice. Media owners also recognized that new technology meant reporters could do more work in less time, leading to reductions in newsroom staffing as employees now had to increase output for multiple platforms. News organizations continue to grapple with both opportunities and problems arising from digital media, including as disinformation online remains a significant concern, raising questions as to the role of journalists in combating falsehoods and misleading information while adapting to ever-changing technology.

Political pressure, greater resources, and calls for police reform meant notable changes in police technology. For example, police body-worn cameras (BWCs) first gained national attention following the shooting of Brown and acquittal of Wilson.[43] The calls got even louder a week later when a Staten Island grand jury did not indict NYPD officer Daniel Pantaleo, who used a chokehold on Eric Garner, killing the unarmed Black man. One proposed solution to help ease tensions and deter future incidents was the implementation of BWCs as a means of documenting interactions between the public and law enforcement and thus bringing greater police accountability, helping rebuild public trust. By 2016, 80 percent of police departments with five hundred or more full-time officers had body cameras, according to the Bureau of Justice Statistics.[44] In total, 47 percent of the 15,328 general-purpose law enforcement agencies in the United States had acquired the cameras.

However, technological developments are not without problems and concerns. Although BWCs purport to show the truth and provide accountability, they also raise privacy concerns, problems of reliability, accuracy, and interpretation, and issues of costs. Furthermore, BWCs and other law enforcement technology are meant to be solutions to a problem that is far more complex than it appears on the surface. The high-profile deaths of unarmed Black men by law enforcement in recent years are certainly significant, but are not the first instances of division and distrust between the Black community and police. It is a conflict woven into the fabric of the nation's history with origins dating back to slavery.

Rapid technological developments in police weapons and defenses have also led to other problems, including police militarization, a trend in which police, through federal, state, and local funding, acquire and use military-style equipment, weapons, and tactics like armored vehicles, assault rifles, flashbang grenades, sniper rifles, and SWAT teams. The purpose behind such equipment and strategies is to purportedly stay one step ahead of criminals, allowing for police to respond to any scene while maintaining officer safety. However, significant consequences also arise when police gain "firepower that is often far beyond what is necessary for their jobs as protectors of their communities," including increased use of force and violence against the public even in cases where it was not necessary.[45]

In his 2013 book *Rise of the Warrior Cop: The Militarization of America's Police Forces, Washington Post* opinion columnist Radley Balko details how the United States, founded on the principles of avoiding having a standing army in American streets, came to have "a dominant military culture within modern police agencies," including "SWAT teams [that] violently smash into private homes more than one hundred times per day."[46] Balko traces the history of police militarization in the United States, including the influence of the War on Drugs and increased federal funding under the Reagan, Clinton, Bush, and Obama administrations. In particular, the 1990s marked a significant increase in the proliferation of military gear and weapons for police, further accelerated following the September 11, 2001, terrorist attacks, which also augmented the emphasis on law and order and increasing police resources. Balko contends that although law enforcement, including SWAT teams, can, and do, accomplish important purposes and functions, reform is needed to ensure that there is adequate accountability through legal, technological, and community-focused means. Balko and police reform advocates also call for greater transparency in the use of advanced weapons and aggressive policing, changes to police culture around the use of force, and a reexamination of when the use of force is needed.

Technological developments, as well as other reform and accountability efforts, also run into a significant roadblock: police unions. Dating back to antecedents in the late nineteenth and early twentieth centuries, these unions make reform, change, and accountability of law enforcement more difficult, namely, due to protections bargained for by police unions in the contracts with their respective cities.[47] Such protections include erasing an officer's disciplinary record after as few as six months, keeping an officer's disciplinary record secret, or delaying any questioning of officers after incidents like police shootings. Police unions are also often vocal opponents of reforms and punishing officers for misconduct, further dividing police and the public, especially marginalized communities.

Current Goals, Purposes, Functions, and
Actions of the Press and Police

Part of the history of the press-police relationship is the ways in which both the press and the police sought to delineate their roles in the United States, including becoming independent professions beginning with the Progressive Era in the early twentieth century. They did so as part of their responses to the societal context around them, including political, economic, social, and technological changes. Over time, the press and police helped shape their normative roles and responsibilities, meaning the ways in which both should, at least ideally, operate, namely, with the public in mind. The result of this trajectory is a series of purposes and functions ascribed to both institutions in the present, each of which necessarily implicates not only each other but also their relationship and the public. Thus, cooperative coexistence and contentiousness, dating back to the American colonies, remain the predominant forms of inter-actions between the press and police in the present.

Michael Schudson articulated seven functions of U.S. journalism, including foremost that the press should inform and educate the public about political, economic, and social information and developments.[48] The second function of the press is "investigation," which requires the press to "probe" the "political world" and hold government accountable. Third, the press should "publicize representative democracy," helping the public to participate in democracy as informed voters. Fourth, the press should help effect change in society through "mobilization." Fifth, the press should act as a "public forum" by fostering debate among members of the public. Sixth, the news media should provide "analysis" to help explain complicated events or processes. Finally, Schudson argued that the press should contribute to "social empathy," meaning journalists should report stories about people in such a manner that all members of society might not only see them but understand their situation. Beyond these functions, the activities of the press are often intertwined with the business functions of media organizations or the owners thereof, including publishing or broadcasting advertising to generate income as well as to draw in readers, listeners, and viewers. In some cases, the press may aim merely to entertain its audience.

Samuel Walker, professor emeritus at the University of Nebraska at Omaha, and Charles Katz, an associate professor in the School of Criminology and Criminal Justice at Arizona State University, articulated four goals of law enforcement, including to prevent crime, conduct investigations and apprehend criminals, maintain order, and provide other miscellaneous services.[49] The American Bar Association provided eleven recommended responsibilities police should carry out, including to "resolve conflict."[50] Much like those of the press, the pre-scribed purposes and functions of police are generally meant to serve and benefit the public.

As detailed later, the purposes and functions of the press and police help begin to explain why, amid the political, social, economic, and technological changes occurring in the final decades of the twentieth century and first decades of the twenty-first century, the press and po-lice saw the return of the emphasis on cooperative coexistence, reflect-ing the 1940s–'50s, while contentiousness also continued, reflecting the 1960s–'70s, as did impersonation and media ride-alongs.

Cooperative Coexistence through Press Coverage of Police Returns Balance to Press-Police Relationship

Cooperative coexistence made a resurgence following the 1960s–'70s as the public remained fascinated by crime and policing, coverage the press was only too willing to provide. Newspapers, both in print and online, along with radio and television stations across the United States, continued traditional crime coverage, including of murders, terrorist incidents, thefts, mass shootings, and more. As police used community-oriented policing and more aggressive tactics to target and address crime throughout the country, the press was there to cover what took place.

The rise of cable news and 24/7 coverage included significant cover-age of crime and police, often through highly emotional coverage, with the press increasingly looking over the shoulder of police and public officials in an effort to gather more news.[51] The significance of this shift was not only increased coverage of police, but also different ways for the press to do so. A notable example came early in this era when CNN covered the attempted assassination of President Ronald Reagan.[52] On March 30, 1981, NBC, CBS, and ABC had their cameras rolling when President Reagan was shot and wounded by John Hinckley Jr. Although CNN did not have a camera to record the shooting, the cable network reported on the shooting four minutes before its broadcast competitors. Additionally, CNN provided continuous coverage of the shooting for the following forty-eight hours, including when it became clear that

President Reagan had been wounded more seriously than previously believed.

As discussed in chapter 5, the coverage of crime and police was also pervasive on local broadcast television beginning in the late 1970s, as viewers across the United States took in coverage of policing daily.[53] As television news became increasingly common and popular in the 1980s–'90s, television reporters and crews frequently conducted live on-the-scene coverage, especially when covering breaking news and crime. In some cases, the press and police even cooperated, such as in tracking down a suspect or finding a missing person.[54]

Why the Press and Police Cooperate and Coexist

Continuing in the present on a daily basis, why do members of the press and the police cooperate or coexist? What accounts for this type of interaction dating back hundreds of years? Ultimately, the commonality between the responsibility of the press and police to work with an eye toward benefiting the public suggests that they need not always find themselves at odds with each other. At the theoretical level, social responsibility theory (SRT) was first officially introduced by the Commission on Freedom of the Press, often referred to as the Hutchins Commission.[55] The commission was formed in 1942 when *Time* magazine founder Henry Luce asked Robert Hutchins, the president of the University of Chicago and his former classmate at Yale, to lead a panel exploring how freedom of the press worked, and ought to work, in the United States. In 1947, the commission published its report, *A Free and Responsible Press*, in which it found that "an overall social responsibility for the quality of press service to the citizen cannot be escaped." In 1956, Frederick S. Siebert, the director of the School of Journalism and Communications at the University of Illinois; Theodore Peterson, an associate professor of journalism and communications at the University of Illinois; and Wilbur Schramm, a professor of journalism and communications at Stanford University, published *Four Theories of the Press: The Authoritarian, Libertarian, Social Responsibility, and Soviet Communist Concepts of What the Press Should Be and Do*, elaborating on the conclusions raised by the Hutchins Commission, claiming that the power possessed by the press requires an obligation to be socially responsible.[56]

The Hutchins Commission was not without its detractors, including from some within the professional press. However, an important ideal arising from its work was the notion that how something ought to operate must be weighed against or balanced with other public interests. For his part, Thomas Scanlon, a professor at Princeton University from 1966 to 1984 and Harvard University from 1984 to 2016, argued that freedom of expression "rests upon a balancing of competing [social] goods."[57] Similarly, Schramm called for "a combination of responsibility and freedom" that ensured a consideration of the public interest, even if doing so partially limited press freedom.[58]

Although most often applied to the news media, SRT can also be applied to police as public servants. Ultimately, SRT demands that an institution act in a way that is responsible to the public, meaning that the public interest trumps and can delimit both the press's and the police's core values or interests. Both institutions must, at times, accommodate the wishes of the other because both are meant to serve to the benefit of the public.

Further explaining why cooperative coexistence exists is the press's balancing of its need for independence and for collaboration. In other words, cooperative coexistence is characterized, on the one hand, by the independence of the press, namely, its ability to carry out its purposes and functions without interference by the government. But on the other hand, cooperative coexistence necessarily includes the press's "collaborative role," namely, "any number of relationships in which the media willingly, sometimes even enthusiastically, participate."[59] This includes the government broadly and law enforcement more specifically, where collaboration includes "an acknowledgment of the state's interest—to which the media accede either passively or unwittingly, reluctantly or wholeheartedly—in participating in the choices journalists make and the coverage they provide."

Effects Arising from Cooperative Coexistence

There are certainly positive effects arising from press coverage of police, including informing, and otherwise serving, the public. These positive effects are reflected in the purposes and functions of the press, as well as press independence under the First Amendment. However, the increase in television crime news in particular also led to problems, especially in relation to underrepresented communities, continuing trends dating back to the 1970s. First, crime coverage often stereotypes Black people, with at least some reporting continuing to "[overrepresent] Black perpetrators, [underrepresent] Black victims, and [overrepresent] White victims."[60] Black individuals are also more often depicted under the physical control of police officers, including being restrained, tackled, and handcuffed. Second, crime coverage, in an effort to build ratings, focuses heavily on crime and can, therefore, create perceptions of rampant crime and unsafe communities while the reality is that crime has declined throughout the late twentieth and early twenty-first centuries. Last, at both the national and the local levels, television crime coverage often lacks context around crimes committed by Black men and women, namely, that they are subject to higher rates of discrimination, unemployment, ineffective schooling, and more.[61] Although research remains ongoing about the extent to which local crime news misrepresents people of color,[62] such concerns continue amid calls for greater racial equity and justice.

Concerns about racial bias and overly favorable views of policing also arise from the continued growth of television crime shows, including *Law & Order: SVU*, *NCIS*, and others.[63] Whereas people of color have often been depicted as suspects rather than victims, law enforcement has generally been depicted as heroes in crime dramas. Similar concerns are also found in film, which frequently "valorize" police officers and depict law enforcement as "heroic."[64] Wrongful police actions, ranging from the use of physical force to illegal searches to overt racism, are often normalized by making them seem routine, harmless, and, in some cases, even noble to bring about justice. Furthermore, television crime dramas leave out real-life problems related to race, such as the disproportionate targeting of people of color and racial profiling, undermining calls for police reform. They also create a gap between audience members' perceptions of crime and reality. Last, women and people of color hold relatively few positions behind the camera, further problematizing film and television entertainment related to crime and policing as important voices and opinions are missing in the production and distribution process.

Contentiousness Persists as Press and Police Continue to Target Each Other

Where the press-police relationship becomes more contentious is when the press seeks to investigate, criticize, or otherwise critically report on the police, including wrongdoing or misconduct. As in past eras, such reporting occurred among a variety of events and developments, though perhaps most notably in journalists and news organizations across the United States reporting on police killings of Black individuals. One such case arose in October 2014 when Chicago Police Department officers approached seventeen-year-old Laquan McDonald and told him to drop the knife he was carrying.[65] McDonald refused and began jogging down a four-lane road. Two officers followed him on foot and in a car for several blocks before Jason Van Dyke, one of the six police officers at the scene, fired his weapon and struck McDonald sixteen times.

Jamie Kalven, an independent journalist based in Chicago, was the first reporter to cover inconsistencies in the CPD's official reports of McDonald's death. Kalven, through an open-records request, obtained the autopsy report detailing the precise number of times Van Dyke shot McDonald, which previously had not been released. Kalven detailed how the autopsy report told a different story than the official police account, finding it was not a simple case of self-defense. His reporting ultimately held law enforcement accountable and helped prompt change and reform. More specifically, Kalven contributed to charges being filed against Van Dyke. In October 2018, the officer was found guilty of second-degree murder and sixteen counts of aggravated battery. Kalven also helped prompt the release of dash-camera footage depicting the shooting after he learned from an anonymous source that the footage existed and was not being released by the CPD. Additionally, Kalven's reporting led to greater calls for police reform and accountability, leading the CPD to expand use of BWCs in an effort to regain public trust.

As in past eras, contentiousness also arises when law enforcement targets, intentionally or not, members of the press, including through arrests. From 2017 to 2021, at least 189 journalists were arrested while performing reporting, including 131 in 2020 alone.[66] Arrests have been made for a variety of reasons under federal and state statutes, including for allegedly interfering in police activities.[67] Often, arrests were made in connection to press purposes and functions,[68] though, as in past eras, some arrests were tied to actions unrelated to journalists' jobs.[69] While being arrested, journalists often faced threats and the use of force, including tear gas and other chemical agents, rubber bullets, riot batons, flashbangs, being tackled to the ground, and more.

In recent years, police have detained, harmed, or threatened journalists, most frequently in connection to protests, demonstrations, and riots. Perhaps the most notable instances in recent years came in the wake of the murder of George Floyd. Amid the protests across the country, journalists faced arrests, use of force, and threats by police. According to the U.S. Press Freedom Tracker, between May 26, 2020, and December 2020, there were more than 800 reported incidents of journalists being "assaulted, arrested or otherwise prevented from documenting history" by police or demonstrators amid the protests across the country for racial justice.[70] The incidents took place across at least seventy-nine cities and included at least 255 physical attacks of journalists by police or protesters and 115 arrests. For example, on May 29, 2020, Minnesota State Patrol officers arrested CNN correspondent Omar Jimenez, photojournalist Leonel Mendez, and producer Bill Kirkos while they were reporting live in south Minneapolis.[71] The arrests were made despite Jimenez identifying himself as a reporter and showing his press credential. He also told police he would comply with their orders. The three were later released once they were confirmed to be members of the media. The arrest of the CNN crew marked only one of numerous incidents between the press and police in Minneapolis during the protests over Floyd's death, which included threats of violence and arrests, as well as use of force against journalists by police using tear gas, rubber bullets, riot batons, flashbangs, tackling journalists to the ground, and more.[72] Similar actions were directed at numerous journalists amid protests across the United States in ensuing days, weeks, and months.

Law enforcement's targeting of the press prompted federal lawsuits from journalists. One such lawsuit was filed by the ACLU on behalf of freelance journalist Jared Goyette and other members of the press arrested or harmed by police.[73] The complaint made several claims, including that the defendants—the City of Minneapolis, Minneapolis chief of police Medaria Arradondo, Minneapolis police lieutenant Robert Kroll, Minnesota Department of Public Safety commissioner John Harrington, and Minnesota State Patrol colonel Matthew Langer, in their official capacities, as well as two unnamed police officers—in deploying chemical agents and less-lethal ballistics, had retaliated against the journalists for "engaging in constitutionally protected [reporting] activity" in violation of the First Amendment. The complaint contended that the actions created a chilling effect on constitutionally protected activity, namely, journalists' ability "to observe and record some events of public interest, including . . . the conduct of law enforcement officers on duty in a public place." The complaint also alleged violations of Fourth Amendment protections against unlawful seizure and excessive force.

Conflict between the press and police escalated once more amid protests stemming from the trial of Derek Chauvin—the Minneapolis police officer who pressed his knee into Floyd's neck—and following the April 11, 2021, police killing of Daunte Wright, a twenty-year-old Black man, in Brooklyn Center, Minnesota. In this case, Officer

Kimberly Potter shot and killed Wright at a traffic stop, claiming that she accidentally grabbed her gun instead of her Taser. On December 23, 2021, Potter was convicted of first- and second-degree manslaughter and was sentenced to sixteen months in prison and six months of supervised release.

On April 16, 2021, District of Minnesota judge Wilhelmina M. Wright issued a temporary restraining order (TRO) requested by the ACLU on behalf of several journalists, including Goyette, which prevented some Minnesota law enforcement agencies from "arresting, threatening to arrest, or using physical force—including through use of flash bang grenades, non-lethal projectiles, riot batons, or any other means—directed against any person whom they know or reasonably should know is a Journalist . . . unless [law enforcement has] probable cause to believe that such individual has committed a crime."[74] Wright weighed newsgathering interests more heavily than those of law enforcement, namely, general dispersal orders.

On February 8, 2022, Wright approved a permanent injunction as part of a settlement agreed to by the Minnesota Department of Public Safety and the Minnesota State Patrol. The settlement included an $825,000 payout to members of the press attacked and injured by the state patrol, as well as requirements that the state patrol improve its training related to journalists and that all state troopers wear BWCs by June 2022, among other provisions.

Meanwhile, on June 10, 2020, Linda Tirado, a freelance journalist who permanently lost vision in one eye after being hit with a rubber bullet while covering the protests in Minneapolis, filed a lawsuit against Arradondo, Kroll, Harrington, Langer, and four unnamed police officers.[75] The complaint alleged that police tear-gassed Tirado even though her press credentials were clearly visible and she was allowed to photograph the protests because news media were exempt from the citywide curfew. Additionally, Tirado yelled "I'm press, I'm press" as the police fired tear gas at protesters and herself. The complaint also argued that Tirado did not break any laws and did not interfere with law enforcement activities. The complaint therefore argued that the police's actions were an affront to freedom of the press, contending that "the police must not shoot journalists reporting on civil protests. Journalists . . . cover the protests and capture any tactics employed by law enforcement. If the press is silenced, . . . nobody can see the police violence committed against citizens for exercising their First Amendment rights." Thus, the complaint asserted that police violated Tirado's First Amendment rights, among other claims.

Like the *Goyette* case, Tirado's lawsuit ended in a settlement, in this case after District of Minnesota chief judge John Tunheim had allowed Tirado's lawsuit to proceed on February 22, 2022. In his ruling, Tunheim found, among other conclusions, that "Plaintiff Tirado's experience as a journalist during the George Floyd protests and her injuries are serious and troubling. That numerous other journalists experienced similar, seemingly unjustified incidents involving less-lethal munitions and other measures is even more troubling, as the allegations plausibly suggest an unconstitutional custom carried out by MPD officers of targeting journalists for unlawful reprisals."[76] Additionally, prior to the settlement, the Minneapolis city attorney served subpoenas at the homes of at least three journalists in the Twin Cities, requesting information and materials related to Tirado's lawsuit and other incidents in the protests following Floyd's murder. While one reporter, Goyette, complied, two journalists, *Minnesota Reformer* deputy editor Max Nesterak and *Minneapolis Star Tribune* reporter Andy Mannix, contested the subpoenas, arguing that they were protected by the reporter's privilege and that the subpoenas inhibited their First Amendment right to gather and report news on law enforcement. Ultimately, the Minneapolis City Council approved a $640,000 settlement with Tirado on May 26, 2022, though the City of Minneapolis denied wrongdoing in reaching the settlement.

Police targeting the press with arrests, threats, and violence has also occurred in other contemporary contexts.[77] Perhaps most notably, on January 6, 2021, protests around the U.S. Capitol erupted into chaos as hundreds of President Trump's supporters forced their way into the Capitol Building. Earlier that morning, President Trump held a rally focused on unfounded claims of election fraud and calling on his supporters to protest the congressional certification of President-Elect Joe Biden's victory. The attack on the Capitol led to the deaths of five people, as well as additional injuries and property damage. Amid the chaos, *Washington Post* video journalist Zoeann Murphy "was detained alongside a colleague [*Post* video journalist Whitney Leaming] while documenting the ongoing riots" in Washington, D.C.[78] Murphy told the *Post* during a live interview that she and Learning were being surrounded by a group of Metropolitan Police Department officers using a technique called "kettling," in which police surround a group of people to prevent anyone from exiting. Independent journalist Talia Jane was also briefly detained in the kettle. Even after Murphy and Learning explained to police that they were members of the press, officers confirmed that they were under arrest for violating a curfew order in Washington, D.C. Eventually, police announced that they were releasing members of the press, after which the journalists continued covering the scene.

In recent decades, law enforcement also continued searches and seizures, as well as enforcing subpoenas, targeting journalists' and news organizations' homes, offices, and newsrooms; phone calls, phone records, emails, and email records; electronic devices, equipment, social media accounts, and location information; and sources, materials, and information. In May 2019, approximately ten San Francisco Police Department officers "banged" on the outer gate of the home of Bryan Carmody, a freelance journalist in the San Francisco Bay Area, attempting to break the gate with a crowbar and sledgehammer.[79] The SFPD executed one search warrant on his home and later a second at his office, seizing his confidential work materials, as well as his computers, cell phones, and other electronic devices. Five San Francisco County Superior Court judges ultimately quashed the warrants they had previously signed allowing for the searches of Carmody's home, office, and phone. The judges generally found that the searches were "breathtakingly broad" and that the SFPD had failed to inform them that Carmody was a freelance journalist.[80] The orders meant that investigators could not use any evidence obtained through the searches and also needed to return any property of Carmody. The judges also ordered that any sealed documents related to the warrants be released.

Newsroom searches, although rare, also still occurred in recent years.[81] For example, in December 2016 New Brunswick Police Department officers in New Jersey executed a search warrant at the *New Brunswick Today*'s offices.[82] The New Brunswick Water Utility, at the center of controversy in the community around allegations of not providing affordable access to safe drinking water, requested that police seize a water meter held by the newspaper as evidence of wrongdoing by the local agency. Detectives told *New Brunswick Today* employees that they were in possession of stolen property. The search warrant, signed by a judge, also would have allowed officers to seize "a memory card or other medium" connected to a recent broadcast discussing the meter and how it demonstrated illegal actions by the utility.

The federal government and law enforcement also obtained journalists' and news organizations' phone and email records, sometimes in cases related to leaks of classified government materials and subsequent federal prosecutions of the leakers under the Espionage Act of 1917 by the Obama and Trump administrations.[83] In 2013, the DOJ seized phone records from at least five numbers associated with Fox News, as well as the personal cell-phone number of Fox News reporter James Rosen.[84] The DOJ named him as a coconspirator in a government leak case against Stephen Jin-Woo Kim, a former State Department contractor. Rosen had protected Kim's identity after using him as a source for a 2009 story reporting that North Korea planned to respond to impending UN sanctions with another nuclear test. Kim ultimately pleaded guilty to one count of violating the Espionage Act in 2014 and was sentenced to thirteen months in prison.

Several cases of the government and law enforcement seizing journalists' phone and email records arose under the Trump administration, such as in 2018 when *New York Times* reporter Ali Watkins was swept up in the DOJ's investigation and prosecution of former U.S. Senate Select Committee on Intelligence director of security James A. Wolfe in connection to an investigation into "multiple unauthorized disclosures of information to one or more members of the news media."[85] Federal prosecutors seized several years' worth of Watkins's Verizon phone and Gmail records, though they did not obtain the content of the messages. The DOJ would later target *Washington Post*, CNN, and *New York Times* reporters, again secretly obtaining their phone and email records.[86]

Federal and state government have also obtained the contents of journalists' phone calls and emails. Federal agencies, in recording domestic phone calls made by the public,[87] may also monitor or record those made by journalists. The monitoring of journalists' phone calls is also possible at the local level, as evidenced by SFPD officers perhaps listening to Bryan Carmody's private calls through warrants of his cell phone.[88] In the case of Rosen, the DOJ obtained full emails from his Gmail account in addition to the phone records the department had also attained.

Law enforcement searches and seizures have also targeted members of the press's electronic devices and equipment, as evidenced in the targeting of Carmody, as well as journalists' social media accounts and location information. From 2017 through 2020, there were at least sixty-one incidents of journalists being subjected to "equipment searches & seizures" by law enforcement, often in connection to arrests.[89] For example, on June 20, 2020, Tulsa, Oklahoma, police officers arrested

Texas-based photojournalist Alan Pogue for "obstructing or interfering with an officer" outside a campaign rally held by President Trump
where he had been documenting arrests of demonstrators for the *Texas
Observer*.[90] The police report claimed that Pogue had followed officers
into a restricted area and refused to leave. Pogue, who was held in a
jail cell until being released on a $500 bond, countered that he obeyed
an officer's order to step back a few feet and identified himself as a
journalist with his business card and a wristband given to him after a
security screening. Law enforcement searched Pogue's cell phone and
camera bag, and also subsequently seized his camera equipment, memory cards, and more, holding them as evidence even after Pogue was
released from police custody. The camera equipment was held until
August 2020 when prosecutors decided not to pursue charges against
him. The Secret Service ultimately returned Pogue's smartphone, but
not until January 2021 after it had been transferred into FBI custody for
undisclosed reasons.

Law enforcement can also use subpoenas to target journalists' electronic devices, equipment, and social media accounts. For example, in
December 2019, the NYPD issued a subpoena seeking information from
New York Post reporter and police bureau chief Tina Moore's Twitter account.[91] The NYPD sought ISP addresses, emails, and other information
affiliated with the account as part of an investigation into the leaking of
crime-scene photos to Moore. It was later revealed that the photos were
given to Moore by freelance photographer Amr Alfiky, who was arrested
for disorderly conduct, despite explaining that he was a journalist, after
he refused to stop taking photographs of the crime scene. After Twitter
refused to comply with the subpoena and notified the *New York Post*, the
NYPD dropped the subpoena.

As in past eras, there have also been several recent cases of government and law enforcement seeking journalists' sources, materials, and
information, often in the course of targeting their homes, newsrooms,
devices, records, and more. Between 2017 and 2020, at least sixty-three
journalists and thirty-nine news organizations were implicated by subpoenas or other legal orders.[92] A particularly notable case arose a decade
earlier in 2006 when federal prosecutors issued a subpoena to freelance
blogger Joshua Wolf to appear before a grand jury.[93] Wolf had recorded a
protest in San Francisco during which an individual struck and seriously injured a police officer with a pipe. Although the video was not aired,
Wolf refused to turn it over. Wolf served 225 days in jail for contempt

after the U.S. Court of Appeals for the Ninth Circuit held that he could not claim the reporter's privilege for nonconfidential materials. Wolf was ultimately released after he agreed to post the video on his website, though it did not depict who had struck the officer.

In rare cases, journalists have served jail time for refusing to disclose their sources and being held in contempt, actions dating back to the nineteenth century. Perhaps the most notable example arose in 2005 when the D.C. Circuit upheld a ruling by the federal district court, which found *New York Times* reporter Judith Miller in contempt after she refused to appear before a federal grand jury investigating who had leaked the identity of CIA agent Valerie Plame.[94] Miller spent eighty-five days in prison before Lewis Libby, Dick Cheney's chief of staff, consented to letting Miller testify that she was the source of the leak.

Finally, journalists and news organizations, like the general public, also faced increased surveillance by the government and law enforcement in the 1980s–2020s.[95] Mass surveillance is made possible at the federal level through different legal mechanisms. Section 702 of the Foreign Intelligence Surveillance Act (FISA)[96] Amendments Act provides authority for the National Security Agency's (NSA) surveillance programs, which gained increased authority following the September 11 terrorist attacks.[97] Section 702 primarily authorizes the U.S. government to monitor electronic communications by non-U.S. citizens "reasonably believed to be located outside the United States" and to compel cooperation from "electronic communication service provider[s]." However, loopholes in Section 702 also allow the collection of U.S. persons' information because they may be connected to data acquisitions of foreigners, known as "backdoor" searches.

Connected to Section 702 is the U.S. Foreign Intelligence Surveillance Court (FISA Court), a secretive panel of eleven federal district court judges provided authority under FISA to approve monitoring, intelligence-related wiretapping, and other surveillance carried out by the FBI and other bodies domestically and abroad.[98] The FISA Court can issue "FISA warrants" allowing for electronic surveillance, physical searches, and other foreign intelligence investigative actions. To protect national security, the court does so in secret, meaning "outside the sort of adversarial judicial process that allows journalists and other targets of regular criminal warrants to eventually challenge their validity."[99]

Experts, including from the Committee to Protect Journalists (CPJ), have asserted that the NSA uses Section 702 and other legal mechanisms to target journalists. Furthermore, CPJ contended that Section 702 allows intelligence agencies to indefinitely store not only communications records, but also "huge amounts of the content of phone calls, texts, and emails."[100] The result is several negative effects on the press. A 2018 study found that journalists increasingly reported that their work had changed due to the "real or perceived threat of mass government surveillance," including under Section 702, making their work more challenging.[101] A related effect is the undermining of journalists' source relationships by damaging communications with sources and making it increasingly challenging to keep identities confidential.[102] Adding to concerns for journalists is that the "circumstances when the government might consider a journalist an agent of a foreign power" remain unclear, as does how law enforcement should handle information risking journalists' sources. Additionally, Section 702 provides federal agents the ability to "recreate a reporter's research, retrace a source's movements, and even retroactively listen in on communications that would otherwise have evaporated forever."

Amendments to Rule 41 of the Federal Rules of Criminal Procedure (Rule 41)[103] also implicate law enforcement's ability to search and surveil journalists.[104] The changes allow the FBI to access computers outside jurisdiction limitations, so long as agents obtain a warrant from a magistrate judge. Reporters Committee for Freedom of the Press (RCFP) fellows Victoria Baranetsky and Selina MacLaren argued that such changes "have an outsized impact on journalists," reasoning that the changes allow law enforcement to obtain remote access to computers where anonymization tools are used, a common practice used by reporters to maintain confidential-source relationships. Law enforcement can, therefore, not only view journalists' information but also remotely manipulate their computer. Additionally, an officer can use such access to impersonate the journalist who owns the device, leading to negative effects arising from police impersonation of the press.

Finally, national security letters (NSLs) are administrative orders through which the FBI is able to obtain certain phone and financial records without judicial oversight.[105] Such orders therefore provide law enforcement the power to compel the disclosure of customer records held by banks, telephone companies, ISPs, and others. What makes NSLs particularly problematic is that the subjects of the searches are prohibited from telling anyone that they received a letter, undermining oversight and transparency. Although the Second Circuit and Northern

District of California have previously held that NSL gag orders violate the First Amendment, the orders have still been used to acquire a significant amount of personal data, often secretly or beyond what is disclosed.

Freedom of the Press Foundation executive director Trevor Timm called NSLs a key tool for surveillance of journalists by the federal government because they allow the FBI to circumvent the DOJ policies regarding subpoenaing journalists "with absolutely no court oversight."[106] Although it is unclear how many journalists have been targeted by NSLs, the federal government admitted in redacted inspector-general reports to using NSLs on unnamed *New York Times* and *Washington Post* reporters during President George W. Bush's administration. In 2014, *Washington Post* reporter Barton Gellman revealed that his phone records had been obtained through an NSL.[107]

Surveillance of the press and public can also be conducted by state and local law enforcement, namely, through new and evolving technologies that raise privacy and other concerns. One type of technology is facial recognition, which has been increasingly employed by police, including in connection to BWCs.[108] Civil liberties and privacy advocates have raised several concerns with facial recognition technology, including that it "provides government with unprecedented power to track people going about their daily lives."[109] Another concern is that it has "algorithmic bias," often returning more false matches for Black than white people, which can result in police harassment, false arrests, and other forms of discrimination and profiling.[110] Conversely, some in law enforcement contend that the technology provides a useful tool in maintaining public safety. Nevertheless, several cities have banned police use of facial recognition software, including San Francisco, Oakland, and Berkeley, California.

Another area of evolving technology raising privacy and security concerns is the Internet of Things. IoT devices collect sensitive information, including financial account numbers, health information, precise geolocation, and more.[111] These devices, because they are connected to the internet, are also susceptible to cyberattacks and hacking. Nevertheless, police across the United States have begun implementing IoT devices.[112] One use is "smart" firearms, which record data every time the gun is fired, among several other examples. Additionally, there have been efforts by police to gain more access to video recordings, such as those collected by Ring, a doorbell-camera firm, which can be stored indefinitely. Last, law enforcement collect data, including through "person-based predictive policing," that allows police to obtain information about people that are perceived as at risk or are seen as more likely to commit a crime.

Why the Press and Police May Be in Conflict

What accounts for the police targeting the press, intentionally or unintentionally, whether at protests, in relation to investigations, or otherwise in recent years? The answer is multifaceted, with one explanation being that such interactions are a carryover from the previous era of adversarial relations between the press and police, as well as other time periods that also saw law enforcement target journalists, especially people of color.[113] The current societal context also provides clues as to why the police continue to target journalists, perhaps even to a greater extent than in previous years. Stemming once again from the 1960s–'70s, the continued emphasis on law and order, as well as increased police resources and presence, means a greater likelihood of the press getting caught up, purposefully or not, in law enforcement actions. Partisanship, polarization, and decreasing trust all also play a role. Antipress rhetoric and actions can influence police officials' and officers' views of, and attitudes toward, the press, in some cases even emboldening individuals to target journalists. Finally, and perhaps most fundamentally, police targeting the press falls as part of larger cases and efforts by law enforcement and government targeting protesters and other members of the public, meaning it is not just journalists who face violence, threats, arrests, and more.

The very nature of the press-police relationship, given their respective roles, necessarily means that conflict can arise. For example, in the course of their daily activities, the police may not want the press to cover certain actions or events, potentially leading to actions like threats or violence in certain cases, especially at chaotic scenes like protests, to prevent certain reporting. Ironically, however, as such attacks continue, press criticism of police only further grows, creating a cycle, of sorts, in which police attitudes may further sour toward news organizations and journalists. In other cases, when the press does cover something, police officials may want access to their information, potentially leading to searches and seizures or subpoenas. The fundamental role of the press, namely, covering dangerous stories and holding the powerful accountable, necessarily increases the risk of being targeted with arrests, violence, or legal orders.

Here, First Amendment theory helps explain why the press and police may be at odds, namely, by illuminating the importance of the concept of the news media as independent of government, free and even encouraged to hold public officials and institutions accountable to the public. One can trace the idea of press independence from government back to the formation of the United States and the drafting of the First Amendment. As early as 1768, Samuel Adams expressed the need for an independent press, writing, "There is nothing so fretting and vexatious, nothing so justly terrible to tyrants, and their tools and abettors, as a free press."[114] James Madison wrote in 1800, "In every State, probably, in the Union, the press has exerted a freedom in canvassing the merits and measures of public men."[115] Scholars have also articulated these ideas, including David Anderson, the Fred & Emily Marshall Wulff Centennial Chair Emeritus in Law at the University of Texas, who wrote that one of the "essential roles" of the Press Clause is to "protect the press from a concerted government campaign to intimidate or control it."[116]

Connected to the press's independence from the government and, by extension, the police, is the normative responsibility of holding public officials and entities accountable, often referred to as the "watchdog" role. Although present in the founders' respective views of what a "free press" meant in the growing republic, the ideal of the press holding the powerful accountable would more fully develop in the twentieth century. In 1917, Zechariah Chafee Jr., a Harvard law professor for nearly forty-one years and champion of free-speech rights, wrote, "Truth can be sifted out from falsehood only if the government is vigorously and constantly cross-examined."[117] In 1984, Jerome H. Skolnick, a criminal justice expert who had a long career as a professor at New York University and the University of California–Berkeley, and Candace McCoy, a professor of criminal justice at the City University of New York, directly applied the press's purpose of holding officials accountable to police, contending that the press can, and should, inform the public about law enforcement, therefore providing accountability and perhaps leading to reform.[118]

In First Amendment theory, the press is often referred to as the "Fourth Estate," suggesting that its role is similar to a fourth branch of government, while remaining independent.[119] The earliest reference was by Thomas Carlyle in 1840 when he wrote that Edmund Burke, a member of English Parliament from 1766 to 1794, had said, "There were Three Estates in Parliament; but, in the Reporters' Gallery yonder, there sat a Fourth Estate more important far than they all."[120] The Fourth Estate concept emphasizes the press's role of holding government accountable, giving the press "a special position within the democratic process."[121]

In 1977, Vincent Blasi, the Corliss Lamont Professor of Civil Liberties at Columbia Law School and free-speech theorist, referred to the watchdog role as the "checking value" of the press.[122] He contended that "a primary purpose of the freedoms of speech and press . . . [is] to check government as a way of preventing abuses." He added that "one of the most important values attributed to a free press by eighteenth-century . . . thinkers was that of checking the inherent tendency of government officials to abuse the power entrusted to them." Blasi provided several reasons the checking value needs to be protected, including that the press is the only institution with the capacity to properly hold government accountable, a crucially important function given that government abuse of power is "an especially serious evil" and that the government can affect the public through "its capacity to employ legitimized violence."

The press as a watchdog also arises under First Amendment theory in that the press must serve as an "instrument of the search for truth."[123] John H. Garvey, former president of the Catholic University of America and a faculty member at several universities, including Notre Dame, and Frederick Schauer, a law professor at the University of Virginia, argued that the "earliest basis for the defense of . . . freedom of the press . . . [and] likely also the most enduring . . . is free speech as the instrument of the search for truth." Ultimately, First Amendment theory has developed over time to emphasize the press's role in holding government, including the police, accountable.

The concept of the press holding government accountable is, however, largely at odds with some tenets of criminal justice theory. In 1964, Herbert L. Packer, a law professor at Stanford University from 1956 to 1969, laid out the "Crime Control Model," based on the premise that "the repression of criminal conduct is by far the most important function to be performed by the criminal process," with the failure to do so resulting in a "breakdown of public order."[124] The model encourages increased police and prosecutorial powers, with a tougher stance taken toward crime over the protection of individual liberties. Although the Crime Control Model is not the only set of values driving policing and has been the subject of criticism, it remains a key consideration in law enforcement, with many jurisdictions increasing police power. This model's advocacy of increased authority puts it at odds with the values of the press, in that police may attempt to limit the ability of the press to hold law enforcement accountable. Furthermore, as has been mentioned, police activities that specifically target journalists and news organizations further put the press and police at odds.

A final explanation for why contentiousness exists is that professions often seek to establish and protect their boundaries, authority, and autonomy. Throughout their respective histories, the press's and police's "boundaries" were "established, sustained, enlarged, policed, breached, and sometimes erased in the defense, pursuit, or denial of epistemic authority" and their autonomy.[125] In this way, the press and police sought to establish "jurisdictional boundaries," falling as part of "a larger context" of an interdependent system of professions whose "history of jurisdictional disputes . . . is the real, the determining history of the professions."[126] Such efforts by the news media and law enforcement to delineate their professions continue in the present. The press, for example, aims to be the source of news and information, necessarily "keeping out non-journalistic informational actors" like public relations experts.[127] At the same time, police, unlike in some past eras, seek to maintain their authority as the institution investigating crimes and ultimately apprehending suspects. The press can go to a crime scene, but are kept at an arm's length in terms of access to locations and to information. The creation of boundaries by each entity therefore necessarily means separating from other institutions. In some cases, this emphasis on independence can lead to coexistence, as each are able to accomplish their own purposes and functions without interfering with the other. However, at other times, this separation can lead to division, including if one entity intrudes upon or targets the other, leading to contentiousness.

Effects Arising from Contentiousness

As detailed earlier, press accountability of police carries enormous benefits, including holding the powerful accountable and, in some cases, contributing to change and reform. In the case of Kalven's reporting, he helped expose the truth of law enforcement actions, as well as changes like the adoption of BWCs. However, press accountability of police can also lead to negative effects, including creating antagonism with law enforcement. One way this can play out is that journalists and news organizations can face legal action related to their coverage and investigations, undermining the press's ability to carry out its important functions in the face of lengthy and costly legal battles. For example, Kalven's reporting did not come without pushback from Van Dyke. At a 2017 hearing, Daniel Herbert, an attorney for the officer, alleged that Kalven had received leaked documents from the now defunct Independent Police Review Authority, which obtained protected statements made by Van Dyke following the shooting. Circuit Court of Cook County judge Vincent M. Gaughan quashed a subpoena brought by Van Dyke and ruled that Kalven did not have to testify about his reporting. Although the decision was hailed by some observers as a First Amendment victory, Kalven contended that the subpoena should have been quashed immediately and that the proceedings affected his credibility.

Another potential area of litigation is defamation lawsuits, such as in May 2018 when Carroll, Iowa, police officer Jacob Smith sued the *Carroll Daily Times Herald*.[128] Reporter Jared Strong had spent months gathering information about Smith, including by obtaining records and conducting interviews, in order to investigate claims that Smith was having inappropriate relationships with underage girls. District of Iowa judge Thomas Bice ultimately dismissed Smith's defamation lawsuit, ruling that the articles published by the newspaper were accurate. However, the $140,000 in legal expenses not covered by libel insurance put the paper's future in doubt, as did a decrease in subscribers who doubted or criticized Strong's reporting.

Another negative effect that can arise from the press providing critical reporting of law enforcement is the loss of access and source relationships with law enforcement due to negative reactions. In several instances, police departments, officials, and officers have pushed against press coverage of misconduct, wrongdoing, or violence, calling it biased or inaccurate.[129] Such claims can undermine the press's credibility if members of the public believe the police's narrative over that of the news media. Furthermore, police departments across the United States spend millions on public relations and marketing efforts, hoping to manipulate or otherwise influence the news.[130] Independent journalist Jeremy Borden perhaps put it best when he wrote that the "relationship between the media and police is naturally fraught with tension and a central ethical quandary: Reporters rely on police to serve as sources on crime and other public safety issues, even as they function as a check on police power."[131] He added, "So long as police accountability is an issue, the relationship between law enforcement and the press will be tense."

Law enforcement targeting the press—intentionally or not through arrests, use of force, threats, searches, seizures, subpoenas, and surveillance—also raises several significant effects. Although such actions can help law enforcement accomplish its goals and functions, they also lead to problematic negative effects, especially for the press. First, journalists face physical harm when being arrested or detained by police. Physical danger is only heightened when law enforcement tackles journalists or uses chemical agents, rubber bullets, flashbangs, riot batons, and more. Second, police targeting the press limit journalists' ability to gather news as they must instead handle being threatened, detained, arrested, harmed, or targeted by a warrant or subpoena. Government interference into the press's important purposes and functions is only worsened when journalists and news organizations face, and go through, potentially lengthy and costly litigation following arrests at events like protests, as was the case for at least four journalists across the United States after being arrested or detained at the protests around the death of George Floyd.[132] Court action further limits the press's ability to carry out its important functions, especially if it causes financial strain or extended absences from journalistic responsibilities. Third, the risk of arrests, use of force, threats, and more, as well as possible legal action stemming from the practices, may also lead some journalists to avoid covering an otherwise important story, creating a "chilling effect" on the press. Finally, police targeting the press can undermine reporters' credibility and source relationships, especially if confidential information is uncovered, legally or not, by police. These actions can also create antipress sentiment as the public sees the news media as the focus of law enforcement efforts often coinciding with targeting criminals.

Police departments, officials, and officers are also affected when journalists and news organizations become the target of police actions. Although law enforcement may be able to further its purposes and functions through targeting the press, the benefits of such practices are undermined if police could have used a different tactic to get the needed information or did not need the information at all. Targeting the press may also shift law enforcement's focus and attention from other important activities and interests. Additionally, departments, officials, and officers may face consequences, including First and Fourth Amendment lawsuits by the press, internal punishments, and shifts in public opinion about policing. Finally, attempts to target the press may also embolden officers in problematic ways, leading to potential cases of misconduct or overreach.

Perhaps most important, law enforcement targeting the news media, like press accountability of police, implicates the press-police relationship and the public. By intentionally or unintentionally targeting journalists and news organizations, police interfere with press purposes and functions, therefore straining their relationship and leading to greater contentiousness. Significantly, if the press is unable to do its job due to law enforcement actions, the public loses its source of information and ability to hold police accountable. At a protest, for example, this can mean that important racial justice messages are not fully communicated and disseminated to the larger public or that law enforcement actions harming members of the public are not held to account. Furthermore, if law enforcement is focused on the press, or the consequences of doing so, officials' and officers' attention may be diverted, meaning they are not fully serving other people or areas needing attention. But despite these negative effects, police targeting the press has continued in the 1980s–2020s, echoing, rather than moving away from, the adversarial 1960s–'70s, necessitating the reevaluation of the use of these practices.

Impersonation and Media Ride-Alongs Pass Century Mark
Amid the balancing of cooperative coexistence and contentiousness between the press and police, impersonation and media ride-alongs largely reflected trends dating back to the nineteenth century. Significantly, police impersonation of the press and press impersonation of police continued to prompt concerns and criticism as they had in previous eras, though it did not eliminate either practice, as they continued through the present. Media ride-alongs, on the other hand, continued in ways in which the perceived benefits of the practice overshadowed its negative effects. It was not until the twenty-first century that criticism of the practice would more fully arise and even to this day remains inadequate, despite negative effects arising for more than a century.

Police Impersonation of the Press
One year after the revelations about the CIA's use and impersonation of journalists, the agency, in 1974, secretly created a loophole allowing the agency to pose as or use journalists under "extraordinary circumstances" with "specific approval" from the CIA director.[133] The loophole was not revealed until 1996 when the *Washington Post* reported that an independent task force of the Council on Foreign Relations proposed reevaluating the limits on the use of "covers" during clandestine activities. Then-CIA director John Deutch told Congress that such a review

was not necessary because the CIA "already had the power to use U.S. reporters as spies," revealing the loophole.

Nevertheless, government at all levels did not eliminate police impersonation of the press, even by the CIA.[134] Following the 1996 revelations, Congress passed a law prohibiting the use of journalists "as agents or assets" for intelligence purposes.[135] However, the president or CIA director can get around the statute through "a written determination that the waiver is necessary to address the overriding national security interest of the United States." Furthermore, the statute stops short of prohibiting impersonation of the press, though it shows that Congress could pass such a law. Also in 1996, President Bill Clinton signed into law the Intelligence Authorization Act of 1997, which, among other provisions, allowed the CIA to use and pose as American journalists when "necessary to address the overriding national security interest of the United States" or when members of the press voluntarily cooperate.[136]

The continuation of police impersonation of the press meant that several negative effects dating back decades also continued into the twenty-first century. First, the 1980s–2020s saw renewed concerns about the undermining of the press's credibility, including in cases where police used impersonation of the press in standoff and hostage cases. In 1980, three Colorado Springs policemen posed as members of a news team to end a standoff with Larry Olsen, who threatened to kill himself and any police officer he saw.[137] After Olsen said he would give up only if he could speak to "the media," the police borrowed a television camera from a local reporter and convinced Olsen to surrender. Deputy police chief Vic Morris said the ruse was used "as a last resort" after Olsen threatened to kill himself and fired four or five rounds from his pistol at officers. But following the episode, KKTV-TV general manager George Jeffrey argued that impersonation "would damage the credibility of reporters" and their ability to report on police. KRDO-TV news director Lloyd Wright added, "We don't impersonate police officers and we don't want them impersonating us."

Recent decades also saw continued instances of police using impersonation of the press to conduct investigations and surveillance, once more raising concerns about undermining the press's credibility.[138] The most widely covered case of local police impersonating the press during this time arose in May 1984 when two men wearing T-shirts and jackets claimed to be a local television cameraman and interviewer as they approached six individuals participating in a "smoke in" protest of state drug laws in Morristown, New Jersey.[139] However, the cameraman was actually a deputy sheriff and the interviewer an assistant county prosecutor. Although the participants were not smoking an illegal substance, they were charged for use of a "look-alike" drug, with the footage and interviews obtained by the undercover sheriff and prosecutor used as evidence. The *New York Times* argued that the actions undermined confidence in not only the press but also the police, resulting in losing "an essential attribute of their value to the community." New Jersey attorney general Irwin I. Kimmelman later admitted in a letter to state prosecutors that police impersonation of the press leads to decreased trust and confidence in the news media.

Second, the 1980s–2010s saw police impersonation of the press continue to undermine reporters' source relationships.[140] In 1986, a woman in Anaheim, California, told the *Los Angeles Times* that she had been arrested by a detective posing as a cameraman for KNBC-TV.[141] The unnamed detective arrested the woman, a prostitution suspect, after showing her a set of counterfeit press credentials seized years earlier by the police in a forgery case. The result, as argued by the *Times* editorial board, was undermining "the confidence and trust" that reporters rely on when forging source relationships. The editorial board added, "That trust is weakened, and every news organization's credibility is undermined, if people get an impression that the press is working for the police, or at least that they cannot tell whether they are talking to reporters or police officers. Facing that, many people will stop talking. And that, in the long run, hurts the press, police and other institutions in a democracy that depends on an informed public and watchdog press to keep the system functioning effectively." And that is exactly how the case played out. The woman explained that the impersonation "upset" her and made her less willing to talk to news outlets, thinking they may be police officers.

Third, editors, reporters, and others expressed concern about the undermining of the press's ability to gather news and press independence.[142] In 1998, NYPD officer Joseph Locurto held a news conference in his lawyer's office to apologize for appearing in blackface during a parade.[143] However, Locurto did not realize that among the reporters was a police sergeant posing as a journalist as part of his investigation into Locurto. The sergeant was taking notes, which led to a report filed with the Internal Affairs Bureau. Locurto was summarily fired, leading to a lawsuit for wrongful termination, which ultimately ended with the Second Circuit ruling against Locurto.[144] Upon learning that the sergeant had posed as a journalist, New York Civil Liberties Union director Norman Siegel, who represented Locurto, denounced the actions, arguing they threatened to chill First Amendment activity and press independence.

A case of police impersonation of the press from 2008 demonstrated how the practice undermines public trust, source relationships, news gathering, and independence. The case arose when a North Carolina sheriff's deputy posed as a *Newsweek* reporter in an attempt to "coax an anonymous source out of a local newspaper journalist."[145] *Jacksonville (NC) Daily News* reporter Lindell Kay handed over the phone number of her confidential source, Robert Sharpe, who was an intern at the local district attorney's office. Kay explained that the source was okay with her providing his phone number to *Newsweek* because he was used to speaking with national media outlets. This example therefore represented a final, and important, purpose of police impersonation of the press: obtaining information law enforcement would otherwise be unable to get or receive. However, after being charged with embezzlement and larceny, Sharpe had "harsh words for *The Daily News*." He said, "I'm supposed to be a confidential source. They screwed me over and offered no help or assistance afterwards. I put my trust in this organization." Although Sharpe later apologized to the news organization after learning about the impersonation, the case demonstrated that he felt he could no longer trust the news outlet, or others, to protect his identity.

Fourth, police impersonation of the press continued to strain the press-police relationship. In August 1987, the "faith of the press" in law enforcement in Indianapolis was undermined when hostage negotiators posed as reporters in order to enter the home of a woman who threatened police officers with a rifle after turning away health inspectors.[146] As in other standoffs leading to impersonation, the woman requested to speak to a member of the press. Law enforcement then posed as reporters from "the Star-News" doing a human-interest story to get inside, ultimately convincing the woman to surrender. The *Indianapolis Star* acknowledged that law enforcement was "well-intentioned" in posing as reporters, but that the police "did a disservice to both [institutions]. . . . In a society that has freedom of the press at its core, police are not expected to impersonate the press under any circumstances. . . . And certainly reporters do not go around claiming to be policemen. That would be violating the law as well as journalistic ethics." The newspaper editorial board added, "It may be no crime to impersonate a reporter, but it will not happen again if Indianapolis police seek the continued respect of the press."

The straining of the press-police relationship was further evidenced in that law enforcement officials sometimes called for or changed department or agency policies, issued apologies, or both. For example, in 1999, an undercover police officer in Westminster, California, used a fake AP credential to surveil a protest over a Vietnamese store's display.[147] Westminster police chief James Cook issued an apology to the AP and reprimanded the officer for using impersonation. Cook also told the AP that he was reviewing policies regarding impersonating journalists, though he did not indicate if any had been or would be changed.

Finally, examples from recent decades, including two high-profile examples involving the FBI and CIA, further demonstrated how and why journalists face greater physical danger as a result of police impersonation of the press.[148] One case arose in 2000 during the highly publicized civil trial against Aryan Nations activist and leader Richard Butler.[149] The lawsuit was filed by the Southern Poverty Law Center on behalf of Victoria Keenan and her son, who were returning from a wedding when their car backfired near the Aryan Nations compound in Idaho, leading Aryan Nations security guards to chase and shoot at the Keenans, striking their vehicle several times and shooting out a tire, causing the vehicle to careen into a ditch. The guards then assaulted the Keenans. More than sixty journalists from various local and national outlets descended upon the small town of Coeur d'Alene to cover the trial, which ended in a $6.3 million jury verdict against the Aryan Nations and Butler for being grossly negligent in selecting and supervising the security guards.

During the trial, Captain Ben Wolfinger, a spokesperson for the sheriff's department, granted seven press passes to FBI and Bureau of Alcohol, Tobacco, Firearms, and Explosives agents, who were monitoring the protests outside the courtroom. Tom Clouse, a reporter for the *Spokane (WA) Spokesman-Review*, uncovered the plan, which he believed was to allow agents to photograph suspected members of the Aryan Nations. Clouse identified several clues that the photographers were not who they claimed to be, including that they promised two- to five-dollar prints for those they had photographed and asked people to pose for the photos. The agents were also using brand-new equipment with barcode stickers still on it, and when asked what organization they worked for, they responded with names different from those appearing on their credentials. Where the ruse became especially problematic, and dangerous, for the journalists at the scene was one of the FBI agents wearing a media badge identifying him as Mike Gordon, a real photographer for the *Spokesman-Review*. Gordon raised the concern that "now all the Aryans will think I am a federal agent," making him a potential target. Clouse added that the agents were "putting us in danger. The Aryan Nation is not somebody you want to mess with."

Two years later, the death of a well-known foreign correspondent demonstrated the significant danger created by impersonation of the press, in this case by the CIA. In 2002, Daniel Pearl, the South Asia correspondent for the *Wall Street Journal*, was kidnapped and killed by extremists in Pakistan.[150] Pearl had been seeking interviews as part of his research linking Pakistani extremists with Richard C. Reid, the man arrested after taking a shoe bomb aboard an international flight in 2001. However, Pearl was unaware that the militants he wished to interview thought he was working undercover for the CIA. Although not confirmed, the blurring of the lines between the press and law enforcement likely cost Pearl his life. To top it off, militants gave the video of the execution to a federal agent who they thought was a reporter, further demonstrating the gravity of police impersonation of the press.

Despite the concerns and negative effects arising from police impersonation of the press, it continued into the twenty-first century, including two revelations in 2014 of the FBI impersonating a reporter and documentary filmmakers. The first instance arose in 2007 when Timberline High School near Seattle received several anonymous bomb threats, prompting daily evacuations of the school.[151] Local law enforcement, unable to identify the source of the threats, called the cybercrime experts at the FBI's Seattle Division to investigate. An FBI special agent summarily contacted the anonymous social media account tied to the threats and identified himself as an AP "staff publisher," requesting the social media user's input into a fake AP news story, suggesting the user had outsmarted the authorities. Unbeknownst to the user, the fake article contained "Computer and Internet Protocol Address Verifier" malware, which, once opened, allowed the FBI to track the suspect's location. Within a few hours, the FBI made an arrest. However, the impersonation was not uncovered until 2014 when an ACLU technologist discovered the FBI's impersonation of an AP reporter in documents released earlier in a Freedom of Information Act (FOIA) request by the Electronic Frontier Foundation.

The second case arose when supporters of Nevada cattle rancher Cliven Bundy clashed with police after the U.S. Bureau of Land Management sought to enforce court orders requiring Bundy to pay withheld grazing fees for his use of federally owned land.[152] Gregory Burleson, one of Bundy's supporters, was sentenced to sixty-eight years in prison for his role in the armed confrontation. During Burleson's trial, FBI special agent Charles Johnson testified that FBI agents had posed as documentary filmmakers to lure suspects into speaking with them. The testimony matched court records showing that FBI agents had impersonated documentary filmmakers, with the DOJ later acknowledging that the FBI did so.

In letters to the DOJ and FBI, the RCFP and the AP raised the concerns found throughout the history of police impersonation of the press, including that it undermines the press's credibility, independence, and ability to gather news and report on law enforcement.[153] Affidavits from two documentary filmmakers also highlighted the potential effects of the impersonation, including undermining public trust in documentary filmmakers and making it more difficult to forge source relationships with members of a community.[154] Filmmaker Abby Ellis went so far as to argue that several of her sources became more distrustful of the media, requiring her to persuade them that she was not working for the government. According to Ellis, some individuals refused to speak to her, thinking she was an undercover FBI agent. Filmmaker David Byars similarly argued that some of his sources likely would have confronted him with physical violence had they thought he was a federal agent.

Press Impersonation of Police

The 1980s–'90s saw a resurgence in documented examples of press impersonation of police, which largely continued trends dating back to the nineteenth century. The most widely covered instance of press impersonation of police, perhaps in its entire history, arose in 1983 when *Potomac News* bureau chief Dave Roman visited the Mecklenburg Detention Center in Virginia to interview death-row inmate John LeVasseur, who was convicted of the 1982 slaying of a Woodbridge woman.[155] Roman alleged that William Britton, the former superintendent of the Prince William–Manassas Regional Jail, provided him with a fake badge and told him he had been sworn in for one day as a sheriff's sergeant. This highly publicized example is significant for three reasons. First, Roman impersonated the police by using a fake badge, suggesting another way in which the press can accomplish impersonation. Second, law enforcement aided in the impersonation, therefore undermining the independence of both institutions, as their purposes and functions overlap in problematic ways. Last, the case marked another instance of a reporter facing punishment or legal action for the impersonation.[156] Roman, Britton, and another jail official were each arrested for their role in the ruse. A Virginia state judge convicted Roman of impersonating an officer, a misdemeanor under state law, imposing a $500 fine and a six-month suspended jail sentence. An appellate court later increased the fine, after which Roman elected to pay $1,000 and begin serving the jail sentence.

During this time period, reporters were also the subject of law enforcement investigations amid allegations of impersonating the police. In 1991, Albuquerque, New Mexico, law enforcement investigated KGGM-TV reporter Bryan Glazer for allegedly impersonating a police officer in order to obtain the address of a security guard, Jerry Archuleta, who fatally shot a robber attempting to hold up a credit union.[157] Archuleta's supervisor, Jackie Garner, asserted that he gave Archuleta's home address and phone number "to a man who telephoned and identified himself as an Albuquerque police Detective Sorenson." Garner alerted Archuleta that a detective would likely visit his home, though a reporter and cameraperson arrived instead. The Albuquerque Police Department, who said there was no "Detective Sorenson" on their force, identified Glazer as the reporter following a news segment in which he attempted to interview Archuleta at his home, which was not listed in the latest phone book and not otherwise publicly available. Glazer denied the report, contending that he had identified himself as a reporter. If it turned out to be a false allegation, the example would demonstrate how the police could make a mistake that would implicate a reporter and lead to an investigation. If the allegation turned out to be true, it would provide an instance of a reporter identifying himself as a police officer in order to gather news, though still leading to the same consequence of facing an investigation and potential legal action.

A particularly noteworthy case in 1999 further showed the range of ways in which press impersonation of police can take place.[158] Channel 5 reporter Derrol Nail, accompanied by a cameraperson and Allison Fraser, a "real" police officer, knocked on the door of Ava Van de Water, not knowing she was a *Palm Beach (FL) Post* reporter and columnist, and identified himself as a detective. Nail also wore a fake police badge and asked if he could enter her home, which Van de Water allowed. Upon entering, Nail summarily identified himself as a reporter, prompting Van de Water to call the police.

In addition to the odd set of circumstances, this case also demonstrated two negative effects of press impersonation of police. First, it represents a clear case of undermining the independence of both the press and the police. Dena Peterson, a police spokesperson, attempted to defend the impersonation by explaining that the department was "assisting the media in educating the public." When one institution aims to help the other conduct impersonation or seeks to benefit from the other doing so, it results in one or both institutions working toward the purposes and functions of the other without accomplishing at least some of their own. The result, rather than educating the public, is that both the press and the police fail to properly serve their communities. Second, resulting from the impersonation was the undermining of the press's and police's credibility and public trust. Van de Water said that given the circumstances, she did not know whether Fraser was actually a real officer or a reporter. Bob Jordan, the general manager of the NBC affiliate, later apologized for the impersonation, acknowledging the problematic nature of the practice.

The 2000s–2010s saw another decrease in instances of press impersonation of police, though two allegations of the practice demonstrate that the practice may still be surreptitiously used. In 2001, an accusation arose that an unknown television reporter had impersonated a Bureau of Alcohol, Tobacco, Firearms, and Explosives agent in order to gain access to the site of the September 11 terrorist attacks.[159] NYPD commissioner Bernard Kerik told the *Akron (OH) Beacon Journal* that he was "so fed up with unauthorized forays into lower Manhattan" that he threatened to arrest any individual for trespassing, suggesting why the practice was rarely used or infrequently reported by the press.

In 2004, the *Inland Valley Daily Bulletin* in Ontario, California, reported an accusation that a *Rancho Cucamonga Voice* reporter had impersonated a police officer.[160] The reporter had allegedly called the San Bernardino County Coroner's Office and identified himself as "a member of a law enforcement agency" in order to obtain information on the cause of death of a teenager who was fatally shot by a security guard. Although the San Bernardino Sheriff's Department announced that it would not investigate the accusation, this instance nevertheless demonstrated that a reporter, by identifying himself as a police officer, sought to gather news, continuing the practice first seen more than a century earlier.

Like in the 1960s–'70s, what accounts for the lack of documented instances of press impersonation of police? The reasons remain largely the same as the past era, namely, the illegality of the practice, combined with its potential effects and consequences, likely deters journalists from using the practice, or at least admitting to doing so. Certainly, it also precludes journalists from discussing the prevalence of the practice. Nevertheless, the previous reporting suggests that like in the 1960s–'70s, the practice is still used covertly. And it remains possible that the press may, in some limited cases, still report on the use of impersonation of police. One explanation for why such reporting would continue to exist is the idea of "paradigm repair." Coined in 1985,[161] this growing body of research posits that "only in those brief moments when the journalistic paradigm is breached that the paradigm really comes into view and that paradigm repair is performed."[162] Applied to press impersonation of police, it is possible that there are occasions where reporters admit to errors of judgment or ethical lapses, such as by breaking the law in impersonating a police officer, in order to rearticulate institutional values, norms, and practices. This was evident in past eras when members of the press would condemn impersonation of police, citing how it can undermine the credibility of the news media as a whole. It remains to be seen whether press impersonation sees a resurgence in use or coverage, but at the very least, the clues that exist demonstrate the practice can continue, raising notable negative effects.

Media Ride-Alongs

In 1999, the U.S. Supreme Court ruled in *Wilson v. Layne* that the presence of a *Washington Post* reporter and photographer during the execution of arrest warrants in the Wilson family's home violated their Fourth Amendment rights. The Court found that unless members of the press aid the police in the execution of a warrant, or obtain consent, they cannot enter a private residence as part of a ride-along. The ruling prompted concern less so about the problems arising from media ride-alongs and more so, from the press and police, that it would mark the end to the practice or, at the very least, would prevent reporters or camera crews from detailing a significant amount of police duties.[163]

However, media ride-alongs not only survived after *Wilson* but also remained largely unchanged, following trends dating back to the first patrol wagons more than a century earlier. As in each previous era, journalists continued to receive invitations or permission to ride with police officers and officials, suggesting once more that police expected something in return for granting access to members of the press. For example, a June 4, 1989, story by the *Orange County Register* quoted an unnamed reporter who praised an Irvine, California, police officer for being "very helpful in allowing me to ride along on his Friday night shift."[164] The give-and-take nature of media ride-alongs arising from the police providing, and in some cases encouraging, access to their vehicles was articulated by *Daily News of Los Angeles* writer Jim Benson when he wrote that media ride-alongs cause a "predicament" for journalists, namely, that they can get increased access to law enforcement, but are also "pressured to write the story a certain way because you have to be back the next day with these same people."[165]

This would play out when reporters used media ride-alongs to cover their experiences, as well as detailing police activities and reporting about police officers.[166] Through such coverage, reporters often included praise or, at the very least, defenses of the police even amid controversy in a community.[167] In 2016, *Issaquah & Sammamish (WA) Reporter* journalist Nicole Jennings detailed her first ride-along with local police, which gave her "a glimpse of the daily life of a law enforcement officer, and the challenges that those charged with ensuring the community's safety face routinely."[168] Jennings quoted Officer Chase Goddard, who contended that people "sometimes criticize [officers'] decisions later." Jennings wrote that she agreed with Goddard that "it is much easier for a person on the outside to make judgments in hindsight than for the officer at the time who is alone, under pressure and facing a threat." Jennings added that she had "a newfound respect for law enforcement" and was "beyond grateful that there are people who are willing to make putting their lives on the line a career so that the rest of us can sleep soundly at night."

Although Jennings's reporting may have been accurate, she still pushed against or dismissed concerns raised by the public by highlighting her positive ride-along experience on a single shift. Concerns arise in her case and others when the alternative critical view of law enforcement is not fully fleshed out or is too quickly dismissed. As in past eras, cases of praise and positive coverage, often coming across as almost PR-like messages, significantly outnumbered examples of such critical coverage over the past four decades. This suggests that the press was not *providing* the public a full or accurate view of law enforcement, including because media ride-alongs generally present the point of view of the police. And because the police may have acted differently, intentionally or not, due to the press's presence, journalists also may not have *received* an accurate view of policing. This also raises questions about whether media ride-alongs are an effective means at getting the complete picture of law enforcement in a community, as well as holding police departments, officials, and officers accountable.

A related negative effect of the press providing the police predominantly favorable coverage is that the news media's goals and purposes becoming more closely aligned with those of law enforcement. More specifically, praise and positive coverage of policing helped improve the police's community relations. In fact, some reporters even helped the police accomplish their functions and actions, including searching for a suspect, tending to an injured man, and helping disperse a violent mob. Similarly, in the give-and-take nature of media ride-alongs, police also helped the press to cover news and human-interest stories. Although the police still had their own purposes and functions at heart, the result was still the two institutions' goals and actions beginning to overlap in problematic ways.

This is not to say that every media ride-along needs to result in critical coverage. It can be important and beneficial to show police activity in a community, whether something bad happened or not; it is part of the two institutions cooperatively coexisting. Additionally, there are certainly instances where detailing police actions can be newsworthy, such as the dangers faced by the police or if such actions had direct effects on the public. However, the almost complete absence of critical coverage suggests that even when a more negative view of police is needed and is, perhaps, witnessed on a ride-along, reporters may not be able to cover it or may choose not to risk straining the press-police relationship, therefore losing access to police vehicles, locations, information, and sources.

During this period, journalists also continued using media ride-alongs to cover news stories, including reporting on reckless driving, a topic of coverage through a media ride-along dating back to at least 1936.[169] Although such reporting contained less explicit praise of police than when reporters specifically undertook to report on their ride-along experience or on the police, it still generally cast law enforcement in, at worst, a neutral light by covering their actions and what was accomplished. Once again, such reporting, without a critical lens of whether these actions were in the best interest of the public, suggests reporting stemming from media ride-alongs may not provide a complete picture of law enforcement or what took place at a scene, therefore also failing to hold police accountable and instead aiding in community-relations efforts.

Recent decades also saw the third purpose for why journalists participated in ride-alongs: aiding police with law enforcement interests. Perhaps the best example came in 2004 when a newspaper in Corpus Christi, Texas, agreed to work with the police in a sting operation targeting individuals soliciting prostitutes. *Caller-Times* reporter Venessa Santos-Garza, during a ride-along, posed as a prostitute, leading to at least two arrests.[170] Although the newspaper initially sought to simply gather information about the operation through a ride-along, newspaper supervisors later agreed with Chief Pete Alvarez that Santos-Garza would take part in the sting. *Caller-Times* editor Libby Averyt later apologized for the decision, calling it a "mistake," adding that "it was concluded that this was not the way we want to go about gathering information." Averyt added, "For us to maintain our watchdog role, we should not get involved in law enforcement activities and will not in the future." Although rare, instances of the press aiding police through a ride-along provides a clear demonstration of how media ride-alongs can lead both institutions to lose their independence as one institution performs the purposes and functions of the other.

A fourth purpose of media ride-alongs also arose: entertainment. In 1989, the television show *Cops* was introduced.[171] It followed a "ride-along style," in which camera crews rode with police in order to purportedly show law enforcement conducting their normal functions and interactions with the public. In the years since the creation of *Cops*, similar television shows have followed, including *The First 48* and *Live PD*, among others. On the surface, the intentions behind shows like *Cops* appear to be different from that of journalists, and to some degree they are. However, delivering entertainment carries the same concern as traditional reporters praising the police in their reporting: providing overly positive coverage of law enforcement, such as "present[ing] excessive force as good policing," in stark contrast to the reality for many people, especially from communities of color.[172] The distorted and unfair view of policing is made only worse in that *Cops* showed a disproportionate number of arrests related to drugs, more than three times the number of such arrests in real life. Furthermore, people of color are disproportionately represented as criminals compared to white people, in addition to cases of stereotyping and portraying marginalized individuals and communities in negative, problematic ways. The result once again is that the public does not receive a full or accurate picture of law enforcement and the ability to hold police accountable.

On top of these issues, the 1980s–2020s also saw additional negative effects of media ride-alongs traced back to the 1880s, including heightened danger to journalists and to police officers. As the *Pueblo (CO) Chieftain* bluntly put it in 1997, one needs only to "look at the plaques on the wall at the jail of . . . officers who died in the line of duty, to know that things can go wrong and officers—or citizens along for the ride—can die."[173]

Given the dangers of ride-alongs, departments took greater precautions during this era, including having participants stay in the car or hide under the dashboard "if things got hairy."[174] Some participants were required to wear bulletproof vests.[175] Nevertheless, dangers remained for reporters riding along with police, such as in the case of *Issaquah & Sammamish (WA) Reporter* journalist Nicole Jennings, who, during her first ride-along, experienced how a scene could change rapidly.[176] She wrote that one suspect "all at once . . . met my gaze and began walking in the direction towards me." Although the man ultimately did not approach the vehicle, Jennings worried that he would become violent, illustrating the heightened danger faced by journalists on ride-alongs.

Journalists also continued to face dangers related to shootings involving police. In fact, in 1989, a news team from Salt Lake City was riding along with police to record a story about Los Angeles gang connections in Utah when they "had to hit the dirt after someone took a pot shot at a police officer" with whom they were riding.[177] One officer grabbed KTVX-Channel 4 camera operator Dennis Kurumada, while another pulled reporter Sheila Hamilton from the patrol car. Sergeant Paul Hernandez explained that Hamilton was "in the killing zone or the danger zone" and was "in the line of fire," though she fortunately suffered only a cut hand.

But in some cases, the result was worse than a cut. In 1998, a Chesapeake, Virginia, police officer accidentally shot a *Cops* cameraman, with the "blast pepper[ing] the photographer's shins with birdshot while the camera was rolling."[178] The cameraman survived, but the situation only further illuminated the myriad possible dangers posed to media members on ride-alongs. The case also demonstrated that when an individual, whether a police officer or a member of the public, is being recorded or otherwise observed by a television crew or members of the press, they may act differently than they otherwise would, potentially leading to more aggressiveness, violence, or, as in this case, mistakes.

Reporters on ride-alongs even witnessed police officers being shot and, in some cases, killed. In 1991, *Jonesboro (KS) Sun* reporter Stan Mitchell rode in a patrol car with Pocahontas, Kansas, patrolman Scott Bennett when responding to a disturbance with a man whom he had arrested for driving under the influence of alcohol two weeks earlier.[179] The man, Dwight Sullinger, had reportedly assaulted his wife. Upon the police arriving at the scene, Sullinger stepped off his front porch holding a shotgun. When he got close to Bennett, Sullinger said, "You deserve this," and he shot the officer before taking his own life. At the end of his article describing what took place, Mitchell wrote, "Only hours earlier [Bennett] was telling me how much he loved his job. He said, 'You've got to love this job. You can't be in it for the money.'"

Another effect seen in recent decades was the threat of legal action stemming from the practice, which has helped garner at least some greater criticism of the practice in recent years.[180] Most notable was *Wilson*, though other federal and state cases also arose, as discussed in the following chapter. New reality television shows and their emphasis on entertainment also raised legal implications for the media and law enforcement, including around consent to be filmed. More specifically, the show's producers generally need to obtain written legal consent from individuals shown on camera.[181] However, several suspects depicted on the show revealed that they did not provide consent, were too inebriated to do so, or were "coerced into signing" a consent form. Some suspects claimed that police threatened to add additional charges if they did not sign.

Newer ride-along television shows have also prompted legal issues, including lawsuits for defamation and other legal claims. For example, in 2018, a Miami man reached a $1.3 million settlement with *The First 48* after the show falsely accused him of murder.[182] Another example arose the same year when a man's vehicle was searched by Greenville, South Carolina, police in front of *Live PD* cameras. He sued production company Big Fish Entertainment and its producers for defamation, intentional infliction of emotional distress, and invasion of privacy, demonstrating the range of legal issues that can arise from reality television ride-alongs. The lawsuit ended in a $9,000 settlement in January 2020.[183]

A different set of legal issues arose in relation to *The First 48* after the show followed Minneapolis police officers as they investigated several serious crimes that had occurred throughout the city in 2015.[184] As several cases related to the recorded investigations went to trial, both prosecutors and defense attorneys sought to compel Kirkstall Road Enterprises, the production company of *The First 48*, to release footage to be used in the trials. The company refused to comply, citing the First Amendment and the Minnesota Free Flow of Information Act, Minnesota's shield law protecting journalists' confidential sources and information. Attorney John Borger, who represented Kirkstall Road Enterprises, argued that the attorneys had not met the three-part test under the statute that could compel disclosure. Hennepin County prosecutor Mike Freeman countered that the statute did not apply to *The First 48* because it was for entertainment, not journalistic, purposes. Although no footage was released, the case represented yet another way in which media ride-alongs can raise legal issues.

In the 2010s, police departments also began conducting virtual and social media ride-alongs as public relations responses, meaning social media users can follow live updates and videos of police activities at a given time. Some police departments in the 2010s began providing "virtual" ride-alongs for those following their social media accounts, allowing viewers to see videos and other materials that showed officers' daily activities.[185] Despite being a safer means of riding along with police, social media ride-alongs can pose many of the same concerns as reality television shows, including raising privacy concerns and allowing police to exclude certain footage that casts them in a negative light. Virtual ride-alongs also raise important considerations for journalists looking to cover police in that they can serve as a source for news gathering, but likely do not provide a complete view of law enforcement. The result is once again limiting the press's ability to use ride-alongs as a means of informing the public and holding police accountable.

Connected to legal action is the final effect of media ride-alongs: undermining public trust in the press and police. When members of the public see journalists working with police, they may be less likely to trust those journalists, especially if they wish to provide confidential information. Such concerns are heightened when the press and police are targeted by litigation over ride-alongs, such as for violating the Fourth Amendment.

Amid these negative effects of media ride-alongs, some potential benefits did arise, including providing viewers with a unique perspective of law enforcement and newsworthy events,[186] granting journalists a way to better understand the internal workings of law enforcement,[187] and allowing some limited instances of the press holding police accountable.[188] However, as in past eras, these potential benefits were undermined by the more prevalent negative effects arising from the practice, including the ineffectiveness of media ride-alongs and undermined independence caused by the practice, as well as the threats of physical danger, legal action, and decreased public trust. The problem remains, however, that such issues are not fully recognized, or at least do not receive adequate criticism, necessitating action.

The press's and police's purposes and functions, as we define them in the twenty-first century, did not develop overnight. Instead, they represent years of political, economic, social, and technological influences, prompting changes and reform by the press and police, sometimes in their control and sometimes not. The 1980s–2020s are no different in that major events and trends once again influenced the news media and law enforcement. Over the past forty years, and continuing in the present, these influences, as well as the purposes and functions of the press and police, play a significant role in their interactions that follow trends dating back hundreds of years. Cooperative coexistence and contentiousness continued at the end of the twentieth century and first decades of the twenty-first century as a combination not seen in the previous sixty years marked first by partnerships and then by conflict. Significantly, the press's and police's respective purposes and functions, in addition to theoretical and practical explanations, begin to explain why the relationship continues to be defined by the same interactions dating back to the very beginnings of the United States. But there is even more to the story: the law around the press-police relationship, intertwined with the history of the relationship and how it continues to operate in the present.

CHAPTER 7

Legal Landscape of the U.S. Press-Police Relationship

GIVEN THE NEGATIVE EFFECTS ARISING from contentiousness, as well as impersonation and media ride-alongs, between the press and police, why do these interactions continue? The history of the press-police relationship and the previous chapter began to answer these questions, but the story of the press-police relationship, and the answer to this key question, is not complete without looking at the contemporary legal landscape. Here, the law of the press-police relationship provides further explanation as to why this has and continues to be the case. More specifically, the law around press coverage of police and press accountability of police demonstrates why the press-police relationship can be cooperative coexistence at one moment, but contentious at the next, raising key effects detailed in chapter 6. The legal landscape around law enforcement targeting the press further explains why contentiousness remains a part of the press-police relationship even after both institutions underwent changes following the 1960s–'70s and despite the negative effects arising from the practice. And finally, the law around the impersonation and media ride-alongs demonstrates how these practices also can, and do, continue despite the problems and issues they raise.

Legal Landscape of Press Coverage and Accountability of Police

The first two interactions between the press and police—press coverage and accountability of police departments, officials, officers, and activities—each of which date back to the American colonies and continue through the present, raise similar legal considerations, including related to press independence from government, news gathering, publication and broadcasting, and editorial control. Together, these legal elements protect the press from government and police intrusion and interference, allowing the news media to report on, and hold accountable, law enforcement. At the same time, the legal landscape also limits these practices, and, therefore, press intrusion into law enforcement interests and activities because of the press's ability to cover and investigate the police does not receive absolute protection under the First Amendment and other areas of U.S. law. The law also allows law enforcement to target the press in certain circumstances. The result is cooperative coexistence at one moment and contentiousness the next. Although press coverage and accountability of police are important in informing the public and holding the powerful accountable, greater contentiousness also raises several significant negative effects outlined in chapter 6.

Independence from Government
The first area of law related to press coverage and accountability of police is court precedent emphasizing the press's independence from government under the First Amendment. The Supreme Court, echoing the values of the founding fathers and First Amendment theory, has emphasized that freedom of the press is inextricably tied to press independence.[1] In his concurring opinion in *New York Times v. United States* (1971), Justice Hugo Black wrote that the First Amendment was drafted to "abolish" the government's "power to censor the press . . . so that the press would remain forever free to censure the Government [and] . . . inform the people."[2]

News Gathering
The second area of law is that around news gathering, a complicated legal landscape that affords the press certain rights and privileges to gather news, but generally does not provide greater protections than members of the public, in some cases favoring law enforcement interests over those of the news media and limiting journalists' access to locations and information. There are several ways in which constitutional, statutory, and common laws have provided the press with greater rights and protections to gather news. First, although the Supreme Court has not definitively ruled that the press's news-gathering function is protected by the First Amendment, it and lower courts have indicated that this may be the case. In *Branzburg v. Hayes* (1972), the Court held that "news gathering is not without its First Amendment protections" and that "without some protection for seeking out the news, freedom of the press could be eviscerated."[3]

Second, journalists receive protection for news gathering from the reporter's privilege protecting members of the press from compelled disclosure of confidential sources and information.[4] *Branzburg* brought the privilege to national attention, but established that it is not absolute under the First Amendment. The Court ruled against the press, though in a limited decision focused only on journalists appearing before a grand jury to reveal confidential sources. Justice Byron White held that because citizens are not constitutionally immune from testifying before a grand jury under a subpoena, the same standard applies to the press. However, the majority did not prevent states from drafting their own statutes, known as shield laws. Forty-nine states currently recognize at least a qualified constitutional-, statutory-, or common-law privilege. All federal circuit courts, as well as some state appellate courts, have recognized at least a qualified reporter's privilege, with some basing the privilege in the First Amendment, while others rely on state laws.

Third, although court precedent and statutory law generally do not provide the press with special access to locations and information, as discussed later in the chapter, there are still some limited ways in which journalists' ability to gather news is promoted over the general public's right of access. More specifically, at least three state laws grant the press a qualified right of access to emergency and disaster scenes, including California, Ohio, and Alaska.[5] Some federal and state courts have held that journalists have a First Amendment right to cover news at crime, accident, or disaster scenes, so long as they do not interfere with law enforcement activities.[6]

In some limited cases, courts have ruled in favor of press interests in news gathering over those of law enforcement. A ruling that illustrates well this balancing is *Channel 10, Inc. v. Gunnarson* (1972), in which the District of Minnesota weighed "a newsman's right to take pictures [and gather news with] the government's power to limit the exercise of that right," ruling in a local news photographer's favor.[7] The case arose when Dennis Anderson, a cameraperson for Channel 10 in Duluth, Minnesota, filmed police activity at the scene of a burglary from a public sidewalk. Two officers ordered Anderson to stop filming and confiscated his camera. The court found these actions unlawful, reasoning that Anderson was allowed to film on public property and did not interfere with police activity.

Journalists also gain special access to restricted areas through press passes, otherwise known as hard passes, press ID badges, or media credentials.[8] Additionally, journalists enjoy greater access through press rooms, press galleries, and press pools. Where police departments have implemented press-pass systems, officials and officers may not "decide arbitrarily who will receive passes and who will not."[9] Instead, there are "narrow and specific standards which advance a compelling state interest."[10] If a department denies a press pass, it must generally provide reasons for doing so and a chance to appeal.

Finally, some laws promote news gathering in ways that go beyond protections afforded to the public. For example, in 1980, Congress passed the Privacy Protection Act in response to the Supreme Court's ruling in *Zurcher v. Stanford Daily* (1978), discussed earlier.[11] The PPA makes it "unlawful for a government officer or employee, in connection with the investigation or prosecution of a criminal offense, to search for or seize any work product materials possessed by a person reasonably believed to have a purpose to disseminate to the public a newspaper, book, broadcast, or other similar form of public communication." The PPA also prohibits the seizure of "documentary materials," which include information that is "recorded, and includes, but is not limited to, written or printed materials, photographs, motion picture films, negatives, video tapes, audio tapes, and other mechanically, magnetically or electronically recorded cards, tapes, or discs." However, the PPA includes exceptions in situations where a journalist is under investigation or a search is needed to "prevent the death of, or serious bodily injury to, a human being." Several federal circuits have applied the PPA to newsroom searches.[12] Additionally, eight states— California, Connecticut, Illinois, Nebraska, New Jersey, Oregon, Texas, and Washington—have their own statutes providing similar or greater protection.

There are also some exceptions for journalists written into federal or state rules or policies, including U.S. Customs and Border Protection's (CBP) Directive No. 3340-049A, titled "Border Searches of Electronic Devices," which provides guidance and procedures for "searching, reviewing, retaining, and sharing information" contained in travelers' electronic devices.[13] The policy includes some exceptions, including when the device contains "possibly sensitive information, such as medical records and work-related information carried by journalists." Print media also receive special postal rates and some exemptions from antitrust laws. Broadcast media get preferential treatment regarding the use of spectrum.[14]

However, the current legal landscape makes clear in several ways that the press often does not enjoy greater rights than members of the general public, even in the course of news gathering. First, the Supreme Court's claims of a First Amendment right for news gathering are generally "empty rhetoric."[15] Instead, the Court has held that the press generally does not receive special privileges, such as for avoiding grand jury subpoenas and newsroom searches.[16] In *Cohen v. Cowles Media Co.* (1991), the Court held that "generally applicable laws do not offend the First Amendment simply because their enforcement against the press has incidental effects on its ability to gather and report the news."[17] The Court held that the First Amendment did not bar the press from being sued for promissory estoppel after two newspaper editors decided to break a verbal contract ensuring confidentiality to Republican campaign associate Dan Cohen, who approached several media outlets with allegations that the Minnesota Democratic-Farmer-Labor Party candidate for lieutenant governor was previously convicted for shoplifting.

Second, some courts have favored law enforcement interests over journalists' interests in gathering news. One such case is *United States v. Matthews* (2000), in which the Fourth Circuit held that the First Amendment did not provide a defense for freelance journalist Larry Matthews, who claimed to be investigating the distribution of child pornography online when he was arrested and charged by the FBI for trafficking such content.[18] The court affirmed the ruling of U.S. District Court for the District of Maryland judge Alexander Williams Jr., who explained that Matthews was subject to the same laws of general applicability as the public and that news gathering is not absolutely protected by the First Amendment.[19] Significantly, Williams weighed the law enforcement interest in protecting children from exploitation over the press's news-gathering function. He ultimately held that the press's interests in investigations and news gathering "is insignificant compared to the government's interest in preventing the exploitation of children," especially when a journalist violates the law.

Finally, the press generally does not enjoy a special right of access to public, restricted, or private locations, as well as to information, or special protection from charges of invasion of privacy, trespassing, wiretapping, and more. Here, too, the press's ability to gather news is often circumscribed when weighed against law enforcement interests.

In general, the First Amendment provides the press and public with the same right to not only be in public spaces but also to record from such locations. For example, multiple federal appellate courts have affirmed a First Amendment right to record police officers in the course of their duties in public places so long as the press does not interfere in police activities.[20] In cases where the government attempts to limit expression on government property, the "public forum doctrine" is employed.[21] In *Perry Education Association v. Perry Local Educators' Association* (1983), the Supreme Court created three categories of public forums, including traditional public forums, limited or designated public forums, and non-public forums.[22] In a traditional public forum, such as a public sidewalk, street, park, or town square, the government's ability to regulate speech is "sharply circumscribed" and is subject to strict scrutiny review, a high legal burden. A designated public forum is one in which a government body designates a space for expressive activities, such as a classroom at a public university. In such forums, content-based restrictions on expression are also subject to strict scrutiny. Finally, nonpublic forums are spaces that are "not by tradition or designation a forum for public communication," including airport terminals and polling places.

However, government bodies can restrict press and public access to certain locations, even public spaces, through "time, place, and manner restrictions." In *Ward v. Rock Against Racism* (1989), the Supreme Court held that such restrictions must be content neutral, narrowly tailored to serve a significant governmental interest, and allow for alternative channels for communication or access.[23] In terms of the press-police relationship, law enforcement interests for restricting access to certain locations include preventing interference in police activities, maintaining public safety, preserving evidence, and protecting privacy.[24]

The only area where the Court has recognized a First Amendment right of access to government proceedings is at criminal trials, though this right is the same for the press and the public. In *Richmond Newspapers, Inc. v. Virginia* (1980), the Court held that "the right to attend criminal trials is implicit in the guarantees of the First Amendment; without the freedom to attend such trials, which people have exercised for centuries, important aspects of freedom of speech and 'of the press could be eviscerated.'"[25] Justice John Paul Stevens wrote in a concurring opinion that "for the first time, the Court unequivocally h[eld] that an arbitrary interference with access to important information is an abridgment of the ... First Amendment."

Similarly, the press and public generally have the same rights of access to public meetings. At the federal level, the Government in the Sunshine

Act was passed in 1976 to require that federal agencies with multiple members conduct their business meetings in public.[26] The U.S. House of Representatives has generally been open to the public since the First Congress, whereas the U.S. Senate was closed until 1794.[27] Although both houses may close with a majority vote, such instances are rare. At the state level, all fifty states and the District of Columbia have passed open-meetings laws. These laws vary in their detail, scope, and enforcement, but all require that public bodies hold meetings where a quorum of members are present in public, though with certain exceptions.

The Supreme Court has generally held that the press also does not enjoy an absolute or special right of access to restricted locations, such as crime, disaster, or emergency scenes. In *Branzburg*, the Court found that journalists "have no constitutional right of access to the scenes of crime or disaster when the general public is excluded."[28] In *Zemel v. Rusk* (1965), the Court similarly held that "the right to speak and publish does not carry with it the unrestrained right to gather information."[29] The Court has also ruled that journalists enjoy only a qualified right of access to some locations where police may be present, such as prisons or jails.[30]

In *New Jersey v. Lashinsky* (1979), the New Jersey Supreme Court balanced the press's right of access to an accident scene against law enforcement interests in promoting safety and conducting investigations.[31] The case arose when *Newark Star-Ledger* photographer Harvey I. Lashinsky took several photographs at the scene of a serious car accident. Soon after, New Jersey state police trooper Eric Herkloz arrived at the scene where an additional forty to fifty people had also gathered. Herkloz ordered everyone to clear the area after he noticed that the vehicle could erupt in flames. He also wished to preserve the scene for investigation. Lashinsky did not leave the scene after several requests by Herkloz, which came even after Lashinsky showed his press card. Lashinsky claimed that Herkloz arrested him immediately, though witnesses alleged that the arrest came after Lashinsky "engaged the trooper in a heated argument."

The New Jersey Supreme Court concluded that there was "ample evidence from which to conclude that the defendant impeded the trooper in the performance of his duties." The court acknowledged the existence of "special constitutional protection" for news gathering, that the court needed to take a journalist's "constitutional prerogatives" into account, and that law enforcement should accommodate the interests of the press whenever possible. However, the court emphasized that news gathering must be balanced with "other important and legitimate government interests," including law enforcement maintaining order and safety. The court also made clear that the First Amendment "does not serve to place the media or their representatives above the law." Justice Morris Pashman took a different view in a dissenting opinion, writing that because Lashinsky "was a news photographer engaged in the task of reporting a newsworthy event," the order for him to leave was unreasonable, including because journalists going to crime, disaster, and emergency scenes benefits the public. Justice Pashman concluded that the majority's ruling "allows the police to remove any newsman from the scene of any accident merely because that newsman is competently performing his job. As such, the press's right of special access is rendered meaningless."

Press access is only further restricted regarding private property or places where people have a "reasonable expectation of privacy."[32] A seminal moment in U.S. privacy law came in 1890 when lawyers Samuel Warren and Louis Brandeis published "The Right to Privacy," expressing concern over "invasion either by the too enterprising press, the photographer, or the possessor of any other modern device for recording or reproducing scenes or sounds."[33] In ensuing years, press access to private locations has been curtailed by two invasion-of-privacy torts: intrusion upon seclusion and publication of private facts. Intrusion provides that any individual "who intentionally intrudes, physically or otherwise, upon the solitude or seclusion of another or [their] private affairs or concerns, is subject to liability to the other for invasion of [their] privacy, if the intrusion would be highly offensive to a reasonable person."[34] Publication of private facts provides that those "who [give] publicity to a matter concerning the private life of another is subject to liability . . . for invasion of his privacy, if the matter publicized is of a kind that (a) would be highly offensive to a reasonable person, and (b) is not of legitimate concern to the public."

Press access is also limited under the federal criminal trespass statute, 25 CFR § 11.411, which provides that an individual commits criminal trespass "if, knowing that he or she is not licensed or privileged to do so, he or she enters or surreptitiously remains in any building or occupied structure." The Electronic Communications Privacy Act is a federal statute prohibiting wiretapping, meaning "any person who . . . intentionally intercepts, endeavors to intercept, or procures any other person to intercept or endeavor to intercept, any wire, oral, or electronic communication."[35] At the state level, criminal trespass laws generally have similar provisions to the federal statute, though punishments vary. State wiretap laws range widely,[36] with each state requiring either one-party consent, two-party consent, or all-party consent to record a conversation. Thirty-eight states and the District of Columbia have one-party consent statutes, allowing individuals to record conversations in which they participate without informing the other members that they are doing so. Twelve states have all-party consent statutes, which generally require the consent of all members of a conversation.

In general, federal[37] and state courts[38] have held that the press does not have a special right of access to private locations. For example, *Shulman v. Group W. Productions, Inc.* (1998) arose following a car accident in 1990, in which Ruth and Wayne Shulman, mother and son, were injured.[39] A rescue helicopter was dispatched to the scene with the pilot, a medic, nurse Laura Carnahan, and Joel Cooke, a video camera operator employed by defendants Group W Productions, Inc., and 4MN Productions. Cooke filmed what took place in the helicopter and "roamed the accident scene, videotaping the rescue," for the entertainment program *On Scene: Emergency Response.* The California Supreme Court ruled against Ruth and Wayne on the claim of public disclosure of private facts, finding that the recording of the accident scene was of a newsworthy event and "of legitimate public interest." Regarding the intrusion claim, the court found two aspects of Cooke's footage problematic, namely, the filming of Ruth in the helicopter and recording her conversations with Carnahan. The court ultimately held that although the government "may not intrude into the proper sphere of the news media to dictate what they should publish and broadcast," the press may not "play tyrant to the people by unlawfully spying on them in the name of newsgathering."

One year later, the California high court was tasked in *Sanders v. ABC* (1999) with determining whether ABC reporter Stacy Lescht violated the state's intrusion tort by obtaining employment at a "telepsychic" company and recording conversations in the private office.[40] Lescht had a small video camera hidden in her hat while working in Psychic Marketing Group's Los Angeles office, videotaping conversations with several coworkers, including plaintiff Mark Sanders. The California Supreme Court held that employees enjoy a limited expectation of privacy in their conversations and interactions taking place in a private office or workplace, even if the conversations could be overheard by other coworkers. The court extended the privacy protections to being "secretly videotaped by undercover television reporters," once again limiting the press's ability to gather news on privacy grounds.

The press may even be singled out under certain legislation that favors privacy over news gathering. In 1998, the California Legislature enacted the Anti-Paparazzi Act, which provided that "a person is liable for physical invasion of privacy when the defendant knowingly enters onto the land of another without permission . . . with the intent to capture any type of visual image, sound recording, or other physical impression."[41] In 2015, despite arguments by news outlets and observers that the law creates penalties for news gathering, the Second District Court of Appeal in Los Angeles held that the statute did not violate the First Amendment.[42]

As with access to locations, the current legal landscape provides the press with the same rights as the public regarding access to government and law enforcement data, records, and information. The Supreme Court and some federal circuits have directly held that the First Amendment does not afford the press special access to information. In *Branzburg*, the Court held that "the First Amendment does not guarantee the press a constitutional right of special access to information not available to the public generally," citing *Zemel*, in which the Court ruled that "the right to speak and publish does not carry with it the unrestrained right to gather information."[43]

Two rulings, one by the Supreme Court and one by the Seventh Circuit, directly addressed the First Amendment and disclosure of law enforcement records, both ruling in favor of law enforcement over news-gathering interests. In *Los Angeles Police Department v. United Reporting Publishing Corporation* (1999), the Supreme Court held that the government may selectively grant access to public record information and that a statute regulating access to government information is not an abridgment of free-speech rights.[44] In *Dahlstrom v. Sun-Times Media, LLC* (2015), the Seventh Circuit held that the *Sun-Times* possessed "no constitutional right either to obtain [police] officers' personal information from government records or to subsequently publish . . . unlawfully obtained information."[45] In balancing government interests versus press interests, the Seventh Circuit concluded that although the

Sun-Times was reporting on a matter of public interest, the publication of an allegation that the Chicago Police Department manipulated a homicide investigation "both intruded on [the] privacy [of the officers] and threatened their safety, while doing little to advance Sun-Times's reporting."

Turning to statutory law, at the federal level, the Freedom of Information Act was signed into law by President Lyndon B. Johnson in 1966 and took effect on July 4, 1967.[46] Congress passed the legislation to create a presumption of public access to the records of federal agencies. In general, federal agencies are required to disclose records unless they fall under one of nine exemptions, including Exemption 7(C), which excuses from disclosure "records or information compiled for law enforcement purposes" if their production "could reasonably be expected to constitute an unwarranted invasion of personal privacy." Although FOIA serves as an important tool for the press, questions remain about its effectiveness for journalists, including after the Supreme Court expanded the breadth of Exemption 7(C) regarding law enforcement records in *U.S. Department of Justice v. Reporters Committee for Freedom of the Press* (1989) and *National Archives and Records Administration v. Favish* (2004).[47]

At the state level, public disclosure laws and open-records statutes, often called Freedom of Information (FOI) laws, generally provide that police records are open unless an exemption allows for police to deny access to the information.[48] However, statutes governing access to police records still vary from state to state. Common law also provides at least some right of access for the press and public to government records. Additionally, most government agencies and departments have written policies covering what information is public.

Nevertheless, in some cases, law enforcement records may be unavailable, incomplete, or unreleased, which may prompt members of the press or media organizations to take legal action to obtain access to police records. However, some observers have argued that this should be used only as "a last resort" because it can result in diminished access offered by police. Therefore, there are circumstances where the press looks to other sources of police information, including detectives' notes, police reports, police radio frequencies, and relevant social media accounts.[49] Journalists also forge source relationships and speak with officials and officers, as well as eyewitnesses, victims, suspects, detained individuals, and others.

Publication and Broadcasting

For news gathering to be effective, there need to be protections for the publishing or broadcasting of the acquired information. One area of precedent protecting publication from government intrusion is the general prohibition of prior restraints. *Near v. Minnesota* (1931)[50] and *New York Times v. United States* (1971),[51] both discussed in previous chapters, established a First Amendment presumption against prior restraints, demonstrating the significance of preventing government intrusion into the press's ability to publish information.[52]

A connected area of jurisprudence concerns the publication of lawfully obtained, truthful information. In what is sometimes referred to as the *Daily Mail* string of cases, the Supreme Court held that statutes prohibiting the media from publishing such information—including the name of a rape victim,[53] the confidential proceedings before a state judicial review commission,[54] a preliminary hearing open to the public and press,[55] and the name of a juvenile defendant[56]—violated the First Amendment. Additionally, in *Bartnicki v. Vopper* (2001), the Supreme Court held that "a stranger's illegal conduct does not suffice to remove the First Amendment shield from speech about a matter of public concern."[57] The Court therefore ruled that, at least in the particular circumstances of the case, the First Amendment right of publication exceeded the government's interests, therefore protecting the press from punishment where it did not participate in, but received, the illegal interception of communications.

A third area of jurisprudence is Supreme Court rulings emphasizing the importance of the free flow of information under the First Amendment so the press and public can criticize and hold accountable the government, including law enforcement. For example, in *New York Times v. Sullivan* (1964), the Court emphasized the "profound national commitment to the principle that debate on public issues should be uninhibited, robust, and wide-open, and that it may well include vehement, caustic, and sometimes unpleasantly sharp attacks on government and public officials."[58] In *Hustler Magazine, Inc. v. Falwell* (1988), the Court held that "at the heart of the First Amendment is the recognition of the fundamental importance of the free flow of ideas and opinions on matters of public interest and concern."[59] Finally, the Court ruled in *Mills v. Alabama* (1966) that "there is practically universal agreement that a major purpose of [the First] Amendment was to protect the free discussion of governmental affairs. . . . The Constitution specifically selected the press . . . to play an important role in the discussion of public affairs."[60]

In *Fields v. Philadelphia* (2017), the Third Circuit connected the free flow of information directly to oversight of law enforcement, holding that "access to information regarding public police activity is particularly important because it leads to citizen discourse on public issues, 'the highest rung of the hierarchy of First Amendment values.'"[61] The court added that obtaining and spreading information about police falls under "special [First Amendment] protection."

The Supreme Court has held that without protection for the circulation and dissemination of materials by the press under the First Amendment, publication would be worthless. In *Ex parte Jackson* (1877), the Court reasoned that "liberty of circulating is as essential to that freedom as liberty of publishing; indeed, without the circulation, the publication would be of little value."[62] The Court reaffirmed these conclusions in *Lovell v. City of Griffin* (1938), finding that a statute, which "in its broad sweep prohibit[ed] the distribution of 'circulars, handbooks, advertising, or literature of any kind,'" was "invalid on its face" because it "str[uck] at the very foundation of the freedom of the press by subjecting it to license and censorship."[63] One year later, in *Schneider v. State* (1939), the Court struck down a similar ordinance in Milwaukee, Wisconsin, as well as those in other cities, after police arrested the petitioner for handing out handbills pertaining to a labor dispute.[64] The Court found that the freedoms of speech and press are "fundamental personal rights" that lie "at the foundation of free government by free men."

However, protections for publication are not without limitations. First, in *Near*, Chief Justice Hughes noted "exceptional" circumstances where prior restraints may be constitutional, including a "hindrance to [the war] effort," such as the "actual obstruction to its recruiting service or the publication of the sailing dates of transports or the number and location of troops"; "obscene publications"; "incitements to acts of violence and the overthrow by force of orderly government"; and "uttering words that may have all the effect of force."[65] Second, court precedent has established that publication and broadcasting can result in liability and subsequent punishment, including for privacy, defamation, intentional infliction of emotional distress, and other areas of law. In *Gitlow v. People of State of New York* (1925), the Supreme Court held that the First Amendment "does not confer an absolute right to speak or publish, without responsibility, whatever one may choose."[66] Finally, radio and television broadcasting face more limitations than print publications, namely, through Federal Communications Commission rules and regulations.[67] Although broadcast networks and stations are protected by the First Amendment and statutory law, three FCC rules implicate the coverage of law enforcement, including "hoaxes"—the broadcasting "of false information concerning a crime or catastrophe"— intentionally distorting the news, and transmitting indecent, profane, or obscene content.

Editorial Control

Protections for news gathering, access, and publication allow the press to not only gather and access information, but also print or broadcast it. However, the Supreme Court has recognized that such protections would be ineffective if the press were unable to make editorial decisions about their reporting and coverage. More specifically, in *Miami Herald v. Tornillo* (1974), the Supreme Court held that the First Amendment protects from government interference "the editorial control and judgement" of a news organization, including the "choice of material to go into a newspaper, and the decisions made as to limitations on the size and content of the paper, and treatment of public issues and public officials—whether fair or unfair."[68] Although broadcast networks and stations receive lesser protections for editorial control, the Court held in *Arkansas Educational Television Commission v. Forbes* (1989) that "when a public broadcaster exercises editorial discretion in the selection and presentation of its programming, it engages in speech activity."[69]

Law Enforcement Targeting the Press Raises Additional Legal Considerations

In much the same way as press investigations can target the police, law enforcement investigations can target or otherwise sweep up journalists and news organizations, practices that continue through the present. And also like press accountability of police, this third type of interaction—law enforcement targeting press—is likely to lead the press-police relationship to be more contentious, among other significant effects outlined in chapter 6. Nevertheless, the contemporary legal landscape allows arrests, use of force, threats, searches and seizures, subpoenas, and surveillance against the press to continue, helping demonstrate how and why these practices lead to contentiousness and, therefore, why change is needed.

Arrests, Use of Force, and Threats
Dating back to the eighteenth and nineteenth centuries, and continuing ever since, police have arrested, threatened, and used force against members of the press, practices that despite their negative effects are able to continue under the current legal landscape. In *Cohen*, the Supreme Court established that the press is subject to "generally applicable laws,"[70] meaning the news media does not have a special privilege to avoid arrests for laws of general applicability, including for invasion of privacy, trespass, wiretap, and more. Journalists also face arrests for theft if they take anything from a crime scene or other location.[71] For example, in 2007, Tom Lyden, a reporter for KMSP-TV in Minnesota, noticed a videotape inside the unlocked vehicle of a boxer suspected of organizing dogfights. Lyden took the tape and used it in preparing a story before returning it to authorities. He was arrested and ultimately pleaded guilty to tampering with a motor vehicle, resulting in a $500 fine, community service, and a year of probation. Lyden also apologized on air.

Arrests largely stem from the "tension [of] allowing the police to do what they need to do to protect public safety and conduct a complete investigation and balancing that with journalists' right to report."[72] For example, in *Matthews*, the Fourth Circuit and District of Maryland weighed the law enforcement interest in protecting children over the press's ability to gather news.[73] In *Lashinsky*, the law enforcement interests in maintaining public safety and preserving an investigation of an automobile accident were favored over a news photographer's ability to take pictures and otherwise gather information, leading to his arrest.

However, if law enforcement arrests a journalist specifically for covering the news, without any other justification, such as breaking the law or interfering with police activities, the detained journalist may potentially bring a civil claim under 42 U.S.C. § 1983, known as a "1983 action." A journalist could file such an action in federal court against police "[claiming] that by unlawfully interfering with [their] newsgathering," such as by denying access "to a public forum for no good reason," the police violated the journalist's First Amendment rights.[74] However, such claims may not always be successful because it can be challenging to establish harm from such interference. Challenges also arise in disproving that a journalist had interfered with police.

Such claims arose following the incidents in Minneapolis around the George Floyd protests, which prompted at least two federal lawsuits against law enforcement in Minnesota, as discussed in chapter 6.[75] Although the cases ended in settlements favoring the press, some observers criticized the final terms, saying they did not go far enough to address the harm suffered by several journalists and the strong potential that the actions could happen again. District of Minnesota judge Wilhelmina M. Wright's orders favoring the press are also not a panacea for several reasons, including that she acknowledged that injunctions in similar cases need to include the requirement that journalists "refrain from impeding law enforcement activities";[76] her rulings applied only to dispersal orders, not to police activities more broadly; and the orders did not apply to all law enforcement agencies responding to the protests in Brooklyn Center. But perhaps most significantly, even in cases where the press is granted a TRO or injunction, violence by law enforcement against members of the press can continue. Following Wright's order, law enforcement continued to detain journalists, many of whom were subjected to photographs of their faces and press credentials.[77] Members of the press also continued to face use of force and threats amid ongoing protests. This demonstrates how the legal landscape allows the police to target members of the press, even in cases of positive court rulings for journalists. Thus, whether a judge rules in favor of journalists or not, such as in a 1983 action or a request for a TRO, the result is that the negative effects of law enforcement targeting the press, again outlined in chapter 6, can, and do, continue, necessitating action or change to address these problems.

Searches, Seizures, and Subpoenas
Another way in which police actions implicate and intrude into the press's purposes and functions is when officers or agents execute searches and seizures, or enforce subpoenas, targeting journalists or news organizations, including their homes, offices, and newsrooms; sources, materials, and information; phone calls, phone records, emails, and email records; and electronic devices, equipment, social media accounts, and location information. Significantly, chapter 6 demonstrated that journalists have recently faced each of these types of searches and seizures. Given their negative effects, which date back to the eighteenth

and nineteenth centuries, why do they continue? Much like with arrests, use of force, and surveillance, the legal landscape allows these practices notwithstanding some limited protections for the press.

Under the Fourth Amendment, law enforcement, in order to search a member of the public or seize their property, generally needs to secure a warrant supported by probable cause and signed by a judge. The "exclusionary rule" provides that evidence obtained through illegal searches and seizures cannot be used in an ensuing trial.[78] However, in *United States v. Leon* (1984), the Court created the "good faith" exception, meaning that if a police officer inadvertently violated a suspect's Fourth Amendment rights during a search, but was acting in good faith, the exclusionary rule no longer applied.[79] There are also some exceptions to the Fourth Amendment warrant requirement, including searches incident to lawful arrests, which allows police to conduct a warrantless search of an arrested person in order to find any possible weapons or to prevent the destruction of evidence. Warrantless searches and seizures are also permitted in "exigent circumstances," meaning that a reasonable officer would have believed the need for the search to be urgent and that securing a warrant was not possible or practical. Other exceptions, including the "plain view doctrine," searches in "open fields" and individuals' vehicles, and the "border search exception," can also apply, with a warrant also not being required if an individual provides consent to the search.

The first area of law raised by law enforcement searches, seizures, and subpoenas is when police execute search warrants against journalists' homes and personal offices. Although the Supreme Court has never heard a Third Amendment case, this constitutional protection—providing that "no Soldier shall, in time of peace be quartered in any house, without the consent of the Owner, nor in time of war, but in a manner to be prescribed by law"—is nevertheless important because it shows the founders' concern about government intrusion into private homes.[80] The Supreme Court similarly raised this apprehension in *Weeks v. United States* (1914), emphasizing "the sanctity of a man's home and the privacies of life."[81] Nevertheless, at the state and local levels, law enforcement can conduct, and have conducted, searches and seizures of journalists' homes and offices, as demonstrated by the 2019 search warrants executed against Bryan Carmody in San Francisco.

A second area of law regarding searches, seizures, and subpoenas targeting the press is journalists' footage, notes, and information through warrants or subpoenas. The Supreme Court ruled in *Branzburg* and

Zurcher that the press does not receive special protection under the First Amendment from subpoenas seeking confidential sources and from newsrooms. Although both rulings opened the door for important statutory protections, lower court precedent, and government guidelines, law enforcement has continued to target members of the press's information and materials. For example, the reporter's privilege provides at least qualified protection from compelled disclosure of confidential sources and information through protections provided by federal and state courts, as well as state shield laws, though journalists have continued to face subpoenas, with cases even increasing compared to previous years.[82] Similarly, although the PPA and some state laws provide protections for the press against newsroom searches and seizures targeting their information and materials, as discussed earlier, such searches have continued, including in New Jersey, Missouri, and Nevada.

The legal landscape allows, or at least does not fully curtail, government and law enforcement seeking to obtain reporters' and news organizations' phone calls, phone records, emails, and email records, resulting in several cases of such actions detailed in the previous chapter. The Supreme Court and lower courts have generally allowed such searches and seizures. In *Smith v. Maryland* (1979), the Supreme Court ruled that law enforcement's use of a "pen register," a mechanical device that records the numbers dialed on a telephone, did not constitute a "search" under the Fourth Amendment and that police could do so without a warrant.[83] In a series of cases, the Supreme Court has "consistently . . . held that a person has no legitimate expectation of privacy in information [they] voluntarily turns over to third parties," which is known as the "third-party doctrine."[84] The D.C. Circuit held in *Reporters Committee for Freedom of the Press v. American Telephone & Telegraph Company* (1978) that the government can subpoena records of journalists' long-distance calls because in making such calls, they "expos[ed] their actions to a third party."[85] The court rejected the argument that journalists "are entitled under the First Amendment to prior notice of toll-call-record subpoenas issued in the course of felony investigations, even if citizens in general have no such right." Similarly, in *New York Times Co. v. Gonzalez* (2006), the Second Circuit held that two *New York Times* reporters' telephone records were not protected by New York's shield law,[86] requiring the journalists to hand over eleven days' worth of records to a grand jury, which was investigating how the reporters learned about planned law enforcement action against two Islamic charities suspected of funding terrorist activities.

Also implicating efforts to obtain journalists' sources, information, and materials is the DOJ's guidelines regarding search warrants and subpoenas targeting journalists.[87] The guidelines, titled "Policy Regarding Obtaining Information from, or Records of, Members of the News Media; and Regarding Questioning, Arresting, or Charging Members of the News Media," were first instituted in 1970 by Attorney General John Mitchell in response to press concerns about the increasing number of subpoenas aimed at compelling journalists to reveal their confidential sources.

The guidelines, which have been amended at least three times since 2013, first provide that the use of "subpoenas, court orders, . . . and search warrants to seek information from, or records of, nonconsenting members of the news media [are] extraordinary measures, not standard investigatory practices." Such measures may be used only after the attorney general has authorized the use; when the information sought is "essential to a successful investigation, prosecution, or litigation"; and after "all reasonable alternative attempts have been made to obtain the information from alternative sources." The guidelines list principles the attorney general is to consider. For example, in criminal matters, there "should be reasonable grounds to believe . . . that a crime has been committed, and that the information sought is essential to the successful investigation or prosecution of that crime." In civil matters, the information sought must also be essential to the litigation. In cases where the attorney general authorized a subpoena or search warrant pursuant to a journalist, the affected individual(s) generally "shall be given reasonable and timely notice," though with some exceptions. The DOJ may also obtain warrants to search "the premises [and] property" of members of the news media, as well as seek the disclosure of "communications records" ("the contents of electronic communications as well as source and destination information associated with communications, such as email transaction logs and local and long distance telephone connection records") and "business records" ("work product and other documentary materials, and records of the activities, including the financial transactions, of a member of the news media related to the coverage, investigation, or reporting of news"). In 2021, the DOJ announced it would no longer seize journalists' phone and email records in connection with government leak investigations, though the new policy included exceptions.[88] The DOJ codified the changes in 2022.

The final area of law related to searches, seizures, and subpoenas of journalists is their electronic devices, social media accounts, and location information, each of which continue to be targeted by the government and law enforcement in the present, as discussed in the previous chapter. A key case focused on searches and seizures of individuals' electronic devices is *Riley v. California* (2014), which arose when officers examined the defendants' cell phones under suspicion that they were involved in gang- or drug-related activities.[89] Chief Justice John Roberts ruled that although "the information on a cell phone is [not] immune from search[es] . . . a warrant is generally required before such a search, even when a cell phone is seized incident to arrest." He reasoned that courts in previous Fourth Amendment cases could not have imagined the large amount of data and information contained within modern cell phones, though Roberts also acknowledged that limiting the police's ability to search electronic devices would affect efforts to combat crime.

However, as Chief Justice Roberts noted, such protections are not absolute. For example, journalists' electronic devices have been the target of warrantless searches and seizures at U.S. borders.[90] Because of the Fourth Amendment border-search exception, as well as a federal circuit split on the issue, journalists "have not received adequate protections against warrantless searches and seizures at U.S. borders and remain confused and uncertain about their rights." Furthermore, the federal government has also compiled information about journalists and other travelers crossing U.S. borders, including in relation to the "migrant caravan," a group of more than five thousand migrants seeking asylum at the U.S.-Mexico border in November 2018.[91]

As in other cases of searches and seizures targeting journalists, the legal landscape also does not curtail warrants subpoenas and other efforts targeting journalists' social media accounts, a practice that although secretive and rare, continues to affect journalists in the present, as discussed in the previous chapter. Although the DOJ and other governmental entities may need to follow several procedural safeguards to "ensure that the identities of innocent persons [and third parties were] not revealed,"[92] this does not eliminate the practice and the burden it can put on journalists and news organizations.

Federal agencies, as well as state and local police departments, may utilize new and evolving technologies to track journalists' past and current locations, including through GPS and cell cite location information (CSLI). Two Supreme Court cases have addressed government use of technology to track the locations of members of the public. In *United States v. Jones* (2012), Justice Antonin Scalia and a plurality of the Court held that the federal government's installation of a GPS device on a vehicle, as well as the subsequent use of the tracker to monitor the vehicle's movements, constituted a "search" within the meaning of the Fourth Amendment and "impinges on expectations of privacy."[93] In *Carpenter v. United States* (2018), the Court addressed government and law enforcement efforts to obtain CSLI, which is historical data from cell-phone carriers detailing the movements and location of a user.[94] Chief Justice Roberts concluded that law enforcement "must generally obtain a warrant supported by probable cause before acquiring [CSLI]."

Surveillance and Evolving Technologies

Surveillance—including "mass" surveillance, wiretapping, and bulk data collection, as well as secretive searches, seizures, and subpoenas, among other practices where government or law enforcement closely observers or spies on the public or press—raises significant concerns for journalists and news organizations beyond conventional warrants and subpoenas. Mass surveillance is made possible at the federal level by Section 702 of the FISA Amendments Act, amendments to Rule 41, and NSLs, as discussed in chapter 6. Through these mechanisms, the federal government and law enforcement are able to obtain warrants and subpoenas that allow for even more invasive surveillance of journalists' sensitive information, phone and email records, electronic devices, communications, and more, raising significant press freedom concerns. At the state and local levels, use of facial recognition technologies and IoT devices by police create further security and privacy concerns for the news media, the press-police relationship, and the public. Ultimately, journalists and news organizations continue to be targeted by the government and law enforcement through surveillance and other means in a legal landscape that provides some protection for the press, though not enough to eliminate or effectively minimize the use of these practices, or, most important, their negative effects outlined in chapter 6.

Impersonation and Media Ride-Alongs Pose
Complicated Legal Landscape

Despite the problems caused by police impersonation of the press, press impersonation of police, and media ride-alongs, these practices continue in the present and will almost assuredly do so in the future. A main reason for this is the legal landscape, which, like with the other interactions between the news media and law enforcement, allows impersonation and media ride-alongs to continue to varying degrees. Worse, the law does not go far enough to address the negative effects they raise, implicating both institutions, their relationship, and the public.

Police Impersonation of the Press

To best understand the complicated legal landscape around police impersonation of the press, the following section walks through a First Amendment claim seeking to prevent the practice. In doing so, this section touches on several of the same legal considerations related to press coverage and investigations of the police, though also touches on other areas of law, demonstrating how the First Amendment claim is unlikely to succeed. The result is the legal landscape will do little to limit police impersonation of the press, requiring alternatives to address the negative effects arising from the practice.

To date, a journalist or news organization has never brought a constitutional challenge, such as under 42 U.S.C. § 1983, against police impersonation of the press.[95] A preliminary but important question is whether a journalist or news organization could establish standing to bring such a claim. To establish standing under Article III of the U.S. Constitution, a plaintiff must show an "injury in fact" stemming from the challenged action by the defendant.[96] The Supreme Court and lower courts have found that "standing is more permissive when First Amendment harms are alleged because First Amendment challenges are necessary for the very functioning of our democracy."[97] Thus, the complaint must demonstrate both a First Amendment violation and potential harms resulting from the violation.

A First Amendment claim against police impersonation of the press would be able to make at least plausible arguments for both. The first argument a journalist or news organization could raise is that police impersonation of the press undermines the independence of the news media, a key effect found throughout the history of the practice. The press could cite Supreme Court and lower court precedent establishing barriers to government intrusion into press independence news gathering, publication and broadcasting, and editorial control. By citing court precedent, as well as First Amendment theory—including the checking value of the press and the Fourth Estate—the news media could argue that police impersonation constitutes government intrusion into the press's independent functions in violation of the First Amendment.

Second, the press could point to examples of special privileges that help journalists and news organizations avoid government intrusion. The most notable example is the reporter's privilege to avoid compelled disclosure of confidential sources and information. Although a qualified protection under the First Amendment and statutory law, this privilege provides protections from government interference, which is what police impersonation of the press represents. The press could also point to journalists' affirmative right to a press pass as an example of greater protection for the news media compared to members of the public. Additionally, the press could note the PPA and DOJ guidelines regarding search warrants and subpoenas targeting journalists, each of which provide additional protections from government intrusion into news gathering not otherwise extended to the public.

Finally, journalists and news organizations could raise several additional harms caused by police impersonation of the press, including undermining journalists' safety, credibility, source relationships, news gathering, and independence. The press could also raise other areas of law, including invasion of privacy, among other claims.[98] The journalist or news-organization plaintiff could argue that because of these effects, police impersonation of the press can, and should, be viewed as equally problematic as police posing as doctors or lawyers, especially because constitutional freedoms and protections are at stake.

However, even if a journalist or news organization can establish standing, a court is more likely to rule against the First Amendment claim for several reasons. First, the legal landscape around press coverage and investigations of police, as well as around police targeting the press, revealed that the news media does not enjoy special privileges not available to the general public in several contexts, including against grand jury subpoenas. Journalists and news organizations also do not receive a special First Amendment right of access to locations and information, especially if they are likely to interfere with police activities. Protections for publication and broadcasting are also not absolute. Additionally, the First Amendment does not protect the press from litigation stemming from crimes applicable to the public. As a result, a court could find that the press does not or cannot have special protection from impersonation by law enforcement, especially if such protections would limit the ability of police to accomplish its interests.

Second, the press's First Amendment claim would be balanced against strong government interests in police impersonation of the press, which include, as the history of the practice revealed, law enforcement conducting investigations and ending standoffs or hostage situations. There is a long history of courts balancing First Amendment rights with government interests,[99] including law enforcement such as in *United States v. Matthews* (2000) and *New Jersey v. Lashinsky* (1979), discussed earlier.

Third, at least one court has addressed whether police officers who impersonated members of the press have qualified immunity, which provides that "government officials performing discretionary functions, such as police officers, are generally shielded from liability for civil damages insofar as their conduct does not violate clearly established statutory or constitutional rights of which a reasonable person would have known."[100] *Spratlin v. Montgomery County* (1991) arose when Paul Spratlin attended a 1988 rally in Rockville, Maryland, to protest enforcement of a zoning ordinance. During the rally, Montgomery County police officers Robert Angelino and Barbara Kunkle posed as a photographer and reporter, respectively, and approached Spratlin after he yelled statements like "Sidney must die" in reference to county executive Sidney Kramer. The Fourth Circuit held that Angelino and Kunkle were entitled to qualified immunity protecting them from civil liability under 42 U.S.C. § 1983. The court found that a reasonable police officer would not find apparent unlawfulness in the officers' use of impersonation and also concluded that there was no apparent unlawfulness in the officers' actions anyway.

Finally, legislative efforts and federal agency policies either only limit police impersonation of the press, rather than ending it, or fail to address the practice altogether, instead authorizing its use. The result is that a court could find that Congress and other bodies have not eliminated the practice, electing to do the same. In 1980, Representative Les Aspin (D-WI) authored a bill that would have prohibited "the paid use of journalists . . . for intelligence purposes," as well as CIA agents posing as journalists.[101] Although this represents the strongest effort to date addressing police impersonation of the press, it did not advance through Congress.

As discussed in the previous chapter, even following the revelations that the CIA had impersonated journalists during the Cold War, authorization of the agency to use the practice in certain circumstances continued. The U.S. Postal Service is the only known federal agency to date that has officially banned impersonation of journalists.[102] Although other federal agencies have adopted or changed their guidelines regarding the practice, they have not ended the practice altogether. For example, in 2016, the FBI amended its guidelines following the revelations that one of its agents impersonated an AP reporter in order to catch the source of several anonymous bomb threats targeting Timberline High School in Washington State. Although then-FBI director James Comey defended the practice,[103] the DOJ and FBI changed the policy to provide greater protection for the press against impersonation and other tools that would undermine news-gathering activities.[104] The policy also required that an FBI agent get approval from the head of their FBI field office and the deputy director, after a review by the Undercover Review Committee, before representing, posing, or claiming to be a member of the press. Nevertheless, the policy still only limited impersonation of the press, rather than ending it, providing little comfort that the FBI would refrain from using the practice in the future. Ultimately, absent a federal court ruling in favor of the press's First Amendment claim or successful legislation prohibiting the practice, the legal landscape will continue to allow police impersonation of the press, including its negative effects.

Press Impersonation of Police

Like with police impersonation of the press, a journalist or news organization can raise a First Amendment claim regarding press impersonation of police. However, in this case, the press would be arguing for the First Amendment right to impersonate the police rather than requesting the prohibition of the practice. More specifically, the journalist or news organization could argue that federal or state statutes prohibiting impersonation of the police are unconstitutional because they chill protected First Amendment activity, namely, undercover reporting. Nevertheless, the result is the same: a First Amendment claim is unlikely to succeed.

Once again, it is possible that a journalist or news organization filing the claim could establish standing, as well as plausibly allege a First

Amendment violation and potential harms. The claim could first raise similar arguments as the complaint targeting police impersonation of the press, including that the First Amendment provides protection from government intrusion into news gathering. The press could point to the finding in *Branzburg* that "news gathering is not without its First Amendment protections,"[105] for example, to argue that the First Amendment should provide protection for impersonation of police as a form of news gathering.

Second, the complaint could focus on undercover reporting and stunt journalism, news-gathering tactics with long histories in the United States and abroad.[106] The press's main argument would be that such reporting is imperative to investigative journalism on matters of public concern and that statutes prohibiting impersonation of police chill journalists' ability to conduct such reporting. Without the ability to conduct such investigations, the press would be unable to fully inform the public and hold government and law enforcement accountable.

At the federal level, 18 U.S.C. § 912, found under chapter 43, "False Impersonation," and titled "Officer or Employee of the United States," provides that anyone who "assumes or pretends" to be a federal "officer or employee" is fined or imprisoned for up to three years, or both. Every state and the District of Columbia also prohibit impersonation of police, though statutes vary about whether doing so is a felony or a misdemeanor.[107] Statutory law also prohibits other actions that can allow an individual to impersonate a police officer, including forging public documents, using emergency lights, and failing to obey a law enforcement officer's order. The press could at least attempt to argue that such laws chill journalists' First Amendment activity, namely, using impersonation of police to conduct undercover reporting.

Recently, the argument that undercover reporting raises key First Amendment implications has been brought up in different contexts. One such context is so-called ag-gag laws, state statutes that generally prohibit individuals or organizations, including the press, from gaining access to and recording agricultural and livestock areas restricted to the general public. In recent years, federal courts have ruled that several states' statutes violated the First Amendment, including in Iowa, Idaho, North Carolina, Wyoming, Utah, and Kansas.[108] Courts have generally found that portions of ag-gag statutes amount to content- and viewpoint-based regulation of speech in violation of the First Amendment that cannot survive strict-scrutiny review. Courts have further held that the laws cause First Amendment harm to plaintiffs seeking to do undercover investigations because protected expression on matters of public concern would result from such investigating. Although the plaintiffs in these cases are generally animal-safety advocacy groups, they nevertheless raised important arguments about the ability to conduct undercover investigations that carry key implications for the press.

Legal questions have also arisen around claims by undercover video makers that they are entitled to First Amendment protection for their controversial hidden camera videos. As with the plaintiffs in ag-gag cases, although these video makers are not traditional journalists, they have raised important First Amendment claims regarding undercover reporting with significant implications for the press. For example, political activist James O'Keefe, an undercover filmmaker known for posting controversial hidden-camera videos on his website, Project Veritas, previously targeted the *New York Times*, the *Washington Post*, CNN, and others. In a 2018 case, the District of Massachusetts ruled that a state statute prohibiting the secret recording of a public official was unconstitutional, reasoning that "the First Amendment protects the right to record audio and video of government officials."[109]

A final area of law that a journalist or news organization could raise in arguing for a First Amendment right to pose as police officers is protection for false speech, such as if a journalist falsely identified themselves as a police officer. In *United States v. Alvarez* (2012), the Supreme Court struck down the Stolen Valor Act, which prohibited lying about receiving military awards or medals, such as the Congressional Medal of Honor.[110] The Court held that "the remedy for speech that is false is speech that is true," not government suppression. The Court further held that false statements are protected by the First Amendment so long as they do not cause a "legally cognizable harm" or provide "material gain" to the speaker, therefore limiting the extent to which false speech is protected.

Although a journalist or news organization could at least plausibly raise a First Amendment claim for protection to impersonate a police officer, they would be unlikely to succeed for several reasons. First, a court would likely cite the finding in *Cohen v. Cowles Media Co.* (1991) that laws of general applicability apply to the press, including those at the federal and state levels that make it a crime to impersonate a law enforcement official or officer.[111] Furthermore, as discussed above, First Amendment protection for news gathering, including undercover reporting, is not absolute.

Second, a court would be unlikely to strike down such statutes on First Amendment grounds. In fact, in *United States v. Chappell* (2012), the Fourth Circuit held that there is no First Amendment right to impersonate a police officer, declining to strike down Virginia's statute.[112] The case arose in October 2009 when Douglas Chappell was pulled over for speeding by a U.S. park police officer in Washington, D.C. To avoid a ticket, Chappell falsely told the officer that he was a Fairfax County deputy sheriff, where he previously worked more than a year earlier. Chappell also provided a false employee identification number before admitting his lie. He was charged with impersonating a police officer in violation of Virginia Code § 18.2-174. Chappell filed a complaint alleging that the statute was unconstitutional on its face under the First Amendment, focusing in particular on the clause prohibiting "falsely assum[ing] or pretend[ing] to be any such officer," under which he was charged. The Fourth Circuit declined to find the statute invalid on its face, reasoning that the law "has a plainly legitimate sweep. By protecting unsuspecting citizens from those who falsely pretend to be law enforcement officers, the statute serves the Commonwealth's critical interest in public safety." The statute also "deters individuals from pretending to be police officers in an attempt to evade fines, incarceration, and other state-imposed sanctions," which was what Chappell admitted he was attempting to do. Conversely, striking down the statute, according to the court, would risk undermining police functions by adding "an untold flock of faux policemen." Thus, the ruling demonstrated that police interests would likely outweigh interests of the news media in attempting to impersonate a police officer, much like a First Amendment claim against police impersonation of the press.

Finally, as revealed by the history of press impersonation of the police, there are several negative effects that could further undermine the news media's arguments, including decreased public trust, the straining of the press-police relationship, and the undermining of the institutions' independence. Taken together, these effects demonstrate the problematic nature of press impersonation of police, potentially further leading a court to rule against a First Amendment claim seeking to allow the practice. However, even though press impersonation of police is illegal across the United States, unlike police impersonation of the press, some journalists may still take the chance of using the practice, bringing with it negative effects needing to be addressed.

Media Ride-Alongs

A seminal moment in media ride-alongs came in 1999 when the Supreme Court ruled in *Wilson v. Layne* that under the Fourth Amendment, members of the press and the media cannot enter private homes while police execute search warrants unless they receive the consent of the homeowner or aid the police in their law enforcement duties.[113] *Wilson* settled a circuit-court split in which the Second Circuit in *Ayeni v. Mottola* (1994) and the Ninth Circuit in *Berger v. Hanlon* (1997) concluded that the presence of the news media during the execution of a search warrant was unreasonable under the Fourth Amendment, whereas the Eighth Circuit held in *Parker v. Boyer* (1996) that media ride-alongs during the execution of a search warrant do not violate the Fourth Amendment.[114]

One ruling that applied the Supreme Court's reasoning in *Wilson* was *Smart v. City of Miami* (2015).[115] The case arose following the murders of two teenagers in a Miami, Florida, apartment. The ensuing investigation was recorded by a camera crew for the reality television show *The First 48*, including the interrogation of plaintiff Taiwan Smart, the prime suspect, who lived in the same apartment. Smart, who was arrested for second-degree murder, filed a lawsuit arguing that the City of Miami had violated his Fourth Amendment rights by allowing its police force to be involved in the production of *The First 48*, without training the police on the proper manner of dealing with the camera crew. Southern District of Florida judge Marcia G. Cooke ultimately held that Smart's "theory that his constitutional rights were violated . . . is sound," applying *Wilson*.

The above rulings—combined with other cases focused on other legal issues like trespass,[116] invasion of privacy,[117] and the permissibility of evidence collected during a media ride along[118]—demonstrate that although some courts have sided with the press or media in cases stemming from media ride-alongs, most have sided with individuals claiming Fourth Amendment and other violations. But despite such rulings, media ride-alongs have continued in recent years, including by major news networks, as well as new reality television shows based on the same concept as *Cops*. As discussed in the previous chapter, these shows raise additional negative effects in relation to media ride-alongs, including legal issues, overly positive views of policing, and stereotyping of marginalized communities. Similar concerns also arise when police conduct virtual or social media ride-alongs.

Given all these concerns arising from media ride-alongs, including complicated legal issues and consequences, why do they still continue more than twenty years after *Wilson*? Perhaps the primary reason is that the ruling and other federal court rulings limited prohibitions of ride-alongs to only the entering of private places without the owner's or a third party's consent. The media remain able to record police activities in public spaces, though consent from those being recorded remains an important consideration, especially to avoid a lawsuit for invasion of privacy or other claims.

Additionally, departments across the United States have implemented policies regarding ride-alongs, which detail the eligibility of participants, how to sign up for a ride-along, instructions and rules, and more.[119] Other policies cover whether to allow ride-along participants to enter certain locations and scenes, including in response to *Wilson*.[120] Some jurisdictions have taken a different approach and have banned reality television crews from riding along with police, including in Detroit in 2010 after a seven-year-old girl was shot and killed during a raid in which *The First 48* accompanied police.[121] Although court precedent, department policies, and local government decisions help mitigate some of the concerns with media ride-alongs, including better protecting the safety of those riding along and avoiding privacy concerns, several negative effects identified by the history of the practice still remain. Such issues include the undermining of trust in both the press and the police, legal consequences in some cases, and limiting the press's ability to fully inform the public and hold law enforcement accountable. Even the safety concerns arising from media ride-alongs cannot be fully eliminated, requiring action to address these negative effects.

Taken as a whole, the legal landscape around the press-police relationship not only adds additional context to the development of the press and police into the institutions we see today, but also helps explain why the two entities interact in the ways that they do. Put simply, the legal landscape allows cooperative coexistence, contentiousness, impersonation, and media ride-alongs to happen and continue, despite the negative effects that some of the press's and police's interactions raise.

But that does not mean that change is impossible. That does not mean the press-police relationship cannot be improved. In fact, it is quite the opposite. Although no quick, magical solution exists, there are steps both the news media and law enforcement can take moving forward that are built on recommendations informed by the history and law of their relationship and, significantly, with the best interests of all members of the public in mind.

The Future of the Press-Police Relationship

BEGINNING IN THE AMERICAN COLONIES and throughout the period in which they began to take their modern forms (1830s–'50s), the press and police have evolved, often in similar ways, in response to numerous political, economic, social, and technological forces that spawned changes ranging from urbanization, immigration, and industrialization in the nineteenth century to the rise of the digital era in the twentieth and twenty-first. In each period, the press and police responded in ways that implicated their relationship, with some eras defined by greater partnerships and trust and others by more division and conflict. But despite all these changes, cooperative coexistence and contentiousness, as well as unique practices like impersonation and media ride-alongs, continuously defined the press-police relationship. Among other factors, the legal landscape ensures that this is the case by allowing, in different ways, each interaction to continue. So, what's next? What can we learn from the history and law of the press-police relationship? Moving forward, although government, advocacy organizations, and other individuals and institutions may play a role, it is up to the news media and law enforcement to shape and improve their relationship, doing so for the benefit of the public.

Balancing Cooperative Coexistence and Contentiousness

Throughout the history of the press-police relationship, three main practices—press coverage of police, press accountability of police, and law enforcement targeting the press—have defined the interactions between the institutions. The first type of interaction, press coverage of police, dates back even further to spoken, written, and printed news, as well as the first publications in the New World. It continued with the penny press, which marked the modern conceptions of news. From then on, coverage of law enforcement remained a fundamental part of print journalism, as well as in or on films, radio, television, and the internet, leading to cooperative coexistence. Press accountability of police, the second type of interaction, followed a similar trajectory, though generally leading to greater contentiousness. The third type of interaction, law enforcement targeting the press, further fuels contentiousness through arrests, use of force, threats, searches and seizures, subpoenas, and surveillance.

Part of the reason such practices have continued despite their problems is the legal landscape. And rightfully so; it's important that the key functions served by the press and the police be preserved to a significant extent. In terms of cooperative coexistence, constitutional, statutory, and common laws provide the press with important protections from government intrusion needed to gather, publish, and disseminate news, including related to law enforcement. The press can therefore carry out its functions largely free from government and police intrusion. However, the legal landscape also prevents press intrusion into law enforcement activities in several ways, including favoring the interests of law enforcement over those of the press. Furthermore, the press generally does not have greater rights or protections than members of the public; it does not, for example, have a special First Amendment right of access to locations and information or special protection from laws of general applicability. By limiting press intrusion, the legal landscape similarly allows law enforcement to perform its important functions free from interference. By allowing significant latitude for both institutions to generally fulfill their responsibilities, even when interacting, the legal landscape creates opportunities for cooperative coexistence.

Where this changes and leads the relationship toward contentiousness is if in the course of their duties one institution ends up specifically targeting the other. More specifically, the legal landscape does not eliminate the press's ability to investigate, criticize, or critically report on the police. The same goes for law enforcement when it targets the news media. Although the legal landscape limits the press and police interfering with each other, it still allows each to fulfill its responsibilities in a way that does not completely prevent them from at times acting in ways that create conflict and divisiveness.

We all rely on the press for garnering and distributing information and holding all citizens, including the powerful, accountable. Law enforcement, too, is supposed to play a crucial role in public safety and order. We therefore need both institutions to perform at their best level, something that is hindered when the press and police are in direct conflict with one another. Recent cases of contentiousness between the press and police, such as during the protests around the murder of George Floyd in 2020, demonstrate that both institutions are still in need of change in order to ensure that both institutions might properly serve the public.

Fortunately, there are tangible steps the press and police can take to this end. The press-police relationship has always worked best and had the least negative effects in periods of cooperative coexistence, so the same is likely the prescription moving forward. In times marked by cooperation, both institutions function without interfering with one another, at least to the point that the press and police do not undermine the other's purposes. To a large degree, the current legal landscape fosters the possibility for press-police cooperation by limiting one's intrusion of the other. It is imperative that members of the press and police respect the important role both institutions play in the United States. Doing so requires open and honest communication, opportunities for shared training, and education about the legality and effects of their actions.

Of course, it is important that cooperative coexistence ends up serving the public and not end up perpetuating racism and sexism and otherwise harming marginalized people and communities, much like what occurred during Jim Crow and other eras. Cooperative coexistence can also become problematic when engaging in certain methods, such as impersonation and media ride-alongs. Issues can also arise if the press provides overly positive coverage of police or knowingly publishes fabricated information released by law enforcement. Cooperative coexistence is therefore not a panacea, but this is where journalism ethics—for example, covering crime only when it is actually newsworthy and providing a complete picture of what took place by using other sources in addition to law enforcement such as community members—and broader reforms of law enforcement tactics become important safeguards to complement cooperative coexistence.

At the same time, contentiousness, although not ideal, will never simply go away. And, to some degree, it is also necessary. Journalists absolutely must continue covering, investigating, and criticizing the police. At a minimum, the press must remain skeptical of police accounts and push the police to answer necessary questions, in order to inform the public and hold law enforcement accountable. The police, too, may in certain exceptionally rare cases need to target members of the press with arrests, use of force, searches and seizures, subpoenas, or surveillance. While the current legal landscape ensures that these actions can continue, it does not adequately address the negative effects these actions might spark.

It is therefore necessary for both the press and the police to take steps to minimize contentiousness to the greatest extent possible without undermining their prescribed roles. At the very least, both institutions should try to ensure that the relationship remain uncontentious unless absolutely necessary. For the press, it is imperative that journalists and news organizations follow ethical guidelines and considerations to the greatest extent possible when covering or investigating matters related to the police. Such principles include fair and accurate reporting, using caution when relying on police sources or access granted by police, recognizing potential harm arising from reporting on law enforcement, and being transparent, all with the good of the public in mind. The result may still be police officials and offers becoming upset at or pushing against the critical reporting targeting them, but in any such cases journalists will have done their best to get the reporting right for their audience in a way that holds the powerful accountable.

Police, in turn, must continue to carry out their duties in ways that avoid targeting the press, especially through secretive and clandestine means. This requires better police training in how to interact with the press, including at the federal, state, and local levels. The same goes for how to address protests, whether peaceful or violent, in which members of the news media are present and the scene has the capacity to become more chaotic. Topics covered during such police training, which could include the presence of members of the press or advocacy groups— or incorporate them as instructors—might include First and Fourth Amendment rights, as well as the negative effects arising practices targeting journalists.[1] Training should also emphasize the importance of independent journalists as critical to ensuring public confidence in government institutions, providing additional motivation for officials and officers to follow what was covered during the training. In the event that training does not go far enough or proves to be ineffective, federal, state, and local government bodies should pass legislation "placing conditions on . . . funding to encourage law enforcement to adopt policy changes to promote better community relations," including with the press.[2] Such policy changes could include disciplinary actions for officers who violate the law or department policies, expanded efforts to collect data on police interactions with the press and public, and an emphasis on reasonable and responsible actions regarding protected First Amendment activity. By taking such actions, the press and police can not only help each other and improve their relationship, but also better serve the public.

Where the Greatest Problems Arise: Impersonation and Media Ride-Alongs

Emphasizing cooperative coexistence over contentiousness is a good place for the press and police to begin improving their relationship. However, the most problematic interactions are those that uniquely bridge cooperative coexistence and contentiousness, raising several negatives that remain in our current moment. Although police impersonation of the press is seen as "rare" by some observers,[3] the practice dates back to at least 1889 and has continued to the present day. Throughout this history, police impersonation of the press raised several significant problems for the latter, including undermining the press's credibility, relationships with key informants, news-gathering ability, safety, and independence. Importantly, the practice also undermines public trust in police departments, officials, and officers, as it undermines public trust in the police. From the first documented instance of press impersonation of police in 1877, the practice has resulted in the discipline of and legal consequences for journalists who employed the practice, as well as undermining press functions, credibility, and safety like when the police use impersonation. Finally, media ride-alongs, which date back to the introduction of the first horse-drawn patrol wagons, raise their own share of concerns, including some of the same ones stemming from impersonation, namely, that the practice precludes the press from fully informing the public or holding police accountable for their actions, as well as undermines journalists' safety, credibility, and independence. Additionally, ride-alongs put journalists at risk of facing legal repercussions.

All the risks notwithstanding, including straining their relationship, the reason the police and the press continue to use impersonation and media ride-alongs is because at times they find the practices effective. In justifying police impersonation of the press, law enforcement can point to public safety, claiming that it helps them conduct investigations and end standoff or hostage situations. For its part, the press employs impersonation of the police as a means of surreptitious news gathering. In the case of media ride-alongs, the purported benefits for both institutions include improved community relations for the police and a hands-on method of covering law enforcement for the press. The problem with these practices is of course the noted negative effects, which have not received adequate attention and are overshadowed by the purported benefits, resulting in them often going undisclosed to the public.

The legal landscape around impersonation and media ride-alongs is deeply complicated and raises issues concerning constitutional, statutory, and common law, as well as federal, state, and local law enforcement agency or department policies and guidelines. As with cooperative coexistence and contentiousness, the law largely allows the practices of impersonation and media ride-alongs to continue. Perhaps most problematic is that the law does not go far enough in curtailing the negative effects of police impersonation of the press, press impersonation of police, and media ride-alongs. As a result, it is left up to both to take actions to address these concerns in the interest of serving the public.

Even if new laws were enacted to limit, but not eliminate, police impersonation of the press, it would not be enough to preclude the possible negative effects of the practice, simply because it is most often done in secret, without the press's knowledge. Instead, law enforcement must completely eliminate its impersonation of the press to improve the press-police relationship and both institutions' relations with the public. More specifically, the DOJ and FBI must take the lead in adopting a policy that eliminates the practice, not just purportedly limiting its use to exceptional cases. In doing so, the federal government and federal law enforcement can set an example for state and local police to follow. Only by categorically prohibiting impersonation of the press can law enforcement assure the news media that the practice has ended and stifle its negative effects.

Certain federal and state laws have already made impersonation of law enforcement illegal, with little hope that a First Amendment newsgathering claim would succeed in allowing the press to use the practice. However, to further ensure that the negative effects do not occur, the press must look to alternatives, much like the police must do instead of continuing to impersonate the press. Certainly, it is important that journalists and news organizations continue to hold law enforcement accountable, but they must do so without blurring the lines dividing the press-police relationship. National news organizations can, and should, take the lead in denouncing the practice and emphasizing that it should be avoided at the regional and local levels as well.

Unlike impersonation, media ride-alongs present potential benefits that are not completely outweighed by the potential problems the practice poses. Nevertheless, action is still needed. For too long, the problems arising from media ride-alongs have not received adequate attention, with the practice garnering generally more praise than criticism. I have therefore sought to go beyond existing literature in demonstrating the long history of these negative effects and make three recommendations for how the press in particular might address the matter. To start, journalists and news organizations should seek alternatives to media ride-alongs whenever possible, particularly through traditional reporting methods such as interviewing multiple sources, obtaining and reviewing police records, and transporting themselves to the location of a news story or investigation. Doing so would mitigate concerns about undermining reporters' safety, credibility, and independence, as well as allow for better opportunities to provide a full, even critical, view of law enforcement. By ceasing to engage in media ride-alongs, the press can decrease its reliance on the police for access to information and reestablish the necessary independence from law enforcement to best inform the public and hold police accountable.

As noted, however, media ride-alongs have been employed for important reasons, such as providing journalists access otherwise unavailable to the police and crime scenes. So, if reporters cannot or choose not to avoid going on media ride-alongs, they should provide greater transparency about the practice, including their specific case-by-case reasons for using it, to their readers or viewers. Journalists also should explain that the ride-along in question was not meant to and cannot provide a complete picture of law enforcement actions, meaning that the coverage does not fully hold police officials and officers accountable. Second, journalists using media ride-alongs should find and utilize alternative ways to examine and report on what in the story may have been left out, missed, or handled differently due to their presence in the vehicle, ensuring they are not simply providing positive public relations for the police. Furthermore, if accountability of the police simply cannot be achieved through media ride-alongs, reporters must take other measures to make sure that it is not completely missing from their reporting. In so doing, the press can complement the more positive or neutral coverage generally stemming from media ride-alongs with important critical reporting, helping to mitigate the possible negative effects arising from the practice.

Reform and change have long been a part of the press-police relationship, sometimes leading to positive effects. But as the press and police face ever-increasing pressure and scrutiny, both institutions are in need of modification and improvement, especially if each party wishes to win back the trust of, as well as properly serve, all members of the public, including from marginalized communities. Amid these broader reforms, more also should be done to improve the press-police relationship. Doing so might minimize negative effects arising from their interactions, implicating not only each other and their relationship but also the public. And this is why these recommendations matter. For years, the press and police have sought to delineate their roles, even though they both ultimately strive to benefit and serve the public. When these institutions fall short of this goal, or fail outright, it is the American public that suffers, especially that part of it living in marginalized communities. It is my hope my recommendations are steps in the right direction.

In May 2020, the press-police relationship in the United States came to the forefront of national attention amid demonstrations following the murder of George Floyd. The public watched as demonstrators as well as journalists faced arrests, use of force, threats, searches, and surveillance by police. Amid the clouds of tear gas and smoke from burning buildings and vehicles, reporters, photographers, and other members of the press covered the scenes, critically reporting on what was taking place, including law enforcement's actions. It was a moment of significant tension and conflict between the press and police, falling as part of a story of the press-police relationship that began with the very foundations of the republic in the American colonies and the creation of the modern forms of both institutions in the 1830s–'50s.

Existing literature has covered different aspects of the press-police relationship;[4] however, its history and law have remained largely unstudied,[5] necessitating this book, which aimed to provide the most comprehensive history and legal analysis of the press-police relationship to date. The story of the press-police relationship in the United States is important to tell, as it describes how two separate entities underwent changes across different eras in response to the societal context around them to carve out their role and authority, continuously defining and redefining their boundaries and eventually becoming the independent institutions as we conceive of them today.[6] Significantly, such efforts came amid the press and police interacting in ways that transcended time periods and major societal upheavals. In this sense, the press and police developed together across different historical moments. The ebb and flow of cooperative coexistence and contentiousness as well as unique practices like impersonation and media ride-alongs continue in the present, in large part due to a legal landscape that permits the press to cover the police and hold them accountable, law enforcement to target the press, and practices of impersonation and ride-alongs to continue to varying degrees.

The press and police remain fundamental and important parts of American society given their normative responsibilities.[7] The press's purposes and functions continue to be important, as the news media is meant to inform the public and hold the powerful accountable. The police also play a crucial role in that law enforcement is meant to pro- tect public safety, maintain order, and more. However, increased tension and scrutiny of both institutions, combined with decreasing public trust and resources, as well as ongoing identity crises and boundary work, have raised questions about the future of both the press and the police, as well as the relationship between the two. For example, as journalists and news organizations, especially at the local level, continue to see re- sources dwindle, the public will increasingly need different sources of information regarding crime. For their part, the police have increased the use of social media and press releases to provide this information. Concerns, however, arise about what is lost when the press is not the one providing this information: Does this, for example, let the police skirt accountability?

Both the news media and law enforcement are the subject of calls for reform, some more significant and wide reaching than others and too wide ranging and complicated to be adequately discussed and an- alyzed herein. But, crucially, amid these broader efforts of reform, it is up to both the press and the police to play a role in improving their relationship to help ensure that they are benefiting and serving the pub- lic, including marginalized communities, to the greatest extent possible. As I have done my best to attest, cooperative coexistence is the ideal way for the press and police to interact, as it allows both institutions to retain their independence yet still, at least ideally, accomplish their important goals. The case studies provided in this book, combined with social responsibility theory,[8] the press's "collaborative role,"[9] and the legal landscape,[10] demonstrate how and why cooperative coexistence can, and will, continue, namely, with proper efforts towards open communication, education, and training.

That said, contentiousness is a natural part of the press-police relationship, one that cannot be completely avoided. Once more, case studies across different eras, including First Amendment theory,[11] criminal justice theory,[12] and the legal landscape,[13] helped explain why contentiousness will continue moving forward. It is imperative that the news media continue to hold law enforcement accountable, even if doing so risks straining the press-police relationship. By the same token, there may be rare, exceptional instances wherein the police may need to target a member of the press or limit news gathering. However, it is imperative that both institutions limit contentious actions to only those they deem absolutely necessary, requiring emphasis on ethics, training, and other actions.

Particular attention needs to be paid to minimizing or, even better, eliminating the significant negative effects arising from the particularly problematic practices that bridge cooperative coexistence and contentiousness. The legal landscape does not go far enough in eliminating impersonation, requiring that both the press and police take necessary steps to cease the practices of impersonating each other. It is also necessary for the press to limit the use of media ride-alongs, or, at the very least, provide transparency and additional reporting when the practice is used.

Can the events surrounding Floyd's death lead to change in the press-police relationship? Even if so, change will come neither easily nor rapidly. Reforms to the press-police relationship must happen across different locations and between different journalists, news organizations, and police departments, officials, and officers, at the local, state, and national levels. Certainly, conflict between the press and police will continue, as will the political, economic, social, and technological problems each faces. But none of this indicates that meaningful change is unattainable. In fact, if history tells us anything, it confirms the opposite. Although there have been entire eras of division and conflict, there have also been just as many of successful cooperation and coexistence between the two institutions that provided the best chance to serve the public well.

In 1833, Benjamin Day did not realize that he had published the first modern crime story, a key moment in the long history between the press and police in the United States. Nearly two centuries later, in 2020, as journalists faced arrests, use of force, threats, searches, and surveillance from law enforcement amid the protests over the murder of George Floyd, the members of both institutions were unlikely to have reflected on the complicated history and legal landscape between the press and police. But these key moments present good opportunities to ponder the important story of the press-police relationship and how both foundational institutions might best serve the public going forward.

NOTES

Introduction
Understanding the U.S. Press-Police Relationship

1. *New York Sun*, September 8, 1833, 2.

2. Michael Schudson, *Discovering the News: A Social History of American Newspapers*, 22. The *New York Sun* is heralded by media historians as the first successful newspaper of the penny press, though it was not the first newspaper to be sold for a penny. For example, the *Boston Transcript* began publication in July 1830 and was sold for four dollars a year. However, it and other antecedents to the *Sun* did not have the longevity or the focus on "modern" news that Day's paper and his competitors would bring.

3. Brandon Stahl, Jennifer Bjorhus, and MaryJo Webster, "Denied Justice: Minnesota's Failed Rape Investigations," *Minneapolis Star Tribune*, July 22, 2018, https://www.startribune.com/denied-justice-series-when-rape-is-reported-and-nothing-happens-minnesota-police-sexual-assault-investigations/487400761/.

4. "Denied Justice Podcast/Postscript: Investigating Rape," *Minneapolis Star Tribune*, March 13, 2019, http://www.startribune.com/follow-the-denied-justice-podcast/488719141/.

5. "Press Freedom in Crisis."

6. *Wilson v. Layne*, 526 U.S. 606, 607 (1999).

7. Wilson v. Layne, 526 U.S. 603 (1999).

8. Alan Vinegrad, "Law Enforcement and the Media: Cooperative Co-existence," 237.

9. Larry E. Sullivan, *Encyclopedia of Law Enforcement*, 303; James E. Guffey, "The Police and the Media: Proposals for Managing Conflict Productively," 33–34; Karen M. Markin, "An 'Unholy Alliance': The Law of Media Ride-Alongs," 33; Nancy L. Trueblood, "Curbing the Media: Should Reporters Pay When Police Ride-Alongs Violate Privacy?"; Patricia A. Kelly, ed., *Police and the Media: Bridging Troubled Waters*; Brian A. Jackson, "Strengthening Trust between Police and the Public in an Era of Increasing Transparency"; Louise Cooke and Paul Sturges, "Police and Media Relations in an Era of Freedom of Information," 407; Steven Chermak and Alexander Weiss, "Maintaining Legitimacy Using External Communication Strategies:

An Analysis of Police-Media Relations"; Rob C. Mawby, "Continuity and Change, Convergence and Divergence: The Policy and Practice of Police Media Relations."

10. Vinegrad, "Law Enforcement and the Media," 237; Larry Jones, "Police and Media Relations: How to Bridge the Gap," 1; Howard Giles, *Law Enforcement, Communication, and Community*, 47; Gerald W. Garner, *The Police Meet the Press*, 1; Pati Hendrickson and Howard Swindle, "The Symbiotic, but Conflicted Relationship between Law Enforcement and the Media: A Case Study," 1; William L. Selke and Marshall G. Bartoszek, "Police and Media Relations: The Seeds of Conflict," 25; Jeremy Borden, "'Cease and Desist': Journalism's Strained Relationship with Police."

11. Kelly, "Police and the Media," 130; Gerald W. Garner, *"Chief, the Reporters Are Here': The Police Executive's Personal Guide to Press Relations*, 4–5; David M. Mozee, "Police/Media Conflict," 141.

12. Seth C. Lewis, "The Tension between Professional Control and Open Participation."

13. Matt Carlson, "Metajournalistic Discourse and the Meanings of Journalism: Definitional Control, Boundary Work, and Legitimation."

14. Commission on Freedom of the Press, *A Free and Responsible Press*; James Melvin Lee, *History of American Journalism*, 430; Frederick S. Siebert, Theodore Peterson, and Wilbur Schramm, *Four Theories of the Press: The Authoritarian, Libertarian, Social Responsibility, and Soviet Communist Concepts of What the Press Should Be and Do*, 74; Thomas Scanlon, "A Theory of Freedom of Expression," 130–32; Wilbur Schramm, *Responsibility in Mass Communication*, 103.

15. Clifford G. Christians et al., *Normative Theories of the Media: Journalism in Democratic Societies*, 196.

16. Ray Surette, *Media, Crime, and Criminal Justice: Images and Realities*, 1st ed., 5–6.

17. For a nonexhaustive assortment of previous literature focusing on different elements of the U.S. press-police relationship, see Jarret S. Lovell, *Good Cop/Bad Cop: Mass Media and the Cycle of Police Reform*, 8; Alan Vinegrad, "Law Enforcement and the Media: Cooperative Co-existence," 237; Sullivan, *Encyclopedia of Law Enforcement*, 303; Guffey, "Police and the Media," 33–34; Markin, " 'Unholy Alliance,'" 33; Trueblood, "Curbing the Media"; Kelly, *Police and the Media*; Jackson, "Strengthening Trust"; Cooke and Sturges, "Police and Media Relations," 407; Chermak and Weiss, "Maintaining Legitimacy"; Mawby, "Continuity and Change"; L. Jones, "Police and Media Relations," 1; Giles, *Law Enforcement, Communication, and Community*, 47; Garner, *Police Meet the Press*, 1; Hendrickson and Swindle, "Symbiotic, but Conflicted Relationship," 1; Selke and Bartoszek, "Police and Media Relations," 25; Borden, "'Cease and Desist'"; Garner, *"Chief, the Reporters Are Here*," 4–5; Mozee, "Police/Media Conflict," 141; Wallace Westfeldt and Tom Wicker, *Indictment: The News Media & the Criminal Justice System*; David D. Perlmutter, *Policing the Media: Street Cops and Public Perceptions of Law Enforcement*; Jerry V. Wilson and Paul Q. Fuqua, *The Police and the Media*; John Lofton, *Justice and the Press*, 71–110; Ray Surette, *Justice and the Media: Issues and Research*; Surette, *Media, Crime, and Criminal Justice*, 1st ed.; Dennis Howitt, *Crime, the Media, and*

the Law; Steven Chermak, Edmund McGarrell, and Jeff Gruenewald, "Media Coverage of Police Misconduct and Attitudes toward Police"; Kenneth Dowler, "Media Consumption and Public Attitudes toward Crime and Justice"; Kenneth Dowler, "Media Influence on Citizen Attitudes toward Police Effectiveness"; Kevin Morrell, "How Does the Media Shape Perceptions of the Police"; Murray Lee and Alyce McGovern, *Policing and Media: Public Relations, Simulations and Communications*, 9; G. Douglas Gourley, "Police Public Relations"; Raymond E. Clift, "Police, Press, and Public Relations"; Anja Johansen, "Police-Public Relations: Interpretations of Policing and Democratic Governance"; Chermak, McGarrell, and Gruenewald, "Media Coverage of Police Misconduct"; Alfred Friendly and Ronald L. Goldfarb, *Crime and Publicity: The Impact of News on the Administration of Justice*; and Roy Lotz, *Crime and the American Press*.

18. There are certainly texts that have included a chapter or section on the history or law (or both) of the press-police relationship. See, for example, Lovell, *Good Cop/ Bad Cop*, 8. Other texts have also separately covered press history and police history. These sources are found throughout chapters 1–6. However, no single text or volume has undertaken to tell the story and law of the U.S. press-police relationship.

Chapter 1
Rise of the Modern Press and Police, 1630s–1850s

1. For discussions of the history of the press prior to the American colonies, see Mitchell Stephens, *A History of News*, 9–20, 31, 91; John Nerone, *Media and Public Life: A History*, 12–13; and Willard Grosvenor Bleyer, *Main Currents in the History of American Journalism*, 3–8, 28.

2. For discussions of the history of the law enforcement prior to the American colonies, see Baillie Reynolds, "The Police in Ancient Rome"; Radley Balko, *Rise of the Warrior Cop: The Militarization of America's Police Forces*, chap. 1; William J. Bopp and Donald O. Schultz, *A Short History of American Law Enforcement*, 5–7; and James A. Conser et al., *Law Enforcement in the United States*, 30–32. The word *police* derives from the Ancient Greek word *polis*, meaning "city."

3. Wm. David Sloan, *The Media in America: A History*, 17. For more on early American publications, see Bleyer, *Main Currents*, 47–51, 74; Christopher B. Daly, *Covering America: A Narrative History of a Nation's Journalism*, 20; Sidney Kobre, *Development of American Journalism*, 9, 45–48; Frank Luther Mott, *American Journalism: A History, 1690–1960*, 8, 40, 48–50; George Henry Payne, *History of Journalism in the United States*, 26, 66; and Wm. David Sloan and Julie Hedgepeth Williams, *The Early American Press, 1690–1783*, 17–19.

4. Stephens, *A History of News*, 131.

5. Payne, *History of Journalism in the United States*, 19.

6. For discussions of the partisan press in New England and developments due to the Revolutionary War and two-party system, see Bleyer, *Main Currents*, 76–79, 90, 93, 101–5, 136; Daly, *Covering America*, 36–37, 45–47; Carol Sue Humphrey, *The Press of the Young Republic, 1783–1833*, 155–58; Kobre, *Development of American Journalism*, 7, 53, 66–72, 106–10, 134; J. Lee, *History of American Journalism*, 82,

100–104, 117–18; Mott, *American Journalism*, 47, 63–64, 71, 95, 101, 113–15, 148; Nerone, *Media and Public Life*, 13–14, 56–57, 60–61, 70–72; Paul Starr, *The Creation of the Media: Political Origins of Modern Communication*, 57, 73–77; Payne, *History of Journalism in the United States*, 86, 101, 117, 135–36, 153, 177–80, 190; and Sloan, *Media in America*, 90–91.

7. Daly, *Covering America*, 35; David Paul Nord, *Communities of Journalism: A History of American Newspapers and Their Readers*, 81.

8. Jean Folkerts, Dwight L. Teeter, and Edward Caudill, *Voices of a Nation: A History of Mass Media in the United States*, 89; Richard R. John, *Spreading the News: The American Postal System from Franklin to Morse*, 1–24.

9. J. Lee, *History of American Journalism*, 143; Mott, *American Journalism*, 168–69.

10. Mott, *American Journalism*, 135; Kobre, *Development of American Journalism*, 276–77.

11. Sloan, *Media in America*, 179, 183–86; Payne, *History of Journalism in the United States*, 190–92, 296; Kobre, *Development of American Journalism*, 282–83, 460–61, 480, 551, 561.

12. For discussions of law enforcement in the American colonies, see Samuel Walker, *Popular Justice: A History of American Criminal Justice*, 13–18, 25–26, 36; Herbert A. Johnson, Nancy Travis Wolfe, and Mark Jones, *History of Criminal Justice*, 105, 121, 202; Bopp and Schultz, *Short History of American Law Enforcement*, 21, 26; Kenneth G. Alfers, *Law and Order in the Capital City: A History of the Washington Police, 1800–1886*, 7; Lionel Pender, ed., *To Serve and Protect: The History of Policing*, 33; Samuel Walker and Charles M. Katz, *The Police in America: An Introduction*, 26; Robert C. Wadman and William Thomas Allison, *To Protect and Serve: History of Police in America*, 8–9; Michael P. Roth and Tom Kennedy, *Houston Blue: The Story of the Houston Police Department*, 2–4; James F. Richardson, *The New York Police: Colonial Times to 1901*, 7; Roger Lane, *Policing the City: Boston, 1822–1885*, 7–8; Westfeldt and Wicker, *Indictment*; Perlmutter, *Policing the Media*; and J. Wilson and Fuqua, *Police and the Media*.

13. For more information on the watch system, see S. Walker and Katz, *Police in America*, 26; S. Walker, *Popular Justice*, 27; Lane, *Policing the City*, 10; Richardson, *New York Police*, 8–11; Wadman and Allison, *To Protect and Serve*, 10, 55–56; Bopp and Schultz, *Short History of American Law Enforcement*, 16, 27; H. Johnson, Wolfe, and Jones, *History of Criminal Justice*, 108–9; Thomas A. Reppetto, *American Police: The Blue Parade, 1845–1945, a History*, 5; and David R. Johnson, *American Law Enforcement: A History*, 5.

14. "The Growth of Cities"; Blake McKelvey, *American Urbanization: A Comparative History*, 37.

15. "Immigration Begins."

16. See, for example, Paul Dolan, "Rise of Crime in the Period 1830–1860."

17. Dolan, "Rise of Crime," 861.

18. Dolan, "Rise of Crime," 864.

19. See Steven Mintz and Sara McNeil, "Policing the Pre–Civil War City."

20. Lovell, *Good Cop/Bad Cop*, 8; Schudson, *Discovering the News*, 22. For discussions of the penny press and the rise of urbanization, industrialization, and immigration, see William Huntzicker, *The Popular Press, 1833–1865*; Sloan, *Media in America*, 127–28; John Nerone, "The Mythology of the Penny Press"; J. Lee, *History of American Journalism*, 163, 187, 201, 223; Mott, *American Journalism*, 215, 222–35, 241–43, 314; Kobre, *Development of American Journalism*, 197–98, 215–26, 262–67; Payne, *History of Journalism in the United States*, 240–59; Bleyer, *Main Currents*, 155–61; Starr, *Creation of the Media*, 169; Edwin Emery, *The Press and America: An Interpretive History of Journalism*, 216–17; and Richard L. Kaplan, *Politics and the American Press: The Rise of Objectivity, 1865–1920*, 11.

21. Bleyer, *Main Currents*, 158, 164, 174, 183.

22. Starr, *Creation of the Media*, 5, 12–13; Daly, *Covering America*, 77, 104–5; Sloan, *Media in America*, 133; Stephens, *A History of News*, 214, 216; J. Lee, *History of American Journalism*, 273–75.

23. For more information on Peel's force, see S. Walker, *Popular Justice*, 53; S. Walker and Katz, *Police in America*, 25; D. Johnson, *American Law Enforcement*, 18–22; Bopp and Schultz, *Short History of American Law Enforcement*, 30–31; Wilbur R. Miller, *Cops and Bobbies: Police Authority in New York and London, 1830–1870*, 2; Richardson, *New York Police*, 21–24; Alfers, *Law and Order in the Capital City*, 1–3; H. Johnson, Wolfe, and Jones, *History of Criminal Justice*, 218–20; and Marilynn S. Johnson, *Street Justice: A History of Police Violence in New York City*, 14.

24. Lovell, *Good Cop/Bad Cop*, 8; Wadman and Allison, *To Protect and Serve*, 17.

25. For more information on the rise of modern police forces, see Richardson, *New York Police*, 15; Lane, *Policing the City*, 1–2, 14, 18, 26, 29–32; S. Walker, *Popular Justice*, 49–51; Reppetto, *American Police*, chaps. 2–3, 5; Wadman and Allison, *To Protect and Serve*, 14–25, 61–62; Bopp and Schultz, *Short History of American Law Enforcement*, 33–38. Lovell, *Good Cop/Bad Cop*, 8; D. Johnson, *American Law Enforcement*, 6–8, 17, 22–24; W. Miller, *Cops and Bobbies*, 4–5, 8; Roth and Kennedy, *Houston Blue*, 7; Alfers, *Law and Order in the Capital City*, 10; H. Johnson, Wolfe, and Jones, *History of Criminal Justice*, 241; M. Johnson, *Street Justice*, 13–14; and James P. Hall, *The History and Philosophy of Law Enforcement*, 82, 88–90.

26. See Olivia B. Waxman, "How the U.S. Got Its Police Force"; Sam Mitrani, "Stop Kidding Yourself: The Police Were Created to Control Working Class and Poor People"; and Gary Potter, "The History of Policing in the United States."

27. Schudson, *Discovering the News*, 26–27; Nerone, *Media and Public Life*, 105–6; Michael Kiernan, "Police vs. the Press: There's Always Tension"; Melanie Magin and Peter Maurer, "Beat Journalism and Reporting," 7; James McGrath Morris, *The Rose Man of Sing Sing: A True Tale of Life, Murder, and Redemption in the Age of Yellow Journalism*.

28. H. Johnson, Wolfe, and Jones, *History of Criminal Justice*, 220; Clark Secrest, "Metal of Honor: A Return to the Days When 'Badgering' Reporters and 'Press Shields' Had a Whole Different Meaning," 48–50; Savannah Jacobson and Keith Henry Brown, "Who Needs a Press Pass? The Origins of an Exclusionary Object."

29. Lovell, *Good Cop/Bad Cop*, 56; S. Walker and Katz, *Police in America*, 27.

30. For more on how political organizations and politicians influenced early police departments, see Richardson, *New York Police*, 45, 53–57, 95; Lane, *Policing the City*, 95, 119; W. Miller, *Cops and Bobbies*, 17, 29, 43–47, 62–63; D. Johnson, *American Law Enforcement*, 26–27; H. Johnson, Wolfe, and Jones, *History of Criminal Justice*, 220–21; Wadman and Allison, *To Protect and Serve*, 63; M. Johnson, *Street Justice*, 3; Bopp and Schultz, *Short History of American Law Enforcement*, 41–43; S. Walker and Katz, *Police in America*, 30–33; Lovell, *Good Cop/Bad Cop*, 56–57; Dennis C. Rousey, *Policing the Southern City: New Orleans, 1805–1889*, 68, 98; and M. Lee and McGovern, *Policing and Media*, 16.

31. Juan González and Joseph Torres, *News for All the People: The Epic Story of Race and the American Media*, 8, 21–22.

32. Mott, *American Journalism*, 317–23; Payne, *History of Journalism in the United States*, 223–29; González and Torres, *News for All the People*, 41–45, 149, 154–57.

33. González and Torres, *News for All the People*, 41. See also Carol A. Stabile, *White Victims, Black Villains: Gender, Race, and Crime News in US Culture*, 5–6.

34. González and Torres, *News for All the People*, 63–64, 109–15; Folkerts, Teeter, and Caudill, *Voices of a Nation*, 107–8.

35. "African American Studies: Newspapers"; "African American & Ethnic Newspapers & Magazines"; "Publisher Charlotta Bass," PBS, accessed July 24, 2022.

36. González and Torres, *News for All the People*, 93–108.

37. Folkerts, Teeter, and Caudill, *Voices of a Nation*, 101–2; González and Torres, *News for All the People*, 69–91, 123–34; Huntzicker, *Popular Press*, 81–82.

38. González and Torres, *News for All the People*, 65.

39. "Immigrants in the United States: Newspapers."

40. Huntzicker, *Popular Press*, 79–89; Folkerts, Teeter, and Caudill, *Voices of a Nation*, 102–5.

41. Karla Kelling Sclater, "The Labor and Radical Press, 1820–the Present."

42. For more on the history of women's magazines, see Anna Luker Gilding, "Preserving Sentiments: American Women's Magazines of the 1830s and the Networks of Antebellum Print Culture," 156; and Janell Ross, "The Remarkable Political History of Women's Magazines," *Washington Post*, August 14, 2015, https://www.washingtonpost.com/news/the-fix/wp/2015/08/14/womens-magazines-go-political-but-really-theyve-been-political-since-1792/; and Amy Beth Aronson, *Taking Liberties: Early Women's Magazines and Their Readers*.

43. González and Torres, *News for All the People*, 119.

44. For more information on police brutality and the divisiveness between law enforcement and marginalized communities in the American colonies, see S. Walker, *Popular Justice*, 27; S. Walker and Katz, *Police in America*, 27; Wadman and Allison, *To Protect and Serve*, 8–9; Richardson, *New York Police*, 6, 11, 30; Lane, *Policing the City*, 26; D. Johnson, *American Law Enforcement*, 8; and W. Miller, *Cops and Bobbies*, 5.

45. Michael A. Robinson, "Black Bodies on the Ground: Policing Disparities in the African American Community—an Analysis of Newsprint from January 1, 2015, through December 31, 2015," 552.

46. Potter, "History of Policing in the United States."

47. Rousey, *Policing the Southern City*, 3–4; Roth and Kennedy, *Houston Blue*, 18; Sally E. Hadden, *Slave Patrols: Law and Violence in Virginia and the Carolinas*, 21; Richard Wade, *Slavery in the Cities: The South, 1820–1860*, 98–100; H. Johnson, Wolfe, and Jones, *History of Criminal Justice*, 223, 225.

48. Rousey, *Policing the Southern City*, 6.

49. K. B. Turner, David Giacopassi, and Margaret Vandiver, "Ignoring the Past: Coverage of Slavery and Slave Patrols in Criminal Justice Texts," 186; Amy Louise Wood and Natalie J. Ring, eds., *Crime and Punishment in the Jim Crow South*, 2–4; Wadman and Allison, *To Protect and Serve*, 36.

50. Mott, *American Journalism*, 12, 49–52; Bleyer, *Main Currents*, 61.

51. Wesley Fiorentino, "Pirates in Boston: The Trial and Execution of John Quelch," *Beehive* (blog), April 9, 2021, https://www.masshist.org/beehiveblog/2015/01/pirates-in-boston-the-trial-and-execution-of-john-quelch/.

52. Nerone, *Media and Public Life*, 32; Daly, *Covering America*, 20; J. Lee, *History of American Journalism*, 67; Mott, *American Journalism*, 49–52; Bleyer, *Main Currents*, 61; Bopp and Schultz, *Short History of American Law Enforcement*, 19, 29.

53. Fisher Ames, "Hercules," 222–25.

54. Bleyer, *Main Currents*, 136; Mott, *American Journalism*, 101. For example, in 1770, the *Connecticut Journal* reported on the frequency of murders in the area, just one example of crime news in the years leading up to, and following, the Revolutionary War.

55. Schudson, *Discovering the News*, 22. For additional research on the rise of crime news brought about by the penny press, see Mott, *American Journalism*, 222, 243–48, 297; Nerone, *Media and Public Life*, 104–6; Huntzicker, *Popular Press*, 3, 19, 26; Stephens, *A History of News*, 184, 216–29; Starr, *Creation of the Media*, 133–35; J. Lee, *History of American Journalism*, 188, 202; Payne, *History of Journalism in the United States*, 240–44; Emery, *Press and America*, 215, 251–52; Bleyer, *Main Currents*, 156, 160–65, 188; Kobre, *Development of American Journalism*, 224–29; Hazel Dicken-Garcia, *Journalistic Standards in Nineteenth-Century America*, 89; and John Lofton, *Justice and the Press*, 71–110.

56. Schudson, *Discovering the News*, 28.

57. Arthur Conan Doyle, *A Study in Scarlet*, 11.

58. *New York Daily Herald*, April 10, 1838.

59. Huntzicker, *Popular Press*, 20–21; Starr, *Creation of the Media*, 133; Daly, *Covering America*, 68; Bleyer, *Main Currents*, 169–70, 181–83; Mott, *American Journalism*, 233; Kobre, *Development of American Journalism*, 225, 234–35; Emery, *Press and America*, 222; Dan Schiller, *Objectivity and the News: The Public and the Rise of Commercial Journalism*, 12–75; Andi Tucher, *Froth & Scum: Truth, Beauty, Goodness, and the Ax Murder in America's First Mass Medium*; Patricia Cline Cohen, *The Murder of Helen Jewett: The Life and Death of a Prostitute in Nineteenth-Century New York*.

60. Roth and Kennedy, *Houston Blue*, 37–38.

61. Stephens, *A History of News*, 165–66; J. Lee, *History of American Journalism*, 32. See also Leonard W. Levy, *Emergence of a Free Press*; and Jeffery A. Smith, *Printers and Press Freedom*.

62. *New York City Gazette*, February 21, 1857; Richardson, *New York Police*, 13.

63. Richardson, *New York Police*, 19.

64. Levy, *Emergence of a Free Press*, 22–37; J. Smith, *Printers and Press Freedom*; Gordon T. Belt, "Jailed & Subpoenaed Journalists: A Historical Timeline"; RonNell Andersen Jones, "Avalanche or Undue Alarm? An Empirical Study of Subpoenas Received by the News Media". See also Nerone, *Media and Public Life*, 60–61; Payne, *History of Journalism in the United States*, 177–80; Kobre, *Development of American Journalism*, 134; J. Lee, *History of American Journalism*, 102–3; and Mott, *American Journalism*, 148.

65. For further discussions of the Zenger trial, see Daly, *Covering America*, 28; Bleyer, *Main Currents*, 64–67; Nerone, *Media and Public Life*, 37; J. Lee, *History of American Journalism*, 40–42; Payne, *History of Journalism in the United States*, 49–58; Nord, *Communities of Journalism*, 66; and Kobre, *Development of American Journalism*, 37–42.

66. Lovell, *Good Cop/Bad Cop*, 8. For additional examples of the press criticizing police during this era, see W. Miller, *Cops and Bobbies*, 42, 61, 71, 151–52; Lane, *Policing the City*, 78; Mark H. Haller, introduction to *History of the Chicago Police*, by John J. Flinn, xv; Alfers, *Law and Order in the Capital City*, 1; Bruce Smith, *Police Systems in the United States*, 1–2; and Edward Eldefonso, Alan Coffey, and Richard C. Grace, *Principles of Law Enforcement*, 6–8.

67. Richardson, *New York Police*, 21–22, 42; *New York Sun*, March 24, 1843.

68. Bopp and Schultz, *Short History of American Law Enforcement*, 41, 46; *Commercial Advertiser*, August 20, 1840; Richardson, *New York Police*, 26.

69. Elliott J. Gorn, "The Wicked World," 11–12; Richardson, *New York Police*, 62; *Police Gazette*, June 12, 19, 1847; Edward Van Every, *Sins of New York as "Exposed" by the Police Gazette*; Gene Smith, "The National Police Gazette."

70. Gorn, "The Wicked World," 11–12.

71. Bopp and Schultz, *Short History of American Law Enforcement*, 34.

72. Emery, *Press and America*, 246–47; Huntzicker, *Popular Press*, 21; Lovell, *Good Cop/Bad Cop*, 61–62; Mott, *American Journalism*, 242–43; Wilbur R. Miller, *The Social History of Crime and Punishment in America*, 1249.

73. Bopp and Schultz, *Short History of American Law Enforcement*, 34; Stephens, *A History of News*, 229, 238.

74. Matthew Pearl, "The Incredible Untold Story of America's First Police Detectives," *Boston Globe*, April 28, 2016; Haia Shpayer-Makov, *Ascent of the Detective: Police Sleuths in Victorian and Edwardian England*, 303; Lane, *Policing the City*, 57, 65.

75. Lovell, *Good Cop/Bad Cop*, 8; Lane, *Policing the City*, 96–99; *Boston Herald*, January 11, 15, 18, 24, 25, 1853.

76. J. Lee, *History of American Journalism*, 206–07.

77. "Charles Torrey: The Most Successful, Least Celebrated Abolitionist"; *American National Biography*, s.v. "Torrey, Charles Turner (1813–1846), Abolitionist," by Harold D. Tallant, February 2000.

78. *Philadelphia Public Ledger*, January 19, 1842.

79. *Philadelphia Public Ledger*, July 12, 1844.

80. See *Brooklyn Daily Eagle*, August 6, 1858; "An Editor Arrested," *Baltimore Daily Exchange*, August 14, 1858; "An Editor Arrested—Served Him Right," *Brooklyn Evening Star*, June 21, 1851; "A Reporter Arrested for Libel," *Brooklyn Times Union*, January 19, 1859; and *Lancaster (PA) Daily Evening Express*, June 2, 1858.

81. "Editor Arrested," *Burlington (VT) Free Press*, July 25, 1855; *Chicago Times*, August 29, 1857; "An Editor Arrested for Mail Robbery," *Chicago Tribune*, February 1, 1860; *Richmond (VA) Dispatch*, December 1, 1857; "Frightful Tragedy," *Cincinnati Enquirer*, June 14, 1857; *Lancaster (PA) Daily Evening Express*, June 8, 1858.

82. See, for example, "An Editor Assaulted by a Judge," *Hartford (CT) Courant*, April 26, 1842; *Louisville (KY) Daily Courier*, August 19, 1858; "An Editor Attacked with a Horsewhip!," *Buchanan County Guardian* (Independence, IA), November 18, 1858; *Baltimore Sun*, July 6, 1859; *Pittsburgh Daily Post*, March 2, 1846; and *New Bern (NC) Daily Progress*, August 15, 1859.

83. "Assaulting an Editor," *New Orleans Times-Picayune*, August 9, 1850. For additional examples, see "Editors Attacked," *Montgomery (AL) Weekly Advertiser*, October 14, 1851; "News Items," *Danville (VT) North Star*, June 17, 1854; and "City Intelligence," *Baltimore Daily Exchange*, June 20, 1859.

84. "Seizure of Arms at the Courier Office," *New Orleans Times-Picayune*, November 5, 1856; "Search Warrants: The Mayor," *New Orleans Daily Crescent*, November 10, 1856; *Cincinnati Enquirer*, June 28, 1857; "The Tail End of the Great Wentworth Drunk," *Chicago Tribune*, July 8, 1859.

85. "Arrest of James O. Brayman, Editor of the Democrat, upon a Charge of Larceny," *Chicago Daily Tribune*, August 22, 1857.

86. Stephen Bates, "*Garland v. Torre* and the Birth of Reporter's Privilege," 98.

87. "The Senate Arrests a Reporter." See also Belt, "Jailed & Subpoenaed Journalists"; and Charles D. Tobin, "From John Peter Zenger to Paul Branzburg: The Early Development of Journalist's Privilege," 33.

88. "Senate Arrests a Reporter."

Chapter 2
New Opportunities, New Problems, 1860s–1890s

1. J. Lee, *History of American Journalism*, 260; Mott, *American Journalism*, 329–30.

2. J. Lee, *History of American Journalism*, 279–83, 318; Payne, *History of Journalism in the United States*, 217, 307–25, 349; Kobre, *Development of American Journalism*, 317; Mott, *American Journalism*, 369; Sloan, *Media in America*, 145; Nerone, *Media and Public Life*, 74–79; Kaplan, *Politics and the American Press*, 23, 48, 72.

3. Kobre, *Development of American Journalism*, 327–31. See also Sloan, *Media in America*, 172–76; J. Lee, *History of American Journalism*, 288–89; and Mott, *American Journalism*, 336–37, 360.

4. Bopp and Schultz, *Short History of American Law Enforcement*, 44; Lane, *Policing the City*, 118, 126; Alfers, *Law and Order in the Capital City*, 25–26; Richardson, *New York Police*, 124–25, 129, 153–55, 136–37.

5. Reppetto, *American Police*, 263–67; D. Johnson, *American Law Enforcement*, 75–81; Bopp and Schultz, *Short History of American Law Enforcement*, 80; H. Johnson, Wolfe, and Jones, *History of Criminal Justice*, 253–54.

6. Rousey, *Policing the Southern City*, 103–7, 111, 114–19; Alfers, *Law and Order in the Capital City*, 25, 33; Wadman and Allison, *To Protect and Serve*, 36.

7. Richardson, *New York Police*, 143.

8. For more information on this wave of urbanization, industrialization, and immigration, see W. Joseph Campbell, *Yellow Journalism: Puncturing the Myths, Defining the Legacies*, 8–9; Schudson, *Discovering the News*, 97–102; Bleyer, *Main Currents*, 389–96; Kobre, *Development of American Journalism*, 349–50; Wadman and Allison, *To Protect and Serve*, 17, 61–62; Bopp and Schultz, *Short History of American Law Enforcement*, 59; Bernard Whalen and Jon Whalen, *The NYPD's First 50 Years: Politicians, Police Commissioners, and Patrolmen*, 40–41; and Richardson, *New York Police*, 165–66. See also W. Miller, *Cops and Bobbies*, 141–43; Alfers, *Law and Order in the Capital City*, 32; Richardson, *New York Police*, 166; and Lane, *Policing the City*, 133–34, 142, 150.

9. "Notable Labor Strikes of the Gilded Age," Weber State University, accessed May 18, 2022; "Labor Wars in the U.S.," PBS, accessed May 18, 2022; "City Life in the Late 19th Century."

10. For more on yellow journalism, see Campbell, *Yellow Journalism*, 11; Lovell, *Good Cop/Bad Cop*, 63; Mott, *American Journalism*, 519, 524; Bleyer, *Main Currents*, 328–29, 338–41; Schudson, *Discovering the News*, 98; and Payne, *History of Journalism in the United States*, 360–61, 363, 370.

11. Schudson, *Discovering the News*, 89, 105.

12. Stephens, *A History of News*, 267; Schudson, *Discovering the News*, 96; Nerone, *Media and Public Life*, 131; Bleyer, *Main Currents*, 396–97.

13. For more on the *New York Times* and serious journalism, see Bleyer, *Main Currents*, 239–51, 405–9; Daly, *Covering America*, 144; Kobre, *Development of American Journalism*, 259–60; Mott, *American Journalism*, 280, 551, 619–20; Sloan, *Media in America*, 217; Folkerts, Teeter, and Caudill, *Voices of a Nation*, 202–4; Lovell, *Good Cop/Bad Cop*, 63; Surette, *Media, Crime, and Criminal Justice*, 1st ed., 53–56; and Stephens, *A History of News*, 243–44.

14. *New York Times*, March 22, 1860; Mott, *American Journalism*, 389.

15. Schudson, *Discovering the News*, 89.

16. Folkerts, Teeter, and Caudill, *Voices of a Nation*, 202–4.

17. Mott, *American Journalism*, 573–74; Daly, *Covering America*, 125–27, 145–47. See, for example, Nellie Bly, "Ten Days in a Mad-House," *New York World*, series, 1887; and Ida B. Wells, *Southern Horrors: Lynch Law in All Its Phases*. Advocacy

journalists sometimes got their stories through "stunt journalism," meaning taking on roles and disguises through misrepresentation in order to uncover stories for certain institutions and industries.

18. "The Woman's Column in the Suffrage Movement: The Suffrage Press"; Jerry E. Claire, "The Role of Newspapers in the Nineteenth-Century Woman's Movement," 22–23.

19. Rousey, *Policing the Southern City*, 2–3, 7–8, 67, 198–99; Richardson, *New York Police*, 123; D. Johnson, *American Law Enforcement*, 27–28; Haller, introduction to *History of the Chicago Police*, by Flinn, v.

20. Lane, *Policing the City*, 118, 210, 219; Richardson, *New York Police*, 109, 176–78, 190, 203, 259, 284; M. Johnson, *Street Justice*, 55–64; Whalen and Whalen, *NYPD's First 50 Years*, 3–4; Roth and Kennedy, *Houston Blue*, 44; H. Johnson, Wolfe, and Jones, *History of Criminal Justice*, 257–59; Rousey, *Policing the Southern City*, 160.

21. W. Miller, *Cops and Bobbies*, 141–43; Alfers, *Law and Order in the Capital City*, 32; Richardson, *New York Police*, 166; Lane, *Policing the City*, 133–34, 142, 150; M. Johnson, *Street Justice*, 13, 37.

22. "Notable Labor Strikes of the Gilded Age"; "Labor Wars in the U.S."

23. William J. Adelman, "The Haymarket Affair"; "Act II: Let Your Tragedy Be Enacted Here". William J. Adelman, the founder of the Illinois Labor History Society and its vice president, contended that "no single event has influenced the history of labor in Illinois, the United States, and even the world, more than the Chicago Haymarket Affair."

24. Adelman, "The Haymarket Affair."

25. Rousey, *Policing the Southern City*, 7, 91.

26. Reppetto, *American Police*, 153, 225; Wadman and Allison, *To Protect and Serve*, 42–56; D. Johnson, *American Law Enforcement*, 89–97, 100; H. Johnson, Wolfe, and Jones, *History of Criminal Justice*, 227–28.

27. Alfers, *Law and Order in the Capital City*, preface, 53. See also "Brief History of the MPDC"; and "Our History."

28. González and Torres, *News for All the People*, 151–53; Kaplan, *Politics and the American Press*, 31–34; Stabile, *White Victims, Black Villains*, chaps. 3–4; Khalil Gibran Muhammad, *The Condemnation of Blackness: Race, Crime, and the Making of Modern Urban America*, 4–5.

29. "Slavery v. Peonage," PBS, accessed May 18, 2022, https://www.pbs.org/tpt/slavery-by-another-name/themes/peonage/.

30. Douglas A. Blackmon, *Slavery by Another Name: The Re-enslavement of Black People in America from the Civil War to World War II*, 1–7, 61–66; Michelle Alexander, *The New Jim Crow: Mass Incarceration in the Age of Colorblindness*, 28–31; Carol Anderson, *White Rage: The Unspoken Truth of Our Racial Divide*, 19.

31. Wood and Ring, *Crime and Punishment in the Jim Crow South*, 3–4; M. Johnson, *Street Justice*, 3–4; Bopp and Schultz, *Short History of American Law Enforcement*, 33–34; W. Miller, *Cops and Bobbies*, 5; Lane, *Policing the City*, 29; Richardson, *New York Police*, 24; Alexander, *New Jim Crow*, 42; Joel Williamson, *A Rage for Order: Black/White Relations in the American South since Emancipation*,

71, 83–84.

32. Williamson, *Rage for Order*, 84–85, 135–39; W. Fitzhugh Brundage, *Lynching in the New South: Georgia and Virginia, 1880–1930*, 180, 238.

33. Williamson, *Rage for Order*, 137. See also M. Johnson, *Street Justice*, 3.

34. J. Lee, *History of American Journalism*, 318; Mott, *American Journalism*, 376, 381; Daly, *Covering America*, 98.

35. Kaplan, *Politics and the American Press*, 118; Mott, *American Journalism*, 411, 434, 523; Kobre, *Development of American Journalism*, 356–57, 388, 428–29; Stephens, *A History of News*, 243–44, 251–53; Schudson, *Discovering the News*, 95, 105; Nerone, *Media and Public Life*, 133; Surette, *Media, Crime, and Criminal Justice*, 1st ed., 53–56; Folkerts, Teeter, and Caudill, *Voices of a Nation*, 202–4; Roth and Kennedy, *Houston Blue*, 37–38; Schudson, *Discovering the News*, 95, 98–99; Bleyer, *Main Currents*, 357; J. Lee, *History of American Journalism*, 382–84.

36. Kobre, *Development of American Journalism*, 259–60.

37. Trevor D. Dryer, "'All the News That's Fit to Print': The *New York Times*, 'Yellow' Journalism, and the Criminal Trial, 1898–1902," 549. See, for example, *New York Evening World*, December 28, 1892; and *New York Journal and Advertiser*, August 22, 1898.

38. *Boston Herald*, February 15–16, 1870; Lane, *Policing the City*, 133–34, 142, 150; Rousey, *Policing the Southern City*, 160.

39. *New York Times*, November 18, 1858; W. Miller, *Cops and Bobbies*, 146–47.

40. Kobre, *Development of American Journalism*, 259–60. See also Bleyer, *Main Currents*, 405; J. Lee, *History of American Journalism*, 29; Bopp and Schultz, *Short History of American Law Enforcement*, 60–61; and Raymond Fosdick, *American Police Systems*, 94.

41. N. R. Kleinfield, "150th Anniversary: 1851–2001; Investigative Reporting Was Young Then," *New York Times*, November 14, 2001.

42. M. Johnson, *Street Justice*, 12–13; *New York Times*, April 20, June 30, July 20, August 25, 1865, August 21, 24, 1866, May 26, 30, 1867.

43. "Local Miscellany," *New-York Tribune*, June 28, 1881.

44. "A Brute in Police Uniform," *New York Times*, June 28, 1881.

45. M. Johnson, *Street Justice*, 13.

46. Paul H. Stuart, "Ida B. Wells-Barnett Confronts 'Excuses for Lynching' in 1901," 208; Keisha N. Blain, "Ida B. Wells Offered the Solution to Police Violence More than 100 Years Ago," *Washington Post*, July 11, 2017.

47. Ida B. Wells, "Lynch Law."

48. Nellie Bly, "Nellie Bly a Prisoner," *New York World*, February 24, 1889.

49. Mott, *American Journalism*, 415; Folkerts, Teeter, and Caudill, *Voices of a Nation*, 202–4; Reppetto, *American Police*, 148; Kobre, *Development of American Journalism*, 380, 392; Starr, *Creation of the Media*, 256. For an example, see *New York Evening World*, October 10, 1887. The *New York Evening World* covered the actions and ensuing trial of policeman Edward Hahn, who was alleged to have shot and killed Captain Jack Hussey.

50. Alfers, *Law and Order in the Capital City*, 44–46.

51. J. Lee, *History of American Journalism*, 360; Kobre, *Development of American Journalism*, 357.

52. *New York Journal*, September 11, 1897; Bleyer, *Main Currents*, 368.

53. See, for example, "Killikelly Caught a Crook," *Boston Globe*, September 18, 1891; and "Risky Reporting," *Reno Gazette-Journal*, December 31, 1878.

54. J. Lee, *History of American Journalism*, 360–61. For example, the *New York World* identified the man who attempted to kill millionaire Russell Sage. *World* reporter Isaac D. White solved the murder after he found "a button from the trousers and a piece of cloth from the clothing of the would-be murderer." The button was stamped "Brooks, Boston," leading White to a tailor named Brooks. He then scoured the "order books" from the store and identified a suspect named "Norcross," whose parents recognized the piece of clothing and identified their son as the perpetrator of Sage's attempted murder.

55. *New York Journal*, July 4, 1897; Bleyer, *Main Currents*, 368. See also Mott, *American Journalism*, 523–24; Paul Collins, "Headless Body in Tabloid City," *New York Post*, June 19, 2011; Paul Collins, "How to Get Ahead in Tabloid Journalism"; Paul Collins, *The Murder of the Century: The Gilded Age Crime That Scandalized a City & Sparked the Tabloid Wars*, 3–7; and "How a New York 'Murder' Sparked the Tabloid Wars," National Public Radio, June 25, 2011, https://www.npr.org/2011/06/25/137351785/how-a-new-york-murder-sparked-the-tabloid-wars.

56. Collins, "How to Get Ahead in Tabloid Journalism."

57. J. Lee, *History of American Journalism*, 361.

58. G. M. Roe, *Our Police: A History of the Cincinnati Police Force, from the Earliest Period until the Present Day*, 390–92.

59. Bleyer, *Main Currents*, 369.

60. *New York Journal*, January 28, 1899.

61. *New York Journal*, January 7, 1899.

62. George Murray, *The Madhouse on Madison Street*, 205–6.

63. "The Philadelphia Detectives' Revenge," *Washington (D.C.) Evening Star*, August 28, 1873. For other examples, see "Had Been to Jacksonville"; and "To Strike First," *Brooklyn Citizen*, November 22, 1893.

64. "A Fatal 'Scoop,'" *St. Louis Post-Dispatch*, November 4, 1887. For additional examples, see "Arrest of Reporters," *Philadelphia Inquirer*, December 6, 1861; *Baltimore Sun*, November 24, 1862; "Newspaper Reporters," *Weekly Oregon Statesman* (Salem), January 28, 1873; *Atchison (KS) Daily Champion*, April 26, 1887; "In the Line of Duty. Arrest of Reporter Clark for Witnessing a Prize Fight," *Nashville Tennessean*, August 3, 1889; "Forgery," Associated Press, July 18, 1891; *Philadelphia Times*, June 15, 1891; "Reporters Arrested," United Press, September 1, 1892; *Alton (IL) Telegraph*, December 17, 1896; "World Reporter Arrested," *Brooklyn Daily Eagle*, August 6, 1897; and "Reporter Arrested on Serious Charge," *Lincoln (NE) Journal Star*, August 8, 1899.

65. "Fallen from Grace," *Chicago Tribune*, March 28, 1883; "Wholesale Arrest of Reporters," *Livingston (MT) Enterprise*, March 20, 1886; "It Cost Him Five Dollars," *Washington (D.C.) Evening Star*, August 20, 1890; "Unjustly Accused."

66. For two examples of police threatening force, see "After the New Police," *San Francisco Chronicle*, March 31, 1868; and *Newton (IA) Daily Republican*, May 28, 1886. For examples of their use of actual force, see "Southern Gossip," *Salisbury (NC) Truth*, May 3, 1888; *Macon (GA) Telegraph*, April 26, 1888; "Policeman vs. Reporter," *Buffalo Evening News*, November 1, 1882; *Chicago Weekly Post and Mail*, January 7, 1875; "A Brutal Policeman," *Brooklyn Daily Eagle*, August 1, 1879; Edgar W. Nye, "An Amateur Sleuth," *Washington (D.C.) Sunday Herald*, September 15, 1889; and "Assaulted a Reporter," *Fall River (MA) Daily Herald*, March 13, 1891.

67. "A Small Fire and a Great Outrage," *Pittsburgh Commercial*, October 1, 1875.

68. For additional examples, see "Reporters Arrested," *Kansas City Star*, June 1, 1885; "A Railway Passenger in Bad Luck," *Altoona (PA) Tribune*, July 2, 1874; "Home from Yucatan," *Boston Globe*, July 13, 1889; and "No Reporter He," *Buffalo Evening News*, May 23, 1891.

69. "'The Fly Cop,'" *New Orleans Daily Picayune*, February 11, 1896.

70. Belt, "Jailed & Subpoenaed Journalists," 2; "A Newspaper Man in Trouble: Asked for His Source of Information about Grand Jury Secrets," *Chicago Daily Tribune*, December 13, 1886; "Knew the Grand Jury's Secrets: A Reporter of a Baltimore Paper Imprisoned for Contempt of Court," *Chicago Daily Tribune*, December 23, 1886; "The Case of Mr. Morris," *Baltimore Sun*, December 23, 1886; Bruce L. Bortz and Laurie R. Bortz, "'Pressing' Out the Wrinkles in Maryland's Shield Law for Journalists," 461–62; *Pledger v. State*, 77 Ga. 242, 3 S.E. 320 (1887); *Ex Parte A. M. Lawrence and L. L. Levings*, 116 Cal. 298, 48 P. 124 (1897). In other jurisdictions, additional cases arose, with subpoenas against the *New-York Tribune* in 1875, the *Defiance* editor A. W. Burnett in 1887, and *San Francisco Examiner* news editor Andrew M. Lawrence and reporter L. L. Levings in 1897.

71. See, for example, "Important Arrests," *Weekly National Intelligencer*, April 26, 1851; *Buffalo Commercial*, March 8, 1856; "An Error Corrected," *Daily Milwaukee News*, October 26, 1860; "Curious Case of Spiritualism," *Brooklyn Union*, August 8, 1868; and "Counterfeiter Arrested," *New Orleans Times-Picayune*, September 21, 1869.

72. The author obtained and compiled these newspaper articles from historical databases following rigorous search parameters and procedures. The author's analysis of the articles followed social science qualitative and quantitative content-analysis research methods. For more information on the methodology around these articles, see Scott Memmel, "Pressing the Police and Policing the Press: The History and Law of the Relationship between the News Media and Law Enforcement in the United States."

73. For more on the CIA's use and impersonation of the press, see Herbert N. Foerstel, *From Watergate to Monicagate: Ten Controversies in Modern Journalism and Media*, 70; "Foreign and Military Intelligence," 179; Carl Bernstein, "The CIA and the Media"; and "CIA Halting Use of U.S. Reporters as Secret Agents," *Washington Star*, February 12, 1976.

74. "Toledo Topics," *Cincinnati Enquirer*, October 29, 1880; "The Hounds of Justice," *Brooklyn Times Union*, March 31, 1887.

75. "Watching the Anarchists," *Cedar Rapids (IA) Gazette*, November 13, 1889.

76. "Police Act," *Buffalo Express*, October 21, 1890.

77. "Those 'Pictures': The Denver Chief of Police Poses as an Art Critic," Associated Press, January 19, 1895.

78. "Were Places Offered in Exchange for Votes?," *Brooklyn Daily Eagle*, December 18, 1896.

79. "Brevities," *Pittsburgh Post-Gazette*, March 30, 1877.

80. "What a 'Scoop' Means," *Reno Gazette*, February 1, 1879.

81. "Much Evidence Excluded," *Indianapolis News*, June 8, 1896.

82. "A Model Patrol Wagon," *Chicago Tribune*, October 26, 1881.

83. "The Patrol Wagon. An Institution of Modern Police Systems. A Night on 'the Red Wagon,'" *Columbus (IN) Republic*, June 20, 1883.

84. "A Model Patrol Wagon."

85. See, for example, *Chicago Tribune*, November 24, 1880.

86. "A Model Patrol Wagon."

87. "An Observant Chief: The Patrol Wagons," *St. Louis Post-Dispatch*, August 23, 1881.

88. "Mob Rule," *Chicago Tribune*, February 28, 1882.

89. "Parading Policemen," *Inter Ocean*, October 18, 1882.

90. "The Patrol Wagon."

91. "The Cedar Block Pavement," *Lincoln (NE) Journal Star*, May 4, 1889.

92. "Police Alarm Signals," *San Francisco Chronicle*, November 30, 1890.

93. Malcolm W. Bingay, "Good Morning," *Detroit Free Press*, October 15, 1952.

94. "The Patrol Wagon."

95. See also "Police Alarm Signals." For additional examples, see "One Day's Ride in a Chicago Patrol Wagon," *Chicago Daily Tribune*, April 24, 1895; and "A Night on the Box with the Patrol Driver," *Washington (D.C.) Evening Star*, Jan 3, 1909.

96. "On the Hoodlum. A Night Spent with the Patrol Wagon Officers in Central District," *St. Louis Post-Dispatch*, July 26, 1884.

97. "On the Hoodlum."

98. "Police Alarm Signals."

99. "The State Capital," *Minneapolis Tribune*, June 22, 1885. For another example, see "Searching for the Cause of Death," *Lincoln (NE) Journal Star*, April 6, 1896.

100. "Gotham Stations," *St. Paul (MN) Globe*, October 6, 1895.

101. "Gathering Strike News: Reporters Were Exposed to Peril Wherever They Went," *New York Times*, March 17, 1895.

102. "Gotham Stations."

103. "Gathering Strike News."

104. "Police Alarm Signals."

105. "A Day with the Patrol," *San Francisco Examiner*, March 15, 1891.

Chapter 3
Reform and Separation, 1900s–1910s

1. Daly, *Covering America*, 149; Folkerts, Teeter, and Caudill, *Voices of a Nation*, 202–4; Mott, *American Journalism*, 575.

2. Leonard Ray Teel, *The Public Press, 1900–1945*, 4; J. Lee, *History of American Journalism*, 401–2; Schudson, *Discovering the News*, 151; Nerone, *Media and Public Life*, 143, 158–59, 162–67; Kaplan, *Politics and the American Press*, 141, 161–63, 184. For discussions of "jazz journalism," see Teel, *Public Press*, 119–20; Sloan, *Media in America*, 289; Mott, *American Journalism*, 666; and Kobre, *Development of American Journalism*, 605–10.

3. Nerone, *Media and Public Life*, 158–69; Daly, *Covering America*, 153–57; Mott, *American Journalism*, 727–28; Kobre, *Development of American Journalism*, 33–34, 734–37; Teel, *Public Press*, 2–3, 115; J. Lee, *History of American Journalism*, 388; Bleyer, *Main Currents*, 389–91.

4. Nerone, *Media and Public Life*, 163.

5. S. Walker, *Popular Justice*, 112–19, 126–34. See also S. Walker and Katz, *Police in America*, 35–37; Wadman and Allison, *To Protect and Serve*, 67–68, 74–77, 131–33; D. Johnson, *American Law Enforcement*, 68–70; Reppetto, *American Police*, 242–54; Lovell, *Good Cop/Bad Cop*, 96–100; Bopp and Schultz, *Short History of American Law Enforcement*, 84–89, 105–6; H. Johnson, Wolfe, and Jones, *History of Criminal Justice*, 306–8; M. Lee and McGovern, *Policing and Media*, 17; John Pope, *Police-Press Relations: A Handbook*; and Orlando W. Wilson, *Police Administration*.

6. Lovell, *Good Cop/Bad Cop*, 96–97; Schudson, *Discovering the News*, 137–140; Kaplan, *Politics and the American Press*, 170; Bopp and Schultz, *Short History of American Law Enforcement*, 89; S. Walker, *Popular Justice*, 135; S. Walker and Katz, *Police in America*, 36–37; Whalen and Whalen, *NYPD's First 50 Years*, 83–84, 90; H. Johnson, Wolfe, and Jones, *History of Criminal Justice*, 306, 309–10; Gene E. Carte and Elaine H. Carte, *Police Reform in the United States: The Era of August Vollmer, 1905–1932*; Gourley, "Police Public Relations"; Ray Surette, "Public Information Officers: The Civilianization of a Criminal Justice Profession," 107–8.

7. S. Walker, *Popular Justice*, 165; Wadman and Allison, *To Protect and Serve*, 108–13, 122; Richardson, *New York Police*, 68–70; Rousey, *Policing the Southern City*, 161; D. Johnson, *American Law Enforcement*, 62, 116; Whalen and Whalen, *NYPD's First 50 Years*, 191–92; Bopp and Schultz, *Short History of American Law Enforcement*, 66.

8. S. Walker, *Popular Justice*, 166; Bopp and Schultz, *Short History of American Law Enforcement*, 67, 77, 85–86; Wadman and Allison, *To Protect and Serve*, 115–16; Lane, *Policing the City*, 203–4; Whalen and Whalen, *NYPD's First 50 Years*, 156, 192, 197; Rousey, *Policing the Southern City*, 161; H. Johnson, Wolfe, and Jones, *History of Criminal Justice*, 318; Pascal Storino, "'What's the Deal': With the Early History of Police Aviation in New York City? Post WWI (1918) though Fixed Wing Aircraft (1950)—Part 3."

9. Wadman and Allison, *To Protect and Serve*, 116–17; M. Johnson, *Street Justice*, 17.

10. H. Johnson, Wolfe, and Jones, *History of Criminal Justice*, 256.

11. Wadman and Allison, *To Protect and Serve*, 101. See also D. Johnson, *American Law Enforcement*, 75–81, 89; and S. Walker, *Popular Justice*, 138, 160.

12. Lane, *Policing the City*, 138; Reppetto, *American Police*, 122–23, 132–33, 141; S. Walker, *Popular Justice*, 140–41; Bopp and Schultz, *Short History of American Law Enforcement*, 44–45, 77–80, 111; D. Johnson, *American Law Enforcement*, 155–64; Wadman and Allison, *To Protect and Serve*, 57–70; Roth and Kennedy, *Houston Blue*, 19–20; H. Johnson, Wolfe, and Jones, *History of Criminal Justice*, 309; Laurence Armand French, *The History of Policing America: From Militias and Military to the Law Enforcement of Today*, 33.

13. For more on the Boston Police Strike and the history of police unions, see Steven Greenhouse, "How Police Unions Enable and Conceal Abuses of Power"; and M. J. Levine, "Historical Overview of Police Unionization in the United States."

14. González and Torres, *News for All the People*, 161–82.

15. González and Torres, *News for All the People*, 163, 181–82.

16. Wadman and Allison, *To Protect and Serve*, 82; M. Johnson, *Street Justice*, 3.

17. Glenda Gilmore, "Postwar Race Riots."

18. U.S. Congress, House of Representatives, Special Committee Authorized by Congress to Investigate the East St. Louis Riots, Report, 1918, 65th Cong., 2nd sess., House Doc. 1231, vol. 114, serial 7444, 8. See also Allen D. Grimshaw, "Actions of Police and the Military in American Race Riots," 274.

19. Grimshaw, "Actions of Police and the Military."

20. "For Action on Race Riot Peril," *New York Times*, October 5, 1919.

21. "Reds Try to Stir Negroes to Revolt," *New York Times*, July 28, 1919.

22. See Silvan Niedermeier, *The Color of the Third Degree: Racism, Police Torture, and Civil Rights in the American South, 1930-1955*.

23. See, for example, Edwin R. Keedy, "The Third Degree and Legal Interrogation of Suspects," 761–63. There were also several instances of groups and organizations, including the Bar of the City of New York in 1928, debating the use of third-degree tactics.

24. *Brown v. Mississippi*, 297 U.S. 278 (1936).

25. Folkerts, Teeter, and Caudill, *Voices of a Nation*, 359; Starr, *Creation of the Media*, 385; Teel, *Public Press*, 76–78; Daly, *Covering America*, 165; Nerone, *Media and Public Life*, 153; Emery, *Press and America*, chap. 27; Bleyer, *Main Currents*, 421; J. Lee, *History of American Journalism*, 423; Mott, *American Journalism*, 625–27; Kobre, *Development of American Journalism*, 576–77.

26. Whalen and Whalen, *NYPD's First 50 Years*, 91–10, 113; Roth and Kennedy, *Houston Blue*, 66–69.

27. "The Crime of the Century," *Los Angeles Times*, October 16, 1910.

28. Lovell, *Good Cop/Bad Cop*, 8–9, 63–65; Nerone, *Media and Public Life*, 136. Both *McClure's* and *Cosmopolitan* ran stories about police accepting bribes and being ineffective against growing crime and unrest. *McClure's* also covered the police's role in corruption in New York around the turn of the century.

29. Lincoln Steffens, "The Shame of Minneapolis"; "How One Magazine Shaped Investigative Journalism in America."

30. M. Johnson, *Street Justice*, 12–13, 58–86; Regina G. Lawrence, *The Politics of Force: Media and the Construction of Police Brutality*.

31. M. Johnson, *Street Justice*, 13.

32. Whalen and Whalen, *NYPD's First 50 Years*, 23, 26, 75–78.

33. Jay Maeder, "Why NYPD Officer Charlie Becker Became the First American Cop to Get the Death Penalty," *New York Daily News*, August 13, 2017.

34. "Posed as Crazy for His Paper," *Arizona Silver Belt* (Globe), January 3, 1901. For additional examples, see "Watching for Vanderbilt; Two Reporters Arrested," *Brooklyn Daily Eagle*, June 12, 1904; "Capsule Factory Fire; Water Sadly Delayed," *Brooklyn Daily Eagle*, May 14, 1909; "Nab 5 Scribes for Riot," *Wisconsin State Journal*, March 10, 1910; and "Decatur Reporter Arrested by Police," *Champaign (IL) Daily Gazette*, July 7, 1910.

35. See *Schenck v. United States*, 249 U.S. 47 (1919); *Debs v. United States*, 249 U.S. 211 (1919); *Abrams v. United States*, 250 U.S. 616 (1919); and *Frohwerk v. United States*, 249 U.S. 204 (1919). Reporters were also arrested on charges of being an "alien enemy" during this time period. See *Baltimore Sun*, July 8, 1917; and "Newark Reporter Arrested as Dangerous Enemy Alien," *Fall River (MA) Evening News*, February 9, 1918.

36. "Slew a Millionaire," *St. Louis Post-Dispatch*, November 26, 1900. For a similar example, see "Reporter Arrested for Causing Death of a Man," *Eau Claire (WI) Leader-Telegram*, September 20, 1903. For more examples, see "Hammerstein Causes Arrests," *New-York Tribune*, January 24, 1909; "Young Reporter Arrested for Alleged Blackmailing," *Wheeling (WV) Intelligencer*, March 22, 1919; "Spurious Associated Press Reporter," *Norwich (CT) Bulletin*, March 25, 1910; "Marked Bills Used," *Harford (CT) Courant*, November 15, 1902; *Spokane (WA) Spokesman-Review*, June 6, 1919; "Jewelry Store Safe Blown Open at Night," *Brooklyn Standard Union*, November 30, 1910; "Mysterious Man before Jury," United Press, June 8, 1911; and "Say Goesman Thug's Victim," *Louisville (KY) Courier-Journal*, November 11, 1918.

37. "Bribery and Blackmail," *Buffalo Evening News*, July 28, 1900.

38. "Reporter Assaulted by Chief of Police," *Topeka (KS) Daily Capital*, March 3, 1910. For additional examples, see "Some New York Policemen," *New York Sun*, January 29, 1905; *Indianapolis News*, December 8, 1914; and "Officer Assaults Reporter," *Kearney (NE) Morning Times*, January 31, 1915. Also like in past eras, some arrests marked efforts to obtain journalists' sources and materials. See "News Reporter Arrested—Hearing at 5 O'Clock," *Charlotte (NC) News*, January 12, 1910.

39. "Officer Attacks Reporter," *Marshalltown (IA) Evening Times-Republican*, October 9, 1913.

40. "Vic Mauberret Assaults Reporter at Second Precinct of Fourth Ward," *New Orleans Times-Democrat*, March 8, 1911. For additional examples, see "Dangers of Journalism," *Marion (OH) Star*, June 14, 1905; and "Physician Reaps Enormous Profit," *Washington Herald*, February 22, 1915.

41. *In re Grunow*, 84 N.J.L. 235, 85 A. 1011 (1913); *Ex Parte Holliway*, 272 Mo. 108 (1917); "Reporter Arrested in Marshall Case," *Rochester (NY) Democrat and Chronicle*, March 4, 1916.

42. Belt, "Jailed & Subpoenaed Journalists"; "Jail Term Price of 'Tip'—Augusta Reporter Protects Policeman Who Gave Him Murder Story," *Washington Post*, March 15, 1911.

43. Folkerts, Teeter, and Caudill, *Voices of a Nation*, 390, 401; Nerone, *Media and Public Life*, 153.

44. "Envoys Seek Dietz. Armistice Is On," Associated Press, October 6, 1910.

45. For an additional example, see "Two Confess; Hit Healey," *Chicago Daily Tribune*, January 10, 1917. In 1917, the *Chicago Daily Tribune* covered the arrest, arraignment, and trial of Chicago police chief Charles C. Healey in connection to a series of bribes and a vice graft ring. It was alleged that "nine policemen, posing as reporters, broke into Chief Healey's home . . . and served him with warrants." In this instance, the police used impersonation of the press in order to go beyond conducting an investigation, but also serve arrest or search warrants (or both).

46. "Larkin Pledges 500 to Communism," *New York Times*, November 29, 1919.

47. *Gitlow v. New York*, 268 U.S. 652 (1925).

48. "Federal Officer Played Reporter," *Macon (MO) Republican*, September 6, 1918.

49. "Judge Fritz Denounces Methods of Professional Charity Workers in Deciding Conspiracy Charge," *San Francisco Call*, June 21, 1901.

50. "Accused Minister Will Have Able Counsel," *Knoxville (TN) Journal and Tribune*, October 22, 1911.

51. "Who Said He Was Chief Lucas? A Reporter? Nevah! But Chief Says It Is Very S-E-R-I-O-U-S, Too," *Tulsa (OK) Democrat*, July 11, 1916.

52. "First in the World. . . Akron's Automobile Patrol Wagon Is about Ready for Use," *Akron (OH) Beacon Journal*, January 6, 1900; "Automobile Police Patrol," *Scranton (PA) Republican*, July 8, 1899. See also "Automobile Police Patrol," *Muncie (IN) Star Press*, January 14, 1900.

53. "That Balking Auto," *Akron (OH) Beacon Journal*, January 20, 1900.

54. See "Police to Use Automobiles," *Washington (D.C.) Evening Times*, September 13, 1899; "Go without Horses," *Iola (KS) Register*, November 10, 1899; "Afraid to Risk Men in Sewer," *Chicago Tribune*, October 1, 1901; "Auto-Patrol Wagon," *Eau Claire (WI) Leader*, August 1, 1901; and "Police Auto Beaten in Thrilling Race," *St. Louis Post-Dispatch*, May 8, 1905.

55. "Police Automobile Balks: Reporters and Chief Walk on Car's Trial Trip," *Indianapolis News*, April 26, 1907.

56. "Evening Tribune Reporter Spends Afternoon in Police Car Chasing the Automobile Speeder," *Des Moines (IA) Evening Tribune*, March 7, 1917.

57. "Outing with the Coppers," *Charlotte (NC) Observer*, May 2, 1905.

58. Reporters also pointed out the limitations of police vehicles, including when reporters praised the trip on the new police wagon with Meltzer, but also reported on its breaking down twice along the way. See "Police Automobile Balks." The same year, the *St. Louis Post-Dispatch* contended that "more speedy police automobiles [were needed to address] the dangers of automobile scorching," meaning motorists

who violated speed limits. However, the criticism matched the calls by Officer William Stinger and others in the police department, therefore making it less about criticizing the police and more about reporting on the changes they wanted to see made. See "Police Autos Are Too Slow to Serve End," *St. Louis Post-Dispatch*, January 7, 1907.

59. "All This in Face of the Police Denials," *San Francisco Chronicle*, February 9, 1901. See also "Wittman Pleads for His Reputation and Makes a Futile Effort to Capture a Chinese Accuser," *San Francisco Call*, February 9, 1901.

60. "Wittman Now to Be Heard," *San Francisco Chronicle*, March 10, 1905; "Wittman Legally Dismissed," *Los Angeles Herald*, October 1, 1905.

61. "Reporters Barred from Police Autos," *Salt Lake Herald-Republican*, August 6, 1912.

62. "A Dead Hero Is the Poorest Sort of a Husband."

63. "A Night on the Box with the Patrol Driver." For another example, see "Evening Tribune Reporter Spends Afternoon in Police Car." A lack of precautions was also apparent during Harrison's ride-along, in which he explained there was "enough danger in chasing the speeder to make it a fascinating game." See also "Detectives Have Narrow Escape," *Butte (MT) Miner*, December 25, 1918.

64. "Speeding Law Far Reaching," *Los Angeles Times*, June 19, 1917.

Chapter 4
Greater Partnerships, 1920s–1950s

1. Starr, *Creation of the Media*, 286. See also Emery, *Press and America*, chap. 28; and Emma Goldman, "Free Speech in the Progressive Era," PBS, accessed October 8, 2022, https://www.pbs.org/wgbh/americanexperience/features/goldman-free-speech-progressive-era-1907-1916/.

2. Norman L. Rosenberg, "Another History of Free Speech: The 1920s and the 1940s," 335–36; *Abrams v. United States*, 250 U.S. 616 (1919) (Holmes, J., dissenting); *Whitney v. United States*, 274 U.S. 257 (1927) (Brandeis, J., concurring).

3. Mott, *American Journalism*, 675; Kobre, *Development of American Journalism*, 565; Daly, *Covering America*, 217; Teel, *Public Press*, 129–30, 137.

4. Kobre, *Development of American Journalism*, 684. See also Folkerts, Teeter, and Caudill, *Voices of a Nation*, 390, 401; Mott, *American Journalism*, 788; Teel, *Public Press*, 214–15; Mott, *American Journalism*, 707–8, 761–68; Kobre, *Development of American Journalism*, 684, 687–88, 697; Nerone, *Media and Public Life*, 175–77; Sloan, *Media in America*, 439; and Daly, *Covering America*, 286.

5. Mott, *American Journalism*, 721.

6. Folkerts, Teeter, and Caudill, *Voices of a Nation*, 433. See also Daly, *Covering America*, 270; and Mott, *American Journalism*, 723, 763.

7. Daly, *Covering America*, 270. See also Teel, *Public Press*, 213; Matthew Pressman, *On Press: The Liberal Values That Shaped the News*, 7–8; James L. Aucoin, *The Evolution of American Investigative Journalism*, 44–48; and Mott, *American Journalism*, 763.

8. Pressman, *On Press*, 7–8, 186.

9. Teel, *Public Press*, 218; Mott, *American Journalism*, 723, 860–61; Kobre, *Development of American Journalism*, 698–70; Emery, *Press and America*, 688; Sloan, *Media in America*, 443; Daly, *Covering America*, 287; David R. Davies, *The Postwar Decline of American Newspapers, 1945–1965*, 36–37.

10. Davies, *Postwar Decline of American Newspapers*, 37; James S. Pope, "U.S. Press Is Free to Print the News but Too Often Is Not Free to Gather It," 9.

11. Schudson, *Discovering the News*, 160–63; Daly, *Covering America*, 299; Kaplan, *Politics and the American Press*, 3. Teel, *Public Press*, 243; Sloan, *Media in America*, 454–55; Mott, *American Journalism*, 835; Kobre, *Development of American Journalism*, 565–66; Pressman, *On Press*, 6–7, 184; Davies, *Postwar Decline of American Newspapers*, 48; James Brian McPherson, *Journalism at the End of the American Century, 1965–Present*, 183–84.

12. Davies, *Postwar Decline of American Newspapers*, 48.

13. Richardson, *New York Police*, 26–27; H. Johnson, Wolfe, and Jones, *History of Criminal Justice*, 221; D. Johnson, *American Law Enforcement*, 143–47; S. Walker, *Popular Justice*, 140, 154, 158–59; Wadman and Allison, *To Protect and Serve*, 99–100; Roth and Kennedy, *Houston Blue*, 77–83; Bopp and Schultz, *Short History of American Law Enforcement*, 93–97; M. Johnson, *Street Justice*, 114–16, 121.

14. Bopp and Schultz, *Short History of American Law Enforcement*, 94. See also D. Johnson, *American Law Enforcement*, 117, 124, 173; M. Johnson, *Street Justice*, 149; and Whalen and Whalen, *NYPD's First 50 Years*, 121–22, 175.

15. Roth and Kennedy, *Houston Blue*, 120–29; Whalen and Whalen, *NYPD's First 50 Years*, 202–9; M. Johnson, *Street Justice*, 192–93, 198.

16. For more on the development of film, see Irving Fang, *Alphabet to Internet: Media in Our Lives*, 183–85; Folkerts, Teeter, and Caudill, *Voices of a Nation*, 322, 338–39; Sloan, *Media in America*, 248, 381–82; Starr, *Creation of the Media*, 295, 304, 315–18, 325; and Kobre, *Development of American Journalism*, 568–69.

17. For more on the development of radio, see Lovell, *Good Cop/Bad Cop*, 92–93; Daly, *Covering America*, 205; Teel, *Public Press*, 171; and Robert McChesney, *The Problem of the Media: U.S. Communication Politics in the Twenty-First Century*.

18. Daly, *Covering America*, 215 (emphasis in the original).

19. For more on the development of television, see McPherson, *Journalism at the End of the American Century*, 177; Stephens, *A History of News*, 273–76; Nerone, *Media and Public Life*, 181; and Daly, *Covering America*, 291–92.

20. For more on the development of the FBI, see S. Walker, *Popular Justice*, 160–64; Reppetto, *American Police*, chap. 8; D. Johnson, *American Law Enforcement*, 172–82; Bopp and Schultz, *Short History of American Law Enforcement*, 114–15, 120, 123; and French, *History of Policing America*, 151.

21. S. Walker, *Popular Justice*, 160.

22. Matthew Cecil, "'Press Every Angle': FBI Public Relations and the 'Smear Campaign' of 1958," 39–42.

23. Richard Weinblatt, "How History Makes the Future of Police Media Relations Clearer"; Amber Brozek, "Relations between Media and Law Enforcement

Have Changed since 1959," *Lawrence (KS) Journal-World*, April 3, 2005; Aucoin, *Evolution of American Investigative Journalism*, 44–47; Lovell, *Good Cop/Bad Cop*, 134–35; Ellen Warren, "The Scene of the Crimes," *Chicago Tribune*, April 15, 2002.

24. Brozek, "Relations between Media and Law Enforcement Have Changed since 1959"; Melinda Henneberger, "How Would Journalists Report the Story of JFK's Assassination Today? Very Differently," *Washington Post*, November 22, 2013; Warren, "Scene of the Crimes." For additional examples of the press being in police departments, see John J. Hickey, *Our Police Guardians: History of the Police Department of the City of New York, and the Policing of Same for the Past One Hundred Years*, 85; Augustine E. Costello, *Our Police Protectors: History of the New York Police from the Earliest Period to the Present Time*, v; Roe, *Our Police*, 392; and Henry Mann, *Our Police: A History of the Providence Force from the First Watchman to the Latest Appointee*, 367.

25. Roth and Kennedy, *Houston Blue*, 131.

26. Ridgely Hunt, "The People vs. the Police," *Chicago Tribune*, September 7, 1969.

27. Daly, *Covering America*, 270. See also Mott, *American Journalism*, 763; Pressman, *On Press*, 8; Weinblatt, "How History Makes the Future of Police Media Relations Clearer"; Brozek, "Relations between Media and Law Enforcement Have Changed since 1959"; Lovell, *Good Cop/Bad Cop*, 134–35; Warren, "Scene of the Crimes"; and Aucoin, *Evolution of American Investigative Journalism*, 44–47.

28. Weinblatt, "How History Makes the Future of Police Media Relations Clearer"; Brozek, "Relations between Media and Law Enforcement Have Changed since 1959"; Lovell, *Good Cop/Bad Cop*, 134; Cooke and Sturges, "Police and Media Relations," 407; Hunt, "People vs. the Police."

29. Mott, *American Journalism*, 700–704, 845; Ray Surette, *Media, Crime, and Criminal Justice: Images, Realities, and Policies*, 4th ed., 10, 12; Teel, *Public Press*, 146–47; Daly, *Covering America*, 205; Sloan, *Media in America*, 294.

30. *Chicago Tribune*, February 29, 1924.

31. For more information, see "Lindbergh Kidnapping"; and Thomas Doherty, *Little Lindy Is Kidnapped: How the Media Covered the Crime of the Century*.

32. "Free Press vs. Fair Trial: The Lindbergh Baby Kidnapping Case."

33. "Free Press vs. Fair Trial."

34. Jarret Bencks, "Covering the Crime of the Century: The Lindbergh Kidnapping and a Media Revolution."

35. See *Richmond Newspapers v. Virginia*, 448 U.S. 555 (1980).

36. Bencks, "Covering the Crime of the Century."

37. John D. Alexander, "Reporters Forced to Steal Cops' Car to Nab Slayer," *Carlsbad (NM) Current-Argus*, April 17, 1955.

38. Sloan, *Media in America*, 249.

39. Starr, *Creation of the Media*, 303. See also Fang, *Alphabet to Internet*, 187, 190–95; and Sloan, *Media in America*, 248, 302–3, 381.

40. *The Front Page*, directed by Lewis Milestone (1931).

41. Surette, *Media, Crime, and Criminal Justice*, 4th ed., 10, 12; Lovell, *Good Cop/Bad Cop*, 92–93; Teel, *Public Press*, 146–47; Daly, *Covering America*, 205; Sloan, *Media in America*, 294; Mott, *American Journalism*, 703; Anthony R. Fellow, *American Media History*, 253.

42. Surette, *Media, Crime, and Criminal Justice*, 4th ed., 11; Fellow, *American Media History*, 251; González and Torres, *News for All the People*, 13; Mel Watkins, "What Was It about 'Amos 'n' Andy'?," *New York Times*, July 7, 1991, https://www.nytimes.com/1991/07/07/books/what-was-it-about-amos-n-andy.html.

43. Surette, *Media, Crime, and Criminal Justice*, 4th ed., 12. See also Lovell, *Good Cop/Bad Cop*, 107, 118; Mcpherson, *Journalism at the End of the American Century*, 82; Davies, *Postwar Decline of American Newspapers*, 50–52; Daly, *Covering America*, 291–92; and Jeremy Lipschultz and Michael Hilt, *Crime and Local Television News: Dramatic, Breaking, and Live from the Scene*, 1.

44. Carol A. Stabile, "During Floyd Protests, Media Industry Reckons with Long History of Collaboration with Law Enforcement." See also Alyssa Rosenberg, "How Police Censorship Shaped Hollywood," *Washington Post*, October 24, 2016, https://www.washingtonpost.com/sf/opinions/2016/10/24/how-police-censorship-shaped-hollywood/; and Fang, *Alphabet to Internet*, 195.

45. Surette, *Media, Crime, and Criminal Justice*, 4th ed., 11; Robert Staples and Terry Jones, "Culture, Ideology, and Black Television Images," 10.

46. Whalen and Whalen, *NYPD's First 50 Years*, 117.

47. M. Johnson, *Street Justice*, 149, 158, 179. See *New York World*, March 8, 1930; *New York Telegram*, March 7, 1930, *New York Herald-Tribune*, March 7, 1930; *New York News*, March 7, 1930; and *New York Times*, March 8, 1930.

48. *New York World-Telegram*, February 16, 1953; *New York Sun*, February 16, 1953; M. Johnson, *Street Justice*, 222.

49. Bopp and Schultz, *Short History of American Law Enforcement*, 126–27, 138; "Special Committee on Organized Crime in Interstate Commerce."

50. *Near v. Minnesota*, 283 U.S. 697, 700 (1931); Minn. Stat. §§ 10112, 10113 (1927).

51. "Police Arrest Negro Reporter as Vagrant at Birmingham, Ala.," Associated Press, March 31, 1952; "'Reporter' Released, Arrest Protested," *Birmingham Post-Herald*, April 1, 1952.

52. "Reporter Arrested Attempting to Take Photos," *Lancaster (PA) New Era*, May 16, 1925; "Reporter Arrested While Testing U.S. Customs Security," United Press, April 21, 1954. For additional examples, see "Police Arrest Reporters," Associated Press, August 13, 1926; "Reporter Arrested," Associated Press, May 19, 1927; "Hoover Urges Big Fund to Insure Prosperity," *San Bernardino County (CA) Sun*, November 22, 1928; *Shreveport (LA) Journal*, May 16, 1929; "Gilbert Defender Must Face Judge for Fight in Café," Associated Press, March 11, 1930; "Reporter Arrested for a Too-Graphic Story," Associated Press, May 8, 1931; "Seattle Police Arrest Reporters," Associated Press, August 2, 1937; "Reporter Arrested," *Louisville (KY) Courier-Journal*, January 29, 1939; and "Reporter Arrested," Associated Press, July

10, 1956. In fact, in one case, a reporter was arrested for speeding and subsequently ordered by a judge to write and publish articles about his offense. See "Sentenced to Pen Big Story," *Fremont (OH) News-Messenger*, June 22, 1925.

53. For another example from this time period, see "Alleged Tactics Ranger Cummings Brings Loss Job," Associated Press, May 7, 1927. Texas governor Dan Moody "ordered that Ranger Cummings . . . be suspended because of his reported part in the arrest of Vic Wagner, a reporter for the Borger Herald." Cummings was also accused of preventing the editor of the newspaper, T. E. Caufield, from sending certain telegrams about what transpired.

54. "Reporter Must Come to Court," *Los Angeles Record*, September 28, 1931. For additional examples, see "Mayor Nominee in Louisville Under Arrest," Associated Press, November 8, 1921; *Boston Globe*, April 18, 1933; *Pottsville (PA) Republican and Herald*, August 6, 1948; Associated Press, December 6, 1953; "Girl Critically Hurt in Head-on Collision," *Miami (FL) News*, June 9, 1957; "Reporter Arrested at Fire," *Madison (WI) Capital Times*, November 29, 1958; and *Boston Globe*, June 19, 1959.

55. "Reporter Sues after Arrest," *Los Angeles Evening Express*, October 9, 1931.

56. "Radicals Are Beaten by Cops," Associated Press, May 28, 1934; "Officer Beats Reporters," Associated Press, June 8, 1923; "Dismiss Police Who Beat Up Reporter," *Pittsburg (KS) Sun*, September 4, 1921; "Police Chief Assaults Reporter; Quits Post," *Norman (OK) Transcript*, October 18, 1925; R. E. Williams, "Jury Secured for Trial of Strike Murder Cases," *Raleigh (NC) News and Observer*, September 5, 1929; "Springfield Calm after Wild Night Following Voting," Associated Press, October 19, 1929; "Reporter Assaulted by New Policeman," United Press, May 19, 1933; "Officer Who Attacked Reporter Loses Job," Associated Press, August 28, 1934; "Reporter Beaten by Two Officers," United Press, May 26, 1955.

57. "And They Called It an Election," *Memphis Commercial Appeal*, August 5, 1928.

58. "Gets 2 Guesses; Fails, Fined $8," *Detroit Free Press*, December 8, 1922.

59. "FBI Agents Searched Reporter's Room in '59," *New York Times*, July 22, 1975.

60. Belt, "Jailed & Subpoenaed Journalists," 3–4; *People ex rel. Mooney v. The Sheriff of New York County*, 269 N.Y. 291 (1936); *Clein v. State*, 52 So. 2d 117 (Fla. 1950).

61. *Garland v. Torre*, 259 F.2d 545 (2nd Cir. 1958). See also Bates, "*Garland v. Torre* and the Birth of Reporter's Privilege."

62. Edward Ranzal, "Woman Reporter Gets Jail Term," *New York Times*, November 13, 1957.

63. Teel, *Public Press*, 215–18; Mott, *American Journalism*, 723; Emery, *Press and America*, 688; Folkerts, Teeter, and Caudill, *Voices of a Nation*, 390, 401.

64. "Gun-Toting Grandma Outfoxed as Police Pose as Reporters," United Press International, August 6, 1958. See also "Deputies' Tactics End Highway Siege," *Valley Times* (North Hollywood, CA), August 6, 1958.

65. "Pinchot May Back Schnader Boom for Post of Governor," International News Service, March 11, 1933.

66. For an additional example, see "Vincennes Rum Probe Widened," *Indianapolis Star*, May 11, 1926. Two federal prohibition agents "pos[ed] as newspaper reporters" to allegedly buy liquor as part of an investigation and possible arrests of several individuals suspected of selling alcohol.

67. "Detective's Ruse in Dry Case Causes Press Club Protest," *Washington Post*, October 13, 1928.

68. "Struggle in Front of White House: Detectives Disguised as Reporters," Reuters, March 7, 1930.

69. See Foerstel, *From Watergate to Monicagate*; Bernstein, "CIA and the Media"; and "Foreign and Military Intelligence," 179.

70. Although the practice was not revealed until the 1960s–'70s, there were some hints for the existence of the secretive use of impersonation of the press by government and law enforcement. See Henry McLemore, "The Lighter Side," *Los Angeles Times*, December 3, 1947. In 1947, syndicated columnist Henry McLemore discussed how he and two fellow infantrymen during World War II had posed as reporters to gather information from military officers. McLemore explained that they "would tell the officer that our newspapers wanted a story and pictures of him." They would also "equip [themselves] with paper and pencils" or "borrow a camera of some kind." Although seemingly innocuous, such actions by agents would later be scrutinized and criticized. See also "'After You,'" *Eugene (OR) Guard*, August 27, 1957. In 1957, the "Chinese Peoples' Daily, a [Chinese government] party organ," alleged that "Secretary Dulles [was] trying to send 24 American spies, disguised as reporters, into the Oriental Workers' Paradise." See also Robert Branson, "Cuban Revels Seek U.S. 'Spy,'" *Lansing (MI) State Journal*, November 30, 1958. In 1958, Cuban rebel agents alleged that an American agent "bluffed his way into rebel headquarters in Cuba as a 'news reporter' and collected secret data for the enemy." The U.S. government denied the allegation and the one a year earlier, though the reports still provided evidence that an agent could, and perhaps did, pose as a reporter.

71. "Foreign and Military Intelligence," 192; Foerstel, *From Watergate to Monicagate*, 72.

72. Bernstein, "The CIA and the Media." See also Alicia Upano, "Will a History of Government Using Journalists Repeat Itself under the Department of Homeland Security?"

73. "Hearst Men in Los Angeles Attempt to Bulldoze Peavey," *New York Age*, March 4, 1922. For another sensational example, see "Overzealous News Sleuthing Causes Detention of Pair," *Brooklyn Daily Eagle*, October 30, 1931. Arthur O'Sullivan (a reporter for the *Daily News*) and Harold McKinley (the proprietor of an Oyster Bay hotel) reportedly visited the home of Amos Dickerson and asked to speak with his son, Conrad. Dickerson complied because the two men had posed as representatives of the district attorney's office and police officers. The two men then allegedly "took Conrad off in an automobile and while driving to Flushing questioned and threatened him." In Flushing, they entered a house where the questioning continued. Thus, this example marks another instance of journalists acting

"overzealous[ly]," but still for the purpose of obtaining information. For additional examples, see "Peaches' Counsel Charges 'Buying' of Two Witnesses," International News Service, February 13, 1927; and "Reporter Poses as U.S. Agent to Get Story," *Miami (OK) Daily News-Record*, January 26, 1927.

74. Murray, *Madhouse on Madison Street*, 105, 205–6; "The Press: Muscle Journalist."

75. Murray, *Madhouse on Madison Street*, 205–10.

76. "Reporter Is Arrested," *New York Times*, September 21, 1928. See also "Reporter Fined at Tuxedo," *New York Times*, September 26, 1928.

77. Sarah Nordgren, "CNB Tells Staff: If Your Mother Says She Loves You, Check It Out," Associated Press, October 3, 1990.

78. Warren, "Scene of the Crimes."

79. Ivana Andonovska, "The First Police Car Was Bought in Akron, Ohio in 1899; Its First Assignment Was to Pick Up a Drunk Man," *Vintage News*, December 4, 2017; Ian Wright, "History of American Police Cars."

80. Harold J. Eager, "Reporter Rode in 'Maria' on Its First Call," *Intelligencer Journal* (Lancaster, PA), November 24, 1954. For a similar invitation, see "Reporter 'Taken for a Ride," *Arlington Heights (IL) Herald*, June 27, 1952.

81. "Reporter on Police Force," *Kenosha (WI) Evening News*, January 2, 1926.

82. Dick Greene, "Seen and Heard in Our Neighborhood," *Muncie (IN) Star Press*, January 16, 1948.

83. "Chief Defends Action of Men in Cell Death of Dougherty," *Harrisburg (PA) Evening News*, November 14, 1938. For additional examples of police officials changing department policies to prohibit media ride-alongs, see "The Strike Affects Reporters," *Minneapolis Tribune*, July 24, 1894; "Reporters Barred from Police Autos," *Salt Lake (UT) Herald-Republican*, August 6, 1912; and W. W. H., "Whisperings of the Wind," *Semi-weekly Spokane (WA) Spokesman-Review*, February 13, 1938.

84. "Reporter on Police Force." For additional examples, see Tait Cummins, "Voice from the Air Directs Police Radio Squad Cars to All Sections of City on Great Variety of Calls," *Cedar Rapids (IA) Gazette*, February 4, 1934; Jack Martin, "A Tour with Prowl Car: Reporter Does Night Beat with Policemen," *Arlington Heights (IL) Herald*, August 6, 1959; and Charlie Granger, "Halloween Quiet, but There Was No Rest for the Coppers," *Minneapolis Star*, November 1, 1935.

85. Dan Brennan, "Reporter Shares Chase: Squad Car Combs Dark City for Crime," *Minneapolis Sunday Tribune*, March 14, 1948.

86. "Police Bull," *Indianapolis News*, July 17, 1928. For another example, see "How Michigan Police Trapped Parolee Slayer: Reporter, in Car, Tells of Radio Orders," *Chicago Tribune*, January 22, 1937.

87. "Chief Defends Action of Men in Cell Death of Dougherty."

88. "One Killed and 13 Injured in Denver Wrecks," *Arizona Republic* (Phoenix), April 3, 1921; "Condition of Two Remains Serious," *Indianapolis News*, March 27, 1928; "Seven Are Hurt in Auto Crash," International News Service, March 27, 1928.

89. "Police Bull."

Chapter 5
Adversarial Relationship, 1960s–1970s

1. Davies, *Postwar Decline of American Newspapers*, 48; Schudson, *Discovering the News*, 163, 180–88; Mcpherson, *Journalism at the End of the American Century*, ix–x, 178; Daly, *Covering America*, 343; Folkerts, Teeter, and Caudill, *Voices of a Nation*, 465, 476; T. Barton Carter, Juliet Lushbough Dee, and Harvey L. Zuckman, *Mass Communication Law in a Nutshell*, 509–10.

2. Pressman, *On Press*, 10–11.

3. Schudson, *Discovering the News*, 163, 180, 189–91. See also Folkerts, Teeter, and Caudill, *Voices of a Nation*, 446–47, 466; Aucoin, *Evolution of American Investigative Journalism*, 49, 52, 56–57, 62; Pressman, *On Press*, 14–15, 185, 188, 190; and Mcpherson, *Journalism at the End of the American Century*, 1–6, 45, 128.

4. Seth Rosenfeld, "The FBI's Secret Investigation of Ben Bagdikian and the Pentagon Papers."

5. *New York Times v. United States*, 403 U.S. 713 (1971).

6. Aucoin, *Evolution of American Investigative Journalism*, 62. See also Folkerts, Teeter, and Caudill, *Voices of a Nation*, 446–47; Mcpherson, *Journalism at the End of the American Century*, 58; Davies, *Postwar Decline of American Newspapers*, 99–110; Pressman, *On Press*, 14, 185, 188, 196; Aucoin, *Evolution of American Investigative Journalism*, 49–53; Oscar Winberg, "When It Comes to Harassing the Media, Trump Is No Nixon," *Washington Post*, October 16, 2017, https://www.washingtonpost.com/news/made-by-history/wp/2017/10/16/when-it-comes-to-harassing-the-media-trump-is-no-nixon/; and Richard Harris, "The Presidency and the Press."

7. Daniel C. Hallin, *The "Uncensored War": The Media and Vietnam*, 5. See also Aucoin, *Evolution of American Investigative Journalism*, 56–57, 62.

8. González and Torres, *News for All the People*, 8, 295, 302, 339; Pressman, *On Press*, 9, 13–14, 149–50, 236.

9. González and Torres, *News for All the People*, 8, 21–22, 41–45, 149–57, 213–25, 266–69; Muhammad, *Condemnation of Blackness*, 11–12; Stabile, *White Victims, Black Villains*, 5–6; Kaplan, *Politics and the American Press*, 31–34; Robert M. Entman and Andrew Rojecki, *The Black Image in the White Mind: Media and Race in America*, 94.

10. González and Torres, *News for All the People*, 264, 274–75.

11. Pressman, *On Press*, 50. See also González and Torres, *News for All the People*, 294–96.

12. González and Torres, *News for All the People*, 9.

13. S. Walker, *Popular Justice*, 172, 180; S. Walker and Katz, *The Police in America*, 41–42, 255; Wadman and Allison, *To Protect and Serve*, 143. See also M. Johnson, *Street Justice*, 177, 185–87, 203–4, 210; and Bopp and Schultz, *Short History of American Law Enforcement*, 135.

14. National Advisory Commission on Civil Disorders, *Report of the National Advisory Commission on Civil Disorders*, 201; Thomas J. Hrach, *The Riot Report and*

the News: How the Kerner Commission Changed Media Coverage of Black America, 4–6.

15. French, *History of Policing America*, 156–57; Bopp and Schultz, *Short History of American Law Enforcement*, 153; D. Johnson, *American Law Enforcement*, 178; H. Johnson, Wolfe, and Jones, *History of Criminal Justice*, 321; President's Commission on Law Enforcement and the Administration of Justice, *The Challenge of Crime in a Free Society: A Report by the President's Commission on Law Enforcement and the Administration of Justice; To Establish Justice, to Ensure Domestic Tranquility: Final Report of the National Commission on the Causes and Prevention of Violence*.

16. S. Walker, *Popular Justice*, 45–46, 194–200; S. Walker and Katz, *The Police in America*, 37–38, 48–49; Wadman and Allison, *To Protect and Serve*, 148–50.

17. Melissa Motschall and Liqun Cao, "An Analysis of the Public Relations Role of the Police Public Information Officer," 154.

18. Stan Macdonald, "An Order Is an Order," *Louisville (KY) Courier-Journal*, November 30, 1971.

19. *Standards for Law Enforcement Agencies: The Standards Manual of the Law Enforcement Agency Accreditation Program*.

20. Lipschultz and Hilt, *Crime and Local Television News*, 13. See also Irving Fang, *Television News, Radio News*, 317.

21. González and Torres, *News for All the People*, 306–7. See also George Gerbner, "TV Violence and What to Do about It."

22. Entman and Rojecki, *Black Image in the White Mind*, 152; Alyssa Rosenberg, "How Police Censorship Shaped Hollywood," *Washington Post*, October 24, 2016.

23. Weinblatt, "How History Makes the Future of Police Media Relations Clearer"; Amber Brozek, "Relations between Media and Law Enforcement Have Changed since 1959," *Lawrence (KS) Journal-World*, April 3, 2005; Lovell, *Good Cop/Bad Cop*, 134–35; McPherson, *Journalism at the End of the American Century*, 47; Pressman, *On Press*, 15, 198.

24. Lovell, *Good Cop/Bad Cop*, 4; Aucoin, *Evolution of American Investigative Journalism*, 52; Weinblatt, "How History Makes the Future of Police Media Relations Clearer"; Brozek, "Relations between Media and Law Enforcement Have Changed since 1959."

25. Pressman, *On Press*, 199–205. A similar shift occurred with the *Los Angeles Times*' relationship with the Los Angeles Police Department (LAPD), which was "once characterized by beat reporters sharing drinks with cops who gave them access to crime scenes." However, the press increasingly questioned or criticized the police, including tactics in working with marginalized communities. Whereas officers were previously sources, they were now being targeted, leading many to characterize newspapers as antipolice. See also Max Felker-Kantor, *Policing Los Angeles: Race, Resistance, and the Rise of the LAPD*, 106–7; and McPherson, *Journalism at the End of the American Century*, 51–52.

26. M. Johnson, *Street Justice*, 273–74; French, *History of Policing America*, 152; Commission to Investigate Alleged Police Corruption, *The Knapp Commission Report on Police Corruption*.

27. French, *History of Policing America*, 151; Ronald Kessler, "FBI Director Hoover's Dirty Files: Excerpt from Ronald Kessler's *The Secrets of the FBI.*"

28. Virgie Hoban, "'Discredit, Disrupt, and Destroy': FBI Records Acquired by the Library Reveal Violent Surveillance of Black Leaders, Civil Rights Organizations," *Berkeley Library News*, January 18, 2021, https://news.lib.berkeley.edu/fbi; Benjamin Hedin, "The FBI's Surveillance of Martin Luther King, Jr. Was Relentless. But Its Findings Paint a Fuller Picture for Historians."

29. Brozek, "Relations between Media and Law Enforcement Have Changed since 1959"; Melinda Henneberger, "How Would Journalists Report the Story of JFK's Assassination Today? Very Differently," *Washington Post*, November 22, 2013; Jon Herskovitz, "How the JFK Assassination Transformed Media Coverage," Reuters, November 21, 2013.

30. Sarah Brady Siff, "Policing the Police: A Civil Rights Story," 1–2; David G. Embrick, "Two Nations, Revisited: The Lynching of Black and Brown Bodies, Police Brutality, and Racial Control in 'Post-racial' Amerikkka," 836–37; C. Anderson, *White Rage*, 43; Lovell, *Good Cop/Bad Cop*, chap. 6.

31. Gene Roberts and Hank Klibanoff, *The Race Beat: The Press, the Civil Rights Struggle, and the Awakening of a Nation*, 386.

32. Lovell, *Good Cop/Bad Cop*, chap. 6; Hallin, *"Uncensored War,"* 4; M. Johnson, *Street Justice*, 260; McPherson, *Journalism at the End of the American Century*, 1–6, 45, 128.

33. Joel, Achenbach, "Did the News Media, Led by Walter Cronkite, Lose the War in Vietnam?," *Washington Post*, May 25, 2018, https://www.washingtonpost.com/national/did-the-news-media-led-by-walter-cronkite-lose-the-war-in-vietnam/2018/05/25/a5b3e098-495e-11e8-827e-190efaf1f1ee_story.html.

34. Colleen Leahy, "Remembering the Dow Protest and Riot 50 Years Later," Wisconsin Public Radio, October 18, 2017, https://www.wpr.org/remembering-dow-protest-and-riot-50-years-later; Tim Morrissey, "Dow Chemical Protests: 50 Years Ago in Madison," WXPR, October 18, 2017, https://www.wxpr.org/news/2017-10-18/dow-chemical-protests-50-years-ago-in-madison. See generally David Maraniss, *They Marched into Sunlight*.

35. Bopp and Schultz, *Short History of American Law Enforcement*, 138; William J. Bopp, *The Police Rebellion*, 173; Jeffrey Osoff, "Year Ago Today: Boston Cleaned Up—Some—since Key Shop TV Show," *Boston Globe*, December 1, 1962.

36. "Police Arrest Reporter While Working on Story," Associated Press, December 6, 1953; "Reporter Arrested at PUC," United Press International, April 17, 1974; "Reporter Arrested in Boston School," Associated Press, October 29, 1975; "U.S. to Prosecute Reporters Arrested on Restricted Island," United Press International, September 8, 1977.

37. For additional examples beyond the 1968 DNC, see "Television Reporter Arrested," *Miami News*, July 15, 1964; "Chester High Reopening Set for Monday," Associated Press, April 24, 1964; and "Court Asked to End Racial Disorders in Chester, Pa.," Associated Press, April 25, 1964. For an additional example, see "Negroes, Reporters Arrested in Nyack Trouble," Associated Press, October 6, 1967.

38. Paul Travis, "Police Arrest Reporter during Beach Disorder," *Fort Lauderdale News*, January 1, 1974. For additional examples, see "Police Arrest, Jail Reporter Covering Beckel Hotel Fire," *Dayton (OH) Daily News*, March 2, 1964; "Reporter Arrested in Newsroom," Associated Press, April 18, 1973; "Reporter Arrested by FBI," *Washington Post*, February 1, 1973; "Hearing Goes to Justice Court," Associated Press, June 15, 1978; and "Reporter Arrested, UPI Protests to Reagan," United Press International, March 3, 1970.

39. See, for example, "Delay Trial of Reporter, Court Asked," Associated Press, July 15, 1964.

40. For more on the violence during the 1968 DNC, see Tom Tiede, "Police and the Press: View from Squad Car"; Tanner Howard, "Journalism Still Carries the Mark of 1968"; David Taylor and Sam Morris, "The Whole World Is Watching," *Guardian*, August 19, 2018, https://www.theguardian.com/us-news/ng-interactive/2018/aug/19/the-whole-world-is-watching-chicago-police-riot-vietnam-war-regan; and Craig Wall, "Former *Newsweek* Reporter Recalls 1968 Democratic Convention," ABC 7, August 28, 2018.

41. Tiede, "Police and the Press."

42. Howard, "Journalism Still Carries the Mark of 1968."

43. "2 Reporters Arrested at Conspiracy Trial," *Los Angeles Times*, November 27, 1969.

44. Heather Hendershot, *When the News Broke: Chicago 1968 and the Polarizing of America.*

45. "Reporter Searched by Police," *Asbury Park (NJ) Press*, October 13, 1974; Associated Press, May 18, 1966.

46. *Zurcher v. Stanford Daily*, 436 U.S. 547, 550 (1978).

47. See *Branzburg v. Hayes*, 408 U.S. 665 (1972); *Zurcher*, 436 U.S. at 547; Linda Moon, Bruce D. Brown, and Gabe Rottman, "New DOJ Reports Provide Detail on Use of Law Enforcement Tools against the News Media"; and R. Jones, "Avalanche or Undue Alarm?," 596. For more examples, see Belt, "Jailed & Subpoenaed Journalists," 4–11; and David K. Shipler, "30 Cases Cited in Which Police or Courts Allegedly Threatened Free Press," *New York Times*, February 18, 1973.

48. Moon, Brown, and Rottman, "New DOJ Reports," 1.

49. Foerstel, *From Watergate to Monicagate*, 65.

50. "Foreign and Military Intelligence," 196; "CIA Halting Use of U.S. Reporters as Secret Agents," *Washington Star*, February 12, 1976.

51. "Foreign and Military Intelligence," 196.

52. Foerstel, *From Watergate to Monicagate*, 84.

53. "Foreign and Military Intelligence," 179.

54. Foerstel, *From Watergate to Monicagate*, 63–64; "Foreign and Military Intelligence," 195.

55. "CIA Halting Use of U.S. Reporters as Secret Agents"; CIA Office of the Director.

56. See Marguaret Genovese, "Impersonation: When Cops Pose as Press, Media Credibility Suffers. But Would a Law against It Only Make Matters Worse?,"

Presstime, October 1984; Gary T. Marx, *Undercover: Police Surveillance in America*, 151; James E. Roper, "Impersonating Journalists"; and "Agents Posing as Reporters Would Taint News," *Providence (RI) Journal*, May 28, 1984.

57. William Raspberry, "Freedom of the Press Endangered by Subpoenas, Police Actions," *Washington Post*, May 27, 1970. For additional examples, which further discuss police impersonation of the press undermining journalists' and news organizations' credibility, see Les Brown, "NBC Denies a Role in F.B.I. 'Newsmen,'" *New York Times*, November 23, 1975; and David Briscoe, "Police Pose as Reporters in Attempt to Arrest Father in Truancy Case," *Tampa Bay Times*, October 21, 1978.

58. "Grand Rapids Paper Protests Police Ruse," Associated Press, June 6, 1970. For additional examples and commentary of police impersonation of the press undermining source relationships, see J. A. Hartenfeld, "Impersonating the Press?," *DeKalb (IL) Daily Chronicle*, November 5, 1970; and "Troopers Shouldn't Pose as Reporters—Thompson," Associated Press, November 15, 1977.

59. "State Investigator Was Wrong to Use Deceptive Tactics," *Fort Lauderdale News*, July 5, 1979. For an antecedent to this problem, see "Reporter Punches Governor on Nose," *Washington Post*, September 9, 1930.

60. Raspberry, "Freedom of the Press." See also "Troopers Shouldn't Pose as Reporters."

61. "State Investigator Was Wrong to Use Deceptive Tactics."

62. See, for example, Hartenfeld, "Impersonating the Press?"

63. Erwin D. Canham, "The Bogus Press," *Christian Science Monitor*, June 5, 1972.

64. "Grand Rapids Paper Protests Police Ruse." For another example, see Hartenfeld, "Impersonating the Press?"

65. "Police at Protest Pose as Newsmen," Associated Press, November 15, 1968; "Policemen Pose as Reporters," Associated Press, November 15, 1968.

66. For additional examples, see "Police Acting as Newsmen Ruled Out," *Washington Post*, July 16, 1970; and John Sheimo, "State Agent Poses as Reporter," *Fond Du Lac (WI) Commonwealth Reporter*, August 2, 1973.

67. "Clark Order Bans FBI Men Posing as Press," *Associated Press*, July 11, 1968.

68. For an example of a police official apologizing for impersonation of the press, see "Officer Poses as Reporter, Police Apologize to UPI," United Press International, March 19, 1977; "Trooper Poses as Newsman in Demonstration," United Press International, November 16, 1977; and "Official Admits Cop Posed as Newsman," Associated Press, November 16, 1977.

69. For another example, see Jack Gould, "Newsmen Are Not FBI Men," *New York Times*, February 15, 1970. Following allegations in 1970 that "governmental investigators [had] pose[d] as reporters" domestically and overseas, Jack Gould, a reporter at the *New York Times*, wrote in an editorial that such actions constitute "a damnable encroachment on the free press." See also Jim Dance, "How Dare They Imitate Reporters?," *Philadelphia Inquirer*, May 26, 1976. Knight News Service reporter Jim Dance perhaps put it best when he called the actions of two Tampa officers, who "identified themselves . . . as newspaper reporters," an "unauthorized incursion into [the press's] estate, which is No. 4."

70. "WHAS Says Police Posed as Newsmen during Rally," *Louisville (KY) Courier Journal*, April 20, 1972.

71. David Ellis, "The Difference Is in the Badge One Wears," *Tulare (CA) Advance-Register*, August 30, 1975.

72. Ellen Warren, "The Scene of the Crimes," *Chicago Tribune*, April 15, 2002.

73. David Shaw, "How Ethical for Newsman to Masquerade for Story?," *Los Angeles Times*, October 8, 1979.

74. Renee Boensch, "Bob Schieffer."

75. "300,000 Burglary Revealed," Associated Press, April 30, 1956.

76. *Oxford English Dictionary*, s.v. "ride-along," accessed April 16, 2021.

77. "Citizens Ride Squad Cars," *Chicago Tribune*, December 11, 1964.

78. "Skokie May Let Citizens Ride Along with Police," *Chicago Tribune*, September 17, 1967; "Law Students to Ride Along with Police," *Chicago Daily Defender*, April 19, 1966; Nancy J. Adler, "Youths on Coast Study the Police: Los Angeles Project Seeks Support for the Law," *New York Times*, August 18, 1968; Don Snyder, "Ride Gives Student New View of Police," *Los Angeles Times*, July 23, 1968; "Police 'Ride-Along' Plan for Teen-Agers Will Be Repeated," *Los Angeles Times* June 25, 1969; "Ride Along Program for Teens Started," *Los Angeles Times*, July 20, 1969; "Police Program Lauded: Police 'Ride Along' Clicks with Youths," *Los Angeles Times*, September 21, 1969; Laura A. Kiernan, "Shootout-Chase Ends Police 'Ride-Along,'" *Washington Post*, February 20, 1975.

79. Ronald Koziol, "Reporter Gets Closer View of Cop's World: He Rides Along thru a Long Night's Work," *Chicago Tribune*, January 31, 1965.

80. Ann Plunkett, "'Ride Along' with Police Gives Insight," *Chicago Tribune*, October 22, 1967. See also Bernard Judge, "VASCAR Is Effective: New Timer Nips Speeders," *Chicago Tribune*, September 18, 1966.

81. Plunkett, "'Ride Along' with Police Gives Insight."

82. For additional examples, see Helen Weiershauser, "Experiences of 3 Hours in a Squad Car," *Muscatine (IA) Journal*, July 8, 1978. *Muscatine (IA) Journal* staff writer Helen Weiershauser detailed her "experiences . . . in a squad car," including what she "heard and saw." Following the experience, Weiershauser praised the police, writing that "the policeman may not appear to be an important part of life to the average citizen. But in a time of crisis that person in uniform could make the different between tragedy and joy, health and disability, life and death." See also John Davies, "Reporter Cruises with Police; Tells Squad Car View of Cicero," *Chicago Tribune*, February 16, 1969; Casey Banas, "Fillmore Is Prime Battleground for Chicago's Police," *Chicago Tribune*, October 2, 1969; John Nunes, "Police Show Runs Quietly in City," *Escondido (CA) Times-Advocate*, August 6, 1978; Edward Moran, "An Arrest That Could've Been Trouble," *Philadelphia Daily News*, April 25, 1986; and Adam Greenberg, "Reporter Rides with Police," *Clifton (NJ) Journal*, October 1, 2010. Positive coverage was further reflected in that some reporters also covered reforms undertaken by law enforcement. See Ronald Koziol, "Tribune Reporter Rides Police Car with a Finger Print Expert: How Cops Try to Solve Store Burglaries," *Chicago Daily Tribune*, February 12, 1962; Robert Wiedrich, "Policemen on New Task Force Play Tag with Death," *Chicago Tribune*, March 5, 1962; Judge, "VASCAR Is

Effective"; Ronald Yates, "VASCAR Computes a Net for Speeders," *Chicago Tribune*, December 20, 1970; and Hal Foust, "Indiana Using Airplanes to Nab Speeders," *Chicago Daily Tribune*, April 15, 1967.

83. Lee Cook, "A Night in a Patrol Car: Quiet, Stark, Tense!," *New York Amsterdam News*, May 20, 1972. For additional examples, see Dean Fosdick, "Police Try 1st All-Female Patrol Team," *Minneapolis Star*, August 16, 1976; and Anita Clark, "'Ride-Along Tastes Patrol Work," *Wisconsin State Journal*, November 28, 1976.

84. Tiede, "Police and the Press."

85. For additional examples, see Lee Margulies, "'Violence in America': Real Blood, Not Catsup," *Los Angeles Times*, December 30, 1976; David Peterson and Joe Logan, "Racist Cop: The Norm or 'Bad Apple'?," *Minneapolis Star*, May 18, 1979; Guy Halverson, "Racing to the Rescue: Reporter Rides Night Patrol Car with Chicago Police," *Christian Science Monitor*, July 31, 1968; and "Greenwood Suit Postponed after Law 'Assurances,'" *Atlanta Daily World*, April 5, 1963.

86. Casey Banas, "'Aggressive' Patrols Used in Crime War," *Chicago Tribune*, October 5, 1969. For another example by the *Chicago Tribune*, see Joseph Boyce, "Gang Leaders Explain Their War on S. Side," *Chicago Tribune*, June 1, 1969.

87. "Police Show Runs Quietly in City."

88. Boyce, "Gang Leaders Explain Their War on S. Side." For another example, see Sarah Tully, "Man Throwing Rocks Is Shot by Deputy," *Arizona Daily Star* (Tucson), December 9, 1994.

89. See, for example, Kevin T. Baldwin, "Going Along for a Ride: Reporter Experiences Night Shift at Police Department," *Worcester (MA) Telegram & Gazette*, March 13, 2008.

90. For an example, see "Greenwood Suit Postponed after Law 'Assurances.'"

Chapter 6
Rebuilding a Complicated Relationship, 1980s–2020s

1. Michael Conway, "Trump's Public Attacks on the 'Enemies of the People' Echo Nixon's Private Press War—Except Worse," *NBC Think*, November 10, 2018, https://www.nbcnews.com/think/opinion/trump-s-public-attacks-enemies-people-echo-nixon-s-private-ncna938481; Scott Memmel, "Federal Judge Orders White House Reinstate Reporter's Press Credential," 4–5.

2. Julia Carrie Wong and Sam Levin, "Republican Candidate Charged with Assault after 'Body-Slamming' *Guardian* Reporter," *Guardian*, May 25, 2017, https://www.theguardian.com/us-news/2017/may/24/greg-gianforte-bodyslams-reporter-ben-jacobs-montana; Kyung Lah, Noa Yadidi, and Carma Hassan, "Gianforte Pleads Guilty to Assault in Incident with Reporter," CNN, June 12, 2017, https://www.cnn.com/2017/06/12/politics/greg-gianforte-assault-plea; Ben Jacobs, "'This Needs to Stop': *Guardian* Reporter Ben Jacobs' Statement to Court," *Guardian*, June 12, 2017, https://www.theguardian.com/us-news/2017/jun/12/ben-jacobs-greg-gianforte-sentence-free-press.

3. See, for example, Christopher Hare and Keith T. Poole, "The Polarization of Contemporary American Politics"; and Richard Walker, "Political Polarization: A Dispatch from the Scholarly Front Lines." There are numerous beneficial studies on

political polarization in the United States, discussing its history, present concerns, and outlook for the future.

4. "Political Polarization in the American Public."

5. "U.S. Is Polarizing Faster than Other Democracies, Study Finds"; https://www.pewresearch.org/short-reads/2022/03/10/the-polarization-in-todays-congress-has-roots-that-go-back-decades/.

6. See Elizabeth Kolbert, "How Politics Got So Polarized."

7. Megan Brenan, "Americans Remain Distrustful of Mass Media."

8. Art Swift, "Americans' Trust in Mass Media Sinks to New Low."

9. Megan Brenan, "Americans' Trust in Media Dips to Second Lowest on Record."

10. Jeffrey Gottfried and Jacob Liedke, "Partisan Divides in Media Trust Widen, Driven by a Decline among Republicans."

11. See generally Jonathan Ladd, *Why Americans Hate the Media and How It Matters*; and Seth Lewis, "Lack of Trust in the News Media, Institutional Weakness, and Relational Journalism as a Potential Way Forward."

12. See generally Wood and Ring, *Crime and Punishment in the Jim Crow South*; and Paul Farhi and Elahe Izadi, "Journalists Are Reexamining Their Reliance on a Longtime Source: The Police," *Washington Post*, June 30, 2020, https://www.washingtonpost.com/lifestyle/media/journalists-are-reexamining-their-reliance-on-a-longtime-source-the-police/2020/06/30/303c929c-b63a-11ea-a510-55bf26485c93_story.html.

13. See, for example, Gabriel Arana, "Decades of Failure"; and Christopher Terry and Caitlin Ring Carlson, "Hatching Some Empirical Evidence: Minority Ownership Policy and the FCC's Incubator Program."

14. González and Torres, *News for All the People*, 363–64.

15. S. Walker, *Popular Justice*, 211.

16. S. Walker, *Popular Justice*, 181–82, citing *Mapp v. Ohio*, 367 U.S. 643 (1961); *Miranda v. Arizona*, 384 U.S. 436 (1966); and *Gideon v. Wainwright*, 372 U.S. 335 (1963).

17. S. Walker, *Popular Justice*, 214, citing *United States v. Leon*, 468 U.S. 897 (1984); and *New York v. Quarles*, 467 U.S. 649 (1984).

18. For more on the history of the War on Drugs, see "A History of the Drug War"; and German Lopez, "The War on Drugs, Explained."

19. "Thirty Years of America's Drug War: A Chronology," PBS, 2014, https://www.pbs.org/wgbh/pages/frontline/shows/drugs/cron/.

20. See, for example, "Law Enforcement Veered Away from Community Policing after 9/11 Attacks"; Emily Dubosh, Mixalis Poulakis, and Nour Abdelghani, "Islamophobia and Law Enforcement in a Post 9/11 World"; Ali Watkins, "How the N.Y.P.D. Is Using Post-9/11 Tools on Everyday New Yorkers," *New York Times*, September 8, 2021; and Toni Smith-Thompson, "Ubiquitous Surveillance and Civil Rights Infringements: A Tragic Legacy of 9/11."

21. S. Walker, *Popular Justice*, 180, 238–39; S. Walker and Katz, *Police in America*, 14–16, 42; M. Lee and McGovern, *Policing and Media*, 15; Wadman and Allison, *To*

Protect and Serve, 151–52; D. Johnson, *American Law Enforcement*, 188; Bopp and Schultz, *Short History of American Law Enforcement*, 154–55; M. Johnson, *Street Justice*, 274–76;.

22. S. Walker, *Popular Justice*, 232–39; M. Johnson, *Street Justice*, 285–89; H. Johnson, Wolfe, and Jones, *History of Criminal Justice*, 322–23.

23. Héctor Tobar, "Tape of L.A. Police Beating Suspect Stirs Public Furor," *Los Angeles Times*, March 6, 1991; "Los Angeles Riots Fast Facts," CNN Library, April 8, 2016, http://www.cnn.com/2013/09/18/us/los-angeles-riots-fast-facts/; Ron Dungee, "The Legacy of Rodney King," *Los Angeles Sentinel*, May 7, 1992.

24. "'Can We All Get Along,'" *Chicago Tribune*, May 2, 1992.

25. For more on mass incarceration, see C. Anderson, *White Rage*, 136–37; Alexander, *New Jim Crow*, 98–99, 134; and Michael Klarman, *From Jim Crow to Civil Rights: The Supreme Court and the Struggle for Racial Equality*, 49, 52–53.

26. C. Anderson, *White Rage*, 136.

27. Larry Buchanan et al., "What Happened in Ferguson?," *New York Times*, August 10, 2015, https://www.nytimes.com/interactive/2014/08/13/us/ferguson-missouri-town-under-siege-after-police-shooting.html; "Timeline of Events in Shooting of Michael Brown in Ferguson," Associated Press, August 8, 2019, https://apnews.com/article/shootings-police-us-news-st-louis-michael-brown-9aa320336 92547699a3b61da8fd1fc62.

28. For more on the murder of Floyd, see Scott Memmel and Jonathan Anderson, "Special Report: Journalists Face Arrests, Attacks, and Threats by Police amidst Protests over the Death of George Floyd"; and Evan Hill et al., "How George Floyd Was Killed in Police Custody," *New York Times*, May 31, 2020, https://www.nytimes.com/2020/05/31/us/george-floyd-investigation.html.

29. Daly, *Covering America*, 426–29.

30. See Terry and Carlson, "Hatching Some Empirical Evidence," 403.

31. Daly, *Covering America*, 430–31.

32. Isabella Simonetti, "Over 360 Newspapers Have Closed since Just before the Start of the Pandemic," *New York Times*, June 29, 2022, https://www.nytimes.com/2022/06/29/business/media/local-newspapers-pandemic.html.

33. Mason Walker, "U.S. Newsroom Employment Has Fallen 26% since 2008."

34. Daly, *Covering America*, 433–34.

35. Penelope Muse Abernathy, "The Expanding News Desert."

36. Philip Bump, "Over the Past 60 Years, More Spending on Police Hasn't Necessarily Meant Less Crime," *Washington Post*, June 7, 2020, https://www.washingtonpost.com/politics/2020/06/07/over-past-60-years-more-spending-police-hasnt-necessarily-meant-less-crime/. See also "Criminal Justice Expenditures: Police, Corrections, and Courts."

37. Lauren-Brooke Eisen, "The Federal Funding That Fuels Mass Incarceration."

38. Nathaniel Lee, "Here's How Two Federal Programs Helped Expand Police Funding by over 200% since 1980," CNBC, June 25, 2020, https://www.cnbc.com/2020/06/25/two-federal-programs-helped-expand-police-funding-by-over-200percent.html.

39. Daly, *Covering America*, 399–406; Folkerts, Teeter, and Caudill, *Voices of a Nation*, 502.

40. For more information on the O. J. case and the role of the media, see Kent Babb, "How the O. J. Simpson Murder Trial 20 Years Ago Changed the Media Landscape," *Washington Post*, June 9, 2014, https://www.washingtonpost.com/sports/redskins /how-the-oj-simpson-murder-trial-20-years-ago-changed-the-media-landscape /2014/06/09/a6e21df8-eccf-11e3-93d2-edd4be1f5d9e_story.html; "O. J. Simpson Trial: Night of the Murders Timeline," CNN, 2007, https://www.cnn.com/2007/ US/law/12/11/court.archive.simpson14/index.html; and Scott Memmel, "34th Annual Silha Lecture Tackles Public and Media Access to Court Proceedings and Records."

41. McPherson, *Journalism at the End of the American Century*, 88; Surette, *Media, Crime, and Criminal Justice*, 1st ed., 56; Pressman, *On Press*, 11–12, 112; H. Johnson, Wolfe, and Jones, *History of Criminal Justice*, 323–25; Mott, *American Journalism*, 803.

42. Daly, *Covering America*, 397, 438, 459; McPherson, *Journalism at the End of the American Century*, 189–92; Folkerts, Teeter, and Caudill, *Voices of a Nation*, 486–87.

43. See Scott Memmel, "Police Body Cameras: Historical Context, Ongoing Debate & Where to Go from Here"; "Considering Police Body Cameras," 1794–95; "A Primer on Body-Worn Cameras for Law Enforcement"; Nancy G. La Vigne et al., "Police Body-Worn Camera Legislation Tracker"; Lindsay Miller, Jessica Toliver, and Police Executive Research Forum, *Implementing a Body-Worn Camera Program: Recommendations and Lessons Learned*; Kami Chavis Simmons, "Body-Mounted Police Cameras: A Primer on Police Accountability vs. Privacy"; and Michael D. White, *Police Officer Body-Worn Cameras: Assessing the Evidence*, 27.

44. Lindsey Van Ness, "Body Cameras May Not Be the Easy Answer Everyone Was Looking For."

45. "Police Militarization."

46. Balko, introduction to *Rise of the Warrior Cop*.

47. Greenhouse, "How Police Unions Enable and Conceal Abuses of Power"; Dylan Matthews, "How Police Unions Became So Powerful—and How They Can Be Tamed"; Samantha Michaels, "The Infuriating History of Why Police Unions Have So Much Power"; Noam Scheiber, Farah Stockman, and J. David Goodman, "How Police Unions Became Such Powerful Opponents to Reform Efforts," *New York Times*, June 6, 2020.

48. Michael Schudson, *Why Democracies Need an Unlovable Press*, 13–17. See also Thomas Emerson, *Toward a General Theory of the First Amendment*, 4–11; and Alexander Meiklejohn, *Free Speech and Its Relation to Self-Government*.

49. S. Walker and Katz, *Police in America*, 3.

50. American Bar Association, *Standards Relating to the Urban Police Function*, 1-31 to 1-32, Standard 1-2.2, "Major Current Responsibilities of Police."

51. Daly, *Covering America*, 406; Pressman, *On Press*, 225; McPherson, *Journalism at the End of the American Century*, 81–88.

52. Lisa Napoli, "'Shots Fired. Hilton Hotel': How CNN's Raw, Unfolding Reagan Coverage Heralded the Nonstop News Cycle"; Tony Schwartz, "Coverage of Shooting Marked by Confusion," *New York Times News*, April 1, 1981.

53. Lipschultz and Hilt, *Crime and Local Television News*, 13; Fang, *Television News, Radio News*, 317; Eleanor Randolph, "Bodybag Journalism," *Chicago Tribune*, November 5, 1989; Melissa Schwartz, "If It Bleeds, It Leads"; McPherson, *Journalism at the End of the American Century*, 82; Simon Van Zuylen-Wood, "Oy, the TRAFFIC. And it's POURING! Do I hear SIRENS?"; Franklin D. Gilliam and Shanto Iyengar, "Prime Suspects: The Influence of Local Television News on the Viewing Public"; Surette, *Media, Crime, and Criminal Justice*, 1st ed., 56.

54. "Milwaukee Police Investigating Report of Missing Woman," WTMJ-TV, February 20, 2020, https://www.tmj4.com/news/local-news/milwaukee-police-investigating-report-of-missing-woman.

55. Commission on Freedom of the Press, *Free and Responsible Press*; J. Lee, *History of American Journalism*, 430.

56. Siebert, Peterson, and Schramm, *Four Theories of the Press*, 74.

57. Scanlon, "Theory of Freedom of Expression," 130–32.

58. Schramm, *Responsibility in Mass Communication*, 103.

59. Christians et al., *Normative Theories of the Media*, 196–97.

60. Entman and Rojecki, *Black Image in the White Mind*, 81; Nazgol Ghandnoosh, "Race and Punishment: Racial Perceptions of Crime and Support for Punitive Policies" 3; Stabile, *White Victims, Black Villains*, 2–4.

61. Entman and Rojecki, *Black Image in the White Mind*, 70.

62. Television news coverage of crime and race has been the subject of numerous studies since the turn of the twenty-first century, some coming to different conclusions than others. For literature reviews on this area of research, see Travis L. Dixon, Cristina L. Azocar, and Michael Casas, "The Portrayal of Race and Crime on Television Network News"; Eileen E. S. Bjornstrom et al., "Race and Ethnic Representations of Lawbreakers and Victims in Crime News: A National Study of Television Coverage"; and Jeremy Lipschultz and Michael Hilt, "Race and Local Television News Crime Coverage." See also Alyssa Rosenberg, "Shut Down All Police Movies and TV Shows. Now," *Washington Post*, June 4, 2020, https://www.washingtonpost.com/opinions/2020/06/04/shut-down-all-police-movies-tv-shows-now/.

63. "Normalizing Injustice: The Dangerous Misrepresentations That Define Television's Scripted Crime Genre," 31–33.

64. Constance Grady, "How 70 Years of Cop Shows Taught Us to Valorize the Police."

65. For more information on the shooting, as well as subsequent reporting and legal battles, see "Dash-Cam Video Released Showing Laquan McDonald's Fatal Shooting," NBC 5 Chicago, November 24, 2015, http://www.nbcchicago.com/news/local/Police-Release-Disturbing-Video-of-Officer-Fatally-Shooting-Chicago-Teen-352231921.html; Jaimie Kalven, "Sixteen Shots"; Megan Crepeau, "Laquan McDonald Reporter Won't Be Forced to Testify at Chicago Cop's Hearing," *Chicago Tribune*, December 13, 2017, https://www.chicagotribune.com/news/laquan-mcdonald

/ct-met-laquan-mcdonald-jamie-kalven-sources-20171212-story.html;
Aamer Madhani, "Chicago Police Officer Jason Van Dyke Guilty of Second-Degree
Murder in 2014 Shooting Death of 17-Year-Old Laquan McDonald," *USA To-
day*, October 5, 2018, https://www.usatoday.com/story/news/2018/10/05/chicago
-police-jason-van-dyke-guilty-murder-death-laquan-mcdonald/1525648002/
; Jason Meisner, Jeremy Gorner, and Steve Schmadeke, "Chicago Releases Dash-
Cam Video of Fatal Shooting after Cop Charged with Murder," *Chicago Tribune*,
November 24, 2015, https://www.chicagotribune.com/news/breaking/ct-chicago
-cop-shooting-video-laquan-mcdonald-charges-20151124-story.html; and Jeremy
Borden, "Jamie Kalven on Why His Court Win Isn't a Free-Press 'Victory.'"

66. "Arrest/Criminal Charge."

67. For several examples, see "Midland Reporter Arrested," Associated Press,
May 28, 1987; "Television Reporter Arrested at Hostage Scene," Associated Press,
December 31, 1988; "Radio Reporter Is Jailed," Associated Press, June 29, 1984;
"NBC Reporter Arrested after Scuffle with Police," Associated Press, October 4,
1985; "Police Arrest 140 at WTO Event," Associated Press, December 1, 2000; and
Rock Island (IL) Argus, June 16, 2008.

68. See, for example, "Television Reporters Arrested," Associated Press, February
26, 1986; "Reporter Arrested for Smuggling Papers," United Press International,
June 15, 1988; "Reporter Arrested on Wiretap Charge," Associated Press, April 23,
1996; and "Columbus Reporter Arrested at Hostage Standoff," *Dayton (OH) Daily
News*, July 19, 1997.

69. See, for example, Linda Moss, "Reporter Arrested for Sexual Assault," *Pas-
saic (NJ) Herald-News*, May 26, 1983; "Editors, Reporters Arrested," *Spokane (WA)
Chronicle*, January 3, 1991; "TV Reporter Arrested," *Indianapolis News*, January 23,
1998; and "Reporter Arrested, Accused of Carrying Methamphetamine," *Baltimore
Sun*, April 21, 2008.

70. "Press Freedom in Crisis."

71. Jason Hanna and Amir Vera, "CNN Crew Released from Police Custody after They Were Arrested Live on Air in Minneapolis," CNN, May 29, 2020,
https://www.cnn.com/2020/05/29/us/minneapolis-cnn-crew-arrested/index.html.
For another example, see "WCCO Photojournalist Tom Aviles Arrested in South
Minneapolis," WCCO, May 30, 2020, https://minnesota.cbslocal.com/2020/05/30/
wcco-photojournalist-tom-aviles-arrested-in-south-minneapolis/.

72. "List of Incidents Involving Police and Journalists during Civil Unrest in
Minneapolis, MN."

73. *Complaint, Goyette v. City of Minneapolis*, No. 0:20-cv-01302-WMW-DTS
(D. Minn., filed June 2, 2020).

74. *Order Granting Plaintiffs' Motion for a Temporary Restraining Order, Goyette
v. City of Minneapolis*, No. 20-cv-1302 (WMW/DTS) (April 16, 2021).

75. *Complaint, Tirado v. City of Minneapolis*, No. 0:20-cv-01338-JRT-ECW (D.
Minn. filed June 10, 2020).

76. *Tirado v. City of Minneapolis*, 521 F. Supp. 3d 833 (D. Minn. 2021).

77. See David Barden, "Journalist Told to 'Act Like a Lady' as Police Handcuff Her for Taking Photos"; James Anderson, "Colorado Journalist Says She Was Detained by Denver Police for Taking Photos," Associated Press, July 6, 2018, https://www.denverpost.com/2018/07/06/colorado-journalist-detained-denver -police/; Christopher Mele, "Reporter Arrested in West Virginia after Persistently Asking Questions of Tom Price," *New York Times*, May 10, 2017, https://www.ny-times.com/2017/05/10/business/media/reporter-arrested-tom-price.html; Camila Domonoske, "West Virginia Reporter Arrested for Yelling Question at HHS Secretary," National Public Radio, May 10, 2017, https://www.npr.org/sections/thetwo -way/2017/05/10/527754346/west-virginia-reporter-arrested-for-yelling-question-at-hhs-secretary; Dan Heyman, "I Was Arrested for Asking Tom Price a Question . I Was Just Doing My Job," *Washington Post*, May 16, 2017, https://www.washing-tonpost.com/posteverything/wp/2017/05/16/i-was-arrested-for-asking-tom-price -a-question-i-was-just-doing-my-job/; and Antonia Noori Farzan, "An Arizona Cop Threatened to Arrest a 12-Year-Old Journalist. She Wasn't Backing Down," *Washington Post*, February 22, 2019, https://www.washingtonpost.com/nation/2019/02/22/an-arizona-cop-threatened-arrest-year-old-journalist-she-wasnt-backing-down/.

78. "*Washington Post* Video Journalists Detained in Police 'Kettle' during D.C. Riot"; "Events Surrounding the U.S. Capitol Insurrection Raise Significant Media Law Issues and Questions."

79. Evan Sernoffsky, "SF Police Raid Journalist's Home in Probe over Leaked Adachi Report," *San Francisco Chronicle*, May 10, 2019, https://www.sfchronicle.com/crime/article/SF-police-raid-journalist-s-home-in-probe-over-13837363.php; Heather Knight, "Adachi Leak: San Francisco Ransacks Its Values with Police Raid on Reporter's Home," *San Francisco Chronicle*, May 18, 2019, https://www.sfchron-icle.com/bayarea/heatherknight/article/Adachi-leak-San-Francisco-ransacks-its-values-13855468.php; Laurel Wamsley, "San Francisco Police Raid Journalist's Home after He Refuses to Name Source," National Public Radio, May 13, 2019, https://www.npr.org/2019/05/13/722745266/san-francisco-police-raid-journalists-home-after-he-refuses-to-name-source. For an additional example from earlier in this era, see "Writer Knew of Escape," Associated Press, August 16, 1980; and "Two Gains for Press Freedom," *Christian Science Monitor*, November 18, 1980.

80. "Police Failed to Tell Judge of Bryan Carmody's Status as Journalist before Obtaining Warrant, Unsealed Records Show"; Eli Rosenberg, "A Judge Signed a Warrant to Search a Journalist. But Police Didn't Tell Her the Whole Story.," *Washington Post*, July 23, 2019, https://www.washingtonpost.com/nation/2019/07/23/judge-signed-warrant-search-journalist-police-didnt-tell-her-whole-story/.

81. Newsroom searches also occurred in Missouri in 1995 and Nevada in 1999, among other cases around that time period. Two additional searches took place in 2010, leading to a settlement in one case and the withdrawal of a warrant in the other. "Prosecutor Fined $1,000 for Newsroom Search in Violation of Federal Law"; "Reno D.A. Orders Searches of Four Newsrooms"; Lucy A. Dalglish, Gregg P. Les-lie, and Wendy Tannenbaum, "Agents of Discovery: A Report on the Incidence of

Subpoenas Served on the News Media in 2001," 9. See also Allan Wolper, "Newsies Aren't Police"; and "Newsroom Searches Occurring Despite Law."

82. Charlie Kratovil, "NBPD Confiscates Water Scandal Evidence from *NBToday* Office," *New Brunswick (NJ) Today*, December 25, 2016, https://newbrunswicktoday.com/2016/12/25/nbpd-confiscates-water-scandal; "Journalists Object to New Brunswick Today Search Warrant," *NJ Today*, January 19, 2017, http://njtoday.net/2017/01/19/journalists-object-new-brunswick-today-search-warrant/.

83. For an example, see Charlie Savage and Leslie Kaufman, "Phone Records of Journalists Seized by U.S.," *New York Times*, May 13, 2013, https://www.nytimes.com/2013/05/14/us/phone-records-of-journalists-of-the-associated-press-seized-by-us.html. In 2013, the DOJ obtained AP telephone records listing incoming and outgoing numbers of AP reporters; the general AP office numbers in New York, Washington, D.C., and Hartford, Connecticut; and the main number for AP reporters in the U.S. House of Representatives press gallery. For more information on Espionage Act prosecutions, see Peter Sterne, "Obama Used the Espionage Act to Put a Record Number of Reporters' Sources in Jail, and Trump Could Be Even Worse"; C. J. Chivers et al., "View Is Bleaker than Official Portrayal of War in Afghanistan," *New York Times*, July 25, 2010, https://archive.nytimes.com/www.nytimes.com/2010/07/26/world/asia/26warlogs.html; and Paul Szoldra, "This Is Everything Edward Snowden Revealed in One Year of Unprecedented Top-Secret Leaks."

84. Ryan Lizza, "The Justice Department and Fox News's Phone Records"; Ann E. Marimow, "A Rare Peek into a Justice Department Leak Probe," *Washington Post*, May 19, 2013, https://www.washingtonpost.com/local/a-rare-peek-into-a-justice-department-leak-probe/2013/05/19/0bc473de-be5e-11e2-97d4-a479289a31f9_story.html.

85. Adam Goldman, Nicholas Fandos, and Katie Benner, "Ex-Senate Aide Charged in Leak Case Where *Times* Reporter's Records Were Seized," *New York Times*, June 7, 2018, https://www.nytimes.com/2018/06/07/us/politics/times-reporter-phone-records-seized.html.

86. Devlin Barrett, "Trump Justice Department Secretly Obtained Post Reporters' Phone Records," *Washington Post*, May 7, 2021, https://www.washingtonpost.com/national-security/trump-justice-dept-seized-post-reporters-phone-records/2021/05/07/933cdfc6-af5b-11eb-b476-c3b287e52a01_story.html; Jeremy Herb and Jessica Schneider, "Trump Administration Secretly Obtained CNN Reporter's Phone and Email Records," CNN, May 20, 2021, https://www.cnn.com/2021/05/20/politics/trump-secretly-obtained-cnn-reporter-records/index.html; Charlie Savage and Katie Benner, "Trump Administration Secretly Seized Phone Records of Times Reporters," *New York Times*, June 2, 2021, https://www.nytimes.com/2021/06/02/us/trump-administration-phone-records-times-reporters.html.

87. See, for example, Evan Dashevsky, "Don't Freak Out, but the Government Records and Stores Every Phone Call and Email."

88. Evan Sernoffsky, "SF Police Got Warrant to Monitor Journalist's Phone Months before Controversial Raid," *San Francisco Chronicle*, June 3, 2019, https://

www.sfchronicle.com/crime/article/SF-police-got-warrant-to-tap-journalist-s
-phone-13912559.php.

89. Peter Sterne, "Editor's Note: Equipment Searches, Seizures, and Damage." See also Vadim Lavrusik, "Social Media and Subpoenas: A Broken System That Puts Journalistic Sources at Risk."

90. "Photojournalist Arrested, Equipment Seized Outside Trump's Tulsa Rally."

91. Craig McCarthy, "NYPD Tried to Subpoena *NY Post* Reporter's Twitter Account Citing Anti-terror Law," *New York Post*, February 13, 2020, https://nypost.com/2020/02/13/nypd-tried-to-subpoena-ny-post-reporters-twitter-account-citing-anti-terror-law/; Ali Watkins, "Why the N.Y.P.D. Subpoenaed a Reporter's Twitter Feed," *New York Times*, February 14, 2020, https://www.nytimes.com/2020/02/14/nyregion/patriot-act-subpoena-nypd.html; Tracy Thomas, "Top Cop Sorry for Subpoena vs. Journalist," *New York Daily News*, February 27, 2020, https://www.pressreader.com/usa/new-york-daily-news/20200227/2816553 72110446; Gabe Rottman, "Special Analysis: Why Did the NYPD Cite an 'Anti-terrorism' Law When It Subpoenaed a Reporter's Twitter Account?"

92. "All Incidents," U.S. Press Freedom Tracker, accessed April 3, 2021, https://pressfreedomtracker.us/all-incidents/?categories=9&date_lower=2017-01-01&date_upper=2020-12-31. For additional examples, see Vivian Wang, "Court Weighs Whether Times Reporter Must Testify in 'Baby Hope' Trial," *New York Times*, June 5, 2018, https://www.nytimes.com/2018/06/05/nyregion/baby-hope-trial-reporter-testify.html; James C. McKinley Jr., "Court Ruling Means Times Reporter Must Testify in 'Baby Hope' Trial," *New York Times*, June 27, 2018, https://www.nytimes.com/2018/06/27/nyregion/baby-hope-reporter-testify.html; Rochelle Olson, "Court of Appeals: *Star Tribune* Isn't Required to Release Source's Identity in Nursing Home Story," *Minneapolis Star Tribune*, September 12, 2016, https://www.startribune.com/court-of-appeals-star-tribune-isn-t-required-to-release-source-s-identity-in-nursing-home-story/393144511/; *Gubarev v. Buzz-Feed*, No. 1:17-cv-60426-UU (S.D. Fla. 2017); and "Seattle Police Subpoena Photos, Video of Protests from Media," Associated Press, July 3, 2020.

93. *In re Grand Jury Subpoena Joshua Wolf* (9th Cir. 2006).

94. *In re Grand Jury Subpoena Judith Miller*, 397 F.3d 964 (D.C. Cir. 2005). For another example of a journalist facing jail time, see *United States v. Sterling*, 724 F.3d 482, 483 (4th Cir. 2013).

95. See Basma Humadi, "Mass Surveillance Threatens Reporting That Relies on Confidential Sources."

96. Foreign Intelligence Surveillance Act, 50 U.S.C. § 1881a (2017).

97. See National Security Agency, "NSA Stops Certain Section 702 'Upstream' Activities"; Ewen Macaskill and Gabriel Dance, "NSA Files: Decoded," *Guardian*, November 1, 2013, https://www.theguardian.com/world/interactive/2013/nov/01/snowden-nsa-files-surveillance-revelations-decoded#section/1; Neema Singh Guliani, "Congress Just Passed a Terrible Surveillance Law. Now What?"; Ellen Nakashima, "NSA Halts Controversial Email Collection Practice to Preserve Larger Surveillance Program," *Washington Post*, April 28, 2017, https://www.washingtonpost.

com/world/national-security/nsa-halts-controversial-email-collection-practice
to-preserve-larger-surveillance-program/2017/04/28/e2ddf9a0-2c3f-11e7-be51
-b3fc6ff7faee_story.html; Philip Bump, "How the Government Can Fix the Spying Problem It Doesn't Want to Fix"; Neema Singh Guliani, "4 Things to Be Worried about in the NSA's New Transparency Report"; and "Statistical Transparency
Report."

98. "About the Foreign Intelligence Surveillance Court."

99. Cora Currier, "Government Can Spy on Journalists in the U.S. Using Invasive
Foreign Intelligence Process," *Intercept*, September 17, 2018, https://theintercept
.com/2018/09/17/journalists-fisa-court-spying/.

100. Geoffrey King, "The NSA Puts Journalists Under a Cloud of Suspicion."

101. Stephenson Waters, "The Effects of Mass Surveillance on Journalists' Relations with Confidential Sources."

102. King, "NSA Puts Journalists Under a Cloud of Suspicion." See also Currier,
"Government Can Spy on Journalists in the U.S."

103. Fed. R. Crim., 41.

104. Victoria Baranetsky and Selina MacLaren, "Recent Rule 41 Changes: A
Catch-22 for Journalists." See also Tim Cushing, "Supreme Court Approves Rule 41
Changes, Putting FBI Closer to Searching Any Computer Anywhere with a Single
Warrant"; and letter from Reporters Committee for Freedom of the Press to Mem-
bers of the Advisory Committee on Criminal Rules, February 17, 2015, https://
www.rcfp.org/wp-content/uploads/imported/2015-02-17-rule-41-comment.pdf.

105. Currier, "Government Can Spy on Journalists in the U.S."; "National Security Letters"; "National Security Letters: FAQ"; Kim Zetter, "Federal Judge Finds National Security Letters Unconstitutional, Bans Them"; Jennifer Valentino-DeVries,
"Secret F.B.I. Subpoenas Scoop Up Personal Data from Scores of Companies," *New
York Times*, September 20, 2019, https://www.nytimes.com/2019/09/20/us/data-
privacy-fbi.html.

106. Trevor Timm, "When Can the FBI Use National Security Letters to Spy on Journalists? That's Classified." See also Cora Currier, "Secret Rules Make It Pretty Easy for the FBI
to Spy on Journalists," *Intercept*, June 30, 2016, https://theintercept.com/2016/06/30/
secret-rules-make-it-pretty-easy-for-the-fbi-to-spy-on-journalists/.

107. Darren Samuelsohn, "Barton Gellman Aware of Legal Risks."

108. See generally Jennifer Valentino-DeVries, "How the Police Use Facial Recognition, and Where It Falls Short," *New York Times*, January 12, 2020,
https://www.nytimes.com/2020/01/12/technology/facial-recognition-police.
html; and Shirin Ghaffary, "How to Avoid a Dystopian Future of Facial Recognition in Law Enforcement." See also Jon Schuppe, "Should Police Body Cameras Have Facial Recognition Tech? Axon, the Largest U.S. Maker of Devices,
Says No," NBC News, June 27, 2019, https://www.nbcnews.com/news/us-news/
should-police-body-cameras-have-facial-recognition-tech-axon.

109. Kate Conger, Richard Fausset, and Serge F. Kovaleski, "San Francisco Bans
Facial Recognition Technology," *New York Times*, May 14, 2019, https://www
.nytimes.com/2019/05/14/us/facial-recognition-ban-san-francisco.
html?smtyp=cur&smid=tw-nytimes.

110. See Evan Greer, "Opinion: Don't Regulate Facial Recognition. Ban It"; Amy Harmon, "As Cameras Track Detroit's Residents, a Debate Ensues over Racial Bias," *New York Times*, July 8, 2019, https://www.nytimes.com/2019/07/08/us/detroit -facial-recognition-cameras.html; and Joseph Goldstein and Ali Watkins, "She Was Arrested at 14. Then Her Photo Went to a Facial Recognition Database," *New York Times*, August 1, 2019, https://www.nytimes.com/2019/08/01/nyregion/nypd -facial-recognition-children-teenagers.html.

111. Jane Kirtley and Scott Memmel, "Rewriting the 'Book of the Machine': Regulatory and Liability Issues for the Internet of Things"; Jane Kirtley and Scott Memmel, "Too Smart for Its Own Good: Addressing the Privacy and Security Challenges of the Internet of Things."

112. Colin Neagle, "How the Internet of Things Is Transforming Law Enforcement," Network World, November 3, 2014, https://www.networkworld.com/article/2842552/how-the-internet-of-things-is-transforming-law-enforcement.html; Bill Searcy, "Tapping into the Internet of Things Will Help Police Departments Turn Smart Cities into Safe Cities"; Peter Swire, "Privacy and Cybersecurity Lessons at the Intersection of the Internet of Things and Police Body-Worn Cameras"; Drew Harwell, "Doorbell-Camera Firm Ring Has Partnered with 400 Police Forces, Extending Surveillance Concerns," *Washington Post*, August 28, 2019, https://www.washingtonpost.com/technology/2019/08/28/doorbell-camera-firm-ring-has -partnered-with-police-forces-extending-surveillance-reach/?arc404=true.

113. Erin McGroarty, "How Police Treatment of Journalists at Protests Has Shifted from Cohabitation to Animosity"; Jon Allsop, "The Police Abuse the Press. Again." See also Marc Tracy and Rachel Adams, "Police Target Journalists as Trump Blames 'Lamestream Media' for Protests," *New York Times*, June 1, 2020, https://www.nytimes.com/2020/06/01/business/media/reporters-protests-george-floyd. html; Trevor Timm, "We Crunched the Numbers: Police—Not Protesters—Are Overwhelmingly Responsible for Attacking Journalists," *Intercept*, June 4, 2020, https://theintercept.com/2020/06/04/journalists-attacked-police-george-floyd -protests/; Bryce Greene, "As Cops Targeted Reporters, Media Grew Increasingly Critical of Police Violence"; and Brian Hauss and Teresa Nelson, "Police Are Attacking Journalists at Protests. We're Suing."

114. Jim Rutenberg, "Independent Press Is under Siege as Freedom Rings," *New York Times*, July 2, 2017, https://www.nytimes.com/2017/07/02/business/media /independent-press-is-under-siege-as-freedom-rings.html.

115. James Madison, *The Writings of James Madison*.

116. David A. Anderson, "Freedom of the Press." See also Rachel Luberda, "Fourth Branch of the Government: Evaluating the Media's Role in Overseeing the Independent Judiciary," 513.

117. Zechariah Chafee, "Freedom of Speech in War Time," 958.

118. Jerome H. Skolnick and Candace McCoy, "Police Accountability and the Media," 531–32.

119. Stuart Allan, *The Routledge Companion to News and Journalism*, chap. 1.

120. Thomas Carlyle, *On Heroes, Hero-Worship & the Heroic in History*.

121. Luberda, "Fourth Branch of the Government," 513.

122. Vincent Blasi, "The Checking Value in First Amendment Theory," 521, 538–40.

123. John H. Garvey and Frederick Schauer, eds., *The First Amendment: A Reader*, 57–58.

124. Herbert L. Packer, "Two Models of the Criminal Process," 9.

125. Thomas F. Gieryn, *Cultural Boundaries of Science*, 17, xi, 17.

126. Andrew Abbott, *The System of Professions: An Essay on the Division of Expert Labor*, 2.

127. Matt Carlson and Seth Lewis, "What Are the Boundaries of Today's Journalism, and How Is the Rise of Digital Changing Who Defines Them?"

128. Meagan Flynn, "A Small-Town Iowa Newspaper Brought Down a Cop. His Failed Lawsuit Has Now Put the Paper in Financial Peril," *Washington Post*, October 10, 2019, https://www.washingtonpost.com/nation/2019/10/10/iowa-newspaper-cop-investigation-leads-libel-lawsuit-financial-peril/.

129. See, for example, Nick Budnick, "Portland Police Union Taking PR Push Nationwide," *Portland (OR) Tribune*, August 29, 2017, https://pamplinmedia.com/pt/9-news/370375-253482-portland-police-union-taking-pr-push-nationwide; and Fran Spielman, "Police Union Accuses 'Media Bias' of Painting Police Shooting as Unjustified," *Chicago Sun-Times*, July 16, 2018, https://chicago.suntimes.com/2018/7/16/18410050/police-union-accuses-media-bias-of-painting-police-shooting-as-unjustified.

130. Alec Karakatsanis (@equalityAlec), "As background, major U.S. police departments spend millions to manipulate the news, but we know almost nothing about it. Los Angeles, for example, has at least 67 full-time employees doing media propaganda work," Twitter, May 5, 2022, 10:06 a.m., https://twitter.com/equalityAlec/status/1522231338790797314.

131. Borden, "'Cease and Desist.'"

132. Kirstin McCudden, "Arrested for Covering Protests, Four Journalists Are Due in Court This Month"; William Morris, "'The Jury Made the Right Decision': Reporter Andrea Sahouri Acquitted in Trial Stemming from Arrest as She Covered Protest," *Des Moines Register*, March 10, 2021, https://www.desmoinesregister.com/story/news/2021/03/10/andrea-sahouri-trial-des-moines-register-reporter-acquitted-george-floyd-protest-arrest/6933780002/.

133. Foerstel, *From Watergate to Monicagate*, 63–64; Kate Houghton, "Subverting Journalism: Reporters and the CIA." See also Walter Pincus, "CIA Official Reveals Agency's Use of Journalists in Secret Operations," *Washington Post*, February 16, 1996; and Walter Pincus, "CIA Can Waive Prohibition against Using U.S. Clergy Abroad for Covert Work," *Washington Post*, February 22, 1996.

134. Intelligence Authorization Act for Fiscal Year 1997, H.R. 3259, 104th Cong., § 309 (1996).

135. 50 U.S. Code § 3324.

136. Intelligence Authorization Act for Fiscal Year 1997.

137. "TV Stations Upset after Police Impersonate Media to Nab Man," Associated Press, July 7, 1980; "Cops Impersonate Media to Capture Armed Man," Associated

Press, July 7, 1980. For additional examples of law enforcement using imperson-ation of the press to end standoffs and, therefore, raising concerns about credibility, see Mike Childs and Joe Foley, "No Impersonators, Please," *St. Petersburg Times*, February 9, 1992; and Heather Palmer, "Police Officer Poses as Photographer to Nab Shooting Suspect during Stand-off."

138. For additional examples of law enforcement using impersonation of the press for surveillance purposes and, therefore, raising concerns about credibility, see "NBC Protests Police Use of Fake Press ID," *Los Angeles Times*, March 16, 1986; Tex O'Neill, "Officer's Disguise Irks Media," *Charlotte (NC) Observer*, November 25, 1986; "Police Shouldn't Pose as Press," *Charlotte (NC) Observer*, December 1, 1986; Chuck Murphy, "Police Posing as Reporters Bother Media," *Tampa Bay Times*, May 2, 1989; Milton Hollstein, "It's Dangerous and Dumb for Police to Impersonate Journalists," *Deseret News* (Salt Lake City), May 15, 1989; "CBS Disturbed by Police 'Cameramen' Filming," *Seattle Times*, May 5, 1989; and "Mayor: Police Shouldn't Pose as Press," Associated Press, April 7, 1994.

139. Jonathan Friendly, "Impersonation of Newsmen Protested," *New York Times*, May 17, 1984; "You're on Police Camera," *New York Times*, May 19, 1984.

140. Jonathan Friendly, "Crossing the Border That Divides Police and the Press," *New York Times*, May 27, 1984. For additional cases and commentary of imperson-ation undermining source relationships, see "New Jersey Journal," *New York Times*, May 27, 1984; Homer Clance, "Police Pledge No More Use of Press Passes," *San Diego Union-Tribune*, June 25, 1987; "Other News to Note: Not One of Us," *Orlando Sentinel*, April 8, 1989; and "Cops and Reporters," *Lancaster (PA) Intelligencer Jour-nal*, April 1, 1996.

141. "When Police Pose as the Press," *Los Angeles Times*, March 16, 1986.

142. Howard Kurtz, "Nabbed in the Newsroom," *Washington Post*, September 5, 1991. An FBI agent posed as a journalist in 1991 to gather information to be used in staging an immigration raid at an Irish newspaper in New York City. Although the raid led to one arrest and was praised by FBI officials, it garnered criticism from observers, including Reporters Committee for Freedom of the Press executive director Jane Kirtley, who argued that the FBI agent's actions "undermine[d] the ability of reporters to do their job [by] blur[ring] the line between law-enforcement agencies and the independent press." For additional examples, see Friendly, "Cross-ing the Border That Divides Police and the Press." Charles W. Bailey, former editor of the *Minneapolis Tribune*, said, "The blurring of old lines and softening of tradi-tional distinctions make it harder for the public to understand the news business." "Media Criticize Graffiti Sting," Associated Press, June 11, 1994.

143. Michael Cooper, "A Police Sergeant Is Accused of Impersonating a Report-er," *New York Times*, September 30, 1998. See also Mike Gallagher, "Media See Dan-gers in Police Posing as Reporters," *Albuquerque Journal*, August 30, 1992.

144. *Locurto v. Giuliani*, 447 F.3d 159 (2nd Cir. 2006).

145. "Deputy Poses as *Newsweek* Reporter to ID Anonymous Source."

146. "Keeping the Faith," *Indianapolis Star*, August 21, 1987.

147. "Orange County Police Officer Posed as AP Photographer to Observe

Demonstration." See also "Official Criticizes Posing as Reporter," *New York Times,* May 18, 1984.

148. For additional examples, see Milford Fryer, "A Risky Police Tactic," *Baton Rouge Advocate,* December 17, 1995; "Journalists, FBI Have Valid Roles That Are Harmed," *Fort Lauderdale Sun Sentinel,* August 10, 1996; Natalie Patton, "Television Station under Fire for Role in Henderson Standoff," *Las Vegas Review-Journal,* May 16, 1997; "Stations O.K. Reporter Impersonation, Helicopter Use in Police"; "Police Impersonate Reporters in Ploy to End Hostage Crisis," 12; "Newark Man Is Charged with Killing Wife and Mother-in-Law and Holding Son, 9, Hostage," *New York Times,* June 14, 2000; Alan Sepinwall, "Not a TV Cameraman, Just Playing One," *Newark (NJ) Star-Ledger,* June 14, 2000; and "Deception Makes Officers, Reporters Less Believable," *Houston Chronicle,* June 23, 2000.

149. "Federal Agents Posed as Photographers to Track Skinheads," Associated Press, September 1, 2000; Thomas Clouse, "Agent Continues Pose Media Credentials Taken from 'Real Photographer,'" *Spokesman-Review* (Coeur d'Alene, ID), September 1, 2000.

150. Phillip Taylor, "Abduction, Death of Pearl Sparks Concern about CIA Agents Impersonating Journalists." For another example involving the CIA, see Joe Davidson, "FBI Impersonation of Journalists Can Be Hazardous to Their Health," *Washington Post,* September 21, 2016. While working on an article on life under apartheid in South Africa, Joe Davidson, a former columnist for the *Washington Post* and the *Wall Street Journal,* was "confronted [by] three young men" from an informal gang, who asked if Davidson was with the CIA. Only after Davidson spoke extensively with the men were they convinced he was not with the CIA, but was, in fact, a journalist. Davidson wrote that the experience "demonstrated the grave risks that can grow from situations that allow people to confuse . . . law enforcement officials with journalists. Being mistaken for an officer, while not having the same resources for protection—a gun and backup assistance, for example—can be hazardous to a reporter's life."

151. Gene Johnson, "FBI Says It Faked AP Story to Catch Bomb Suspect," Associated Press, October 28, 2014, https://perma.cc/ZH7W-XBFS; Ellen Nakashima and Paul Farhi, "FBI Lured Suspect with Fake Web Page, but May Have Leveraged Media Credibility," *Washington Post,* October 28, 2014, https://perma.cc/A5NX-UXE2; *Complaint, Rep. Comm. for Freedom of the Press v. Fed. Bureau of Investigation,* No. 1:15-cv-01392 (D.D.C. filed August 27, 2015); letter from Reporters Committee for Freedom of the Press to Attorney General Eric Holder (November 6, 2014), https://perma.cc/NEB5-F6LK; Filipa Ioannou, "FBI Apprehended Suspect by Pretending to Be the AP"; *Rep. Comm. for Freedom of the Press v. Fed. Bureau of Investigation,* No. 20-5091 (D.C. Cir. 2021); *Rep. Comm. for Freedom of the Press v. Fed. Bureau of Investigation,* 877 F.3d 399 (D.C. Cir. 2017); *Rep. Comm. for Freedom of the Press v. Federal Bureau of Investigation,* 369 F.Supp.3d 212 (D.D.C. 2019).

152. *Complaint, Rep. Comm. for Freedom of the Press v. Fed. Bureau of Investigation,* No. 1:17-cv-01701 (filed August 21, 2017); Jenny Wilson, "Bundy Defendants Interviewed in Undercover FBI Operation," *Las Vegas Review-Journal,* March 22,

2017, https://perma.cc/WZE8-NK4P; Andrew Blake, "FBI Posed as Documentary Filmmakers to Conduct Interviews with Bundy Ranch Supporters," *Washington Times*, March 24, 2017, https://perma.cc/3TK6-8HYY; Trevor Aaronson, "Even the FBI Agrees: When Undercover Agents Pose as Journalists, It Hurts Real Journalists' Work," *Intercept*, August 7, 2018, https://theintercept.com/2018/08/07/fbi-undercover-journalist-documentary-bundy-longbow-chill/.

153. Letter from Reporters Committee for Freedom of the Press to Holder; letter from Karen Kaiser, General Counsel Associated Press, to Attorney General Eric Holder (October 30, 2014).

154. *Declaration of David G. Byars, Reporters Committee for Freedom of the Press v. Federal Bureau of Investigation*, No. 1:17-cv-01701-RC (D.D.C. filed September 14, 2018); *Declaration of Abby Ellis, Reporters Committee for Freedom of the Press v. Federal Bureau of Investigation*, No. 1:17-cv-01701-RC (D.D.C. filed September 14, 2018).

155. John Burgess, "Newsman Guilty of Posing as Officer to Gain Entry to Prison in Virginia," *Washington Post*, April 9, 1983; "Reporter Is Set to Go to Jail for Impersonation," Associated Press, September 9, 1983; Beth Waters, "The Saga of a Reporter behind a Badge," *Washington Post*, April 20, 1983; Beth Waters, "Prince William Jail Chief Resigns after His Arrest," *Washington Post*, February 6, 1983.

156. For another example, see David Corcoran, "Reporters' Gleaming Image Tarnishes with Time," *Hackensack (NJ) Record*, March 7, 1985.

157. "Police Suspect TV Reporter Impersonated an Officer," Associated Press, April 14, 1991.

158. Rob Hayes, "Real Reporter Trips Up TV's Fake Detective," *Palm Beach Post*, June 23, 1999; Bob Betcher, "Reporter Impersonates Officer," *Jupiter (FL) Courier*, June 27, 1999.

159. "Round the Nation: National Tragedy Followed by Scams," *Akron (OH) Beacon Journal*, September 17, 2001.

160. "Matter Closed to Reporter, Officer Claim," *Inland Valley Daily Bulletin* (Ontario, CA), January 16, 2004.

161. W. Lance Bennett, Lynne A. Gressett, and William Haltom, "Repairing the News: A Case Study of the News Paradigm."

162. Tim P. Vos, "The Paradigm Is Dead, Long Live the Paradigm"; Tim P. Vos and Joseph Moore, "Building the Journalistic Paradigm: Beyond Paradigm Repair."

163. See Sara Hammond, "Court Ride-Along Ruling Draws Media," *Arizona Daily Star* (Tucson), May 25, 1999; Jim Adams, "Twin Cities Police Say They'll Still Let Journalists Ride Along, Observe from Afar," *Minneapolis Star Tribune*, May 25, 1999; "Justices Curtail Police Observers," *Baltimore Sun*, May 25, 1999; and Warren Richey, "Reporting on a Raid: Permission Slips Now Required," *Christian Science Monitor*, May 26, 1999.

164. Pat Riley, "Officer, Reporter Stress Different Aspects of Irvine Teens," *Orange County Register* (Santa Ana, CA), June 4, 1989. For another example, see Laura Simmons, "On the Roads with the Law," *Knoxville News-Sentinel*, November 2, 1992.

165. Jim Benson, "Prime Time Is Crime Time: Are Reporters in Squad Cars Taking Viewers for a Ride?," *Daily News of Los Angeles*, May 7, 1989.

166. See, for example, Gordon Hickey, "'An Average Night' on the City Beat," *Richmond (VA) Times-Dispatch*, August 20, 1987; "Gunshot Interrupts TV Interview," Associated Press, October 15, 1989; Simmons, "On the Roads with the Law"; Sue Fishkoff, "All's Quiet on the Western Front: A Coast Weekly Ride Along in Downtown Monterey," *Monterey County (CA) Weekly*, March 26, 1998; "On Patrol, from 'Man Down' to Teen Woes, Squad Car Ride Gives Slice of Life and Police Work in Easthampton," *Daily Hampshire Gazette* (Northampton, MA), September 21, 2005; Mark Holan, "Brooklyn Police Bicycle Unit Is a Powerful Force on Two Wheels," *Cleveland (OH) Plain Dealer*, July 19, 2013; Haley Viccaro, "Ride-Along Offers Glimpse at Life on Patrol," *Schenectady (NY) Daily Gazette*, July 14, 2015; Laura Weiss, "Citizen's Police Academy," *Westport (CT) News*, November 4, 2016; Steve Bagley, "One Night on the Beat with Officer Bartolomucci," *Watertown (MA) TAB & Press*, October 3, 2008; and Jonathan Hettinger, "Riding Shotgun," *Champaign (IL) News Gazette*, May 26, 2015.

167. See, for example, Jared DuBach, "Serve, Protect: Reporter Takes Ride Along with Elko Police," *Elko (NV) Daily Free Press*, February 6, 2009; "24 Hours on Patrol," *Idaho Falls Post Register*, May 2, 1999; Tara Pugh, "In Parkesburg, Police Work Is Serious business," *Parkesburg Post Ledger* (Quarryville, PA), September 6, 2007; "Ride with Policeman," *Anniston (AL) Star*, February 18, 1996; Gina Covelli, "Citizen Covelli: Ride-Along Contradicts Police Career Thoughts," *Sun Prairie (WI) Star*, October 22, 2009; Tracey LeFevre, "Through Different Eyes," *Cookeville (TN) Herald-Citizen*, May 25, 1998; Ari Kramer, "Photog Swept Up in Shooting Aftermath," *Gary (IN) Post Tribune*, October 25, 1998; Kevin T. Baldwin, "Going Along for a Ride: Reporter Experiences Night Shift at Police Department," *Worcester (MA) Telegram & Gazette*, March 13, 2008; Bill Fonda, "The Things You See in a Police Car," *Marshfield (MA) Mariner*, February 10, 2010; Raquel Royers, "The Adventures of a Police Ride Along in Anderson," *Anderson (CA) Valley Post*, July 31, 2012; Sarah Hogsed, "Even Routine Traffic Stops Can Hold Hazards for Police: Reporter Gest New Perspective from Ride-Along," *Richmond (KY) Register*, January 28, 2013; and Cindy Jackson, "Going on a Ride Along," *Fernandina Beach (FL) News Leader*, December 20, 2017.

168. Nicole Jennings, "Police Ride-Along: The True Meaning of Police Work," *Issaquah & Sammamish (WA) Reporter*, August 13, 2016.

169. Howard Wentworth, "Post's Cruising Reporter Given Thrill in Chase," *Washington Post*, January 15, 1936. For additional examples, see Jim Mason, "Chase Is Accelerated in Ticketing Speeders," *Richmond (VA) Times-Dispatch*, July 11, 1988; Stephen C. Fehr, "Sometimes, a Shoulder to Drive On," *Washington Post*, June 21, 1993; and Jill Bryce, "Troopers Target Aggressive Drivers," *Schenectady (NY) Daily Gazette*, February 16, 2005.

170. "First Prostitution Sting Nets Four Arrests: Reporter's Involvement a Mistake, Editor Says," *Corpus Christi (TX) Caller-Times*, December 23, 2004.

171. Benson, "Prime Time Is Crime Time"; Francesca Chapman, "Keeping the Focus on Philly's Finest 'Cops' Gets in the Back Seat," *Philadelphia Daily News*, August 14, 1992; Mike Mather, "Cops in Hampton Roads Popular TV Show Is Hitting the Streets with Area Police, Capturing the Good, the Bad and the Ugly on Tape," *Virginian-Pilot* (Norfolk), July 25, 1998.

172. Dan Taberski, "Is the Show 'Cops' Committing Crimes Itself?," *New York Times*, June 18, 2019, https://www.nytimes.com/2019/06/18/opinion/cops-podcast -investigation-abuse.html?action=click&module=Opinion&pgtype=Homep- age. See also Adam H. Johnson, "Media Frame: Time to Ban Ride-Along Po- lice TV," *Appeal*, June 24, 2019, https://theappeal.org/media-frame-time-to-ban -ride-along-police-tv/.

173. "Drug Raid Can Start Your Heart Pumping," *Pueblo (CO) Chieftain*, June 29, 1997.

174. Hogsed, "Even Routine Traffic Stops Can Hold Hazards for Police"; Colin Murphy, "WPD Ride-Along: WDN Reporter Experiences a Day on Patrol," *Weath- erford (OK) Daily News*, June 24, 2015.

175. Greenberg, "Reporter Rides with Police."

176. Jennings, "Police Ride-Along."

177. "Gunshot Interrupts TV Interview." For another example, see Casey Banas, "Fillmore Is Prime Battleground for Chicago's Police," *Chicago Tribune*, October 2, 1969.

178. Mather, "Cops in Hampton Roads."

179. "Arkansas Reporter Witnesses Shooting Death of Patrolman," Associated Press, April 17, 1991. See also Walk Belcher, "'Cops' Finds Its Niche, Cruises to Success," *Tampa Tribune*, November 24, 1995.

180. "Speeding Law Far Reaching," *Los Angeles Times*, June 19, 1917.

181. Taberski, "Is the Show 'Cops' Committing Crimes Itself?" See also Ann- Derrick Gaillot, "A Live Version of 'Cops' Is the Most Disturbing Show on TV."

182. A. Johnson, "Media Frame."

183. Daniel J. Gross, "Man Sues Sheriff's Office after Vehicle Search on 'Live PD,'" *Greenville (SC) News*, August 18, 2018, https://www.greenvilleonline.com/story/ news/crime/2018/08/15/livepd-lawsuit-greenville-county-sheriffs/999494002/; Daniel J. Gross, "'Live PD' Lawsuit: Greenville Man Gets Settlement in Case against Sheriff's Office," *Greenville (SC) News*, January 9, 2020, https://www.greenvilleon- line.com/story/news/local/south-carolina/2020/01/09/live-pd-tv-show-lawsuit -greenville-sc-man-wins-settlement-against-sheriffs-office/2842356001/. See, for example, "Settlement Reached in $30-Million Geraldo Suit," United Press Inter- national, July 20, 1990, https://www.latimes.com/archives/la-xpm-1990-07-20 -ca-422-story.html; and Christopher Coble, "Man Sues 'Live PD,' Cops Following Aired Arrest."

184. Andy Mannix, "'The First 48' Won't Hand over Footage in Minneapolis Double Homicide Case," *Minneapolis Star Tribune*, January 30, 2016, http://www. startribune.com/the-first-48-won-t-hand-over-footage-in-minneapolis-double -homicide-case/367052501/; Andy Mannix, "Battle over 'First 48' TV Footage

Now Embroils Up to 12 Court Cases," *Minneapolis Star Tribune*, March 18, 2016, http://www.startribune.com/battle-over-first-48-footage-turning-into-drama-for-prosecutors/372623831/; Scott Memmel, "Television Program's Refusal to Disclose Footage Raises Questions over Minnesota Shield Law"; Minnesota Free Flow of Information Act, Minn. Stat. § 595.021 *et seq.* (2019).

185. Kristy Dalton, "What Is a Twitter Ride-Along?" See, for example, Gordon Severson, "Police Statewide Host 'Virtual Ride-Alongs,'" KARE 11, February 16, 2019, https://www.kare11.com/article/news/police-statewide-host-virtual-ride-alongs /89-0d637229-ff48-4ddc-a0b8-c504334542b2; and Matt Vandenlangenberg, "Be 'Social' with UWPD."

186. See, for example, Hammond, "Court Ride-Along Ruling Draws Media Concern"; Adams, "Twin Cities Police Say They'll Still Let Journalists Ride Along, Observe from Afar"; John McCutcheon Jr., "District Police Kept on the Go by Varied Tasks," *Chicago Daily Tribune*, April 28, 1949; and Brynn Gingras, "Inside the Intense World of a New York Police Hostage Negotiator," CNN, November 10, 2017, https://www.cnn.com/2017/11/10/us/new-york-police-hostage-negotiation-team-beyond-the-call-of-duty/index.html.

187. Hogsed, "Even Routine Traffic Stops Can Hold Hazards for Police."

188. Ed Bark, "Channel 8 Does Bang-Up Job on 'Blues,'" *Dallas Morning News*, May 17, 1988.

Chapter 7
Legal Landscape of the U.S. Press-Police Relationship

1. *Roth v. United States*, 354 U.S. 476, 488 (1957).

2. *New York Times v. United States*, 403 U.S. 713, 717 (1971) (Black, J. concurring).

3. *Branzburg v. Hayes*, 408 U.S. 665, 681, 707 (1972). For additional cases and examples, see *Houchins v. KQED*, 438 U.S. 1, 32 (1978) (Stevens, J. dissenting); *ACLU of Illinois v. Alvarez*, 679 F.3d 583, 595, 597 (7th Cir. 2012); *In re Shain*, 978 F.2d 850, 855 (4th Cir. 1992) (Wilkinson J., concurring); and *City of Oak Creek v. King*, 148 Wis.2d 532 (Wis. 1989).

4. For general discussions of the current state of the reporter's privilege in the United States, see "Sources and Subpoenas (Reporter's Privilege)"; "Absolute or Qualified Privilege"; and *First Amendment Encyclopedia*, s.v. "reporter's privilege," by John O. Omachonu and Deborah Fisher, https://www.mtsu.edu/first-amendment/article/1146/reporter-s-privilege. See also *Zerilli v. Smith*, 656 F.2d 705, 711 (D.C. Cir. 1981), citing *Grosjean v. American Press Co.*, 297 U.S. 233, 250 (1936). In 1981, the D.C. Circuit emphasized the importance of recognizing at least some level of First Amendment protection because "compelling a reporter to disclose the identity of a confidential source raises obvious First Amendment problems." The court found that "the press' function as a vital source of information is weakened whenever [the ability] to gather news is impaired,'" including limiting journalists' reliance on informants and confidentiality.

5. Cal. Penal Code § 409.5(a) (2004); Ohio Rev. Code Ann. § 2917.13(B) (2004); Alaska Stat. § 26.23.200(2) (2004).

6. *Westinghouse Broadcasting Corp. v. Nat'l Transp. Safety Board*, 670 F.2d 4 (1st Cir. 1982). See also *Connell v. Town of Hudson*, 733 F.Supp. 465, 468 (D.N.H. 1990). For a case outside the First Amendment context, but still ruling on news gathering at disaster scenes, see *Leiserson v. City of San Diego*, 184 Cal.App.3d 41, 51 (Cal. Ct. App. 1986).

7. *Channel 10, Inc. v. Gunnarson*, 337 F.Supp. 634, 635 (D. Minn. 1972).

8. D. Anderson, "Freedom of the Press," 528.

9. Lucy A. Dalglish, *The First Amendment Handbook*, 62. See also D. Anderson, "Freedom of the Press," 482, 510.

10. Michael Roffe, "Journalist Access," citing *Quad-City Community News Serv. v. Jebens*, 334 F.Supp. 8 (S.D. Iowa 1971); and *Consumers Union of U.S. v. Periodical Correspondents' Ass'n*, 515 F.2d 1341 (D.C. Cir. 1975). See also *Sherrill v. Knight*, 596 F.2d 124, 129 (D.C. Cir. 1977); and D. Anderson, "Freedom of the Press," 491.

11. Privacy Protection Act, 42 U.S.C. § 2000aa *et seq.* (1980).

12. See "A Newsroom Searches"; and "Legal Protections for Journalists' Sources and Information."

13. U.S. Customs and Border Protection, Border Search of Electronic Devices, CBP Directive No. 3340-049A, at § 1 (January 4, 2018).

14. D. Anderson, "Freedom of the Press," 432.

15. Erwin Chemerinsky, "Protect the Press: A First Amendment Standard for Safeguarding Aggressive Newsgathering."

16. *Branzburg*, 408 U.S. at 665; *Zurcher v. Stanford Daily*, 436 U.S. 547 (1978).

17. *Cohen v. Cowles Media Co.*, 501 U.S. 663, 669 (1991). For additional examples, see *Pennekamp v. Florida*, 328 U.S. 331, 364 (1946); and *Clift v. Narragansett Television LP*, 688 A.2d 805, 811 (R.I. 1996).

18. *United States v. Matthews*, 209 F.3d 338, 350 (4th Cir. 2000).

19. *United States v. Matthews*, 11 F.Supp.2d 656, 661 (D.Md.1998)

20. *Glik v. Cunniffe*, 655 F.3d 78, 84 (1st Cir. 2011); *Project Veritas Action Fund v. Rollins*, No. 19-1586 (1st Cir. 2020); *Fields v. Philadelphia*, 862 F.3d 353 (3rd Cir. 2017); *Turner v. Driver*, 848 F.3d 678 (5th Cir. 2017); *ACLU of Illinois*, 679 F.3d at 583; *Fordyce v. City of Seattle*, 55 F.3d 436, 439 (9th Cir. 1995); *Adkins v. Limtiaco*, 537 Fed.Appx. 721, 722 (9th Cir. 2013); *Askins v. U.S. Dept. of Homeland Security*, 899 F.3d 1035 (9th Cir. 2018); *Smith v. Cumming*, 212 F.3d 1332, 1333 (11th Cir. 2000).

21. *First Amendment Encyclopedia*, s.v. "public forum doctrine," by David L. Hudson Jr., January 8, 2020, https://www.mtsu.edu/first-amendment/article/824/public-forum-doctrine.

22. *Perry Education Association v. Perry Local Educators' Association*, 460 U.S. 37, 46–49 (1983). See also *Hague v. Committee for Industrial Organization*, 307 U.S. 496, 515 (1939).

23. *Ward v. Rock against Racism*, 491 U.S. 781 (1989).

24. Roffe, "Journalist Access."

25. *Richmond Newspapers, Inc. v. Virginia*, 448 U.S. 555, 580 (1980), citing *Branzburg*, 408 U.S. at 681.

26. Government in Sunshine Act, 29 CFR § 1612.1 *et seq.* (1976).

27. Christopher M. Davis, "Secret Sessions of the House and Senate: Authority, Confidentiality, and Frequency."

28. *Branzburg*, 408 U.S. 665 at 684–85. See also *Chavez v. City of Oakland*, 414 Fed.Appx. 939 (9th Cir. 2011).

29. *Zemel v. Rusk*, 381 U.S. 1, 16–17 (1965).

30. See *Houchins v. KQED*, 438 U.S. 1 (1978) (plurality opinion); *Pell v. Procunier*, 417 U.S. 817 (1974); and *Saxbe v. Washington Post Co.*, 417 U.S. 843 (1974).

31. *New Jersey v. Lashinsky*, 81 N.J. 1, 6 (N.J. 1979).

32. *Katz v. United States*, 389 U.S. 347 (1967).

33. Samuel D. Warren and Louis D. Brandeis, "The Right to Privacy."

34. Restatement of the Law, Second, Torts, § 652B-652D (1977).

35. Electronic Communications Act, 18 U.S.C. § 2511(1)(a) (1986).

36. "State-by-State Recording Laws"; Al Tompkins, "What to Do When Police Tell You to Stop Taking Photos, Video." Some states have exceptions for police or exceptions for recording in public places (or both). Furthermore, thirty states prohibit audio recording in certain situations, such as when an individual or group is unaware of being recorded. However, some states allow, or at least do not prohibit, video recordings of an individual without their consent so long as there is no audio recording.

37. *Dietemann v. Time, Inc.*, 449 F.2d 245, 249 (9th Cir. 1971); *Food Lion v. Capital Cities/ABC*, 194 F.3d 505 (4th Cir. 1999); *United States v. Maldonado-Norat*, 122 F. Supp. 2d 264, 265 (D.P.R. 2000). See also *Desnick v. Am. Broadcasting Co., Inc.*, 44 F.3d 1345, 1347 (7th Cir. 1995). Conversely, in *Desnick v. American Broadcasting Companies, Inc.* (1995), the Seventh Circuit rejected a trespass claim after ABC reporters with hidden cameras posed as patients at the offices of the Desnick Eye Center, though it did not rule on First Amendment protections.

38. *Arizona v. Wells*, No. LC2003000566001DT, 2004 WL 1925617 (Ariz. Super. 2004); *Stahl v. Oklahoma*, 665 P.2d 839, 840 (Okla.App. 1983); *JB Pictures, Inc. v. Dept. of Defense*, 86 F.3d 236, 238 (D.C. Cir. 1996).

39. *Shulman v. Group W Productions, Inc.*, 955 P.2d 469, 475 (Cal. 1998).

40. *Sanders v. ABC*, 978 P.2d 69 (Cal. 1999).

41. Cal. Civ. Code § 170.8 (West 2015).

42. *Raef v. Super. Ct. of Los Angeles Cty.*, 240 Cal.App.4th 1112, 1119 (2015).

43. *Branzburg*, 408 U.S. at 684, citing *Zemel*, 381 U.S. at 16–17. See also *Pell*, 417 U.S. at 819; *Houchins*, 438 U.S. at 3; and *Putnam Pit, Inc. v. City of Cookeville, Tenn.*, 221 F.3d 834 (6th Cir. 2000).

44. *Los Angeles Police Dept. v. United Reporting Pub. Corp.*, 528 U.S. 32, 41 (1999).

45. *Dahlstrom v. Sun Times*, 777 F.3d 937, 940 (7th Cir. 2015). See also *Travis v. Reno*, 163 F.3d 1000, 1007 (7th Cir. 1998), citing *Houchins*, 438 U.S. at 14.

46. Freedom of Information Act, 5 U.S.C. § 552 (2006). See also "History of FOIA"; and "Exemption 7(C)."

47. *Dept. of Justice v. Rep. Comm. for Freedom of the Press*, 489 U.S. 749, 757 (1989); *National Archives and Records Administration v. Favish*, 541 U.S. 157 (2004).

48. For more discussion of state FOI laws, see Harold L. Cross, *The People's Right to Know: Legal Access to Public Records and Proceedings*, 95–96; and "Police Records," https://www.rcfp.org/wp-content/uploads/imported/POLICE.pdf, 4. For more discussion of common law, see *Nowack v. Fuller*, 243 Mich. 200 (Mich. 1928); Joseph Regalia, "The Common Law Right to Information"; and Daniel J. Solove, "Access and Aggregation: Privacy, Public Records, and the Constitution."

49. Lyle W. Denniston, *The Reporter and the Law: Techniques of Covering the Courts*, 84–88; Dalglish, *The First Amendment Handbook*, 14; *Scheetz v. The Morning Call, Inc.*, 946 F.2d 202 (3rd Cir. 1991).

50. *Near v. Minnesota*, 283 U.S. 697, 714–16 (1931), citing *Patterson v. Colorado*, 205 U.S. 454, 462 (1907); and *Respublica v. Oslwald*, 1 U.S. 319 (1788).

51. *New York Times v. United States*, 403 U.S. 713 (1971).

52. See *CBS v. Davis*, 510 U.S. 1315 (Blackmun, Cir. Justice, 1994); *Nebraska Press Ass'n v. Stuart*, 427 U.S. 539 (1976); *United States v. The Progressive*, 467 F. Supp. 990 (W.D. Wis. 1979); *Alexander v. United States*, 509 U.S. 544 (1993); and *United States v. Providence Journal Co.*, 485 U.S. 693 (1988).

53. *Florida Star v. B. J. F.*, 491 U.S. 524 (1989); *Cox Broadcasting Corp. v. Cohn*, 420 U.S. 469 (1975).

54. *Landmark Communications, Inc. v. Virginia*, 435 U.S. 829 (1978).

55. *Oklahoma Publishing Co. v. Oklahoma County District Court*, 430 U.S. 308 (1977).

56. *Smith v. Daily Mail Publishing Co.*, 443 U.S. 97, 103 (1979).

57. *Bartnicki v. Vopper*, 532 U.S. 514, 517 (2001). See also *Peavy v. WFAA-TV*, 221 F.3d 158 (5th Cir. 2000).

58. *New York Times v. Sullivan*, 376 U.S. 254 (1964). See also *Terminiello v. Chicago*, 337 U.S. 1, 4 (1949); and *Garrison v. Louisiana*, 379 U.S. 64, 77 (1964).

59. *Hustler Magazine, Inc. v. Falwell*, 485 U.S. 46, 50–51 (1988), citing *Curtis Publishing Co. v. Butts*, 388 U.S. 130, 164 (1967) (Warren, J., concurring). See also *Baumgartner v. United States*, 322 U.S. 665, 673–74 (1944).

60. *Mills*, 384 U.S. at 218–19. For additional cases emphasizing the importance of the free flow of information so that the public can be informed about important issues, see *Thornhill v. Alabama*, 310 U.S. 88, 95, 101–02 (1940); and *First National Bank of Boston v. Bellotti*, 435 U.S. 765 (1978). See also *Boos v. Barry*, 485 U.S. 312 (1988); *Police Dept. of Chicago v. Mosley*, 408 U.S. 92, 95 (1972); *Harte-Hanks Communications, Inc. v. Connaughton*, 491 U.S. 657, 686 (1989); *Arizona Free Enterprise Club v. Bennett*, 564 U.S. 721, 755 (2011); and *Buckley v. Valeo*, 424 U.S. 1, 14 (1976).

61. *Fields v. Philadelphia*, 862 F.3d 353, 359 (3rd Cir. 2017), citing *Snyder v. Phelps*, 562 U.S. 443, 452 (2011); and Connick v. Myers, 461 U.S. 138, 145 (1983).

62. *Ex parte Jackson*, 96 U.S. 727, 733 (1877).

63. *Lovell v. City of Griffin*, 303 U.S. 444, 452 (1938).

64. *Schneider v. New Jersey*, 308 U.S. 147 (1939).

65. *Near*, 283 U.S. at 716.

66. *Gitlow v. People of State of New York*, 268 U.S. 652, 666 (1925), citing *Robertson v. Baldwin*, 165 U.S. 275 (1897); *Fox v. Washington*, 236 U.S. 273, 276 (1915);

Schaefer v. United States, 251 U.S. 466, 474 (1920); and *Gilbert v. Minnesota*, 254 U.S. 325, 332 (1920). See also *R.A.V. v. St. Paul*, 505 U.S. 377, 382–83 (1992).

67. "The Public and Broadcasting"; "Obscene, Indecent and Profane Broadcasts." See also *Miller v. California*, 413 U.S. 15 (1973); and *Federal Comm. Comm'n v. Pacifica Found.*, 438 U.S. 726 (1978).

68. *Miami Herald v. Tornillo*, 418 U.S. 241, 258 (1974).

69. *Arkansas Educational Television Commission v. Forbes*, 523 U.S. 666, 674 (1998), citing *Turner Broadcasting System, Inc. v. FCC*, 512 U.S. 622, 653 (1994); *Los Angeles v. Preferred Communications, Inc.*, 476 U.S. 488, 494 (1986); and *Turner Broadcasting System, Inc. v. FCC*, 520 U.S. 180 (1997).

70. *Cohen*, 501 U.S. at 669. See also *Pennekamp*, 328 U.S. at 364.

71. "Tips for Covering Protests"; Neal Justin, "The Adventures of Tom Lyden," *Minneapolis Star Tribune*, March 17, 2008, https://www.startribune.com/the-adventures-of-tom-lyden/16686151/; "Taking a Plea."

72. Ellyn Angelotti, "During Protests, Police May Balance Journalists' Rights with Public Safety."

73. *Matthews*, 209 F.3d at 350; *Matthews*, 11 F.Supp.2d at 661–63.

74. Jonathan Peters, "Journalists in Ferguson: Know Your Rights."

75. For additional examples of 1983 actions in recent years, see *Complaint, Faulk v. St. Louis*, No. 4:18-cv-308 (E.D. Mo. filed February 23, 2018); and *Complaint, Faulk v. St. Louis*, No. 4:18-cv-308 (E.D. Mo. filed February 23, 2018).

76. Order Granting Plaintiffs' Motion for a Temporary Restraining Order. See also *Index Newspapers LLC v. U.S. Marshals Serv.*, 977 F.3d 817, 834 (9th Cir. 2020), holding that the government would not be irreparably harmed by a narrowly tailored injunction that, among other things, exempts journalists from general dispersal orders; allows officers to arrest anyone, including journalists, based on probable cause to believe a crime is being committed; and prevents journalists from interfering with the lawful activities of the officers.

77. See "Members of the Press Detained and Targeted with Use of Force by Law Enforcement Despite Court Order amid Racial Justice Protests."

78. *Weeks v. United States*, 232 U.S. 383, 398 (1914).

79. *United States v. Leon*, 468 U.S. 897, 905–06 (1984), *citing Mapp v. Ohio*, 367 U.S. 643, 651, 655–57 (1961); and *Olmstead v. United States*, 277 U.S. 438, 462–63 (1928).

80. Balko, *Rise of the Warrior Cop*, 11–14.

81. *Weeks*, 232 U.S. at 391, citing *Boyd*, 116 U.S. at 616; and *Adams v. New York*, 192 U.S. 585 (1904).

82. R. Jones, "Avalanche or Undue Alarm?," 596.

83. *Smith v. Maryland*, 442 U.S. 735 (1979).

84. *Smith*, 442 U.S. at 743–44, citing *Couch v. United States*, 409 U.S. 322, 335–36 (1973); *United States v. White*, 401 U.S. 745, 752 (1971) (plurality opinion); *Hoffa v. United States*, 385 U.S. 293, 302 (1966); and *Lopez v. United States*, 373 U.S. 427 (1963). See also *United States v. Miller*, 425 U.S. 435, 442–44 (1976).

85. *Rep. Comm. for Freedom of Press v. Am. Tel. & Tel. Co.*, 593 F.2d 1030, 1057 (D.C. Cir. 1978).

86. *New York Times Co. v. Gonzalez*, 459 F.3d 160 (2nd Cir. 2006); N.Y. CVR § 79-h.

87. 28 CFR § 50.10. See also Moon, Brown, and Rottman, "New DOJ Reports"; and John Solomon, "Rosenstein, DOJ Exploring Ways to More Easily Spy on Journalists."

88. Veronica Stracqualursi, "Biden's Justice Department Says It Will No Longer Seize Reporters' Records for Leak Investigations," CNN, June 5, 2021, https://www.cnn.com/2021/06/05/politics/justice-department-leak-investigations-reporters-new-york-times/index.html; "New Justice Department Policy Marks 'Historic Shift' in Press Protection."

89. *Riley v. California*, 573 U.S. 373 (2014).

90. Scott Memmel, "Crossing Constitutional Boundaries: Searches and Seizures of Journalists' and Other Travelers' Electronic Devices at U.S. Borders," 29.

91. Tom Jones, Mari Payton, and Bill Feather, "Source: Leaked Documents Show the U.S. Government Tracking Journalists and Immigration Advocates through a Secret Database," NBC San Diego, March 6, 2019, https://www.nbcsandiego.com/investigations/Source-Leaked-Documents-Show-the-US-Government-Tracking-Journalists-and-Advocates-Through-a-Secret-Database-506783231.html.

92. *Complaint, In the Matter of the Search of Information Associated with Facebook Accounts*, No. 17 CSW 658-660 (filed November 9, 2011).

93. *United States v. Jones*, 565 U.S. 400, 401 (2012).

94. *Carpenter v. United States*, 585 U.S. 2206 (2018).

95. Letter from Reporters Committee for Freedom of the Press to Attorney General Eric Holder, November 6, 2014.

96. *Virginia v. American Booksellers Association*, 484 U.S. 383, 392 (1988); *Spokeo, Inc. v. Robins*, 578 U.S. 330 (2016).

97. Brief of Amici Curiae, *Wikimedia Foundation v. National Security Agency*, No. 1:15-cv-662-TSE (D. Md. filed September 3, 2015).

98. Andy T. Wang, "Stealing Press Credentials: Law Enforcement Identity Misappropriation of the Press in the Cyber Era," 49–56; Bernard W. Bell, "Secrets and Lies: News Media and Law Enforcement Use of Deception as an Investigative Tool"; letter from Senator Patrick J. Leahy, Chairman, Senate Judiciary Committee, to Eric Holder, Attorney General, October 30, 2014; *Complaint, New York Times v. Contessa Bourbon*, No. 656843/2017 (N.Y. App. Div. filed November 9, 2017); Erik Wemple, "New York Times Sues Woman for Allegedly Impersonating *Times* Reporter," *Washington Post*, November 10, 2017, https://www.washingtonpost.com/blogs/erikwemple/wp/2017/11/10/new-york-times-sues-woman-for-allegedly-impersonating-times-reporter/?; Daniel M. Faber, "Coopting the Journalist's Privilege: Of Sources and Spray Paint."

99. *Schneider v. State*, 308 U.S. 147, 161 (1939). See also *Dennis v. United States*, 341 U.S. 494 (1951); and Laurent B. Frantz, "The First Amendment in the Balance."

100. *Spratlin v. Montgomery County*, 941 F.2d 1207 (4th Cir. 1991). See also Elizabeth E. Joh, "Bait, Mask, and Ruse: Technology and Police Deception."

101. George Lardner Jr., "Aspin Plans to Introduce New CIA Charter Proposal," *Washington Post*, March 17, 1980. See also Undercover Operations Act of 1983, S.

804, 98th Cong. (1983). Conversely, a bill introduced in 1983 restricted undercover activities by federal agents, but authorized undercover agents to "infiltrate news organizations or impersonate journalists . . . when the government has 'probable cause' to believe it is on the trail of specific crimes." Once again, Congress did not pass the bill.

102. Upano, "Will a History of Government Using Journalists Repeat Itself?," 10.

103. Letter from James B. Comey, Director, Federal Bureau of Investigation, to the Editor, *New York Times* (November 6, 2014).

104. "A Review of the FBI's Impersonation of a Journalist in a Criminal Investigation"; Policy Regarding Obtaining Information from, or Records of, Members of the News Media; and Regarding Questioning, Arresting, or Charging Members of the News Media, 79 F.R. § 10989-01 (2014). See also Jenn Topper, "Reporters Committee Troubled by FBI's Stance on Impersonating Journalists"; Hannah Bloch-Wehba, "FBI Failed to Follow Its Own Rules When It Impersonated the Associated Press in a 2007 Investigation"; and John Ashcroft, "The Attorney General's Guidelines on Federal Bureau of Investigation Undercover Operations."

105. *Branzburg*, 408 U.S. at 707.

106. Brief of Scholars of First Amendment and Information Law as Amici Curiae in Support of Plaintiffs-Appellees, *Animal Legal Defense Fund v. Reynolds*, No. 19-1364 (8th Cir. 2019); Brooke Kroeger, *Undercover Reporting: The Truth about Deception*.

107. See, for example, D.C. Code § 22-1404 (2013); Minn. Stat. § 609.475 (2017); Wis. Stat. § 946.70 (2017); Wis. Stat. § 125.105 (2001); Tex. Penal Code Ann. § 37.11 (2017); N.Y. Penal Law § 190.25–190.26 (McKinney 2008); and Cal. Penal Code § 538d (West 2015).

108. See *Animal Legal Defense Fund v. Reynolds*, No. 4:19-cv-00124–JEG-HCA (S.D. Iowa 2019); *Animal Legal Defense Fund v. Reynolds*, 353 F.Supp.3d 812 (S.D. Iowa 2019); *Animal Legal Defense Fund v. Reynolds*, No. 4:17-cv-362 (S.D. Iowa 2017); *Animal Legal Defense Fund v. Wasden*, 878 F.3d 1184 (9th Cir. 2018); *Animal Legal Defense Fund v. Otter*, 118 F.Supp.3d 1195 (D. Idaho 2015); *People for the Ethical Treatment of Animals v. Stein*, 737 Fed.Appx. 122 (4th Cir. 2018); *Western Watersheds Project v. Michael*, 869 F.3d 1189 (10th Cir. 2017); *Western Watersheds Project v. Michael*, 353 F.Supp.3d 1176 (D. Wyo. 2018); *Animal Legal Defense Fund v. Herbert*, 263 F.Supp.3d 1193 (D. Utah 2017); and *Animal Legal Defense Fund v. Kelly*, No. 18-2657-KHV, 2020 WL 362626 (D. Kan. 2020).

109. *Martin v. Gross*, 340 F.Supp.3d 87, 98 (D. Mass. 2018). See also *Sorrell v. IMS Health Inc.*, 564 U.S. 552, 570 (2011).

110. *United States v. Alvarez*, 567 U.S. 709, 730 (2012); Stolen Valor Act, 18 U.S.C.§§ 704 (b)(c) (2011).

111. *Cohen*, 501 U.S. at 664.

112. *United States v. Chappell*, 691 F.3d 388 (4th Cir. 2012).

113. *Wilson*, 526 U.S. at 614.

114. *Ayeni v. Mottola*, 35 F.3d 680 (2nd Cir. 1994); *Parker v. Boyer*, 93 F.3d 445 (8th Cir. 1996), *cert. denied*, 117 S. Ct. 1081 (1997); *Berger v. Hanlon*, 129 F.3d 505, 507 (9th Cir. 1997).

115. *Smart v. City of Miami*, F. Supp. 3d 1271 (S.D. Fla. 2015).

116. *Florida Publishing v. Fletcher*, 340 So.2d 914, 915 (Fla. 1976). The Florida Supreme Court held that a news photographer had not trespassed when he was invited by law enforcement into the scene of a house fire and took a photograph of a deceased victim.

117. *Baugh v. CBS, Inc.*, 828 F. Supp. 745, 749 (N.D. Cal. 1993). Northern District of California judge Fern M. Smith held that CBS had not violated the tort regarding disclosure of private facts, finding that although the broadcast contained private facts that a reasonable person would not want disclosed, the majority of the broadcast was on newsworthy matters of legitimate public interest. Smith also rejected the trespass and intrusion upon seclusion claims, finding that "no California cases indicate that the consent must be knowing or meaningful," even if consent to enter a home was fraudulently induced. See also *Best v. Malec*, No. 09 C 7749, 2010 WL 2364412 at *1 (N.D. Ill. 2010). Conversely, Northern District of Illinois judge Matthew F. Kennelly held that the broadcasting of a photograph depicting a police officer's dash computer screen that displayed personal details about a suspect included private facts that, if revealed, would be highly offensive to a reasonable person, including by revealing at least one arrest when the plaintiff was a minor.

118. *United States v. Hendrixson*, 234 F.3d 494, 495 (11th Cir. 2000).

119. See, for example, Minneapolis Police Department, "Policy & Procedure Manual § 6-400 Ride-Along Program"; and Milwaukee Police Department, "Standard Operating Procedure § 580.00 *et seq.* Ride-Along Program."

120. See, for example, Madison Police Department, *Standard Operating Procedure Tours, Visitors and Ride-Alongs.*

121. Kate Abbey-Lambertz, "How a Police Officer Shot a Sleeping 7-Year-Old to Death." For additional examples, see Doug Nadvornick, "Spokane City Council Restricts Reality-Based Police TV Programs," Northwest Public Broadcasting, March 6, 2018, https://www.nwpb.org/2018/03/06/spokane-city-council-restricts-reality -based-police-tv-programs/; and Dave Collins, "3 Cities End Their 'Live PD' Roles over Public Image Concerns," Associated Press, January 16, 2018, https://www. policeone.com/patrol-issues/articles/3-cities-end-their-live-pd-roles-over-public -image-concerns-hQxPPmgatkUjqiyu/.

Conclusion
The Future of the Press-Police Relationship

1. See "SDX Foundation Funds National Police, Journalist Training"; Gabe Rottman and Chris Young, "Reporters Committee Letter to Minnesota Officials Demands End to Police Attacks against Journalists"; and "Reporters Committee Letter Calls on Denver Officials to End Police Attacks on Journalists at Protests."

2. "What Role Might the Federal Government Play in Law Enforcement Reform?"

3. Jack Shafer, "Stop or I'll Write! Why Cops Shouldn't Fake Being Reporters," Reuters, November 11, 2014, http://blogs.reuters.com/jackshafer/2014/11/11/stop -or-ill-write-why-cops-shouldnt-fake-being-reporters/.

4. See note 16.

5. See note 17.

6. See, for example, Lewis, "Tension between Professional Control and Open Participation"; Carlson, "Metajournalistic Discourse and the Meanings of Journalism"; Gieryn, *Cultural Boundaries of Science*, 17; Abbott, *System of Professions*, 2; Carlson and Lewis, "What Are the Boundaries of Today's Journalism?"; and Vos and Moore, "Building the Journalistic Paradigm."

7. See broadly Surette, *Media, Crime, and Criminal Justice*, 1st ed., 5–6; Schudson, *Why Democracies Need an Unlovable Press*, 13–17; Emerson, *Toward a General Theory of the First Amendment*, 4–11; Meiklejohn, *Free Speech and Its Relation to Self-Government*; and S. Walker and Katz, *Police in America*, 3.

8. Commission on Freedom of the Press, *Free and Responsible Press*; J. Lee, *History of American Journalism*, 430; Siebert, Peterson, and Schramm, *Four Theories of the Press*, 74; Scanlon, "Theory of Freedom of Expression," 130–32; Schramm, *Responsibility in Mass Communication*, 103.

9. Christians et al., *Normative Theories of the Media*, 196.

10. Sources for the legal landscape can be found throughout chapter 7.

11. Jim Rutenberg, "Independent Press Is under Siege as Freedom Rings," *New York Times*, July 2, 2017, https://www.nytimes.com/2017/07/02/business/media/independent-press-is-under-siege-as-freedom-rings.html; Madison, *Writings of James Madison*; D. Anderson, "Freedom of the Press," 429; Luberda, "Fourth Branch of the Government," 513; Chafee, "Freedom of Speech in War Time," 958; Skolnick and McCoy, "Police Accountability and the Media," 531–32; Allan, *Routledge Companion to News and Journalism*, chap. 1; Thomas Carlyle, *On Heroes, Hero-Worship & the Heroic in History*; Blasi, "Checking Value in First Amendment Theory," 521, 538–40; Garvey and Schauer, *First Amendment*, 57–58.

12. See, for example, Packer, "Two Models of the Criminal Process," 9.

13. Sources for the legal landscape can be found throughout chapter 7.

BIBLIOGRAPHY

Abbey-Lambertz, Kate. "How a Police Officer Shot a Sleeping 7-Year-Old to Death." *HuffPost*, September 17, 2014. https://www.huffpost.com/entry/aiyana-stanley-jones-joseph-weekley-trial_n_5824684?guccounter=1.

Abbott, Andrew. *The System of Professions: An Essay on the Division of Expert Labor.* Chicago: University of Chicago Press, 1988.

Abernathy, Penelope Muse. "The Expanding News Desert." Center for Innovation and Sustainability in Local Media, 2018. https://www.usnewsdeserts.com/reports/expanding-news-desert/loss-of-local-news/.

"About the Foreign Intelligence Surveillance Court." U.S. Foreign Intelligence Surveillance Court. Accessed February 28, 2020. https://www.fisc.uscourts.gov/about-foreign-intelligence-surveillance-court.

"Absolute or Qualified Privilege." Reporters Committee for Freedom of the Press. Accessed February 21, 2020. https://www.rcfp.org/privilege-sections/b-absolute-or-qualified-privilege/.

"Act II: Let Your Tragedy Be Enacted Here." Dramas of Haymarket. Accessed May 18, 2022. http://www.chicagohistoryresources.org/dramas/act2/act2.htm.

Adelman, William J. "The Haymarket Affair." Illinois Labor History Society. Accessed May 18, 2022. http://www.illinoislaborhistory.org/the-haymarket-affair.

"African American & Ethnic Newspapers & Magazines." USC Libraries. Accessed May 18, 2022. https://libguides.usc.edu/c.php?g=234932&p=1561804.

"African American Studies: Newspapers." Princeton University Library. Accessed May 18, 2022. https://libguides.princeton.edu/c.php?g=84280&p=544320.

Alexander, Michelle. *The New Jim Crow: Mass Incarceration in the Age of Colorblindness.* Rev. ed. New York: New Press, 2012.

Alfers, Kenneth G. *Law and Order in the Capital City: A History of the Washington Police, 1800–1886.* Washington, D.C.: George Washington Studies, 1976.

Allan, Stuart. *The Routledge Companion to News and Journalism.* London: Routledge, 2009.

"All Incidents." U.S. Press Freedom Tracker. Accessed April 3, 2021. https://pressfreedomtracker.us/all-incidents/?categories=9&date_lower=2017-01-01&date_upper=2020-12-31.

Allsop, Jon. "The Police Abuse the Press. Again." *Columbia Journalism Review* (June 1, 2020). https://www.cjr.org/the_media_today/the-police-abuses-the-press-again.php.

American Bar Association. *Standards Relating to the Urban Police Function*. 2nd ed. Boston: Little, Brown, 1980.

Ames, Fisher. "Hercules." In *Works of Fisher Ames*, 222–25. Boston: T. B. Wait, 1809.

Anderson, Carol. *White Rage: The Unspoken Truth of Our Racial Divide*. New York: Bloomsbury, 2016.

Anderson, David A. "Freedom of the Press." *Texas Law Review* 80, no. 3 (2002): 429–530. https://www.questia.com/library/journal/1P3-110217487/freedom-of-the-press.

Angelotti, Ellyn. "During Protests, Police May Balance Journalists' Rights with Public Safety." Poynter, August 14, 2014. https://www.poynter.org/reporting-editing/2014/during-protests-police-may-balance-journalists-rights-with-public-safety/.

Arana, Gabriel. "Decades of Failure." *Columbia Journalism Review* (2018). https://www.cjr.org/special_report/race-ethnicity-newsrooms-data.php.

Aronson, Amy Beth. *Taking Liberties: Early Women's Magazines and Their Readers*. Westport, CT: Praeger, 2002.

"Arrest/Criminal Charge." U.S. Press Freedom Tracker. Accessed April 3, 2021. https://pressfreedomtracker.us/arrest-criminal-charge/?categories=4.

Ashcroft, John. "The Attorney General's Guidelines on Federal Bureau of Investigation Undercover Operations." Washington, D.C.: U.S. Department of Justice, 2013. http://www.justice.gov/sites/default/files/ag/legacy/2013/09 /24/undercover-fbi-operations.pdf.

Aucoin, James L. *The Evolution of American Investigative Journalism*. Columbia: University of Missouri Press, 2005.

Balko, Radley. *Rise of the Warrior Cop: The Militarization of America's Police Forces*. New York: PublicAffairs, 2014.

Baranetsky, Victoria, and Selina MacLaren. "Recent Rule 41 Changes: A Catch-22 for Journalists." *Just Security*, December 23, 2016. https://www.justsecurity.org/35804/rule-41-changes-catch-22-journalists/.

Barden, David. "Journalist Told to 'Act Like a Lady' as Police Handcuff Her for Taking Photos." *HuffPost*, August 30, 2018. https://www.huffpost.com/entry/denver-journalist-handcuffed-act-like-a-lady_n_5b877d9ee4b0511db3d4ac5d.

Bates, Stephen. "*Garland v. Torre* and the Birth of Reporter's Privilege." *Communication Law and Policy* 15, no. 2 (2010): 91–128.

Bell, Bernard W. "Secrets and Lies: News Media and Law Enforcement Use of Deception as an Investigative Tool." *University of Pittsburgh Law Review* 60, no. 3 (1999): 745–838.

Belt, Gordon T. "Jailed & Subpoenaed Journalists: A Historical Timeline." First Amendment Center, February 2010. https://www.freedomforuminstitute.org/wp-content/uploads/2016/10/Jailed-subpoenaed-timeline1.pdf.

Bencks, Jarret. "Covering the Crime of the Century: The Lindbergh Kidnapping and a Media Revolution." BrandeisNow, December 18, 2020. https://www.brandeis.edu/now/2020/december/lindbergh-doherty-qa.html.

Bennett, W. Lance, Lynne A. Gressett, and William Haltom. "Repairing the News: A Case Study of the News Paradigm." *Journal of Communication* 35, no. 2 (June 1985): 50–68.

Bernstein, Carl. "The CIA and the Media." *Rolling Stone*, October 20, 1977.

Bjornstrom, Eileen E. S., Robert L. Kaufman, Ruth D. Peterson, and Michael D. Slater. "Race and Ethnic Representations of Lawbreakers and Victims in Crime News: A National Study of Television Coverage." *Social Problems* 57, no. 2 (2010): 269–93.

Blackmon, Douglas A. *Slavery by Another Name: The Re-enslavement of Black People in America from the Civil War to World War II*. New York: Doubleday, 2008.

Blasi, Vincent. "The Checking Value in First Amendment Theory." *American Bar Foundation Research Journal* 2, no. 3 (1977): 521–649. http://www.jstor.org/stable/827945.

Bleyer, Willard Grosvenor. *Main Currents in the History of American Journalism*. Cambridge, MA: Riverside Press, 1927.

Bloch-Wehba, Hannah. "FBI Failed to Follow Its Own Rules When It Impersonated the Associated Press in a 2007 Investigation." Reporters Committee for Freedom of the Press, April 28, 2016. https://www.rcfp.org/browse-media-law-resources/news/fbi-failed-follow-its-own-rules-when-it-impersonated-associated-pres.

Boensch, Renee. "Bob Schieffer." *Texas Monthly*, February 1997.

Bopp, William J. *The Police Rebellion*. Springfield, IL: Charles C. Thomas, 1971.

Bopp, William J., and Donald O. Schultz. *A Short History of American Law Enforcement*. Springfield, IL: Charles C. Thomas, 1975.

Borden, Jeremy. "'Cease and Desist': Journalism's Strained Relationship with Police." *Columbia Journalism Review* (October 18, 2017). https://www.cjr.org/united_states_project/chicago-police-union-reporters.php.

———. "Jamie Kalven on Why His Court Win Isn't a Free-Press 'Victory.'" *Columbia Journalism Review* (January 24, 2018). https://www.cjr.org/united_states_project/kalven-laquan-mcdonald-van-dyke-trial.php.

Bortz, Bruce L., and Laurie R. Bortz. "'Pressing' Out the Wrinkles in Maryland's Shield Law for Journalists." *University of Baltimore Law Review* 8, no. 3 (1979): 461–95. https://scholarworks.law.ubalt.edu/cgi/viewcontent.cgi?article=1204&context=ublr.

Brenan, Megan. "Americans Remain Distrustful of Mass Media." Gallup, September 30, 2020. https://news.gallup.com/poll/321116/americans-remain-distrustful-mass-media.aspx.

"Americans' Trust in Media Dips to Second Lowest on Record." Gallup, October 7, 2021. https://news.gallup.com/poll/355526/americans-trust-media-dips-second-lowest-record.aspx.

"Brief History of the MPDC." Metropolitan Police Department. Accessed April 10, 2021. https://mpdc.dc.gov/page/brief-history-mpdc.

Brundage, W. Fitzhugh. *Lynching in the New South: Georgia and Virginia, 1880–1930.* Urbana: University of Illinois Press, 1993.

Bump, Philip. "How the Government Can Fix the Spying Problem It Doesn't Want to Fix." *Atlantic,* June 7, 2018. https://www.theatlantic.com/politics/archive/2013/06/nsa-privacy-government-fixes/314487/.

Campbell, W. Joseph. *Yellow Journalism: Puncturing the Myths, Defining the Legacies.* Westport, CT: Praeger, 2001.

Carlson, Matt. "Metajournalistic Discourse and the Meanings of Journalism: Definitional Control, Boundary Work, and Legitimation." *Communication Theory* 26, no. 4 (2016): 349–68.

Carlson, Matt, and Seth Lewis. "What Are the Boundaries of Today's Journalism, and How Is the Rise of Digital Changing Who Defines Them?" NiemanLab, April 27, 2015. https://www.niemanlab.org/2015/04/what-are-the-boundaries-of-todays-journalism-and-how-is-the-rise-of-digital-changing-who-defines-them/.

Carlyle, Thomas. *On Heroes, Hero-Worship & the Heroic in History.* London: James Fraser, 1840.

Carte, G. E., and E. H. Carte. *Police Reform in the United States: The Era of August Vollmer, 1905–1932.* Berkeley: University of California Press, 1975.

Carter, T. Barton, Juliet Lushbough Dee, and Harvey L. Zuckman. *Mass Communication Law in a Nutshell.* St. Paul, MN: West Academic, 2014.

Cecil, Matthew. "'Press Every Angle': FBI Public Relations and the 'Smear Campaign' of 1958." *American Journalism* 19, no. 1 (2002): 39–58.

Chafee, Zechariah. "Freedom of Speech in War Time." *Harvard Law Review* 32, no. 8 (1919): 932–73.

"Charles Torrey: The Most Successful, Least Celebrated Abolitionist." New England Historical Society. Accessed May 17, 2022. https://www.newenglandhistoricalsociety.com/charles-torrey-successful-least-celebrated-abolitionist/.

Chemerinsky, Erwin. "Protect the Press: A First Amendment Standard for Safeguarding Aggressive Newsgathering." *University of Richmond Law Review* 33 (2000): 1145–65.

Chermak, Steven, Edmund McGarrell, and Jeff Gruenewald. "Media Coverage of Police Misconduct and Attitudes toward Police." *Policing: An International Journal of Police Strategies & Management* 29, no. 2 (2006): 261–81.

Chermak, Steven, and Alexander Weiss. "Maintaining Legitimacy Using External Communication Strategies: An Analysis of Police-Media Relations." *Journal of Criminal Justice* 33, no. 5 (2005): 501–12. https://doi.org/10.1016/j.jcrimjus.2005.06.001.

"Chicago Police Department." Chicagology. Accessed February 2, 2019. https://chicagology.com/chicagopolice/.

Christians, Clifford G., Theodore L. Glasser, Denis McQuail, Kaarle Nordenstreng, and Robert A. White. *Normative Theories of the Media: Journalism in Democratic Societies.* Urbana: University of Illinois Press, 2009.

CIA Office of the Director. Statement, February 11, 1976. https://www.archives.gov/
files/research/jfk/releases/docid-32403785.pdf.

"City Life in the Late 19th Century." Library of Congress. Accessed May 18, 2022.
https://www.loc.gov/classroom-materials/united-states-history-primary
-source-timeline/rise-of-industrial-america-1876-1900/
city-life-in-late-19th-century/.

Claire, Jerry, E. "The Role of Newspapers in the Nineteenth-Century Woman's
Movement." In *A Voice of Their Own: The Woman Suffrage Press, 1840–1910*,
edited by Martha M. Solomon. Tuscaloosa: University of Alabama Press, 1991.

Clift, Raymond E. "Police, Press, and Public Relations." *Journal of Criminal Law and
Criminology* 39, no. 5 (1949): 667–74.

Coble, Christopher. "Man Sues 'Live PD,' Cops Following Aired Arrest." *FindLaw*,
May 8, 2019. https://blogs.findlaw.com/celebrity_justice/2019/05/man-sues
-live-pd-cops-following-aired-arrest.html.

Cohen, Patricia Cline. *The Murder of Helen Jewett: The Life and Death of a Prostitute
in Nineteenth-Century New York*. New York: Alfred A. Knopf, 1998.

Collins, Paul. "How to Get Ahead in Tabloid Journalism." *Slate*, July 19, 2011.
https://slate.com/culture/2011/07/news-of-the-world-scandal-murdoch-s-
tabloid-minions-have-nothing-on-the-journalists-of-1897.html.

———. *The Murder of the Century: The Gilded Age Crime That Scandalized a City &
Sparked the Tabloid Wars*. New York: Crown, 2011.

Commission on Freedom of the Press. *A Free and Responsible Press*. Chicago: University of Chicago, 1947. https://archive.org/details/freeandresponsib029216mbp.

Commission to Investigate Alleged Police Corruption. *The Knapp Commission Report on Police Corruption*. New York: George Braziller, 1973.

Conser, James A., Gregory D. Russell, Rebecca Paynich, and Terry E. Gingerich.
Law Enforcement in the United States. Burlington, MA: Jones & Bartlett Learning, 2005.

"Considering Police Body Cameras." In "Developments in the Law: Policing." Special issue, *Harvard Law Review* 128 (2014–15): 1794–1817.

Cooke, Louise, and Paul Sturges. "Police and Media Relations in an Era of Freedom
of Information." *Policing & Society* 19, no. 4 (2009): 406–24.

Costello, Augustine E. *Our Police Protectors: History of the New York Police from the
Earliest Period to the Present Time*. New York, 1885.

Crime and Punishment in the Jim Crow South. Edited by Amy Louise Wood and
Natalie J. Ring. Urbana: University of Illinois Press, 2019.

"Criminal Justice Expenditures: Police, Corrections, and Courts." Urban Institute. Accessed September 8, 2022. https://www.urban.org/policy-centers/cross-center
-initiatives/state-and-local-finance-initiative/state-and-local-backgrounders/
criminal-justice-police-corrections-courts-expenditures#:~:text=From%20
1977%20to%202019%2C%20in,an%20increase%20of%20179%20percent.

Cross, Harold L. *The People's Right to Know: Legal Access to Public Records and Proceedings*. Morning Heights, NY: Columbia University Press, 1953.

Cushing, Tim. "Supreme Court Approves Rule 41 Changes, Putting FBI Closer to Searching Any Computer Anywhere with a Single Warrant." Techdirt, April 29, 2016. https://www.techdirt.com/articles/20160429/04233634312/supreme-court-approves-rule-41-changes-putting-fbi-closer-to-searching-any-computer-anywhere-with-single-warrant.shtml.

Dalglish, Lucy A. *The First Amendment Handbook*. Edited by Gregg P. Leslie. Arlington, VA: Reporters Committee for Freedom of the Press, 2011. https://www.rcfp.org/wp-content/uploads/imported/FAHB.pdf.

Dalglish, Lucy A., Gregg P. Leslie, and Wendy Tannenbaum. "Agents of Discovery: A Report on the Incidence of Subpoenas Served on the News Media in 2001." Reporters Committee for Freedom of the Press, 2003. https://www.rcfp.org/wp-content/uploads/imported/agents-of-discovery.pdf.

Dalton, Kristy. "What Is a Twitter Ride-Along?" Government Social Media, January 3, 2014. http://governmentsocialmedia.com/2014/01/03/what-is-a-twitter-ride-along/.

Daly, Christopher B. *Covering America: A Narrative History of a Nation's Journalism*. Amherst: University of Massachusetts Press, 2012.

Dashevsky, Evan. "Don't Freak Out, but the Government Records and Stores Every Phone Call and Email." TechHive, May 6, 2013. https://www.techhive.com/article/2037632/don-t-freak-out-but-the-government-records-and-stores-every-phone-call-and-email.html.

Davies, David R. *The Postwar Decline of American Newspapers, 1945–1965*. Westport, CT: Praeger, 2006.

Davis, Christopher M. "Secret Sessions of the House and Senate: Authority, Confidentiality, and Frequency." Congressional Research Service, December 30, 2014. https://fas.org/sgp/crs/secrecy/R42106.pdf.

Denniston, Lyle W. *The Reporter and the Law: Techniques of Covering the Courts*. New York: Columbia University Press, 1992.

"Deputy Poses as *Newsweek* Reporter to ID Anonymous Source." Reporters Committee for Freedom of the Press, August 18, 2008.

Dicken-Garcia, Hazel. *Journalistic Standards in Nineteenth-Century America*. Madison: University of Wisconsin Press, 1989.

Dixon, Travis L., Cristina L. Azocar, and Michael Casas. "The Portrayal of Race and Crime on Television Network News." *Journal of Broadcasting & Electronic Media* 47, no. 4 (2003): 498–523.

Doherty, Thomas. *Little Lindy Is Kidnapped: How the Media Covered the Crime of the Century*. New York: Columbia University Press, 2020.

Dolan, Paul. "Rise of Crime in the Period 1830–1860." *Journal of Criminal Law and Criminology* 30, no. 6 (1940): 857–64.

Dowler, Kenneth. "Media Consumption and Public Attitudes toward Crime and Justice." *Policing and Society* 12, no. 3 (2002): 109–26.

———. "Media Influence on Citizen Attitudes toward Police Effectiveness." *Policing and Society* 12, no. 3 (2002): 227–38.

Doyle, Arthur Conan. *A Study in Scarlet*. London: Ward Lock, 1887.

Dryer, Trevor D. "'All the News That's Fit to Print': The *New York Times*, 'Yellow' Journalism, and the Criminal Trial, 1898–1902." *Nevada Law Journal* 8, no. 2 (2008): 541–69.

Dubosh, Emily, Mixalis Poulakis, and Nour Abdelghani. "Islamophobia and Law Enforcement in a Post 9/11 World." *Islamophobia Studies Journal* 3, no. 1 (2015): 138–57.

Eisen, Lauren-Brooke. "The Federal Funding That Fuels Mass Incarceration." Brennan Center, June 7, 2021. https://www.brennancenter.org/our-work/analysis -opinion/federal-funding-fuels-mass-incarceration.

Eldefonso, Edward, Alan Coffey, and Richard C. Grace. *Principles of Law Enforcement*. New York: John Wiley & Sons, 1968.

Embrick, David G. "Two Nations, Revisited: The Lynching of Black and Brown Bodies, Police Brutality, and Racial Control in 'Post-racial' Amerikkka." *Critical Sociology* 41, no. 6 (2015): 835–43.

Emerson, Thomas. *Toward a General Theory of the First Amendment*. New York: Random House, 1966.

Emery, Edwin. *The Press and America: An Interpretive History of Journalism*. 2nd ed. Englewood Cliffs, NJ: Prentice-Hall, 1962.

Emery, Edwin, and Michael Emery. *The Press and America: An Interpretive History of the Mass Media*. 5th ed. Englewood Cliffs, NJ: Prentice-Hall, 1984.

Entman, Robert M., and Andrew Rojecki. *The Black Image in the White Mind: Media and Race in America*. Chicago: University of Chicago Press, 2015.

"Events Surrounding the U.S. Capitol Insurrection Raise Significant Media Law Issues and Questions." Silha Center for the Study of Media Ethics and Law, January 11, 2021. https://hsjmc.umn.edu/news/2021-01-11-events-surround ing-us-capitol-insurrection-raise-significant-media-law-issues-and.

"Exemption 7(C)." Department of Justice Guide to the Freedom of Information Act, July 23, 2014. https://www.justice.gov/sites/default/files/oip/lega-cy/2014/07/23/exemption7c_0.pdf.

Faber, Daniel M. "Coopting the Journalist's Privilege: Of Sources and Spray Paint." *New Mexico Law Review* 23, no. 1 (1993): 435–50.

Fang, Irving. *Alphabet to Internet: Media in Our Lives*. 3rd ed. New York: Routledge, 2015.

———. *Television News, Radio News*. St. Paul, MN: Rada Press, 1985.

Felker-Kantor, Max. *Policing Los Angeles: Race, Resistance, and the Rise of the LAPD*. Chapel Hill: University of North Carolina Press, 2018. https://www.jstor.org/ stable/10.5149/9781469646855_felker-kantor.

Fellow, Anthony R. *American Media History*. 2nd ed. Boston: Wadsworth, 2010.

Foerstel, Herbert N. *From Watergate to Monicagate*. Santa Barbara, CA: Greenwood, 2001.

Folkerts, Jean, Dwight L. Teeter, and Edward Caudill. *Voices of a Nation: A History of Mass Media in the United States*. Boston: Pearson/Allyn and Bacon, 2009.

"Foreign and Military Intelligence." Washington, D.C.: Select Senate Committee to Study Governmental Operations, April 26, 1976. https://www.intelligence. senate.gov/sites/default/files/94755_I.pdf.

Fosdick, Raymond B. *American Police Systems*. New York: Century, 1920.

Frantz, Laurent B. "The First Amendment in the Balance." *Yale Law Journal* 71, no. 8 (1962): 1424–50. https://www.jstor.org/stable/pdf/794500.pdf.

"Free Press vs. Fair Trial: The Lindbergh Baby Kidnapping Case." Constitutional Rights Foundation. Accessed September 2, 2022. https://www .crf-usa.org/bill-of-rights-in-action/bria-10-1-a-free-press-vs-fair-trial-the -lindbergh-baby-kidnapping-case.

French, Laurence Armand. *The History of Policing America: From Militias and Military to the Law Enforcement of Today*. Lanham, MD: Rowman & Littlefield, 2018.

Friendly, Alfred, and Ronald L. Goldfarb. *Crime and Publicity: The Impact of News on the Administration of Justice*. New York: Twentieth Century Fund, 1967.

Gaillot, Ann-Derrick. "A Live Version of 'Cops' Is the Most Disturbing Show on TV." *Outline*, July 17, 2017. https://theoutline.com/post/1923/ live-pd-cops-ae-policing-reality-tv?zd=2&zi=xv6hw3js.

Garner, Gerald W. *"Chief, the Reporters Are Here": The Police Executive's Personal Guide to Press Relations*. Springfield, IL: Charles C. Thomas, 1987.

———. *The Police Meet the Press*. Springfield, IL: Charles C. Thomas, 1984.

Garvey, John H., and Frederick Schauer, eds. *The First Amendment: A Reader*. St. Paul, MN: West, 2002.

Gerbner, George. "TV Violence and What to Do about It." *Nieman Reports* 50 (1996): 10–13.

Ghaffary, Shirin. "How to Avoid a Dystopian Future of Facial Recognition in Law Enforcement." *Vox*, December 10, 2019. https://www.vox.com /recode/2019/12/10/20996085/ai-facial-recognition-police-law-enforcement -regulation.

Ghandnoosh, Nazgol. "Race and Punishment: Racial Perceptions of Crime and Support for Punitive Policies." Sentencing Project, 2014. https://www.sentencing-project.org/wp-content/uploads/2015/11/Race-and-Punishment.pdf.

Gieryn, Thomas F. *Cultural Boundaries of Science*. Chicago: University of Chicago Press, 1999.

Gilding, Anna Luker. "Preserving Sentiments: American Women's Magazines of the 1830s and the Networks of Antebellum Print Culture." *Journal of History & Criticism* 23, no. 2 (2013).

Giles, Howard. *Law Enforcement, Communication, and Community*. Amsterdam: John Benjamins, 2002.

Gilliam, Franklin D., and Shanto Iyengar. "Prime Suspects: The Influence of Local Television News on the Viewing Public." *American Journal of Political Science* 44, no. 3 (2000): 560–73. https://doi.org/10.2307/2669264.

Gilmore, Glenda. "Postwar Race Riots." Bill of Rights Institute. Accessed December 13, 2022. https://billofrightsinstitute.org/essays/postwar-race-riots.

González, Juan, and Joseph Torres. *News for All the People: The Epic Story of Race and the American Media.* London: Verso, 2011.

Goodale, James C. "More than a Data Dump." *Harpers,* April 2019. https://harpers.org/archive/2019/04/more-than-a-data-dump-julian-assange/.

Gorn, Elliott J. "The Wicked World." In *The Culture of Crime,* edited by Craig L. LaMay and Everette E. Dennis, 9–21. New Brunswick, NJ: Transaction, 1995.

Gottfried, Jeffrey, and Jacob Liedke. "Partisan Divides in Media Trust Widen, Driven by a Decline among Republicans." Pew Research Center, August 30, 2021. https://www.pewresearch.org/fact-tank/2021/08/30/partisan-divides-in-media-trust-widen-driven-by-a-decline-among-republicans/.

Gourley, G. Douglas. "Police Public Relations." *Annals of the American Academy* 291 (1954): 135–42. https://journals.sagepub.com/doi/pdf/10.1177/000271625429100118.

Grady, Constance. "How 70 Years of Cop Shows Taught Us to Valorize the Police." *Vox,* June 3, 2020. https://www.vox.com/culture/2020/6/3/21275700/police-show-procedurals-hollywood-history-dragnet-keystone-cops-brooklyn-nine-nine-wire-blue-bloods.

Greene, Bryce. "As Cops Targeted Reporters, Media Grew Increasingly Critical of Police Violence." *Fairness & Accuracy in Reporting* (July 1, 2020). https://fair.org/home/as-cops-targeted-reporters-media-grew-increasingly-critical-of-police-violence/.

Greenhouse, Steven. "How Police Unions Enable and Conceal Abuses of Power." *New Yorker,* June 18, 2020. https://www.newyorker.com/news/news-desk/how-police-union-power-helped-increase-abuses.

Greer, Evan. "Opinion: Don't Regulate Facial Recognition. Ban It." *BuzzFeed News,* July 18, 2019. https://www.buzzfeednews.com/article/evangreer/dont-regulate-facial-recognition-ban-it.

Grimshaw, Allen D. "Actions of Police and the Military in American Race Riots." *Phylon* 24, no. 3 (1963): 271–89. http://www.jstor.org/stable/273402.

"The Growth of Cities." Digital History, 2021. https://www.digitalhistory.uh.edu/disp_textbook.cfm?smtID=2&psid=3514#:~:text=During%20the%201820s%20and%201830s,the%20country%20as%20a%20whole.

Guffey, James E. "The Police and the Media: Proposals for Managing Conflict Productively." *American Journal of Police* 9, no. 1 (1992): 33–52.

"Had Been to Jacksonville." *American,* October 13, 1888.

Hadden, Sally E. *Slave Patrols: Law and Violence in Virginia and the Carolinas.* Cambridge, MA: Harvard University Press, 2001.

Hall, James P. *The History and Philosophy of Law Enforcement.* Dubuque, IA: Kendall/Hunt, 1975.

Haller, Mark H. Introduction to *History of the Chicago Police,* by John J. Flinn, i–xviii. Montclair, NJ: Patterson Smith, 1973.

Hallin, Daniel C. *The "Uncensored War": The Media and Vietnam.* Berkeley: University of California Press, 1989.

Hare, Christopher, and Keith T. Poole. "The Polarization of Contemporary American Politics." *Polity* 46, no. 3 (2014): 411–29.

Harold, Christine, and Kevin Michael DeLuca. "Behold the Corpse: Violent Images and the Case of Emmett Till." *Rhetoric & Public Affairs* 8, no. 2 (2005): 263–86. https://muse.jhu.edu/article/189491/summary.

Harris, Richard. "The Presidency and the Press." *New Yorker*, September 24, 1973.

Hauss, Brian, and Teresa Nelson. "Police Are Attacking Journalists at Protests. We're Suing." American Civil Liberties Union. Accessed December 13, 2022. https://www.aclu.org/news/free-speech/police-are-attacking-journalists -at-protests-were-suing.

Hedin, Benjamin "The FBI's Surveillance of Martin Luther King, Jr. Was Relentless. But Its Findings Paint a Fuller Picture for Historians." *Time*, January 18, 2021.

Hendershot, Heather. *When the News Broke: Chicago 1968 and the Polarizing of America*. Chicago: University of Chicago Press, 2022.

Hendrickson, Pati, and Howard Swindle. "The Symbiotic, but Conflicted Relationship between Law Enforcement and the Media: A Case Study." *Quarterly Journal of Ideology* 32 (March 2010); 1–23.

Hickey, John J. *Our Police Guardians: History of the Police Department of the City of New York, and the Policing of Same for the Past One Hundred Years*. New York, 1925. https://babel.hathitrust.org/cgi/pt?id=miua.1135158.0001 .001&view=1up&seq=5.

"History of FOIA." Electronic Frontier Foundation. Accessed September 27, 2019. https://www.eff.org/issues/transparency/history-of-foia.

"A History of the Drug War." Drug Policy Alliance. Accessed September 6, 2022. https://drugpolicy.org/issues/brief-history-drug-war.

Houghton, Kate. "Subverting Journalism: Reporters and the CIA." Committee to Protect Journalists (1996). https://cpj.org/attacks96/sreports/cia.html.

Howard, Tanner. "Journalism Still Carries the Mark of 1968." *Columbia Journalism Review* (September 13, 2008). https://www.cjr.org/analysis/chicago-dnc-1968. php.

Howitt, Dennis. *Crime, the Media, and the Law*. West Sussex: John Wiley & Sons, 1998.

"How One Magazine Shaped Investigative Journalism in America." Longreads, January 5, 2014. https://longreads.com/2014/01/05/how-one-magazine-helped -shape-investigative-journalism-in-america/.

Hrach, Thomas J. *The Riot Report and the News: How the Kerner Commission Changed Media Coverage of Black America*. Amherst: University of Massachusetts Press, 2016.

Humadi, Basma. "Mass Surveillance Threatens Reporting That Relies on Confidential Sources." Reporters Committee for Freedom of the Press, September 30, 2019. https://www.rcfp.org/nsa-mass-surveillance-against-journalist/.

Humphrey, Carol Sue. *The Press of the Young Republic, 1783–1833*. Westport, CT: Greenwood Press, 1996.

Huntzicker, William. *The Popular Press, 1833–1865*. Westport, CT: Greenwood Press, 1999.

"Immigrants in the United States: Newspapers." MSU Libraries. Accessed May 18, 2022. https://libguides.lib.msu.edu/c.php?g=96158&p=625932.

"Immigration Begins." Digital History, 2021. https://www.digitalhistory.uh.edu/disp_textbook.cfm?smtID=2&psid=3522.

Ioannou, Filipa. "FBI Apprehended Suspect by Pretending to Be the AP." *Slate*, November 7, 2014. https://slate.com/news-and-politics/2014/11/fbi-impersonates-a-journalist-james-comey-defends-against-ap-new-york-times-criticism.html.

Jackson, Brian A. "Strengthening Trust between Police and the Public in an Era of Increasing Transparency." *RAND Office of External Affairs* (October 2015).

Jacobson, Savannah, and Keith Henry Brown. "Who Needs a Press Pass? The Origins of an Exclusionary Object." *Columbia Journalism Review* (2021). https://existential.cjr.org/press-pass-history-comic/.

Joh, Elizabeth E. "Bait, Mask, and Ruse: Technology and Police Deception." *Harvard Law Review Forum* 128 (2014): 246–52.

Johansen, Anja. "Police-Public Relations: Interpretations of Policing and Democratic Governance." In *The Oxford Handbook of the History of Crime and Criminal Justice*, edited by Paul Knepper and Anja Johansen. Oxford: Oxford University Press, 2016.

John, Richard R. *Spreading the News: The American Postal System from Franklin to Morse*. Cambridge, MA: Harvard University Press, 1995.

Johnson, David R. *American Law Enforcement: A History*. St. Louis: Forum Press, 1981.

Johnson, Herbert A., Nancy Travis Wolfe, and Mark Jones. *History of Criminal Justice*. 4th ed. Newark, NJ: Matthew Bender, 2008.

Johnson, Marilynn S. *Street Justice: A History of Police Violence in New York City*. Boston: Beacon Press, 2003.

Jones, Larry. "Police and Media Relations: How to Bridge the Gap." *Florida Department of Law Enforcement*. Accessed June 29, 2019. http://www.fdle.state.fl.us/FCJEI/Programs/SLP/Documents/Full-Text/jones-larry-final-paper.

Jones, RonNell Andersen. "Avalanche or Undue Alarm? An Empirical Study of Subpoenas Received by the News Media." *Minnesota Law Review* 93, no. 2 (2008): 585–669. https://digitalcommons.law.byu.edu/cgi/viewcontent.cgi?article=1001&context=faculty_scholarship.

Kalven, Jaimie. "Sixteen Shots." *Slate*, February 10, 2015. https:perma.cc/X5BN-KQQ6.

Kaplan, Richard L. *Politics and the American Press: The Rise of Objectivity, 1865–1920*. Cambridge: Cambridge University Press, 2002.

Keedy, Edwin R. "The Third Degree and Legal Interrogation of Suspects." *University of Pennsylvania Law Review* 85, no. 8 (1937): 761–77.

Kelly, Patricia A., ed. *Police and the Media: Bridging Troubled Waters*. Springfield, IL: Charles C. Thomas, 1987.

Kessler, Ronald. "FBI Director Hoover's Dirty Files: Excerpt from Ronald Kessler's *The Secrets of the FBI*." *Daily Beast*, July 13, 2017. https://www.the-dailybeast.com/fbi-director-hoovers-dirty-files-excerpt-from-ronald-kesslers-the-secrets-of-the-fbi.

Kiernan, Michael. "Police vs. the Press: There's Always Tension." In *Police and the Media: Bridging Troubled Waters*, edited by Patricia A. Kelly. Springfield, IL: Charles C. Thomas, 1987.

King, Geoffrey. "The NSA Puts Journalists under a Cloud of Suspicion." Committee to Protect Journalists, February 2014. https://cpj.org/2014/02/attacks-on-the-press-surveillance-storage.php.

Kirtley, Jane, and Chris Ison. *Media Ethics Today: Issues, Analysis, Solutions*. San Diego: Cognella Academic, 2016.

Kirtley, Jane, and Scott Memmel. "Rewriting the 'Book of the Machine': Regulatory and Liability Issues for the Internet of Things." *Minnesota Journal of Law, Science & Technology* 19, no. 2 (2018): 455–513. https://scholarship.law.umn.edu/mjlst/vol19/iss2/5/.

———. "Too Smart for Its Own Good: Addressing the Privacy and Security Challenges of the Internet of Things." *Journal of Internet Law* 22, no. 4 (2018): 1, 19–30.

Klarman, Michael. *From Jim Crow to Civil Rights: The Supreme Court and the Struggle for Racial Equality*. New York: Oxford University Press, 2004.

Kobre, Sidney. *Development of American Journalism*. Dubuque, IA: Wm. C. Brown, 1969.

Kolbert, Elizabeth. "How Politics Got So Polarized." *New Yorker*, January 3, 2022. https://www.newyorker.com/magazine/2022/01/03/how-politics-got-so-polarized.

Kroeger, Brooke. *Undercover Reporting: The Truth about Deception*. Evanston, IL: Northwestern University Press, 2012.

Ladd, Jonathan. *Why Americans Hate the Media and How It Matters*. Princeton, NJ: Princeton University Press, 2011.

Lane, Roger. *Policing the City: Boston, 1822–1885*. Cambridge, MA: Harvard University Press, 1967.

La Vigne, Nancy G., Margaret Ulle, Tim Meko, Ben Chartoff, Fiona Blackshaw, and Dan Matos. "Police Body-Worn Camera Legislation Tracker." Urban Institute, January 2017. http://apps-staging.urban.org/features/body-camera-update/.

Lavrusik, Vadim. "Social Media and Subpoenas: A Broken System That Puts Journalistic Sources at Risk." *Mashable*, January 11, 2011. https://mashable.com/2011/01/11/journalism-social-media-loophole/.

"Law Enforcement Veered Away from Community Policing after 9/11 Attacks." Arizona State University School of Criminology and Criminal Justice, September 7, 2021.

Lawrence, Regina G. *The Politics of Force: Media and the Construction of Police Brutality*. Berkeley: University of California Press, 2000.

Lee, James Melvin. *History of American Journalism*. Garden City, NY: Garden City, 1923.

Lee, Murray, and Alyce McGovern. *Policing and Media: Public Relations, Simulations and Communications*. Oxford: Routledge, 2014.

"Legal Protections for Journalists' Sources and Information." Student Press Law Center, September 1, 2000. https://splc.org/2000/09/legal-protections -for-journalists-sources-and-information/.

Levine, M. J. "Historical Overview of Police Unionization in the United States." *Police Journal* 61, no. 4 (1988): 334–43.

Levy, Leonard W. *Emergence of a Free Press*. New York: Oxford University Press, 1985.

Lewis, Seth. "Lack of Trust in the News Media, Institutional Weakness, and Relational Journalism as a Potential Way Forward." *Journalism* 20, no. 1 (2019): 44–47.

———. "The Tension between Professional Control and Open Participation." *Information, Communication & Society* 15, no. 6 (2012): 836–66.

"Lindbergh Kidnapping." FBI. Accessed September 2, 2022. https://www.fbi.gov/history/famous-cases/lindbergh-kidnapping#:~:text=The%20Kidnapping,home%20near%20Hopewell%2C%20New%20Jersey.

Lipschultz, Jeremy, and Michael Hilt. *Crime and Local Television News: Dramatic, Breaking, and Live from the Scene*. Mahwah, NJ: Lawrence Erlbaum, 2002.

———. "Race and Local Television News Crime Coverage." *Communication Faculty Publications* 3, no. 4 (2003): 1–11.

"List of Incidents Involving Police and Journalists during Civil Unrest in Minneapolis, MN." Silha Center for the Study of Media Ethics and Law, June 3, 2020. https://hsjmc.umn.edu/news/2020-06-02-list-incidents-involving-police-and-journalists-during-civil-unrest-minneapolis-mn.

Lizza, Ryan. "The Justice Department and Fox News's Phone Records." *New Yorker*, May 21, 2013. https://www.newyorker.com/news/news-desk/the-justice -department-and-fox-newss-phone-records.

Lofton, John. *Justice and the Press*. Boston: Beacon Press, 1966.

Lopez, German. "The War on Drugs, Explained." *Vox*, May 8, 2016. https://www.vox.com/2016/5/8/18089368/war-on-drugs-marijuana-cocaine-heroin-meth.

Lotz, Roy. *Crime and the American Press*. New York: Praeger, 1991.

Lovell, Jarret S. *Good Cop/Bad Cop: Mass Media and the Cycle of Police Reform*. Boulder, CO: Lynne Rienner, 2010.

Luberda, Rachel. "Fourth Branch of the Government: Evaluating the Media's Role in Overseeing the Independent Judiciary." *Notre Dame Journal of Law, Ethics & Public Policy* 22, no. 2 (2008): 507–13.

Madison, James. *The Writings of James Madison*. Edited by Gaillard Hunt. New York: G. P. Putnam's Sons, 1900.

Madison Police Department. *Standard Operating Procedure Tours, Visitors and Ride-Alongs*. August 13, 2018. https://www.cityofmadison.com/police/documents/sop/ToursVisitorsRidealongs.pdf.

Magin, Melanie, and Peter Maurer. "Beat Journalism and Reporting." In *Oxford Research Encyclopedia of Communication* (2019). https://oxfordre.com.

Mann, Henry. *Our Police: A History of the Providence Force from the First Watchman to the Latest Appointee*. Providence, RI, 1889.

Maraniss, David. *They Marched into Sunlight*. New York: Simon and Schuster, 2003.

Markin, Karen M. "An 'Unholy Alliance': The Law of Media Ride-Alongs." *Journal of Communications Law and Policy* (2004): 33–60.

Marx, Gary T. *Undercover: Police Surveillance in America*. Berkeley: University of California Press, 1988.

Matthews, Dylan. "How Police Unions Became So Powerful—and How They Can Be Tamed." *Vox*, June 24, 2020. https://www.vox.com/policy-and-politics /21290981/police-union-contracts-minneapolis-reform.

Mawby, Rob C. "Continuity and Change, Convergence and Divergence: The Policy and Practice of Police Media Relations." *Criminology and Criminal Justice* 2, no. 3 (2002): 303–24.

"McCarthyism and the Red Scare." Miller Center. Accessed August 12, 2019. https:// millercenter.org/the-presidency/educational-resources/age-of-eisenhower/ mcarthyism-red-scare.

McChesney, Robert. *The Problem of the Media: U.S. Communication Politics in the Twenty-First Century*. New York: Monthly Review Press, 2004.

McCudden, Kirstin. "Arrested for Covering Protests, Four Journalists Are Due in Court This Month." Freedom of the Press Foundation, February 25, 2021. https://freedom.press/news/arrested-covering-protests-four-journalists -are-set-face-trial-month/.

McGrath Morris, James. *The Rose Man of Sing Sing: A True Tale of Life, Murder, and Redemption in the Age of Yellow Journalism*. New York: Fordham University Press, 2005.

McGroarty, Erin. "How Police Treatment of Journalists at Protests Has Shifted from Cohabitation to Animosity." Poynter, June 14, 2022. https://www.poynter.org/ reporting-editing/2022/police-journalists-protects-press-freedom-attacks/.

McKelvey, Blake. *American Urbanization: A Comparative History*. Glenview, IL: Scott, Foresman, 1973.

McPherson, James Brian. *Journalism at the End of the American Century, 1965– Present*. Westport, CT: Praeger, 2006.

Meiklejohn, Alexander. *Free Speech and Its Relation to Self-Government*. New York: Harper Brothers, 1948.

"Members of the Press Detained and Targeted with Use of Force by Law Enforcement Despite Court Order amid Racial Justice Protests." *Silha Center for the Study of Media Ethics and Law* (April 19, 2021). https://hsjmc.umn. edu/news/2021-04-18-members-press-detained-and-targeted-use-force-law -enforcement-despite-court-order.

Memmel, Scott. "34th Annual Silha Lecture Tackles Public and Media Access to Court Proceedings and Records." *Silha Bulletin* 25, no. 1 (2019): 38–40. https:// conservancy.umn.edu/handle/11299/209996.

———. "Crossing Constitutional Boundaries: Searches and Seizures of Journalists' and Other Travelers' Electronic Devices at U.S. Borders." *Communications Law & Policy* 25, no. 1 (2020): 25–75.

———. "Federal Judge Orders White House Reinstate Reporter's Press Credential." *Silha Bulletin* 25, no. 1 (2019). https://conservancy.umn.edu/handle/11299/209996.

———. "Police Body Cameras: Historical Context, Ongoing Debate & Where to Go from Here." Master's thesis, University of Minnesota, 2017. https://conservancy.umn.edu/bitstream/handle/11299/188779/Memmel_umn_0130M_18106.pdf?sequence=1&isAllowed=y.

———. "Pressing the Police and Policing the Press: The History and Law of the Relationship between the News Media and Law Enforcement in the United States." PhD diss., University of Minnesota, 2020.

———. "Television Program's Refusal to Disclose Footage Raises Questions over Minnesota Shield Law." *Silha Bulletin* 21, no. 6 (2016): 12–13. https://conservancy.umn.edu/handle/11299/184721.

Memmel, Scott, and Jonathan Anderson. "Special Report: Journalists Face Arrests, Attacks, and Threats by Police amidst Protests over the Death of George Floyd." *Silha Bulletin* 25, no. 2 (2020): 3–15. https://conservancy.umn.edu/handle/11299/213922.

Michaels, Samantha. "The Infuriating History of Why Police Unions Have So Much Power." *Mother Jones*, September–October 2020. https://www.motherjones.com/crime-justice/2020/08/police-unions-minneapolis/.

Miller, Lindsay, Jessica Toliver, and Police Executive Research Forum. *Implementing a Body-Worn Camera Program: Recommendations and Lessons Learned.* Washington, D.C.: Office of Community Oriented Policing Services, 2014. https://www.justice.gov/iso/opa/resources/472014912134715246869.pdf.

Miller, Wilbur R. *Cops and Bobbies: Police Authority in New York and London, 1830–1870.* Chicago: University of Chicago Press, 1977.

———. *The Social History of Crime and Punishment in America.* London: Sage, 2012.

Milwaukee Police Department. "Standard Operating Procedure § 580.00 *et seq.* Ride-Along Program." September 14, 2017. https://www.city.milwaukee.gov/ImageLibrary/Groups/cityFPC/agendas5/171102_IV_A.pdf.

Minneapolis Police Department. "Policy & Procedure Manual § 6-400 Ride-Along Program." Accessed March 12, 2020. http://www.ci.minneapolis.mn.us/police/policy/mpdpolicy_6-400_6-400.

Mintz, Steven, and McNeil, Sara. "Policing the Pre–Civil War City." Digital History. Accessed November 14, 2023. https://www.digitalhistory.uh.edu/teachers/historyonline/policing.cfm.

Mitrani, Sam. "Stop Kidding Yourself: The Police Were Created to Control Working Class and Poor People." Lawcha, December 29, 2014. http://www.lawcha.org/2014/12/29/stop-kidding-police-created-control-working-class-poor-people/.

Moon, Linda, Bruce D. Brown, and Gabe Rottman. "New DOJ Reports Provide
    Detail on Use of Law Enforcement Tools against the News Media." Reporters
    Committee for Freedom of the Press, November 9, 2018. https://www.rcfp.org/
    new-doj-reports-provide-detail-use-law-enforcement-tools-against-new/.
Morrell, Kevin. "How Does the Media Shape Perceptions of the Police." Warwick
    WBS Research Projects, October 26, 2015 .
Motschall, Melissa, and Liqun Cao. "An Analysis of the Public Relations Role of the
    Police Public Information Officer." *Police Quarterly* 5, no. 2 (2002): 152–80.
Mott, Frank Luther. *American Journalism: A History, 1690–1960.* New York: Mac-
    millan, 1968.
Mozee, David M. "Police/Media Conflict." In *Police and the Media: Bridging Trou-
    bled Waters,* edited by Patricia A. Kelly. Springfield, IL: Charles C. Thomas,
    1987.
Muhammad, Khalil Gibran. *The Condemnation of Blackness: Race, Crime, and the
    Making of Modern Urban America.* Cambridge, MA: Harvard University Press,
    2011.
Murphy, Kirsten. "Fair Reporting." *News Media & the Law* (Winter 2004): 14.
Murray, George. *The Madhouse on Madison Street.* Chicago: Follett, 1965.
Napoli, Lisa. "'Shots Fired. Hilton Hotel': How CNN's Raw, Unfolding Reagan Cov-
    erage Heralded the Nonstop News Cycle." *Vanity Fair,* April 27, 2020. https://
    www.vanityfair.com/news/2020/04/cnns-raw-unfolding-ronald-reagan
    -coverage-heralded-the-nonstop-news-cycle.
National Advisory Commission on Civil Disorders. *Report of the National Advisory
    Commission on Civil Disorders.* Washington, D.C.: U.S. Government Printing
    Office, 1968.
National Security Agency. "NSA Stops Certain Section 702 'Upstream' Activities."
    Press release, April 29, 2017. https://www.nsa.gov/news-features/press-room/
    Article/1618699/nsa-stops-certain-section-702-upstream-activities/.
"National Security Letters." Electronic Privacy Information Center. Accessed Feb-
    ruary 28, 2020. https://epic.org/privacy/nsl/.
"National Security Letters: FAQ." Electronic Frontier Foundation. Accessed Febru-
    ary 28, 2020. https://www.eff.org/issues/national-security-letters/faq#18.
Nerone, John C. *Media and Public Life: A History.* Cambridge: Polity, 2015.
———. "The Mythology of the Penny Press." *Critical Studies in Mass Communi-
    cation* 4, no. 4 (1987): 376–405. https://doi.org/10.1080/15295038709360146.
"New Justice Department Policy Marks 'Historic Shift' in Press Protection." Report-
    ers Committee for Freedom of the Press, October 26, 2022. https://www.rcfp.
    org/doj-news-media-guidelines-policy/.
"A Newsroom Searches." Reporters Committee for Freedom of the Press. Accessed
    June 9, 2020. https://www.rcfp.org/privilege-sections/a-newsroom-searches/.
"Newsroom Searches Occurring Despite Law." *News Media & the Law* (Sum-
    mer 2010): 16. https://www.rcfp.org/journals/the-news-media-and-the-law
    -summer-2010/newsroom-searches-occurring/.

Niedermeier, Silvan. *The Color of the Third Degree: Racism, Police Torture, and Civil Rights in the American South, 1930–1955*. Chapel Hill: University of North Carolina Press, 2019.

Nord, David Paul. *Communities of Journalism: A History of American Newspapers and Their Readers*. Urbana: University of Illinois Press, 2001.

"Normalizing Injustice: The Dangerous Misrepresentations That Define Television's Scripted Crime Genre." Color of Change, January 2020. https://hollywood. colorofchange.org//wp-content/uploads/2020/02/Normalizing-Injustice _Complete-Report-2.pdf.

"Notable Labor Strikes of the Gilded Age." Weber State University. Accessed May 18, 2022. https://faculty.weber.edu/kmackay/notable_labor_strikes_of_the _gil.htm.

"Obscene, Indecent and Profane Broadcasts." Federal Communications Commission. Accessed February 24, 2020. https://www.fcc.gov/consumers/guides/ obscene-indecent-and-profane-broadcasts.

"Orange County Police Officer Posed as AP Photographer to Observe Demonstration." *News Media & the Law* (Spring 1999).

"Our History." United States Capitol Police. Accessed April 10, 2021. https://www. uscp.gov/the-department/our-history.

Packer, Herbert L. "Two Models of the Criminal Process." *University of Pennsylvania Law Review* 113, no. 1 (1964): 1–68.

Palmer, Heather. "Police Officer Poses as Photographer to Nab Shooting Suspect during Stand-off." *News Media & the Law* (Fall 2001): 17.

Payne, George Henry. *History of Journalism in the United States*. New York: D. Appleton, 1920.

Pender, Lionel, ed. *To Serve and Protect: The History of Policing*. New York: Britannica Educational, 2017.

Perlmutter, David D. *Policing the Media: Street Cops and Public Perceptions of Law Enforcement*. Thousand Oaks, CA: Sage, 2000.

Peters, Jonathan. "Journalists in Ferguson: Know Your Rights." *Columbia Journalism Review* (August 21, 2014). https://archives.cjr.org/united_states_project/ press_rights_in_ferguson.php.

"Photojournalist Arrested, Equipment Seized Outside Trump's Tulsa Rally." U.S. Press Freedom Tracker, June 20, 2020. https://pressfreedomtracker.us/all-incidents/ photojournalist-arrested-equipment-seized-outside-trumps-tulsa-rally/.

"Police Failed to Tell Judge of Bryan Carmody's Status as Journalist before Obtaining Warrant, Unsealed Records Show." First Amendment Coalition, July 23, 2019. https://firstamendmentcoalition.org/2019/07/police-failed-to-tell -judge-of-bryan-carmodys-status-as-journalist-before-obtaining-warrant-un sealed-records-show/.

"Police Impersonate Reporters in Ploy to End Hostage Crisis." *News Media & the Law* (Summer 2000).

"Police Militarization." ACLU. Accessed September 9, 2022. https://www.aclu.org/ issues/criminal-law-reform/reforming-police/police-militarization.

"Political Polarization in the American Public." Pew Research Center, June 12, 2014. https://www.pewresearch.org/politics/2014/06/12/political-polarization-in-the-american-public/.

Pope, James S. "U.S. Press Is Free to Print the News but Too Often Is Not Free to Gather It." *Quill*, July 1951.

Pope, John. *Police-Press Relations: A Handbook*. Fresno, CA: Academy Library Guild, 1954.

Potter, Gary. "The History of Policing in the United States." Police Studies Online, 2013. https://ekuonline.eku.edu/blog/police-studies/the-history-of-policing-in-the-united-states-part-1/.

President's Commission on Law Enforcement and the Administration of Justice. *The Challenge of Crime in a Free Society: A Report by the President's Commission on Law Enforcement and the Administration of Justice*. Washington, D.C.: U.S. Government Printing Office, 1967.

"The Press: Muscle Journalist." *Time*, March 31, 1941.

"Press Freedom in Crisis." U.S. Press Freedom Tracker. Accessed April 16, 2021. https://pressfreedomtracker.us/george-floyd-protests/.

Pressman, Matthew. *On Press: The Liberal Values That Shaped the News*. Cambridge, MA: Harvard University Press, 2018.

"A Primer on Body-Worn Cameras for Law Enforcement." U.S. Department of Justice Office of Justice Programs National Institute for Justice, 2012.

"Prosecutor Fined $1,000 for Newsroom Search in Violation of Federal Law." Reporters Committee for Freedom of the Press, February 7, 1995. https://www.rcfp.org/prosecutor-fined-1000-newsroom-search-violation-federal-law/.

"The Public and Broadcasting." Federal Communications Commission. Accessed February 24, 2020. https://www.fcc.gov/media/radio/public-and-broadcasting.

Regalia, Joseph. "The Common Law Right to Information." *Richmond Journal of Law and the Public Interest* 18, no. 2 (2015): 90–132. https://scholars.law.unlv.edu/cgi/viewcontent.cgi?article=2258&context=facpub.

"Reno D.A. Orders Searches of Four Newsrooms." Reporters Committee for Freedom of the Press, January 25, 1999. https://www.rcfp.org/reno-da-orders-searches-four-newsrooms/.

"Reporters Committee Letter Calls on Denver Officials to End Police Attacks on Journalists at Protests." Reporters Committee for Freedom of the Press, June 16, 2020. https://www.rcfp.org/briefs-comments/denver-police-protest-attacks/.

Reppetto, Thomas A. *American Police: The Blue Parade, 1845–1945, a History*. New York: Enigma Books, 2011.

"A Review of the FBI's Impersonation of a Journalist in a Criminal Investigation." Washington, D.C.: Office of the Inspector General, U.S. Department of Justice, September 2006. https://oig.justice.gov/reports/2016/o1607.pdf.

Reynolds, Baillie. "The Police in Ancient Rome." *Police Journal* 1, no. 3 (1928): 432–42.

Richardson, James F. *The New York Police: Colonial Times to 1901*. New York: Oxford University Press, 1970.

Roberts, Gene, and Hank Klibanoff. *The Race Beat: The Press, the Civil Rights Struggle, and the Awakening of a Nation*. New York: Vintage Books, 2007.

Robins-Early, Nick. "Assange's Espionage Act Charge Sets Up a Fight over the First Amendment." *HuffPost*, May 24, 2019. https://www.huffpost.com/entry/assange-espionage-first-amendment_n_5ce8457ae4b00e03656dfc5e.

Robinson, Michael A. "Black Bodies on the Ground: Policing Disparities in the African American Community—an Analysis of Newsprint from January 1, 2015, through December 31, 2015." *Journal of Black Studies* 48, no. 6 (2017): 551–71.

Roe, G. M. *Our Police: A History of the Cincinnati Police Force, from the Earliest Period until the Present Day*. Cincinnati: n.p., 1890.

Roffe, Michael. "Journalist Access." Freedom Forum Institute, May 25, 2004. https://www.freedomforuminstitute.org/first-amendment-center/topics/freedom-of-the-press/journalist-access/.

Roper, James E. "Impersonating Journalists." *Editor & Publisher*, May 26, 1984.

Rosenberg, Norman L. "Another History of Free Speech: The 1920s and the 1940s." *Minnesota Journal of Law & Inequality* 7, no. 3 (1989): 333–66.

Rosenfeld, Seth. "The FBI's Secret Investigation of Ben Bagdikian and the Pentagon Papers." *Columbia Journalism Review* (August 29, 2018). https://www.cjr.org/investigation/ben-bagdikian-pentagon-papers.php.

Roth, Michael P., and Tom Kennedy. *Houston Blue: The Story of the Houston Police Department*. Denton: University of North Texas Press, 2012.

Rottman, Gabe. "Special Analysis: Why Did the NYPD Cite an 'Anti-terrorism' Law When It Subpoenaed a Reporter's Twitter Account?" Reporters Committee for Freedom of the Press, February 21, 2020. https://www.rcfp.org/nypd-patriot-act-subpoena/?utm_campaign=02_23_2020&utm_medium=email&utm_source=tpfp.

Rottman, Gabe, and Chris Young. "Reporters Committee Letter to Minnesota Officials Demands End to Police Attacks against Journalists." Reporters Committee for Freedom of the Press, June 2, 2020. https://www.rcfp.org/minnesota-police-attacks-letter/.

Rousey, Dennis C. *Policing the Southern City: New Orleans, 1805–1889*. Baton Rouge: Louisiana State University Press, 1996.

Samuelsohn, Darren. "Barton Gellman Aware of Legal Risks." *Politico*, February 25, 2014. https://www.politico.com/blogs/media/2014/02/barton-gellman-aware-of-legal-risks-183998.

Scanlon, Thomas. "A Theory of Freedom of Expression." In *The First Amendment: A Reader*, edited by John H. Garvey and Frederick Schauer. St. Paul, MN: West, 2002.

Schiller, Dan. *Objectivity and the News: The Public and the Rise of Commercial Journalism*. Philadelphia: University of Pennsylvania Press, 1981.

Schramm, Wilbur. *Responsibility in Mass Communication*. New York: Harper & Brothers, 1957.

Schudson, Michael. *Discovering the News: A Social History of American Newspapers*. New York: Basic Books, 1978.

———. *Why Democracies Need an Unlovable Press*. Cambridge: Polity Press, 2008.

Schwartz, Melissa. "If It Bleeds, It Leads." *HuffPost*, May 29, 2014. https://www.huffpost.com/entry/if-it-bleeds-it-leads_b_5407863.

Sclater, Karla Kelling. "The Labor and Radical Press, 1820–the Present." University of Washington Labor Press Project, 2001. https://depts.washington.edu/labhist/laborpress/Kelling.shtml.

"SDX Foundation Funds National Police, Journalist Training." NPPA, October 1, 2013. https://nppa.org/news/sdx-foundation-funds-national-police-journalist-training.

Searcy, Bill. "Tapping into the Internet of Things Will Help Police Departments Turn Smart Cities into Safe Cities." *Police Chief*. Accessed February 27, 2020. https://www.policechiefmagazine.org/tapping-internet-things/.

Secrest, Clark. "Metal of Honor: A Return to the Days When 'Badgering' Reporters and 'Press Shields' Had a Whole Different Meaning." *Editor & Publisher* 137, no. 7 (2004). https://archive.org/details/sim_editor-publisher_2004-07_137_7/page/n47/mode/2up.

Selke, William L., and G. Marshall Bartoszek. "Police and Media Relations: The Seeds of Conflict." *Criminal Justice Review* 9, no. 2 (1984): 25–30.

"The Senate Arrests a Reporter." U.S. Senate, March 26, 1848. https://www.senate.gov/artandhistory/history/minute/The_Senate_Arrests_A_Reporter.htm.

Shermer, Kerry, and Michael Meyer. "Theodore Roosevelt in New York." New York State Library, January 2019. https://www.nysl.nysed.gov/collections/teddyroosevelt/.

Shpayer-Makov, Haia. *Ascent of the Detective: Police Sleuths in Victorian and Edwardian England*. Oxford: Oxford University Press, 2012.

Siebert, Frederick S., Theodore Peterson, and Wilbur Schramm. *Four Theories of the Press: The Authoritarian, Libertarian, Social Responsibility, and Soviet Communist Concepts of What the Press Should Be and Do*. Urbana: University of Illinois Press, 1956.

Siff, Sarah Brady. "Policing the Police: A Civil Rights Story." *Origins: Current Events in Historical Perspective* 9, no. 8 (2016). http://origins.osu.edu/article/policing-police-civil-rights-story.

Simmons, Kami Chavis. "Body-Mounted Police Cameras: A Primer on Police Accountability vs. Privacy." *Howard Law Journal* 58 (2014–15): 882–83.

Simonite, Tom. "The Best Algorithms Struggle to Recognize Black Faces Equally." *Wired*, July 22, 2019. https://www.wired.com/story/best-algorithms-struggle-recognize-black-faces-equally/.

Singh Guliani, Neema. "4 Things to Be Worried about in the NSA's New Transparency Report." *Speak Freely*, May 7, 2018. https://www.aclu.org/blog/national-security/privacy-and-surveillance/4-things-be-worried-about-nsas-new-transparency.

———. "Congress Just Passed a Terrible Surveillance Law. Now What?" *Speak Freely*, January 18, 2018. https://www.aclu.org/blog/national-security/privacy-and-surveillance/congress-just-passed-terrible-surveillance-law-now-what.

Skolnick, Jerome H., and Candace McCoy. "Police Accountability and the Media." *American Bar Foundation Research Journal* 9, no. 3 (1984): 521–57.

Sloan, Wm. David. *The Media in America: A History*. Northport, AL: Vision Press, 2008.

Sloan, Wm. David, and Julie Hedgepeth Williams. *The Early American Press, 1690–1783*. Westport, CT: Greenwood Press, 1994.

Smith, Bruce. *Police Systems in the United States*. New York: Harper & Brothers, 1949.

Smith, Gene. "The National Police Gazette." *American Heritage* 23, no. 6 (1972). https://www.americanheritage.com/national-police-gazette#1.

Smith, Jeffery A. *Printers and Press Freedom*. New York: Oxford University Press, 1988.

Smith-Thompson, Toni. "Ubiquitous Surveillance and Civil Rights Infringements: A Tragic Legacy of 9/11." *NYCLU*, September 10, 2021. https://www.nyclu.org/en/publications/ubiquitous-surveillance-and-civil-rights-infringements-tragic-legacy-911.

Solomon, John. "Rosenstein, DOJ Exploring Ways to More Easily Spy on Journalists." *Hill*, January 14, 2019. https://thehill.com/opinion/judiciary/425189-rosenstein-doj-exploring-ways-to-more-easily-spy-on-journalists.

Solove, Daniel J. "Access and Aggregation: Privacy, Public Records, and the Constitution." *Minnesota Law Review* 86, no. 1 (2002): 1137–1218.

"Sources and Subpoenas (Reporter's Privilege)." Reporters Committee for Freedom of the Press. Accessed November 12, 2018. https://www.rcfp.org/digital-journalists-legal-guide/sources-and-subpoenas-reporters-privilege.

"Special Committee on Organized Crime in Interstate Commerce." U.S. Senate. Accessed October 8, 2022. https://www.senate.gov/about/powers-procedures/investigations/kefauver.htm.

Speech of Mr. John Milton for the Liberty of Unlicensed Printing, to the Parliament of England. New York: Grolier Club, 1890.

Stabile, Carol A. "During Floyd Protests, Media Industry Reckons with Long History of Collaboration with Law Enforcement." *Conversation*, June 11, 2020. https://theconversation.com/during-floyd-protests-media-industry-reckons-with-long-history-of-collaboration-with-law-enforcement-140221?utm_medium=email&utm_campaign=.

———. *White Victims, Black Villains: Gender, Race, and Crime News in US Culture*. London: Routledge, 2006.

Standards for Law Enforcement Agencies: The Standards Manual of the Law Enforcement Agency Accreditation Program. Fairfax, VA: Fairfax Commission on Accreditation for Law Enforcement Agencies, 1999.

Staples, Robert, and Terry Jones. "Culture, Ideology, and Black Television Images." *Black Scholar* 16, no. 3 (1985): 10–20.

Starr, Paul. *The Creation of the Media: Political Origins of Modern Communication*. New York: Basic Books, 2004.

"State-by-State Recording Laws." MSI Detective Services. Accessed March 7, 2017. http://www.detectiveservices.com/2012/02/state-by-state-recording-laws/.

"Stations O.K. Reporter Impersonation, Helicopter Use in Police." Reporters Committee for Freedom of the Press, June 2, 1997.

"Statistical Transparency Report." Office of the Director of National Intelligence, 2017. https://www.dni.gov/files/documents/icotr/2018-ASTR-CY2017 -FINAL-for-Release-5.4.18.pdf.

Steffens, Lincoln. "The Shame of Minneapolis." *McClure's*, January 1903.

Stephens, Mitchell. *A History of News*. Oxford: Oxford University Press, 2007.

Sterne, Peter. "Editor's Note: Equipment Searches, Seizures, and Damage." U.S. Press Freedom Tracker, January 24, 2018. https://pressfreedomtracker.us/ blog/editors-note-equipment-searches-seizures-and-damage/.

———. "Obama Used the Espionage Act to Put a Record Number of Reporters' Sources in Jail, and Trump Could Be Even Worse." Freedom of the Press Foundation, June 21, 2017. https://freedom.press/news/obama-used-espionage-act -put-record-number-reporters-sources-jail-and-trump-could-be-even-worse/.

Storino, Pascal. "'What's the Deal': With the Early History of Police Aviation in New York City? Post WWI (1918) though Fixed Wing Aircraft (1950)—Part 3." History of Policing in New York, 2017. http://nypdhistory.com/whats-the- deal-with-the-early-history-of-police-aviation-in-new-york-city-post-wwi- 1918-though-fixed-wing-aircraft-1950-part-3/.

Stuart, Paul H. "Ida B. Wells-Barnett Confronts 'Excuses for Lynching' in 1901." *Journal of Community Practice* 28, no. 3 (2020): 208–18. https://doi.org/10.10 80/10705422.2020.1805220.

Sullivan, Larry E. *Encyclopedia of Law Enforcement*. Thousand Oaks, CA: Sage, 2005.

Surette, Ray. *Justice and the Media: Issues and Research*. Springfield, IL: Charles C. Thomas, 1984.

———. *Media, Crime, and Criminal Justice: Images and Realities*. 1st ed. Pacific Grove, CA: Brooks/Cole, 1992.

———. *Media, Crime, and Criminal Justice: Images, Realities, and Policies*. 4th ed. Belmont, CA: Wadsworth, Cengage Learning, 2011.

———. "Public Information Officers: The Civilianization of a Criminal Justice Profession." *Journal of Criminal Justice* 29, no. 2 (2001): 107–17.

Swift, Art. "Americans' Trust in Mass Media Sinks to New Low." Gallup, September 14, 2016. https://news.gallup.com/poll/195542/americans-trust-mass-media- sinks-new-low.aspx.

Swire, Peter. "Privacy and Cybersecurity Lessons at the Intersection of the Internet of Things and Police Body-Worn Cameras." *North Carolina Law Review* 96 (2018): 101–45. https://papers.ssrn.com/sol3/papers.cfm?abstract_id=3168089.

Szoldra, Paul. "This Is Everything Edward Snowden Revealed in One Year of Unprecedented Top-Secret Leaks." *Business Insider*, September 16, 2016. https:// www.businessinsider.com/snowden-leaks-timeline-2016-9.

"Taking a Plea." *Broadcasting & Cable* (August 7, 2000). https://www.nexttv.com/ news/taking-plea-87138.

Taylor, Phillip. "Abduction, Death of Pearl Sparks Concern about CIA Agents Impersonating Journalists." *News Media & the Law* (2002).

Teel, Leonard Ray. *The Public Press, 1900–1945.* Westport, CT: Praeger, 2006.

Terry, Christopher, and Caitlin Ring Carlson. "Hatching Some Empirical Evidence: Minority Ownership Policy and the FCC's Incubator Program." *Communication Law and Policy* 24, no. 3 (2019): 403–32.

Tiede, Tom. "Police and the Press: View from Squad Car." Newspaper Enterprise Association, September 28, 1968.

Timm, Trevor. "When Can the FBI Use National Security Letters to Spy on Journalists? That's Classified." *Columbia Journalism Review* (January 11, 2016). https://www.cjr.org/criticism/national_security_letters.php.

"Tips for Covering Protests." *News Media & the Law* (Spring 2003): 10. https://www.rcfp.org/journals/the-news-media-and-the-law-spring-2003/tips-covering-protests/.

Tobin, Charles D. "From John Peter Zenger to Paul Branzburg: The Early Development of Journalist's Privilege." Media Law Resource Center, August 2004.

To Establish Justice, to Ensure Domestic Tranquility: Final Report of the National Commission on the Causes and Prevention of Violence. Washington, D.C.: U.S. Government Printing Office, 1969.

Tompkins, Al. "What to Do When Police Tell You to Stop Taking Photos, Video." Poynter, June 9, 2010. https://www.poynter.org/reporting-editing/2010/what-to-do-when-police-tell-you-to-stop-taking-photos-video/.

Topper, Jenn. "Reporters Committee Troubled by FBI's Stance on Impersonating Journalists." Reporters Committee for Freedom of the Press, September 15, 2016. https://www.rcfp.org/reporters-committee-troubled-fbis-stance-impersonating-journalists/.

Trueblood, Nancy L. "Curbing the Media: Should Reporters Pay When Police Ride-Alongs Violate Privacy?" *Marquette Law Review* 84, no. 2 (2000): 541–70.

Tucher, Andi. *Froth & Scum: Truth, Beauty, Goodness, and the Ax Murder in America's First Mass Medium.* Chapel Hill: University of North Carolina Press, 1994.

Turner, K. B., David Giacopassi, and Margaret Vandiver. "Ignoring the Past: Coverage of Slavery and Slave Patrols in Criminal Justice Texts." *Journal of Criminal Justice Education* 17, no. 1 (2006): 181–95.

"Unjustly Accused." *Kansas Farmer*, December 31, 1896.

Upano, Alicia. "Will a History of Government Using Journalists Repeat Itself under the Department of Homeland Security?" *News Media & the Law* (Winter 2003): 10.

"U.S. Is Polarizing Faster than Other Democracies, Study Finds." Brown University, January 21, 2020. https://www.brown.edu/news/2020-01-21/polarization.

Vandenlangenberg, Matt. "Be 'Social' with UWPD." UW–Madison Police Department, October 16, 2017. https://uwpd.wisc.edu/news/be-social-with-uwpd/.

Van Every, Edward. *Sins of New York as "Exposed" by the Police Gazette.* New York: F. A. Stokes, 1930.

Van Ness, Lindsey. "Body Cameras May Not Be the Easy Answer Everyone Was Look-
    ing For." Pew, January 14, 2020. https://www.pewtrusts.org/en/research-and
    -analysis/blogs/stateline/2020/01/14/body-cameras-may-not-be-the-easy
    -answer-everyone-was-looking-for.
Vinegrad, Alan. "Law Enforcement and the Media: Cooperative Co-existence." *An-
    nual Survey of American Law* 2 (1999): 237–64.
Vos, Tim P. "The Paradigm Is Dead, Long Live the Paradigm." *Journalism & Com-
    munication Monographs* 19, no. 4 (2017): 260–323.
Vos, Tim P., and Joseph Moore. "Building the Journalistic Paradigm: Beyond Para-
    digm Repair." *Journalism* 21, no. 1 (2020): 3–148.
Wade, Richard. *Slavery in the Cities: The South, 1820–1860*. New York: Oxford Uni-
    versity Press, 1964.
Wadman, Robert C., and William Thomas Allison. *To Protect and Serve: History of
    Police in America*. Upper Saddle River, NJ: Pearson Prentice Hall, 2004.
Walker, Mason. "U.S. Newsroom Employment Has Fallen 26% since 2008." Pew
    Research Center, July 13, 2021. https://www.pewresearch.org/fact-tank/2021
    /07/13/u-s-newsroom-employment-has-fallen-26-since-2008/.
Walker, Richard. "Political Polarization: A Dispatch from the Scholarly Front Lines."
    Issues in Governance Studies (December 2006).
Walker, Samuel. *Popular Justice: A History of American Criminal Justice*. Oxford:
    Oxford University Press, 1998.
Walker, Samuel, and Charles M. Katz. *The Police in America: An Introduction*. New
    York: McGraw-Hill, 2008.
Wang, Andy T. "Stealing Press Credentials: Law Enforcement Identity Misappropri-
    ation of the Press in the Cyber Era." *University of Miami National Security &
    Armed Conflict Law Review* 6 (2016): 25–61.
Warren, Samuel D., and Louis D. Brandeis. "The Right to Privacy." *Harvard Law
    Review* 4, no. 5 (1890): 193–220.
"*Washington Post* Video Journalists Detained in Police 'Kettle'
    during D.C. riot." U.S. Press Freedom Tracker, January 8, 2021.
    https://pressfreedomtracker.us/all-incidents/washington-post
    -video-journalists-detained-in-police-kettle-during-dc-riot/.
Waters, Stephenson. "The Effects of Mass Surveillance on Journalists' Relations
    with Confidential Sources." *Digital Journalism* 6, no. 10 (2018): 1294–1313.
    https://www.tandfonline.com/doi/full/10.1080/21670811.2017.1365616.
Waxman, Olivia B. "How the U.S. Got Its Police Force." *Time*, May 18, 2017. https://
    time.com/4779112/police-history-origins/#.
Weinblatt, Richard. "How History Makes the Future of Police Media Relations Clear-
    er." PoliceOne, April 3, 2005. https://www.policeone.com/media-relations
    articles/98373-How-history-makes-the-future-of-police-media-relations
    -clearer/.
Wells, Ida B. *Southern Horrors: Lynch Law in All Its Phases*. New York: New York
    Age Print, 1892.

Westfeldt, Wallace, and Tom Wicker. *Indictment: The News Media & the Criminal Justice System*. Washington, D.C.: First Amendment Center, 1998.

Whalen, Bernard, and Jon Whalen. *The NYPD's First 50 Years: Politicians, Police Commissioners, and Patrolmen*. Lincoln, NE: Potomac Books, 2014.

"What Role Might the Federal Government Play in Law Enforcement Reform?." Congressional Research Service, June 1, 2020. https://fas.org/sgp/crs/misc/ IF10572.pdf.

White, Michael D. *Police Officer Body-Worn Cameras: Assessing the Evidence*. Washington, D.C.: Office of Community Oriented Policing Services, 2014.

Whitfield, Stephen J. *A Death in the Delta: The Story of Emmett Till*. New York: Free Press, 1988.

Williamson, Joel. *A Rage for Order: Black/White Relations in the American South since Emancipation*. New York: Oxford University Press, 1986.

Wilson, Christopher P. *Cop Knowledge: Police Power and Cultural Narrative in Twentieth-Century America*. Chicago: University of Chicago Press, 2000.

Wilson, Jerry V., and Paul Q. Fuqua. *The Police and the Media*. Boston: Little, Brown, 1975.

Wilson, Orlando W. *Police Administration*. New York: McGraw-Hill, 1963.

Wolper, Allan. "Newsies Aren't Police." *Editor & Publisher* (July 3, 1999).

"The Woman's Column in the Suffrage Movement: The Suffrage Press." Albert M. Greenfield Digital Center for the History of Women's Education, 2014. http://greenfield.brynmawr.edu/exhibits/show/the-womans-column/the -womans-column-and-the-suff/the-suffrage-press.

Wright, Ian. "History of American Police Cars." CarBuzz, October 7, 2019. https:// carbuzz.com/features/history-of-american-police-cars.

Zetter, Kim. "Federal Judge Finds National Security Letters Unconstitutional, Bans Them." *Wired*, March 15, 2013. https://www.wired.com/2013/03/ nsl-found-unconstitutional/.

Zuylen-Wood, Simon Van. "Oy, the TRAFFIC. And it's POURING! Do I Hear SIRENS?" *Columbia Journalism Review* (Spring 2017). https://www.cjr.org/ local_news/tv-news-broadcast-jacksonville.php.

INDEX